Black Freedom

Also by CARLETON MABEE
The American Leonardo:
A Life of Samuel F. B. Morse
(PULITZER PRIZE)

The Seaway Story

BLACK FREEDOM

The Nonviolent Abolitionists from
1830 Through the Civil War

CARLETON MABEE

The Macmillan Company
Collier-Macmillan Limited, London

Library of Congress Catalog Card Number: 79-78969

Second Printing 1970

The Macmillan Company

866 Third Avenue, New York, N.Y. 10022

Collier-Macmillan Canada Ltd., Toronto, Ontario

Printed in the United States of America

Preface

THIS IS THE story of the Americans before the Civil War who tried to abolish slavery and racial discrimination by nonviolent means.

From the overwhelmingly large records of the nonviolent abolitionists I have tried to construct for the general reader an account of what they did, particularly what they did in the form of direct action. I have tried to tell the story largely as they themselves saw it and felt it, and at the same time select aspects of the story relevant to the present.

Among the methods the nonviolent abolitionists used, as this book shows, were methods strikingly similar to those used by nonviolent activists for Negro rights in the twentieth century, including sit-ins, boycotts, refusing to cooperate with the government in war, refusing to obey unjust laws, and gladly going to jail.

I write with sympathy for nonviolent action for freedom. I have taken a small part in nonviolent action to improve the status of blacks—in sit-ins, marches, and voter-registration drives in the North and South. I have studied nonviolence in the recent black protest movement and written a little about it. It was while I was doing this writing that I began to inquire about precedents for nonviolence among earlier advocates of Negro rights in America. I gradually became aware that nonviolence was a major element in the abolitionist movement and that few people knew much about it.

From the perspective of the twentieth-century nonviolent black protest movement, I came to wonder whether historians have given due attention to the abolitionists' direct-action methods in comparison with their conventional methods of agitation and politics. I came to wonder whether historians have adequately presented the black role in the abolitionist movement. Especially I came to wonder if historians have not underrated or unduly disparaged the abolitionists' nonviolence.

The record of the nonviolent abolitionists is a sober reminder to present-day America that in the effort to establish equal opportunity for Negroes, nonviolent as well as violent action has been tried in many forms, over many years, with only limited success. The nonviolent abolitionists succeeded in contributing significantly to the awakening of the North to the injustice of slavery; they succeeded in making minor gains in improving the position of Northern Negroes; but they did not succeed in abolishing either slavery or racial discrimination.

Their record should sound a piercing alarm for us today—an alarm both to Americans who are now seeking to abolish racial inequality and to those who are making it difficult for them to do so. As the supporters of slavery stiffened their opposition to the abolitionists and the abolitionists themselves became increasingly convinced that they were not making adequate progress by nonviolent means, both parties turned increasingly to violence until the Civil War came.

Is something similar happening again? Are both those who demand justice for blacks and those who prefer to emphasize law and order turning increasingly to violence, with results that will parallel the dubious results of the Civil War?

History, examined with an open mind, does not often provide dogmatic answers to current questions. The opportunities for nonviolence to succeed among some people under some circumstances may not be at all the same as among other people under other circumstances. Yet the parallels are many between the methods of the abolitionists in the nineteenth century and those of their counterparts in the twentieth century, and the study of such parallels is not only intriguing in itself, but may suggest methods to try or methods to avoid in the continuing struggle to reduce man's inhumanity to man.

New Paltz, New York   CARLETON MABEE

Contents

Part II. Direct Action Against Discrimination

Part III. Direct Action Against Slavery

Part IV. Tragic Denouement

PART I

Abolitionists Choose Nonviolence

The principles of the Founding Fathers "led them to . . . spill blood like water, in order to be free. Ours forbid the doing of evil that good may come."
—William Lloyd Garrison in the *Declaration of Sentiments,* 1833

1. Three Schools of Abolitionists

◇◇◇◇◇◇◇◇◇◇◇◇

THERE WERE THREE major schools of deliberately nonviolent abolitionists. All three agreed in principle to reject violence in their own strictly abolitionist activity, to discourage slave revolts, and to seek emancipation by peaceful means.

Two of these nonviolent schools, the Quakers and Garrisonians, were well recognized at the time as coherent groups. The third school was less coherent and was without a generally accepted name, but for the purpose of this book we have chosen to call them Tappanites, after a major long-term leader of this group, Lewis Tappan.

The Quakers had always been, ever since their origin in the seventeenth century, "complete nonresistants," that is, dedicated to nonviolence in all aspects of life, even to the extent of being conscientious objectors to war.[1] By the mid-1830's, the major Garrisonian leaders had also come to be recognized as complete nonresistants.

At about the same time the major Tappanite leaders came to be recognized as committed to nonviolence in a less complete form. They were only "limited nonresistants," that is, they were committed to using nonviolence in their strictly abolitionist work but not necessarily in other aspects of their lives; they were not necessarily opposed to violent self-defense under extreme provocation, and they were not necessarily conscientious objectors to war.

Among Quakers nonviolent discipline was strong. For example, a Quaker who became a soldier, unless he repented, was likely to be expelled from his meeting. Among the Garrisonians and Tappanites the nonviolent discipline was weak, and it was possible to be recognized as being part of the school—if one associated with leaders of that school or were part of its organizations—without sharing the views of the leaders of the school on nonviolence. It was even possible to be a Garrisonian leader and also be only an "occasional nonresistant," as the Boston blue blood Wendell Phillips was—that is, to be deliberately nonviolent in abolitionist action when it would work, but when it would not work, to become reluctantly violent.

The Garrisonians were led by editor William Lloyd Garrison, and their center was Boston. The Garrisonians were so well known as "nonresistants" that when abolitionists used the term, they sometimes unjustly applied it to Garrisonians alone.

Organizationally the Garrisonians were identified especially with the Massachusetts Antislavery Society, and from 1840, when they captured control of the American Antislavery Society, they were identified with it as well.

In their nonviolent abolitionist activity the Garrisonians were insistent on separating themselves from any institutions that in any way upheld slavery, including the church and the government. Thus their tendency was toward negative forms of nonviolent direct action, such as "coming out" of slavery-sanctifying churches, refusing to vote under the slavery-supporting United States Constitution, and boycotting segregated schools. More positively, the Garrisonians appealed to all who supported slavery, North and South, asking them to repent and free the slaves.

The strength of the Garrisonians was their uncompromising perseverance. Their weakness was their inclination to a spirit so severe that it helped to arouse antagonism.

For the Quakers, or the religious Society of Friends, the traditional center was Philadelphia, with other centers in North Carolina and Indiana.

The Quakers were less strident than the Garrisonians; they were more careful to distinguish between condemning slavery and condemning slave owners. Following what the Quaker poet John Greenleaf Whittier called their only distinctive doctrine, belief in "the Light within," Quakers emphasized the forgiveness of enemies, the capacity of man to do good, and the value of a quiet, simple life apart from the world.

Quakers had a long tradition of nonviolent abolitionism. During the 1600's, they had begun to protest against slavery. During the

1700's, especially under the lead of the New Jersey tailor, John Wool-man, they had gradually cleared their own members, North and South, from all slaveholding, a feat that no large denomination was to accomplish even up to the Civil War. During the early 1800's, Quakers led the abolitionist cause for Americans at large, but they usually did so along quiet paths, allowing most citizens to evade the question of slavery.

During the main period of abolitionist activity, from 1830 to the Civil War, the largest bodies of Quakers continued to act on their antislavery convictions quietly. Officially they petitioned legisla-tures, asking for the abolition of slavery and for Negroes' right to vote, and they helped create private schools for Negroes. But offi-cially these bodies could not agree to urge their members to partici-pate in more controversial forms of direct action, such as the boycott of slave produce or the Underground Railroad, even though it was Quakers who led in these actions; it was usually only the more concerned Quakers who as individuals took part in them. Similarly, the larger bodies of Quakers could not agree to recommend partici-pation in Garrisonian or Tappanite activities. Most Quakers were likely to believe that Garrisonians and Tappanites, despite their non-violence, were worldly and too much given to controversy; they believed that for Quakers to identify with them would compromise Quaker principles. It was only a few of the more daring Quakers who as individuals took part in Garrisonian activities, and some of them —like Lucretia Mott—did so to such an extent that they can be called both Quakers and Garrisonians.

Garrison sometimes praised the Quakers warmly. Despite many of them dragging their feet, he said, a higher proportion of Quakers labored for the freedom of the slaves than the proportion of any other denomination.

Even together the two schools of complete nonresistants, the Gar-risonians and Quakers, were a minority in the abolitionist move-ment. However, when the larger school, the limited nonresistant Tappanites, cooperated with them, as they sometimes chose to do, nonviolence often predominated over violence in the abolitionist movement.

Lewis Tappan, after whom the Tappanites are named, was a phil-anthropic New York City merchant. The Tappanites' major center was New York City, and their peripheral centers included Oneida Institute in upstate New York and Oberlin College in Ohio. Organi-zationally, the Tappanites were identified during the 1830's with the executive committee of the American Antislavery Society, and after the Garrisonians won control of that society, Tappanites were identified instead with two new agencies of their own: the American and Foreign Antislavery Society, founded in 1840, and the American Missionary Association, founded in 1846.

While the Tappanites were deliberately nonviolent in their strictly abolitionist actions, they varied considerably among themselves in the degree of their nonviolence in the rest of their lives. For example, Lewis Tappan and S. S. Jocelyn refused to use force to defend their own property from anti-abolitionist mobs, while Arthur Tappan and Alvan Stewart did use it. Though not necessarily conscientious objectors to war, the Tappanites were likely to be sympathetic to the peace movement, particularly to its conservative wing associated with the American Peace Society, which did not clearly condemn defensive war.

Unlike the Garrisonians, the Tappanites often worked through political parties and churches. Politically they were strong among supporters of the abolitionist Liberty party, and religiously they were strong among Congregationalists and Presbyterians. The forms of nonviolent direct action they emphasized included refusing fellowship to churchmen who supported slavery, creating new antislavery religious organizations to rival slavery-supporting ones, and creating interracial schools and colleges.

Of course there were nonviolent abolitionists who do not fall clearly into any of the three schools. For example, the Massachusetts naturalist Henry David Thoreau and the Connecticut blacksmith Elihu Burritt were both in their own way complete nonresistants— Thoreau briefly, Burritt throughout his career—but both were too individualistic to identify themselves with any school of abolitionists. There were also nonresistants who, while belonging primarily to one school, were close to another. The poet Whittier, for example, was not only a Quaker but also at first was close to the Garrisonians and later close to the Tappanites. There were other nonresistants who moved from school to school or moved in and out of the nonviolent movement. The escaped slave Frederick Douglass began his abolitionist career as a complete nonresistant Garrisonian, but by the 1850's he had become only an occasional nonresistant.

Opposing the nonviolent abolitionists were those who believed that violence was essential to abolishing slavery. Among them were the Virginia slave, religious mystic Nat Turner, who led a slave revolt; the Kentucky aristocrat Cassuis M. Clay, who openly used pistols and knives to defend his right to speak against slavery; and of course the stalwart Yankee tanner, sheep herder, and guerrilla fighter, John Brown.

By 1859, when Brown raided the federal arsenal at Harper's Ferry, a considerable number of once nonviolent abolitionists, having lost much of their confidence in peaceful methods, welcomed Brown's violence as opening the way to end slavery, while a few continued to doubt even through the Civil War that violence could bring genuine freedom to Negroes.

In the 1830's most abolitionists tended to agree on emphasizing the nonviolent method of "moral suasion," as they called it, that is, essentially agitation by appeals to the "truth" or to conscience.

In the 1840's and 1850's most abolitionists, including most Tappanites, were turning increasingly to the method of politics, while many Garrisonians and Quakers were reluctant to do so, preferring to continue to emphasize moral suasion.

But in addition, all through the 1830's, 1840's, and 1850's many nonviolent abolitionists were using the method of nonviolent direct action. It is this aspect of abolitionist activity that is stressed in this book rather than the more conventional, more often written about methods of agitation and politics.

Not themselves using the term nonviolent direct action—it is a term that the nonviolent actionists brought into common use in the 1940's—the nonviolent abolitionists often thought of such action as intended primarily to persuade others to their views. Sometimes they also thought of it—especially in its more negative forms, such as boycotting slave products—as intended to purify themselves personally from responsibility for slavery. Many nonviolent abolitionists hesitated to think of nonviolent direct action primarily as coercion. While many of them were aware that such action often inevitably involved coercion, they were likely to avoid the idea that coercion was their primary purpose.

In their direct action, the nonviolent abolitionists found themselves facing formidable dilemmas—such as choosing between persuasion or coercion, order or justice, personal integrity or effectiveness in bringing about change, giving outside help to the oppressed or waiting for the oppressed to help themselves, demanding complete change immediately despite furious opposition or accepting small gains for the present while working for more change by common consent.

Despite the dilemmas often involved, over a period of many years the abolitionists developed nonviolent direct actions of imagination and range. Some actions were mainly individual, like refusing to vote under the slavery-supporting Constitution, while others were mainly group actions, like creating antislavery, interracial churches. Some brought violent reprisals, as the church speak-ins did; others got participants into trouble with the law, as refusing to pay taxes or do military service did. Some actions had immediate, easily measured objectives related to the surface of society, as the boycott of segregated railroads did, while others had more long-range, more difficult to measure objectives aimed at changing the fundamental institutions of society, as creating interracial socialist communities did. Some were brief, single acts, such as refusing to invite a pro-slavery pastor to preach, while others involved slow, painstaking action over many years, such as founding and nourishing interracial schools. Some of the actions could be quiet and restrained, like inviting Negroes into one's home, while others could be noisy and rough and at times seemed to threaten the whole social order, like defiance of the officials who tried to seize fugitive slaves and return them to the South.

From the great variety of direct actions, this book emphasizes a few as particularly characteristic, dramatic, or revealing.

2. A Nonviolent Declaration

◇◇◇◇◇◇◇◇◇◇◇

IN 1833, A GROUP OF abolitionists called a convention in the city of Philadelphia. They hoped to carry further the work that the Revolutionary Fathers—meeting in the same city in the Constitutional Convention fifty-seven years earlier—had left unfinished: the work of creating a free nation. The abolitionists intended to free the nation's blacks from slavery and discrimination, and to do so not by the violence by which the Revolutionary Fathers had freed the nation's whites from the British, but by the nobler means of nonviolence.

The immediate purpose of the abolitionists in calling a convention was to draw together the local abolitionist work already going forward and to give it a fresh start on the national level. For several years they had already been trying to revive the abolitionist movement.

The movement needed reviving. During the American Revolution and shortly afterward, there seemed to be some chance for the abolition of slavery throughout the country. The Northern states, where the economy depended little on slavery, gradually abolished it, but after 1800 it increasingly became apparent that Southern planters, finding cotton more and more profitable, believed that slavery was essential to their prosperity and did not intend to abolish it any time soon. The abolitionist movement, led by conservative Quakers, had become discouraged and ineffectual. Its calls for gradual abolition allowed many people to postpone serious thought about the question. It allowed the major humanitarian concern over slavery to become deflected into the deceptive colonization plan—to remove Negroes from the United States by transplanting them to settlements of their own abroad, preferably in Africa—a plan endorsed by many of the nation's leading clergy, educators, and politicians.

By 1833, Garrison in New England and the Tappan brothers in New York had become major figures in the abolitionist revival. They borrowed the term "immediate" from the British abolitionsits who had used it successfully in their recent peaceful campaign to abolish slavery in the British West Indies, and they insisted on "immediate" abolition in the United States. They opposed colonization, arguing that Negroes, brought to America as slaves against their will, should be allowed to stay as free men if they wished.

About this time increasing faith in democracy was giving many Americans new energy, and striving for something better was a mood of the day. Some men sought a better life by moving West and taking up land. Some sought it in religious revivalism. Many sought it in reform—"A restless, prying conscientious criticism broke out in unexpected quarters," said Emerson. Reformers earnestly believed, more than reformers in the previous generation had believed, that society could be reformed quickly and permanently. With great optimism, reformers were trying utopian communities like Brook Farm, Fruitlands, or Oneida. They were trying religious reform such as Unitarianism. They were trying diet reform, land reform, prison reform, women's rights, temperance, peace, or the abolition of slavery.

Reform was in the air of America, but so was hostility to reform, and the hostility was often expressed in violence. Many Americans could easily become violent. When they felt their way of life threatened by abolitionists, it was natural for them to defend themselves by joining an anti-abolitionist mob, and powerful interests had reasons at least to tolerate, if not to encourage, them in doing so. The abolitionists' determination to be nonviolent was in part the attempt of a weak band of reformers to protect themselves from establishment-condoned popular violence, North and South.

The three groups of nonviolent abolitionists were represented at the Philadelphia convention—Quakers, Garrisonians, and Tappanites—and together they dominated the convention. The differences among the three groups, not yet very clear, were only beginning to be felt.

Of the approximately sixty delegates, one-third were Quakers, and they were the largest distinct group at the convention.

By the early 1830's the Quakers had been weakened by theological disputes among themselves and had divided into two branches, the more conservative Orthodox and the more liberal Hicksites. Thus, much of their energy was turned inward, in debilitating contention among themselves, rather than outward toward reform.

In 1833 many of the more conservative Quakers were uneasy about the revived abolitionist program. They feared that to most Americans "immediate" emancipation would mean that Negroes would be freed at once to cut the throats of those who oppressed them. They feared that only in combination with plans to colonize Negroes abroad could Southern planters be induced to participate in emancipation, albeit slowly.

Such conservative Quakers were not represented at the Philadelphia convention. While all Quakers agreed on the use of nonviolent methods, it was only the more liberal, activist minority, those who were willing to risk great public hostility to bring justice to the Negro, who came to the convention. Among them were the young Massachusetts farmer, poet, and politician, John Greenleaf Whittier, who was as yet little known; the clear and eloquent preacher Lucretia Mott, dressed in plain Quaker garb, who was also as yet little known; and her husband James Mott, a Philadelphia merchant. These Quakers agreed with Garrison and the Tappans on setting emancipation in motion at once, even if it took some time to complete it, and on keeping Negroes in America if they wished to stay.

A major figure at the 1833 convention was William Lloyd Garrison, a young Bostonian of manly carriage and grit. By this time Garrison was already dedicated to nonresistance. Russian nonresistant Tolstoy, the novelist, was to say many years later that Garrison was the first to proclaim nonresistance "as a rule for the organization of the life of men. . . . Therefore Garrison will forever remain one of the greatest reformers and promoters of true human progress."[1]

To Garrison, once his thinking had matured, applying nonresistance to abolition meant first of all doing right himself, including dissociating himself from any action or institution that in any way supported slavery. It also meant not using violence to free the slave, not even the legal violence of government coercion. It also meant not using any mundane methods, such as trying to prove that slavery was unprofitable or trying to manipulate one political interest against another. Rather, applying nonresistance to abolition meant freeing the slave by "moral suasion." It meant convincing the nation that slavery was sin.

Garrison came to advocate nonviolence in considerable part through his association with Quakers. Yet to some Quakers, Garrison seemed violent in spirit at the same time that he advocated nonviolence. He seemed both abusive in his language to opponents and insistent on forgiving them. He seemed at once fanatical in his courting of martyrdom and gentle in his love of children, home life, and the oppressed of the world.

Garrison's pinched childhood may help to explain his paradoxical nature. He was born in Newburyport, Massachusetts, in 1805, shortly after his parents emigrated from the British province of New Brunswick. His father was a rough sailing master who, when he could not find employment, turned to drink, which his proud wife, a convert from lenient Anglicanism to the demanding standards of the Baptists, could not endure. After at least one scene of violence between the father and mother, the father deserted her and her three small children. When still small, Lloyd was required to beg scraps of food for his family while his playmates jeered. He was deprived of all but rudimentary schooling. From the age of eight he was placed as an apprentice at various trades in which he found himself a failure. At the age of twelve he was finally placed at a trade at which he could excel: he was apprenticed as a printer to a Newburyport newspaper publisher and lived in his family. Lloyd did not see his mother from the time he was eleven till he was eighteen.

Lloyd's older brother James responded to his childhood deprivations by rebelling against his mother; he eventually ran away to become a dissolute sailor like his father. Lloyd, whose deprivations were probably greater than James's, responded to them differently: he became defensively harsh to opponents, anxious for the security of a stable family, and, perhaps rejecting his father, he became, unlike him, personally gentle, disciplined, and determined to find recognition in an honorable career. For James the major way out of frustration was alcohol; for Lloyd it was work.

In his early twenties, when Garrison made a political speech and a Boston paper taunted him for being unknown, he replied, "If my life be spared, my name shall one day be known to the world, at least to such an extent that common enquiry shall be unnecessary."[2] Like the young Benjamin Franklin, another Yankee printer, Garrison was ambitious, but, having been inoculated with his mother's inclination to personal purity, he was not ambitious in a wordly sense. Unlike

Franklin, Garrison remained poor through virtually all his turbulent life.

Beginning in 1826, Garrison's printing experience led him to become editor of various small New England newspapers. As an editor, he increasingly came to advocate temperance reform, and, since both his brother and father were alcoholics, he had some personal knowledge of what he was writing about. He also became increasingly drawn to advocate peace. In 1826 he published in his Newburyport paper the first poem that the shy farm youth, John Greenleaf Whittier, ever had published. Thereafter Garrison published many of Whittier's poems and became acquainted with Whittier's Quakerism, including its emphasis, in contrast to Garrison's Puritanism, on man's capacity for doing good, even to the extent of abolishing war; Garrison called Whittier the noblest youth in the land. About the same time Garrison met the evangelical William Ladd of Maine, the huge, genial Harvard graduate and former sea captain who was soon to found the American Peace Society; Garrison predicted that Ladd would prove the foremost philanthropist of the age. Early in 1828 in Boston, when Garrison was only twenty-two years old, he met Benjamin Lundy, a somewhat deaf, undersized, New Jersey–born Quaker, a zealot who edited an antislavery paper in Baltimore and walked thousands of miles about the country, North and South, in poverty, agitating against both war and slavery. "We have never met with a more extraordinary being," the ardent Garrison wrote of Lundy at the time; "no one who succeeded so well in grafting his feeling upon our own." Lundy enlisted Garrison's devotion to the antislavery cause and perhaps to the nonresistance cause as well. It was soon after meeting Lundy that Garrison announced publicly that no matter where he was, he would direct his life to the overthrow of intemperance, slavery, and war.[3]

For several years Garrison had not appeared for compulsory training with the Massachusetts militia because he was excused for nearsightedness. In 1829, a year after first meeting Lundy, he again did not appear for militia duty. For not doing so and for neglecting to present a certificate of his nearsightedness as an excuse, he was ordered to pay a fine, and—in an act that may have had a significant bearing on his future advice to conscientious objectors to pay such fines—he paid it.[4]

In a letter to a friend about this incident, Garrison did not indicate that he had refused militia service because he was conscientiously opposed to bearing arms. But this may have been an additional reason, for a few months later, in September, 1829, two years after meeting Whittier and Ladd and more than a year after meeting Lundy, Garrison recounted in Lundy's paper the story of his not appearing for militia duty and explained that he had decided to refuse all military duty because he was conscientiously opposed to it. "I am not professedly a Quaker," he said, "but I heartily, entirely and practically embrace the doctrine of nonresistance. . . . I now solemnly declare that I will never obey any order to bear arms, but rather cheerfully suffer imprisonment and persecution."[5] From this time Garrison publicly maintained his nonresistant position, and he continued to do so even during the Civil War.

Most of Garrison's service to the antislavery cause was as an editor —briefly in 1829 and 1830 with Lundy in slave-owning Baltimore, where he was imprisoned for seven weeks for writing what he thought of a slave trader, and from 1831 for over thirty years in Boston where he was editor of his own antislavery weekly, the *Liberator*.

Though the *Liberator* emphasized nonviolence, ironically it became famous largely because Southern-vested interests chose to regard it as a violent threat to them. In its first year of publication, as Garrison took pleasure in making known, a North Carolina grand jury indicted him for publishing material likely to incite slaves to rebellion.

Even in the North, Garrison's language was often considered inflammatory. The *Liberator*'s "vocabulary of vituperation," said the Boston *Courier*, "is probably the richest and finest in the world."[6]

Garrison sometimes defended himself from such charges by referring to the strong language of Jesus in rebuking the scribes and Pharisees as "blind guides," "serpents," and "vipers." When even his nonresistant friend Samuel J. May told him that he was hurting his cause by his language, Garrison defended himself in another way. Do the slaves "think my language too severe or misapplied?" Garrison asked May. "Do that wretched husband and wife," who have just been separated for life, for sale on the auction block, "think my denunciation of their master too severe?" This answer shook May.[7] He was compelled to agree with Garrison that American slavery deserved severe denunciation. American slavery, the abolitionists at the Philadelphia convention claimed and a recent scholar confirms,[8] was perhaps the most terrible slavery the world has ever known— for denying slaves the right to marry, to learn to read, to worship, or to accumulate property with which to purchase their freedom.

However, some of Garrison's fellow nonresistants persisted in doubting that his style was appropriate for a nonresistant. His Quaker mentor Lundy scolded him publicly for being "too hasty in his criticisms and too indiscriminate in his charges." Lewis Tappan wrote him that sometimes his spirit was "not sufficiently kind and Christlike." Even his warm friend Samuel J. May wrote him that in his quarrels with the Tappanites, he was "not consistent with the nonresistant, patient, long suffering spirit of the Gospel."⁹

Garrison was broad in his reform interests. Besides supporting peace, temperance, and antislavery, he supported many other controversial reforms, like women's rights, the vegetarian Graham diet, and water cures; he favored abolishing not only corporal punishment for children, but also capital punishment for criminals, imprisonment for debt, and the use of tobacco. Whittier and Lewis Tappan were among those who believed he would be more effective if he did not mix his abolitionist activities with too many other reforms, but Garrison, inclined to be heady, would not accept their advice.

In religion Garrison moved from orthodoxy to liberalism. He was brought up by his lonely mother as a stern, Calvinist-inclined Baptist, and his passionate moral attack on slavery always bore the marks of that heritage. During his early years in Boston, Garrison expected churches to lead the antislavery crusade. Later, partly in reaction to the reluctance of churches to oppose slavery and partly under the influence of such liberal Quakers as James and Lucretia Mott, he gradually became a religious liberal. Eventually Garrison rejected observance of the Sabbath, baptism, and communion, and denied that the Bible, since it attributes contradictory opinions about slavery and war to God, could clearly represent the word of God; he came to believe that men should accept nothing on authority. But in the late 1840's he attended—without joining—the independent Unitarian church of his abolitionist friend Theodore Parker. Garrison's liberal religious views provided excuse for conservative churchmen to call him incorrectly an "infidel," which was a common slippery epithet at the time, like "pink" or "pro-Communist" at a later time, used to discredit any opponent. Charging that abolitionists were infidels "is an old device," explained Garrison wearily in 1860, "to divert attention from the true issue."¹⁰

Garrison's enemies were so successful in molding a false image of him as an incendiary and infidel that even his fellow nonresistants were affected by it. Abolitionist Angelina Grimké told a story about a Quaker friend of hers who felt disinclined to work with Garrison, believing from what he had heard that he was "uncouth." However, the Quaker, after talking in the *Liberator* office with a person he did not know and "whose benevolent countenance and benignant manner he . . . much admired," later discovered to his amazement that he had been talking to Garrison. The Quaker grieved that he had allowed himself to be so prejudiced against a person who was so different from what his enemies had represented, and he soon became a co-worker with Garrison.[11]

Both in his time and since, observers have raged at each other about who Garrison really was. The truth appears to be that under his placid exterior many natures churned and, like many people, he never succeeded in bringing them into harmony. As his perceptive associate Bronson Alcott, the transcendentalist, said, "Garrison has not yet won . . . self-victories."[12] He could be vengeful to those who deserted his camp, but he could also seem forgiving. He could be clear in sorting out complicated situations—defining the issues for abolitionists was one of his major contributions—yet he allowed himself to be duped by assorted medical quacks and hypnotists. At a meeting he could seem coldly self-righteous, yet there is abundant evidence that at times he was personally warm, generous, and lovable. He was persistent in advocating nonviolence, yet even in doing so he could use bloody verbal images. Among complete nonresistants he at times pushed his ideas to extremes, yet in practice he was often more moderate than many of them.

In relation to the world at large, his abolitionist position was uncompromising, and his effectiveness often depended on that trait. In large part because of the vigor of his words, his confidence in the righteousness and ultimate victory of the antislavery cause, and his devotion to principles regardless of consequences to himself, rightly or wrongly the nation came to think of him as the leader of abolitionism. For many of those who either blessed or cursed him, the nonviolent Garrison had already become by the time of the 1833 convention, and was to remain throughout the Civil War, abolitionism incarnate.

In addition to Garrison, another major nonviolent leader at the convention was Lewis Tappan. In the early 1830's, Lewis Tappan and his brother Arthur were wealthy New York silk merchants. While they were to have business failures, they sometimes did a million dollars' worth of business a year, and they believed that they did so because of their business integrity. At a time when other merchants did not always give true weights or measures and varied their prices according to customers, the Tappans gave true weights and measures and kept to the same price for all; Lewis said that slave owners, even though they well knew the Tappans' abolitonist views, were still satisfied to trade with them.

The Tappan brothers were brought up by earnest, Calvinist parents in the small town of Northampton, Massachusetts. As children, they lived near a Negro woman who took a kindly interest in them, and they responded affectionately to her; this laid a foundation, Lewis believed, for their later concern for Negroes. As he remembered it long afterward, Lewis as a child was outgoing, busy caring for the family garden and cow, anxious for the Sabbath to be over so he could romp again. At the age of twelve, he left school to work in his father's goldsmith and dry goods shop. As young men, the Tappan brothers served in the federal army as part of President Jefferson's preparation for war with France; according to Lewis' account, they seem to have had no scruples against participation in war at that time.[13]

Lewis Tappan left home in 1804 to become apprenticed to a Boston importer of dry goods. In Boston he rose rapidly. By the time he was thirty-five years old in 1823, he was a financial agent for various New England factories and treasurer of the Boston and Liverpool Packet Company. In public affairs, he served on the building committee of the Athenaeum Lecture Room, was superintendent of a Sunday school, and was a member of the Boston Common Council. He complained that he did not have time enough for his family—he was rearing a large family, lived in a large house, and kept several servants —but somehow he found time to read a good deal, to take part in a religious discussion group that met in members' homes, and at least twice on Sundays he attended his Unitarian church.[14] (To his parents' distress, Lewis, like his brothers, had become a Unitarian.[15]) As in many other circles in which he became active, he was so diligent and careful about details that he attained some prominence in Unitarian circles: he helped edit a Unitarian journal, was a founder in 1825 of the American Unitarian Association, and was chosen its treasurer.

It was during his Boston period that Lewis Tappan was drawn into the peace movement, the reform movement that was just rising at this time in both Europe and America as a reaction to the Napoleonic Wars. Lewis' pastor, William Ellery Channing, the most eminent Unitarian pastor in the nation, probably helped awaken his concern for peace. "I have been engaged on a committee of the [Massachusetts] Peace Society," Lewis wrote in his journal in 1817. "My pastor,

Mr. Channing, takes a lively interest in this society. May it greatly increase!" His brother John, also a member of Channing's church, may have been another influence on Lewis' thinking, for he had been a founder of the Massachusetts Peace Society. For several years Lewis' journal reflects his continued concern for the peace cause. It was "the great subject which agitates the minds of the community," Lewis wrote in 1819. In 1820 he made a visit to nearby Brighton, to the home of the nearly complete nonresistant, Congregational pastor Noah Worcester, a national figure in the peace cause, whom he admired for his "meekness, benevolence, and piety." Like Channing, Tappan himself was by no means a complete nonresistant at this time. He continued to glory in the American victory at Bunker Hill and to take pride in the American warships in the Charlestown navy yard just below Bunker Hill. In 1823, when asked by Noah Worcester for his judgment of one of his manuscripts advocating that soldiers "throw down their arms," Tappan replied that peace societies could not abolish war but they could "gradually excite an abhorrence of wars, especially offensive wars"; until then it was "premature" to ask soldiers to disarm.[16] As for interest in the antislavery movement, it seems that during his residence in Boston, Tappan did not develop any clear bent in that direction, although Channing, his pastor, had antislavery leanings.

After business reverses in Boston, Lewis Tappan moved to New York in 1828 to join his older brother Arthur as a junior partner in his prosperous cloth business. As part of the move, Lewis made the difficult change from liberal Unitarianism, which was strong in Boston and was the church of his two brothers there, to moderately conservative Presbyterianism, which was strong in New York and was the church of his brother Arthur. It was a difficult switch for such a prominent Unitarian to make, and of course he was charged with making it for business reasons—a charge that, considering his willingness to support unpopular causes through much of his life, scarcely seems well-founded. In reply to the charge, Lewis Tappan wrote a pamphlet explaining that he had independently decided that Unitarians were less zealous than more orthodox Christians, were less careful stewards of their wealth, less devotional in frame of mind, and less scrupulous in observing the Sabbath.[17] While Garrison during the course of his abolitionist career was to move gradually from religious orthodoxy to liberalism, Lewis Tappan, before his abolitionist career had begun, had already moved from orthodoxy to liberalism and then back to a middle position.

In New York City both Lewis and Arthur Tappan were drawn into the theologically moderate revivalism—not heavily Calvinistic —which was led by the evangelist Charles G. Finney and was strong among Congregational and Presbyterian churches, and like many of their associates, the Tappan brothers found in it a source of energy for reform. The brothers became leaders in the "benevolent empire," the national religious reform societies whose headquarters were often in New York. Through these societies, the Tappans and other evangelical Christians expressed their social concerns—in promoting home and foreign missions, Bible and tract distribution, temperance, and education.

In accordance with their Puritan family tradition, the New York Tappan brothers, much like Garrison, were hard working, frugal, and severe. They supervised their store clerks' lives as well as their work—they did not permit them to drink, attend theater, or stay out after ten o'clock at night, and insisted that they attend church twice on Sunday. Arthur disciplined himself rigorously, Lewis said; he took only crackers and water for lunch, and at work, while he received visitors courteously, he would not provide chairs for them or say very much, so they didn't stay long. Arthur had a kind heart, but he was taciturn, Lewis admitted, and somewhat impatient, as might be expected of a man plagued with continuous headaches. While Lewis was the more agreeable of the two, he himself had an annoying habit of reproving others. By 1820 he had frankly recognized his habit, and to check it for a time he fined himself whenever he spoke too impatiently, but his habit persisted. In 1827 one of his pastors warned him that his mind had a "constitutional ardor" and that he was too hasty. Similarly, in 1836 his abolitionist associate Theodore Weld wrote him that it was a peculiarity of his mind that he came to unfavorable conclusions about men "on too slight grounds, too summarily."[18]

Of the two brothers Arthur was the wealthier, the more prominent before the public, at least in the 1830's, and the one we know more about because Lewis wrote his biography. Lewis, however, was the more articulate, the one who had the greater influence in the long run in the antislavery movement, and was the more clearly nonviolent.

For Lewis and Arthur, participation in both the antislavery and peace movements was a natural combination, as it also came to be for their two brothers in Boston and for many of their reform associates in New York State.

Already exposed to the peace movement in Boston, Lewis continued to be exposed to it after coming to New York. In 1828, shortly after he arrived in New York, the American Peace Society was founded there as an amalgamation of various state societies, and the next year Lewis was chosen as a member of its board of directors, along with his brother John of Boston.[19]

In addition, after being drawn into the abolitionist movement in New York, Arthur and Lewis could scarcely escape the pervasive Quaker presence in it. Arthur met Quaker Lundy as early as 1828 and offered funds to his antislavery paper by 1830. Just before the Philadelphia convention, Arthur distributed five thousand copies of a pamphlet by Quaker Whittier which insisted on abolishing slavery without "violence and blood."[20] At the convention itself, Lewis eulogized Lundy and was able to make an allusion to English Quaker history in an apparently impromptu speech. But the Tappans' belief in nonviolence was essentially a part of their own commitment to the New Testament as they rather literally understood it, as was also their commitment to honest measure, frugality, the stewardship of wealth, and racial brotherhood.

By 1831, Arthur had broken with the American Colonization Society because, for one reason, it permitted gunpowder to be among the leading articles of trade for its colony of Liberia in Africa. Many years later, Lewis Tappan said Arthur was "fond of peace, and much as he hated slavery he had never desired that the slaves should gain their freedom by the effusion of blood."[21]

But Lewis became a more dedicated peace man than Arthur. As historians have little noticed, Lewis Tappan, like Garrison, strongly committed himself to peace principles and was persistent in his commitment. From 1829, Lewis was an officer of the American Peace Society at various times for twenty-five years. By 1833, having become a more absolute pacifist than while he was in Boston, Tappan believed "that all resort to bloody weapons is anti-Christian."[22] In 1843 he was a delegate of the American Peace Society to the world peace congress, the first of its kind, in London. Although while he was living in Boston he had gloried in the American Revolution, at least by the early 1840's he had come to question the use of violence so sharply that, when funds were being raised to complete the building of a monument to honor the soldiers who fought at Bunker Hill, he declined to contribute, "because of my peace principles," he explained.[23] In 1846, when war between the United States and Britain threatened over Oregon, Tappan secured the signatures of four hundred New Yorkers to a statement that it would be better for Oregon to sink to the bottom of the ocean than for Britain and the United States to go to war over it, "to the disgrace of civilization, Christianity, and rational freedom."[24] In 1858, when an abolitionist proposed encouraging slave revolts, Tappan replied: "I do not approve the course you recommend. I am a Christian, and a peace-maker, and object to all resort to deadly weapons to secure our rights. I believe in the overruling providence of God . . . and in Him who has said, 'vengeance is mine.' "[25] Like most members of the American Peace Society, Lewis Tappan was not clearly a conscientious objector to all war, but he was very close to being one.

As a peace man, Lewis Tappan could not advocate warlike methods to achieve freedom for the slaves. He advised abolitionists not to retaliate against violence, not even to the extent of taking court action against those who attacked them, arguing that "unresisting deportment" would win more friends for the cause.[26] In the 1830's, like most abolitionists, he was a "moral suasionist." Even in the 1840's, when many abolitionists were turning to political action as the major means to free the slaves, he was so sensitive to the danger of diluting what he considered the religious nature of the abolitionist cause by mixing it with the crass methods of politics that, though less absolute about it than Garrison, he was for several years reluctant to become involved in politics at all. Similarly, although active in the rough world of business himself, he distrusted the coercion of economic pressure against slave owners as a means to free the slaves; he believed it would not lead slave owners to the repentance that was necessary to establish justice. His major reliance, like Garrison's, was on appeals to conscience.

Lewis Tappan was essentially of the same stony, Puritan stuff as Garrison. He was, like Garrison, a moralist rather than an intellectual. He believed, like Garrison, that it was his duty to persuade all Americans to accept his own view of Christ and the just, sober, righteous life. He was a little milder in his language than Garrison; he was not under the same compulsion to seek recognition for himself; he was not as anti-institutional; he was closer to the mainstream of American life in his church, business, and political relations. But on slavery he was often as uncompromising as Garrison, and on the question of violence in the antislavery movement he believed, much as Garrison and the Quakers did, in the well-known, little-tried, revolutionary method of forgiveness of enemies, turning the other cheek, and sacrificing oneself for the "truth."

Before the convention met in Philadelphia in 1833, each of the three groups of nonviolent abolitionists—Quakers, Garrisonians, and Tappanites—already had organizations under their control which were pledged to work for abolition by nonviolence.

The Quakers, of course, were organized in the Society of Friends, which had long insisted on working for the abolition of slavery by nonviolent means.

In 1832 the Garrisonians had led in forming the New England Antislavery Society. It adopted a constitution pledging it to operate only by "peaceful" means and to "give no countenance to violence or insurrection."

In October, 1833, just two months before the Philadelphia convention, the Tappanites had led in forming the New York City Antislavery Society. Its constitution said that the society would never "countenance the oppressed in vindicating their rights by resorting to physical force." The society promptly issued an address saying, "Our very object precludes the idea of all resort to force. We have no force but the force of truth."[27]

As the delegates arrived in Philadelphia in December, 1833, one of them, the ardent Samuel J. May, a Unitarian pastor from a little town in Connecticut, studied the others. He inquired who they were, noted their bearing and expression, and listened to what they said. Among them were three Negroes, two or three Unitarians, ten or twelve evangelical ministers, and twenty-one Quakers. By far most of the delegates were young—young enough to survive to see the failure of their nonviolent campaign in the Civil War. They came from ten different states, all in the North. May approved of most of what he observed. The delegates were serious, he decided; many of them were ready to die if need be for the abolition cause.[28]

Even as the delegates met, violence threatened them. The Philadelphia public was so hostile that the police recommended that the convention meet only in the daytime, and the delegates agreed. But the convention admitted visitors just the same. Lewis Tappan told the convention that a young man at the door had said that if he had the opportunity, he would dip his hand in Garrison's blood.

To reduce public hostility toward the convention, a committee of delegates tried to persuade two respectable, conservative Philadelphia Friends to act as chairman of the convention, but both declined. Instead the convention fell back on one of the delegates, the Tappanite Presbyterian minister Beriah Green, for chairman. He was plain and unimpressive in appearance, but able; he had recently been selected as president of a Tappan-supported interracial school, Oneida Institute, in upstate New York. In a gesture to the crucial role of Negroes in the abolitionist movement, when Green himself wished to participate in the convention debate, he turned the chair over to Negro delegate James McCrummell, a Philadelphia barber and dentist.

Sitting on the platform on one side of Green was the well-dressed Lewis Tappan, who served as one of the secretaries. Delegates observing Tappan decided variously that he was "jaunty," "intellectual-looking," and had a fine voice that inspired hope.[29]

Sitting on the other side of Green was Whittier, who also served as secretary. A delegate amused himself with the idea that Whittier, though a Quaker, looked military; he was handsome, with dark, flashing eyes and black whiskers.

Once in session, the convention decided to create the new American Antislavery Society, as it was expected to do. For the new society the convention adopted a constitution that included a clause stating that the society would never "countenance the oppressed in vindicating their rights by resorting to physical force"—the identical words used in the constitution of the Tappanite New York Antislavery Society.[30] The convention chose as president of the society Arthur Tappan, who had been unable to attend. They also elected a board of managers for the society, which in turn elected an executive committee, including the two Tappan brothers and many of their New York associates, and decided to place the office of the society in the Tappans' home city of New York. It was clear that the Tappanites were to have a major influence in the new organization.

If the convention seemed to be shunting Garrison aside, at least it felt obliged to talk about its most notorious delegate. Chairman Green reported that many Americans were saying that Garrison was "imprudent." Lewis Tappan, though uneasy about Garrison, responded with a warm defense of him, asking what prudence is. "Is it holding back a faithful expression of the whole truth, until the people are ready to say amen? Was that the prudence of the Apostle Paul, when he stood before the Roman Governor? Was that the prudence of William Penn, when he poured contempt on the regalia of kings by wearing his broad beaver?"

One of the black delegates, the impetuous Robert Purvis of Philadelphia—a handsome young man who had inherited wealth from his white father—spoke up for Garrison as among those whites who had sacrificed themselves for Negroes: "Their memories will be cherished when pyramids . . . shall have crumbled."

Another delegate read aloud a poem that Whittier had written in defense of Garrison:

> *They tell me thou art rash and vain*
> *A searcher after fame—*
> *That thou art striving but to gain*
> *A long enduring name—*
> *That thou hast nerved the Afric's hand*
> *And steeled the Afric's heart,*
> *To shake aloft his vengeful brand,*
> *And rend his chain apart. . . .*
>
> *And shall the slanderer's demon breath*
> *Avail with one like me,*
> *To dim the sunshine of my faith*
> *And earnest trust in thee?*

Without deliberately intending to, the convention provided a role for the controversial Garrison when it decided to issue a declaration describing the new society's purposes, a declaration that was to become a landmark for the nonviolent abolitionists. The convention first chose a large committee to write it. This committee met and, after discovering it was making little progress, appointed a smaller committee to make the first draft—a committee of three, the Quaker Whittier, aged twenty-five, Garrison, aged twenty-seven, and the Garrisonian May, aged thirty-six, all complete nonresistants.

In the evening these three went to a Negro's home where Garrison was staying. After talking till ten o'clock, the three decided that Garrison should compose the draft, and Whittier and May left, saying they would return about eight the next morning.

When they returned in the gray light of morning, they climbed upstairs to Garrison's small room. They found Garrison's lamp still burning, his "fine, intellectual head," as Whittier called it, still bent over his table. Garrison was just finishing the last paragraph of the draft; evidently he had worked on it all night.

The three carefully read the draft several times and made a few slight alterations. At nine o'clock, as planned, they took it to the large committee. In a room next to where the convention itself was in session the committee considered the draft for three hours, while from time to time they received appeals from the convention to report the declaration as soon as possible. Committeemen kept asking questions and making suggestions. Garrison was patient, as the generous May remembered afterward. Only once did he offer any resistance to the alterations that were suggested, and that was to May's proposal to drop much of the severe passage Garrison had written condemning the movement to colonize Negroes in Africa. May considered it unnecessary because, he explained, the colonization movement could not long survive, and the committe decided to drop the passage. The other alterations the committee decided to make were insignificant.

By afternoon the committee was finally ready to present the declaration to the convention. As the Quaker chairman of the committee read it aloud, May thought to himself that he had never in his life known a deeper impression to be made by words. The declaration began with a passage praising the goals of the American Revolution but rejecting its violence:

Declaration of Sentiments

. . . More than fifty-seven years have elapsed since a band of patriots convened in this place to devise measures for the deliverance of this country from a foreign yoke. The cornerstone upon which they founded the Temple of Freedom was broadly this—"that all men are created equal . . . " At the sound of their trumpet-call, three millions of people rose up as from the sleep of death, and rushed to the strife of blood; deeming it more glorious to die instantly as freemen, than desirable to live one hour as slaves. They were few in number—poor in resources; but the honest conviction that Truth, Justice, and Right were on their side, made them invincible. . . .

Their principles led them to wage war against their oppressors, and to spill human blood like water, in order to be free. Ours forbid the doing of evil that good may come, and lead us to reject, and to entreat the oppressed to reject, the use of all carnal weapons for deliverance from bondage; relying solely upon those which are spiritual, and mighty through God to the pulling down of strongholds.

Their measures were physical resistance—the marshalling in arms —the hostile array—the mortal encounter. Ours shall be such only as the opposition of moral purity to moral corruption—the destruction of error by the potency of truth—the overthrow of prejudice by the power of love—and the abolition of slavery by the spirit of repentance.

The declaration went on to state some of the nonviolent methods the new society would use. It named nonviolent *indirect* methods already familiar in the long history of abolitionism, such as speaking, publishing, and political action. In addition, the declaration specifically endorsed one nonviolent *direct* action method that Quakers were already using, the boycott of slave-produced goods. The declaration pointed to issues over which other major nonviolent direct actions were to develop, such as church participation in the guilt of slavery, denial of educational opportunity to Negroes, and Northern assistance in returning fugitive slaves to the South.

In an invitation to civil disobedience, the declaration boldly announced that all laws that supported slavery were "before God, utterly null and void." Just what such disobedience could mean to abolitionists in practice the declaration did not say.

At the conclusion of the reading, the convention was silent for several minutes, profoundly silent it seemed to May. Then followed discussion. Quaker Thomas Shipley said that calling slave owners "manstealers" was too harsh; but he was mollified with the explanation that it was a biblical phrase and by the decision to state the source—Exodus 21:16—in the declaration text. A woman in a plain Quaker bonnet at the back of the room—Lucretia Mott, the future women's rights leader—rose to speak. It was the first time many of the non-Quaker delegates had ever heard a woman speak in a public assembly. Lucretia Mott began diffidently, but chairman Green encouraged her to continue. She suggested transposing the items in one statement so that the emphasis was on God rather than on the Declaration of Independence, and the convention accepted her suggestion. No one proposed fundamental changes in the declaration.

The delegates debated the nonviolent pledge. A few of them were personally not nonresistants and they hesitated to support it.

According to Tappan's recollection in 1837, these doubters were permitted to sign the declaration with the understanding that they were pledging themselves not to use "weapons of death to advance the cause, nor approve of the slaves resorting to arms to achieve their independence" but that they were not pledging themselves "not to resist, in any legal way, assaults upon themselves or their property."

In 1839, when it seemed to Garrison that some of the delegates had fallen away from nonviolence, he was to admit that in endorsing the declaration they did not all "understand how far they had, in fact, committed themselves" to nonviolence.

According to May many years later, when a few of the delegates were reluctant "to say that they would not fight if they should be roughly used by the opponents of our cause . . . it was strenuously urged in reply that, whatever might be true as to the right of self-defense, in the prosecution of our great undertaking, violent resistance to the injurious treatment we might receive would have a disastrous effect. It was insisted that we ought to go forth to labor for the abolition of slavery, in the spirit of Christian reformers, expecting to be persecuted, and resolved never to return evil for evil."[31]

After the debate was over and the convention had agree to accept the declaration, pastor May read it to the convention again, his "persuasive voice" faltering, according to Whittier, "with the intensity of his emotions." A silence followed, in the Quaker manner. Then as one of the secretaries called the names of the delegates, each one rose, walked to the platform, signed the declaration, and returned to his seat in silence.

All the delegates signed—that is, all the convention participants but the women who, accepting the custom of the times, did not even think of signing.[32] Despite ambiguities in their understanding of what nonresistance meant, the convention delegates were unanimous in pledging themselves to abolish slavery without violence.

President Green rose to make the concluding address. It seemed to Whittier long afterward the most powerful address he had ever heard. Green reviewed the work of the convention, its earnestness, its union, its refreshing atmosphere. "But now we must . . . breathe another atmosphere," he said. "The chill hoar frost will be upon us. . . . The waves of persecution will dash against our souls. Let us be prepared for the worst. Let us fasten ourselves to the throne of God with hooks of steel. If we cling not to Him, our names to that document will be but as dust."

Despite their unanimity in signing the declaration, several years later abolitionists disputed what it meant. While they agreed that the declaration prohibited them from using offensive violence to end slavery, they differed over whether the declaration prohibited them from using defensive violence to protect themselves when opponents of abolition attacked them personally. They also differed over whether the declaration was a pledge of nonviolence binding on the whole American Antislavery Society, in the same way the society's constitution was, or binding only on those who signed it. Pastor May believed it was binding on the whole society, while Lewis Tappan at least for a time believed it was binding only on those who signed it. Nevertheless the society continued to publish the declaration along with its constitution as if they both represented its policy, and it was still doing so during the Civil War.

By 1840 the Tappanites had split off from the American Antislavery Society, leaving it in Garrisonian control. The Tappanites wished to avoid association with Garrison's harsh language, to work through political parties and churches more than the Garrisonians wished to do, and to follow custom by limiting women's participation in the movement as the Garrisonians did not wish to do.

Nonviolence as such was not an issue in the split. In a tribute to the Declaration of Sentiments, both the Garrisonians' American Antislavery Society and the Tappanites' new American and Foreign Antislavery Society claimed that it was more faithful than the other to the principles of the declaration.

Many years later, when Whittier's black whiskers had turned white and his poems were known throughout the land, he said that he valued his name on the Declaration of Sentiments more than on the title page of any of his books.[33]

3. Absorbing Violence

In the 1830's and 1840's, Northern crowds repeatedly harassed abolitionists. They insulted them, stoned their houses, and blocked the doors of the buildings where they spoke. On the streets of New York City they beat the son of Quaker Isaac Hopper, who was known for aiding fugitive slaves. In Utica, New York, a crowd led by a member of Congress heckled an abolitionist meeting to a stop, and, by holding a cane over the head of the clergyman who acted as secretary, they forced him to surrender his records. In Cincinnati anti-abolitionists threw into the Ohio River the printing press of Tappanite abolitionist James Birney, the former Alabama planter who had freed his slaves. In Trumbull County, Ohio, they tarred and feathered a young abolitionist minister and struck him until he was unconscious; he never fully recovered.

The respectable forces of the North, including officials, merchants, editors, and preachers, often did not feel called upon to curb such violence. They considered the abolitionists to be "fanatical"; they believed false rumors about their desire to mix races; and moreover, they did not wish to offend the South, with which they had strong economic, political, and church ties. After a Philadelphia mob had burned down a hall built for abolitionists meetings, an official city investigating committee said, much as Southern officials were often to say in the mid-twentieth century, that the violence was not the fault of those who performed it, but of pro-Negro agitators who advocated doctrines repulsive to the community.[1]

It was hazardous for abolitionists to act openly in the North, but it was even more so below the Mason and Dixon line. The South scarcely made a pretense of respecting a free speech against slavery. When the aristocratic South Carolinian, Angelina Grimké, moved North and became an active Quaker abolitionist, the mayor of Charleston announced that city police would prevent her from ever returning to her home city even to visit her family. In 1835 a New York physician, the mild-mannered Dr. Reuben Crandall, who was visiting Washington to lecture on botany, was charged with circulating "incendiary" American Antislavery Society literature. Washington's unpeaceful district attorney, colonizationist Francis Scott Key, the author of the words of the already well-known unpeaceful song, "The Star-Spangled Banner," thought Crandall should be put to death for this crime. While awaiting trial, Crandall was held in prison, and, though acquitted by a jury and released after nine months, he died from the illness he contracted there.[2]

Southerners often harassed those they suspected of abolitionist opinions, especially Northerners. They whipped them, ducked them in rivers, tarred and feathered them, or shaved their heads. Garrison estimated that in the South over a twenty-one-year period there were three hundred cases of violent vigilante punishment for antislavery opinions, and a recent student of the subject thinks Garrison's estimate reasonable.[3] In 1835 the American Antislavery Society, in the hope of reducing such punishment, announced that it employed no agents in the slave states; in 1836, pastor Samuel J. May explained that abolitionists sent no literature, even by mail, to Negroes south of Washington and that abolitionist publications "uniformly condemn a resort to violence."[4] Still the harassment of abolitionists in the South continued.

When they were subjected to violence either in the North or South, the abolitionists, in accordance with their public pledges of nonviolence, usually responded nonviolently, and deliberately so, especially in the 1830's. Most abolitionists, if not complete nonresistants like Quakers and Garrisonians or limited nonresistants committed to nonviolence in their abolitionist activities like the Tappanites, were at least "occasional" nonresistants, willing for the time being to try nonviolence to see if it would work.

One night while an abolitionist agent on a tour of Connecticut was sleeping, enemies shaved his horse and cut off its ears. Said the agent the next day to an abolitionist meeting: "Those who have done it are known, but I shall not hurt a hair of their heads. I hope the Lord may forgive them."[5]

One of the nonviolent black leaders who was associated with the Tappans, Presbyterian pastor Theodore S. Wright, had studied at Princeton Theological Seminary where he had felt he was among friends. Once when he returned to Princeton to attend a meeting in the chapel, a Southern student seized him by the collar and kicked him, shouting, "Out with the nigger!" Wright did not retaliate. He continued quietly on his way, and later in a public statement protesting the violence he prided himself on having been faithful to the "self-denying doctrine of nonresistance."[6]

One evening a crowd collected outside a Haverhill, Massachusetts, church to harass the Garrisonian minister May, who was giving an abolitionist talk inside. May, who had helped Garrison write the nonviolent Declaration of Sentiments, was always remarkably disarming and courteous, but the crowd was hostile to him just the same, which suggests that it was not true that abolitionists brought violence on themselves only if they used fierce denunciation. The crowd hooted and threw stones through the church windows, forcing the meeting to dissolve. As it did, an abolitionist girl, the poet Whittier's sister, protected May by using a method the nonresistants often used. She simply took his arm and walked with him out of the church and through the crowd.[7]

When the British nonresistant abolitionist George Thompson visited Boston to speak, tough pro-slavery "truckmen" carrying horse whips came to the meeting. They were prepared to seize Thompson as he left the meeting and whisk him to a ship bound for South Carolina where, abolitionists feared, he would be lynched. As Thompson spoke, hostile men in the audience cried out to him, "It's all a lie," and, "If we had you down South, we'd cut off your ears." After Thompson had finished speaking, according to a plan arranged by pastor May, twenty-five or thirty abolitionists clustered around him, asking questions. As Thompson talked with them, they imperceptibly moved with him toward a curtained rear door through which, before the truckmen knew what was happening, he escaped to a back street and a waiting carriage.[8]

During the 1834 anti-Negro riot in New York City, when mobs wrecked Negro houses, Negro churches, and white churches that favored abolition, friends warned Isaac Hopper, a Quaker bookseller, to remove the display of antislavery literature from his window. He refused, saying that he was not "such a coward as to forsake my principles . . . at the bidding of a mob." Eventually a mob, bent on destruction, came down the street to his shop. Hopper walked out onto his steps and stood there looking calmly at the mob until it became irresolute and, after a pause, moved on.[9]

Quaker Thomas Shipley, a Philadelphia merchant and signer of the Declaration of Sentiments, was well known among Negroes as their friend—his name was whispered reverently, Whittier said, even in the slave cabins of Maryland. In the summer of 1835, when whites mobbed Philadelphia Negroes, invading their houses and plundering their furniture, police did not interfere. Shipley disguised himself and mingled with the white rioters to discover their plans and identify their leaders.

At first Negroes did not resist the rioters, but as the riots continued unchecked, they became desperate, and a group of Negroes gathered arms in a hall. One night when this fact became known to the white mob, they planned to attack the hall. Shipley, in the mob, heard the plan. To avert an open battle, he ran to the hall where the Negroes were gathered, identified himself as Shipley, and urged them not to use force because it would increase their troubles. Knowing him as their friend, the Negroes accepted his advice and left the hall. Shortly afterward Shipley reported to the authorities who the leaders of the mob were, and they were arrested.[10]

At a New Haven antislavery meeting, every time the speaker mentioned slavery, a group of white youths loudly interrupted him. Tappanite Simeon S. Jocelyn, the white minister of a colored church in New Haven, remonstrated with the youths, but to no avail.

When the meeting was over, the noisy youths followed Jocelyn to his house. After he had gone inside, the youths knocked down his fence. When a neighbor objected, the youths told him to mind his own business or they would knock his house down. Pastor Jocelyn opened his door and asked the youths what they wanted. They said they would let him know what they wanted. Then they showered the house with stones, shattering windows, and, picking up large stones from a wall in the yard, they pounded them against the blinds.

But Jocelyn, who was a signer of the nonviolent Declaration of Sentiments, did not retaliate in any way, not even by sending for the police—as Quaker Shipley might have done. Jocelyn wrote a New Haven paper afterward: "As this outrage upon myself and my associates is purely on account of the principles of liberty which we promulgate, and to which we religiously adhere . . . I have not resorted to carnal weapons of defense nor to the civil power."[11]

Like Jocelyn, abolitionist Lucretia Mott—the wary, tactful little Quaker saint—refused to appeal for police protection, not even, according to one of her close friends, when howling mobs showered stones through the windows of the meeting places where she was.

When a mob broke up an annual meeting of the American Antislavery Society in New York, Lucretia Mott showed her strength. As the audience left the hall in confusion, she saw that toughs were roughing up some of the women. She asked the gentleman escorting her to help some of them. "But who will take care of you?" he asked.

"This man," she answered, quietly laying her hand on the arm of one of the toughest of the toughs. Though astonished, the man replied by conducting her through the mob to safety.

As if that were not enough, the next day Lucretia Mott returned to the neighborhood of the meeting, entered a restaurant, and, recognizing a leader of the mob at the table, sat down with him to talk and won his respect.[12]

In the summer of 1835 abolitionist Amos Dresser, a Northern student, was selling Bibles in the South to raise funds to continue his education. As he drove about with his horse and barouche, he carried his Bibles wrapped with antislavery papers to prevent them from rubbing each other. As he admitted afterward, he intended to distribute the antislavery papers "as suitable opportunities should present."

While he was selling Bibles in Nashville, he took his carriage to a shop for repairs. In the shop the workmen discovered the antislavery papers and spread the rumor that he was circulating "incendiary" literature among slaves to incite them to revolt. Eventually a city officer took Dresser to the mayor, who asked him to appear before an extralegal vigilance committee. "To this I replied," wrote Dresser afterward, that "it would give me pleasure to do so, as I wished it understood just what I had done and what I had not done."

The extralegal trial was held that evening in a courtroom before the mayor, sixty members of the vigilance committee, and spectators. The committee brought in Dresser's trunk and examined the contents. They read his business and private letters—some of them aloud—including references to abolition, and Dresser admitted he had been a member of the antislavery society at Lane Theological Seminary in Cincinnati. After six or seven hours of trial, Dresser was called on for his defense. "Whilst I told them," he wrote afterward, that "I believed slaveholding to be inconsistent with the Gospel, and a constant transgression of God's law, I yet said, that in bringing about emancipation the interests of the master were to be consulted as well as those of the slave. . . . In reference to my demeanor toward the slave, [I said] that in the few instances in which I had casually conversed with them, I had recommended quietness, patience, submission; teaching them to render 'good for evil.' "

The committee sent Dresser into another room while it deliberated on his case. He remained composed. He believed he had not violated any law. Moreover, he knew that among those trying him were "a great portion of the respectability of Nashville . . . [including] most of the elders of the Presbyterian church, from whose hands, but a few days before, I had received the emblems of the broken body and shed blood of our blessed saviour."

The committee called him back into the courtroom and announced a decision that dismayed him. They found him guilty, as Dresser reported it, "first, of being a member of an antislavery society in Ohio, second, of having in my possession periodicals published by the American Antislavery Society, and third, they believed I had circulated these periodicals and advocated in the community the principles they inculcated." Their sentence was twenty lashes on his bare back and an order to leave town in twenty-four hours.

By then it was late at night, but the committee at once directed the crowd to proceed to the public square. There the committee formed the crowd into a ring and led Dresser into the center of it. While they were stripping off his shirt, someone moved that he be let go, and someone else seconded the motion. But others yelled furiously, "No," and swore at those who would let him go. Amid confusion, Dresser knelt to receive his punishment. City officer Broughton lashed him with a heavy cowskin twenty times.

When the lashing was finished, as Dresser related later, "an involuntary feeling of thanksgiving to God for the fortitude with which I have been enabled to endure it, arose in my soul, to which I began aloud to give utterance." For an instant the crowd fell silent, listening to him. Then someone protested: "God damn him, stop his praying."

A moment later the committee dismissed Dresser. City officer Broughton raised him to his feet and conducted him to his lodging. The next morning Dresser fled the city in disguise, leaving much of his property behind.

Afterward Dresser wrote without vengeance of the man who had lashed him, "I take pleasure here in stating of Mr. Broughton, that . . . he exhibited to me, throughout the whole of this melancholy affair, the kindest and most delicate deportment."

The Nashville *Banner* admitted that Dresser had not broken any law. But the Augusta, Georgia, *Chronicle* insisted that Dresser should have been hung up as high as Haman to rot until the wind whistled through his bones. The cry of the whole South, said the *Chronicle*, should be death, instant death, to the abolitionists whenever they are caught.[13] Such "chivalrous" Southern comment merely served to heighten the effect of Dresser's nonviolence. Garrison praised Dresser, and Dresser's story, frequently retold, became an abolitionist legend.[14]

Theodore Weld, one of the most impressive American Antislavery Society agents and a close associate of the Tappans, was a limited nonresistant. Like many Tappanites, Weld did not clearly rule out the possibility of his participation in war, but he described himself, publicly and privately, as advocating the "doctrine of personal nonresistance." When he first became an antislavery agent, Weld was pelted with eggs and struck on the head with stones; for months, he said, he was called to "test" his nonresistance principles "almost every day."[15]

Weld's greatest danger was whenever he emerged from a meeting into the street where a mob awaited him. Sometimes his friends would form a bodyguard to see him to his room. More often Weld protected himself simply by folding his arms and looking directly at the mob—he had learned that mobs hesitate to attack a man with folded arms.[16]

In 1836, Weld was in a Presbyterian church in Lockport, New York, leading a meeting called to form a Niagara County antislavery society. However, most of the people attending the meeting came in order to prevent the formation of such a society, and when Weld rose to speak, they began to hiss and stamp. Weld informed them that the antislavery forces had the permission of the church's officials—most of whom were present—to hold a meeting to form a society, and he tried to continue speaking. But his opponents, including some of the county's "high judicial and executive officers," began hissing and stamping again, and Weld, determined to be patient, took his seat. The opposition took control of the meeting. For some four hours they proceeded, without interference from the abolitionists, to elect their own officers and to pass resolutions opposing any discussion of slavery as dangerous to the unity of the nation. When the opposition finally wore out and left the church, most of the abolitionists remained in their seats and at last proceeded to form their county society.

The abolitionists' restraint apparently had its effect. A year later, looking back on the formation of their society, one of the society's representatives wrote the state antislavery paper: "We abstain from repeating the names of the actors in these oppressive proceedings, believing that many of them sincerely regret the part they took on that memorable day. We willingly draw the veil, the more cheerfully as amendment has followed repentance, and the sentiments so ably advocated by T. D. Weld have since been treated by this community with much respect."[17]

Garrison regarded such restraint in abolitionist meetings as typical. "The Society of Friends aside," he wrote in the *Liberator*, "what other body of men, whether political or religious, besides abolitionists, would suffer themselves to be insulted and outraged, and their meetings forcibly suppressed or systematically interrupted by their opponents, without making a prompt and violent appeal to the *lex talionis?* . . . Thanks be to God that the abolitionists are generally men of peace."[18]

Garrison himself, by his own example of nonviolence under stress, impressed on some minds the relevance of nonviolent methods to what was essentially a moral campaign.

After a mob had broken up a meeting at the Massachusetts Antislavery Society office in Boston in 1835, the mob began shouting for Garrison. But Garrison remained sitting placidly in the office at a desk. As complete nonresistant C. C. Burleigh, who was there, reported it, Garrison showed "no sign of alarm, either in deed, word, or look."

The mob—composed, as a Boston newspaper said, not of idlers but of "gentlemen of property and standing"—was determined to preserve the city from "incendiaries," and threatened to lynch Garrison. At this point one of Garrison's abolitionist friends, fearing for Garrison's life, renounced nonviolence and said he would defend him. But Garrison refused his help, asking what value principles have if they are not to be used.

By this time the Boston mayor was in the building, and he advised Garrison to escape by climbing out a back window. When abolitionist friends also advised him to do so, Garrison climbed out and hid in a carpenter shop. Police then announced to the mob that Garrison was not in the building. However, somehow they learned where he was. The mob, now numbering in the thousands, seized him and hauled him through the streets. As Burleigh said, "I saw Garrison between two men who held him and led him along, while the throng pressed him on every side, as if eager to devour him alive." The mob tore his coat, his stock, his trousers.

When the mob came opposite the city hall, the police and some in the mob who at least were trying to prevent Garrison from being killed steered him into the city hall.

The mob, however, remained outside, still clamoring for Garrison, and its mood was so fierce that the mayor decided the city hall would be endangered by keeping Garrison in it. To be able to move him to jail in another building, the mayor, with Garrison's consent, arrested him for disturbing the peace, and police took him out to a hack. The mob then rushed "like a whirlwind upon the frail vehicle in which I sat," Garrison wrote afterward, and tried "to drag me out of it. They clung to the wheels—dashed open the doors—seized hold of the horses—and tried to upset the carriage. They were, however, vigorously repulsed by the police . . . and the driver, lustily using his whip upon the bodies of his horses and the heads of the rioters, happily made an opening through the crowd."

The police finally succeeded in putting Garrison in jail. Whittier and May visited him there, finding him in high spirits. The three men most responsible for writing the Declaration of Sentiments had an opportunity to consider together where their determination to "overthrow prejudice by the power of love" was leading them. Garrison slept well that night and left jail in the morning.

In the whole Garrison mob scene, wrote Burleigh, as far as he could observe, the abolitionists "remained true to their principle of rather suffering wrong than doing wrong. Not one raised his hand to repel violence by violence, though they were sufficiently numerous and possessed enough of physical power to have wreaked bloody vengeance upon their injurers had they acted on the common principles of retaliation."[19]

It was soon after the violence to Dresser and Garrison that abolitionists seemed to reach a peak of awareness that they were responding to violence with nonviolence. The Quaker convert Angelina Grimké claimed that abolitionists never used violence. They had "proved themselves to be emphatically peace men," she said, "by never resisting the violence of mobs, even when driven by them from the temple of God, and dragged by an infuriated crowd through the streets of the emporium of New England, or subjected by slaveholders to the pain of corporal punishment." In Missouri, when the Southern Presbyterian abolitionist preacher, David Nelson, was threatened with violence, he said that abolitionists, unlike pro-slavery men, "never talk of burning houses, killing, tarring, feathering, whipping, or burning men." William Ladd, the founder of the American Peace Society, wrote: "Every antislavery man is a peace man; or at least I have known but two or three exceptions."[20]

At about the same time abolitionists were relating their nonviolence to the peace cause at large. Former Alabama planter James Birney wrote: "A large and growing number" of abolitionists "have embraced what are beginning to be known by the name of peace principles. These principles deny to nations the right of making war, either offensive or defensive, and to individuals the right of assaulting others in any case, or of defending their persons or property, if it must be done at the expense of the guilty trespasser's life." Similarly, in the summer of 1837, a leading Garrisonian Negro abolitionist, Pennsylvania lumber dealer William Whipper, said, "There have been many faithful advocates of peace since the apostolic age, but none have ever given a more powerful impetus to the cause of peace, than the modern abolitionists." Whipper agreed with Angelina Grimké that abolitionists were completely nonviolent: "They have been beaten and stoned, mobbed and persecuted from city to city," he said, "and never returned evil for evil."[21]

Of course violence hurt some abolitionists: it interrupted their meetings, bruised their bodies, destroyed their property, and, as a sign of the scorn of the community, it disturbed their pride. On the other hand, the violence brought attention to their cause, a cause that many people preferred to forget. Moreover, many abolitionists believed that by not retaliating they were turning the violence into a positive benefit to their cause. When they did not retaliate, abolitionists won the sympathy people often give the underdog. Also, when they did not retaliate, it became clear to many observers that the abolitionists had put themselves in a better moral position than their attackers.

When Philadelphia rioters burned down the abolitionists' newly built Pennsylvania Hall, Whittier said the fire had "greatly awakened curiosity in regard to a cause which its enemies dare not meet in the fair field of free discussion."

After Boston mobbed Garrison, the effects were a boost in the *Liberator*'s circulation and new recruits for abolitionism, including a young physician of a prominent Massachusetts family, Henry Ingersoll Bowditch.

When an abolitionist tried to speak in Mansfield, Massachusetts, and a band came into the gallery to drown him out, the result, one abolitionist wrote, was that the disturbance had "done the work of twelve lectures": nearly 250 people joined the local antislavery society.

A riot against abolitionists in Utica, New York, helped to revolutionize the city for abolition: 1200 citizens signed petitions to abolish slavery in the District of Columbia, and one of the leading philanthropists of the state, Gerrit Smith, resenting the rioters' attempt to curb free speech, finally converted from colonization to abolition.

The New York City riot created thousands of abolitionists, said a white abolitionist clergyman who was forced to flee his house. "The blood of the abolitionists is the salvation of the slave," he explained, paraphrasing the traditional church maxim.

Editor Lydia Maria Child of the *National Antislavery Standard* said violence against abolitionists had "conspired to do our work, in a manner perceptible enough to us, though not to the world."

The 1830's, the period when the abolitionists were the most clearly nonviolent, was a period of rapid growth for abolitionism. In 1833 there were but a handful of antislavery societies. By 1835 there were about 500, and by 1838 the American Antislavery Society claimed there were 1350 societies with a membership of perhaps 250,000. The ability of the underdog abolitionists to absorb the repeated acts of violence against them, usually without retaliation, was undoubtedly a cause of that spectacular growth.

However, the growth was nearly all in the North. The abolitionists could not claim similar results in the South when nonresistants like Amos Dresser suffered violence there. In the South apparently the economic and political support for slavery was too overwhelming, the pulpit and press too self-serving, to permit the same effect to occur. Were there impassable limits for nonviolence?

Pastor May seemed to believe so when he wrote in 1842: "A free man cannot live the other side of Mason and Dixon's line. . . . He must therefore speak for God and humanity here, or nowhere in our land."[22] But some nonresistants, notably the Tappanites, did not agree with him. They believed the gains they were making by not retaliating to violence could be extended even to the South, and particularly in the 1850's, when the sectional fissure gaped wider than ever, they were to test their belief.

4. Lovejoy Tries Guns

◇◇◇◇◇◇◇◇◇◇◇

DESPITE THE CLAIMS that abolitionists in the mid-1830's never used violence, a few of them in fact did so, among them some of the most prominent abolitionists in the country. But whether they used violence in ways that the Declaration of Sentiments meant to reject was a question on which abolitionists differed.

During the 1834 riot in New York City, a pro-slavery mob gathered in front of Lewis Tappan's home. By the next night Tappan had taken his family out of town. That night rioters smashed his windows, ransacked his house, and hauled much of his furniture into the street to burn. When Tappan and his wife returned to the house after the destruction, his wife laughed to see that the big mirror over the living room fireplace, which he had often thought was too extravagant, had at last been broken. They were all safe, Tappan reported in a letter to Theodore Weld, and they had not disgraced "the glorious cause of antislavery." The only weapon Lewis Tappan had carried during the several days of rioting was a New Testament.[1] Lewis Tappan—after whom the Tappanite nonresistants are named—had remained nonresistant.

However, during the same riot Lewis Tappan's less peaceful brother Arthur, the president of the American Antislavery Society, resorted to violence. As reported in New York papers and in the *Liberator* at the time,[2] Arthur Tappan, fearing damage to his silk warehouse, armed his clerks with guns. He ordered them to fire only if the rioters entered the warehouse and only at their legs in order to spare their lives. For several days and nights the clerks successfully guarded the warehouse. Rioters broke windows but never entered the building.

Afterward abolitionists elsewhere praised New York abolitionists for being nonviolent during the riot, and the executive committee of the American Antislavery Society, including President Arthur Tappan, signed a statement on the riot affirming that they would live and die by their society's constitution and Declaration of Sentiments. Despite their apparent concern for nonviolence, abolitionists did not raise an issue over the use of arms by their president, and neither did the general public. Perhaps abolitionists did not censure Tappan because the guns were not actually fired and because he had acted on the advice of the mayor, thus making it in a sense a police action. Perhaps they did not censure him also because many abolitionists regarded their commitment to the use of nonviolence as not extending to self-defense or defense of personal property but only to their positive action to abolish slavery.

There were other cases of defensive violence by abolitionists, particularly, as was to be expected, by those who were more closely associated with the limited nonresistant Tappanites than with the completely nonresistant Garrisonians or Quakers.

Alvan Stewart, an upstate New York lawyer, was one of the Tappanites who believed that abolitionists should not use violence to interfere with slavery. He was peace conscious; he was even a leader in the American Peace Society. But he still believed that abolitionists had a right to use defensive violence.

In 1835, after Stewart had applied unsuccessfully to Utica city authorities to protect an abolitionist convention from a mob, the mob broke up the convention. That evening the mob also demolished the antislavery printing office in Utica, strewing its type in the streets. When it was rumored that the mob would also attack Stewart's house, Stewart employed carpenters to barricade its doors and windows, armed friends with muskets to protect it, and directed the defenses himself. According to the editor of Stewart's writings, one of those assisting him suddenly realized what he was doing. "Mr. Stewart," he said, "I can't stay with you. I am a peace man."

"So am I," replied Stewart, "but . . . it is my duty to defend this household, and I shall do it. I am captain of this fort, and if they come, I'll mow down fifty of them, in the name of the Lord."

Some of the mob came to Stewart's house and, after spying out its defenses, decided not to attack.[3] Like Arthur Tappan, Stewart did not need to fire his guns.

Afterward abolitionists did not scold Stewart for his use of violence. In fact they honored him by choosing him both as president of the state antislavery society and as chairman of the convention that launched the national abolitionist Liberty party.

Another prominent Tappanite abolitionist who used defensive violence was former Alabamian James G. Birney, the mild and courteous editor of an abolitionist paper in Cincinnati. Beriah Green, who had presided at the nonviolent convention of 1833, was so unashamed of Birney's violence that he described it in a tract intended to help elect Birney as President of the United States on the Liberty party ticket. According to Green, one night in 1836 after a mob had wrecked the office of Birney's paper, Birney heard that his house would be attacked. He soothed the fears of his wife as well as he could, Green said, and then "proceeded, like the man he was, to put his castle into a state of defense. Arms were there, and heroes. But probably aware of the danger to which any such attack would expose them, his adversaries forebore, and kept their distance." Like both Arthur Tappan and Stewart, Birney did not need to fire his guns. But for about two years afterward, Birney and his family, living in constant expectation of attack, kept muskets and other weapons in their house to defend it.

Birney's use of arms did not prevent the Liberty party from twice nominating him for the Presidency or prevent the American Antislavery Society from choosing him to be one of its major executive officers. Nor did it prevent Birney from continuing to be a leader in insisting on exterminating slavery without violence; abolitionists, he said, "are fighting only with the weapons of truth."[4]

It was not until 1837, six years after the *Liberator* began advocating nonviolent abolitionism and four years after the signing of the nonviolent Declaration of Sentiments, that abolitionists at large frankly faced the issue of whether defensive violence was consistent with their public pledges not to use violence to free the slaves. The occasion was Lovejoy's attempt to defend his right to publish an abolitionist paper. In this case Lovejoy and his friends not only armed themselves with guns, but they also fired them, and the result was murder.

The Reverend Elijah Lovejoy, the young editor of a Presbyterian abolitionist paper, had been hounded out of Missouri, a slave state, by pro-slavery mobs and had moved up the Mississippi River to Alton, Illinois, a free state, where he hoped that he would be safer. Under the influence of Garrison, Lovejoy at the time was a complete nonresistant—as Arthur Tappan, Stewart, and Birney never had been. When a hostile Alton crowd surrounded Lovejoy, threatening to tar and feather him, Lovejoy replied, "I am in your hands, and you must do with me whatever God permits you to do." The crowd let him go that time, but did destroy his press.

Lovejoy appealed to the law to protect his property and his freedom of speech, but Alton's mayor said he did not have the necessary police to protect him, and Alton's leading men advised him to leave town. Mobs destroyed his press three times and repeatedly invaded his house, even four times in one night, until his wife became hysterical. Finally Lovejoy felt obliged to abandon nonviolence as a failure. To protect himself and his family, he brought guns into his house. "I have had inexpressible reluctance to resort to this method of defense," he wrote in a letter published in the *Liberator*. "But dear-bought experience has taught me that there is at present no safety for me, and no defense in this place, either in the laws or the protecting aegis of public sentiment. . . . Every night when I lie down, it is with the deep settled conviction that there are those near me and around me who seek my life. I have resisted this conviction as long as I could, but it has been forced upon me."[5]

In November, 1837, Lovejoy's fourth new press arrived on a Mississippi River boat, and he stored it for safety in a stone warehouse near the river. To guard it, Lovejoy, with the permission of the Alton mayor, armed himself and his friends, and they took turns staying inside the warehouse. The next night an armed mob arrived to seize the press. Both the mob and the defenders fired, and one of the mob was killed. Immediately afterward the mayor arrived and ordered the mob to go home, but, incensed at the killing, they refused. The mayor then told Lovejoy and his defenders again, as he had before, that they had the right to shoot to defend their property. Meantime some of the mob had placed a ladder against the warehouse, and one of them, carrying a flaming torch, climbed the ladder and set fire to the wooden shingles of the roof. Lovejoy, seeing someone on the ladder, came out of the building and aimed a gun at him. Before Lovejoy could shoot, several in the mob fired at Lovejoy. He staggered back into the warehouse and died.

The news of the Alton tragedy brought out among abolitionists for the first time a general debate on their commitment to nonviolent methods.

Quaker and Garrisonian abolitionists generally deplored Lovejoy's willingness to arm himself. The Massachusetts Quaker schoolteacher, Abby Kelley, later to be a leading abolitionist orator, wrote her family: "It was shocking to learn that Lovejoy defended himself —he had better have died as did our Saviour saying, 'Father, forgive them, they know not what they do.'" The conservative *Friend* grieved that Lovejoy had violated both the precepts of the gospel and the "avowed pacific policy, often expressed, of the antislavery associations." The more radical Quaker Lundy, Garrison's early mentor, also disapproved of Lovejoy's violence. "while we are sensible that many others will disagree with us," Lundy explained in his paper, "we still feel ourselves bound to protest against the use of deadly weapons, for any purpose, in advocating or promoting the cause of emancipation." Similarly, the Garrisonian H. C. Wright, a former Congregational minister, wrote that he was anguished, "not so much that one of our numbers has fallen in our holy cause, but that he fell as he did. . . . Sorrow hath drunk up my spirits, that that dear brother was in the act of violating the solemn commands of his Saviour when he was shot down." Garrison himself wrote in the *Liberator* that Lovejoy had set a dangerous precedent, and added bluntly, "In the name of Jesus of Nazareth, who suffered himself to be unresistingly nailed to the cross, we solemnly protest against any of his professed followers resorting to carnal weapons under any pretext or in any extremity whatever."[6]

Some other abolitionists who were less dedicated to complete nonviolence under all circumstances nevertheless also deplored Lovejoy's resort to violence. Lewis Tappan wrote Garrison that he believed that Lovejoy "made a great mistake" in using bloody weapons, and "the result appears to show it. . . . In my judgment, God permitted such a failure of the war principle to show abolitionists the folly of their using carnal weapons." While Tappan was judging essentially on the basis of principle, other abolitionists were more pragmatic. When the Revolutionary War veteran Seth Sprague, a merchant and long a member of the Massachusetts legislature, first heard of Lovejoy's death, he only regretted that Lovejoy and his friends had not defended themselves more effectively. But the more he had thought about it afterward, said Sprague at a county antislavery meeting, and the more he considered its probable influence on the antislavery cause, the more he felt it to be important that Lovejoy's "resort to physical resistance in the last extremity, should not be countenanced by the true friends of our great moral enterprise."[7] Lewis Tappan's former pastor, William Ellery Channing, known as a critic of both war and slavery but not as either a complete nonresistant or a complete abolitionist, wrote an open letter to abolitionists warning them that because of the fierce passions their attacks on slavery aroused, they could not use violence successfully. If, on the night Lovejoy died, he and his friends had shot enough of their assailants to protect the press, Channing wrote, they still would not have protected themselves for the future. "The following morning would have revealed the street strewn with dead bodies," Channing explained. "Relatives, friends, the whole people of the surrounding country, would have rushed to the spot. . . . All who have been engaged in the defense of the press, would probably have been torn limb from limb."[8]

But Lovejoy was defending his press under the authority of the Alton mayor, and for some abolitionists this made a difference. The Dover, New Hampshire, *Morning Star*, the organ of the abolitionist Free Will Baptists whose national conference had only recently endorsed the nonviolent Declaration of Sentiments, argued that to censure Lovejoy for defending himself when he was sustaining civil authority "strikes at the root of all civil government." To the Garrisonian May, however, government authority for Lovejoy's action made no difference; the question was simply whether Lovejoy acted "in violation of the avowed principle on which the [American] Antislavery Society commenced."[9] To the Garrisonian H. C. Wright it also made no difference; the question was, has God delegated to man the right to take another man's life, whether through government authority or not? On the issue of government authority Garrison took a middle position between May and Wright's disapproval of violence under any circumstances on the one hand and the *Morning Star*'s approval of violence in enforcing civil law as an exception on the other hand. For Garrison personally, the fact that Lovejoy acted under government authority made no difference; for him, a Christian could not resort to violence under any circumstances. But Garrison realized that acting under government authority did make a difference to many abolitionists. Unless an abolitionist, said Garrison, "has given in his adherence to the doctrine that no man ought to support the laws by physical force, even in obedience to the 'powers that be,'" he should not repudiate Lovejoy for using force.[10]

If anyone was to repudiate Lovejoy for his use of violence, the question remained whether it was the American Antislavery Society's function to do so. Shortly after Lovejoy's death, a group of Quakers called at the society's office in New York to urge it to issue a repudiation. But, as one of them wrote Garrison in alarm, all they could learn at the office was that abolitionists differed on the question. The Quakers foresaw an inevitable division of abolitionists into "fighting" and "pacific" wings.[11]

The society's executive committee, dominated by Tappanites, found itself about equally divided between those who were complete nonresistants and those who thought that taking human life in extreme cases of self-defense was justified. They also found themselves divided over what the society had pledged on the question. Because they were divided, according to one of the society's officers, the committee decided they could not either censure or endorse Lovejoy's use of violence. They could only pledge themselves "strictly to adhere to the pacific principles of the society in all our active measures for the overthrow of slavery."[12]

Disturbed by the committee's divisions, Lewis Tappan wrote Garrison asking for his help to clarify what the society had pledged. Many members, wrote Tappan, "consider that non-combatant principles are obligatory upon every member of the American Antislavery Society," but he himself did not think so, perhaps in deference to the use of violence by his brother Arthur, the president of the society. It seemed to him that the nonviolent Declaration of Sentiments, which some members, including himself, had signed when the society was formed, was a pledge only for those who signed it, and not all members were required to sign it. Moreover, Lewis Tappan said, the constitution of the society, to which all members were pledged, "says nothing about the subject of nonresistance, so far as abolitionists are concerned."[13]

Pastor May flatly disagreed with Tappan. May interpreted the Declaration of Sentiments, which he had helped Garrison write, as a pledge to the world that the society would use nonviolent methods. It was binding on all members, May believed, and Lovejoy as a member had violated it.[14] Later May said that until after the Lovejoy murder he had never heard anyone doubt that the declaration was binding.[15] Moreover, May interpreted the society's constitution as also demanding nonviolence. The constitution, he reminded members in the *Liberator*, says abolitionists "will never, in any way, countenance the oppressed in vindicating their rights by resorting to physical force." If members themselves resorted to physical force, May asked, was not that countenancing the slaves in doing so too?

Garrison again stepped into a middle position—this time a rather muddy middle—between Tappan and May. Garrison did not say, as Tappan did, that the Declaration of Sentiments was not binding on all members. On the other hand, he did not regard the declaration, as May did, as insisting that abolitionists be nonviolent even when they were acting under the authority of government. None of the signers of the declaration—including himself—had rejected the use of violence under civil law at the time they signed it, he believed, though since then he had come to reject it. "Not one of those who signed the Declaration of Sentiments at Philadelphia (however much the views of a few may have since altered), we presume meant to be understood as repudiating that government in defense of which Mr. Lovejoy perished." Therefore in their official capacities the officers of the American Antislavery Society could not "reprobate, distinctly and strongly, the course pursued by Mr. Lovejoy and his associates." Garrison had no intention of trying to make his own newly absolute brand of nonresistance a test for membership in the society. Still he wished to persuade abolitionists that they had already committed themselves to considerable nonresistance. He agreed with the logic of May's interpretation of the clause of the constitution that forbade abolitionists to encourage slaves to revolt, and he asked, if abolitionists believe that slaves are not justified in appealing to physical force for their freedom, "how can they justify others of a different complexion in doing the same thing?"

Among abolitionists, Garrison had taken a middle position on the question of self-defense under government authority, and he had also taken a middle position on the question of whether the American Antislavery Society should repudiate Lovejoy's use of violence. In addition, Garrison took a middle position on the question of whether Lovejoy should be called a martyr.

A substantial portion of the American public was calling Lovejoy a martyr. Developing this idea, President Beriah Green of Oneida Institute, the chairman of the convention that had adopted the Declaration of Sentiments, gave Lovejoy a eulogy at a large Lovejoy commemoration meeting in New York in which he called him a Christian martyr like Stephen. Disturbed, Unitarian pastor May replied that Lovejoy was not a martyr at all and certainly not like Stephen; he asked Green, "Did Stephen throw stones at the mob that pelted him to death?" Garrison, taking a position between Green and May, admitted that Lovejoy because of his use of violence should not be called a Christian martyr, but he decided he could call him a martyr of a kind—a patriotic martyr like General Warren at Bunker Hill.[16]

Garrison, firm in his own nonviolent principles, was conciliatory among abolitionists at large, apparently trying to head off a developing split into a May-Wright wing that would insist on complete nonviolence and a Tappan wing that would temper nonviolence with an acceptance of the right, if not the wisdom, of self-defense. Ideologically Garrison was an absolutist; organizationally he was not.

Evidently either neutral or leaning in the direction of the Tappan point of view were a considerable number of abolitionist statements on Lovejoy which omitted any expression of regret that he had used violence. A statement by the executive committee of the American Antislavery Society, which praised Lovejoy and noted the opportunity his martyrdom provided for more antislavery activity, did not express regret; nor did Beriah Green's address at the Lovejoy commemoration meeting, which the American Antislavery Society published; nor did memorial meetings held by New York and Boston Negroes.[17] Also not deploring the violence were editorials in the New York Negro paper, the Tappan-supported *Colored American*, and in a Methodist abolitionist paper, *Zion's Watchman*.[18] Orange Scott, a prominent New England Methodist minister who had already lost a church post because of his aggressive abolitionism, was concerned that someone should continue to publish Lovejoy's antislavery paper in Alton; whether this was to be done by violence or not was secondary to Scott. In continuing Lovejoy's paper, Scott said, "if the principles of nonresistance be the best (and this I am inclined to believe), then let it be adopted. But if it be thought best to defend our rights, property, and lives, by physical force, as we are authorized to do by our Constitution and laws, then let our preparation be made to do it effectually."

On the other hand, many antislavery societies issued statements deploring that Lovejoy had been armed. Since such statements, publicly issued, could reduce the strategic value of Lovejoy's martyrdom to the cause, it is a sign of the strength of the nonviolent element in abolitionism that many societies issued them. The statements ranged widely in intensity. They came especially from the Garrisonian center, Massachusetts, and the Quaker center, Pennsylvania. Most were expressed at least partly in religious terms, like that of the Bucks County, Pennsylvania, society, which said nonresistance was "the great distinguishing characteristic of the Christian religion."[19] Others were more pragmatic, arguing that they had found that nonviolence worked.

The Massachusetts Antislavery Society issued a carefully worded, moderate, pragmatic statement. It did not, like the Western New York Antislavery Society, insist on "strict fidelity" to the nonviolent Declaration of Sentiments. It did not, like the Plymouth County (Massachusetts) Society, categorically pledge its members to the use of nonviolence alone. It was not a strong enough statement to satisfy Quaker Sarah Grimké. But Garrison endorsed it,[20] and other antislavery societies in Pennsylvania and New England adopted identical statements.[21] The statement, issued by the Massachusetts Society's Board of Managers, recognized the right of self-defense but pointed out advantages in nonviolence: "While it is not in the province of this board to determine for the friends of universal emancipation, how far or under what circumstances, it is right to use arms in self-defense; and while it is certain that no body of men have ever had a better right to do so than did Mr. Lovejoy and his associates, in view of the dreadful provocations and perils with which they were assailed; yet, as abolitionists, we are constrained to believe, that if the doctrine of nonresistance had been practically carried out by our brethren in Alton, as it has been by the friends of the colored race in Boston, New York, and many other places, a similar deliverance and victory would, in the providence of God, have been the result; or, if not, that the spilling of the blood of defenseless men would have produced a more thrilling and abiding effect."[22]

Six months after Lovejoy's death, when abolitionists had had ample time to reflect on the wisdom of his resort to violence, pastor May brought up the issue at the 1838 annual meeting of the American Antislavery Society in New York. As chairman of the committee on resolutions, he moved: "That we consider the Declaration of Sentiments made by the convention at Philadelphia, Dec. 4, 1833, a declaration of the principles of the American Antislavery Society." Joshua Leavitt, an editor of abolitionist publications, opposed the motion on the ground that everybody accepted it already. May then admitted that he planned to follow it with another motion saying that Lovejoy's action was inconsistent with the declaration, and Leavitt said he would reject such a motion on principle. With the sympathetic Gerrit Smith presiding, May's original motion was discussed all one morning and then temporarily set aside. When it came up again in the evening, Garrison, H. C. Wright, Gerrit Smith, and others deeply interested in nonviolence were attending a concurrent peace meeting, and the motion was defeated by a large majority.[23]

Whittier, at the time the editor of the Pennsylvania Antislavery Society's paper, was upset by the defeat. "The whole aspect of the society is changed by it," he said to May, as May recalled it later. As a substitute strategy, Whittier proposed to May that they try to persuade the society at least to endorse a continuation of the general policy of advising agents and members to use pacific methods. Quickly Whittier drew up another resolution[24] and submitted it to the resolutions committee: "We earnestly desire that the agents and members of this Society, while engaged in advocating the pure and pacific principles of emancipation, may continue patient under their manifold provocations, forgiving their enemies, not relying upon physical strength for their defense against the violence of others, but by their patient endurance of evil, evince the spirit of their Master whose mission was one of 'peace on earth and good will to men.' "

The committee reported Whittier's resolutions to the delegates, and, with Arthur Tappan, the president who had defended his store with guns, in the chair, they debated it. Among those speaking for the resolution was, of course, Unitarian pastor May; among those speaking against it were editor Leavitt and others who said it would prevent abolitionists from applying to government for protection against mob violence.[25] While Garrison was still absent, the delegates voted Whittier's resolution down.

"Not a few of us left that annual meeting in sorrow," pastor May wrote afterward, "feeling that the glory, the Christian character of the society, had departed, and foreboding only evil from the change."[26]

Explaining the rejection of Whittier's resolution, Tappanite William Goodell, editor of the New York State Antislavery Society's paper, who said later that his peace principles were like those of Friends,[27] wrote, "Its language seems to abjure all dependence on the penal laws of civil government, a sentiment which not even William Penn himself would have sanctioned."[28]

Another factor in the rejection was that, while both Garrison, the complete nonresistant, and Lewis Tappan, the limited nonresistant, believed that Lovejoy's use of guns was a great error, they also believed it would not be wise to make nonresistance, of any degree, a test of membership in the American Antislavery Society.

The meeting not only rejected both May's and Whittier's resolutions, but it also did not adopt any moderate criticism of Lovejoy, as the Massachusetts Society had. It did not even indicate any regret that Lovejoy had been armed. In fact, a statement by the society's executive committee, read at the meeting, claimed that "our principles [are] now speaking through the blood of the martyred Lovejoy." On the other hand, there was no group attempt either at the meeting or later to repudiate the Declaration of Sentiments or to repeal the clause of the society's constitution which discouraged slaves from securing their freedom by violence. Moreover, at the meeting James Birney, who had defended his Cincinnati house with guns, restated his faith in nonviolence as the means to free the slaves: we are trying to abolish slavery, he said, "not by force, not by power, not even by countenancing the oppressed in any way in vindicating their own rights by physical violence, but by 'a more excellent way.' "[29] In addition, the American Antislavery Society, in appointing its agents, continued after this convention, as it had previously, to say that the Declaration of Sentiments was a statement of the society's principles which it expected its agents to follow. The society's paper, the *Emancipator*, soon reprinted the declaration along with the society's constitution,[30] thus further indicating that both documents were still regarded as official, and the society continued to publish both documents into the Civil War period.

It is notable that during the whole debate about Lovejoy, while there was considerable argument in favor of abolitionists using defensive violence under special circumstances, there was no significant argument in favor of abolitionists using more nearly offensive violence in the sense of encouraging war or slave insurrections as means to abolish slavery. Nearly all abolitionists still considered themselves broadly committed to nonviolence and particularly committed not to employ offensive violence, but, since the American Antislavery Society had found itself unable to agree on precisely what nonviolence meant beyond that, it was left to individuals or auxiliary societies to decide. The abolitionists were frankly admitting that their commitment to nonviolence involved an area of ambiguity. While some abolitionists continued until the Civil War to believe that members of the American Antislavery Society were pledged to reject even defensive violence in their abolitionist work, and from time to time the society and some of its auxiliary societies continued to urge the advantages of defensive nonviolence on their members, Garrison and Lewis Tappan's tolerant view that no specific degree of nonviolence should be a test for membership came to prevail.

As the number of abolitionists grew and the slave interests became increasingly aggressive, the degree of abolitionist nonviolence declined. Never again was there to be as much agreement among abolitionists not to return violence for violence as there was during the period from 1831, when Garrison's *Liberator* began to tout nonviolence, until 1837, when Lovejoy chose guns.

5. Should Slaves Revolt?

◇◇◇◇◇◇◇◇◇◇◇◇

THE QUESTION OF what attitude they should have toward slave revolt
was a major one for abolitionists, black and white.

In the 1830's abolitionist leaders overwhelmingly opposed slave
revolt. Abolitionists repeatedly referred to the peaceful emancipation of slaves in the British West Indies, begun in 1833, as their model,
not to the earlier violent emancipation by slave revolt in Haiti. When
President Andrew Jackson, reflecting popular distrust of abolitionists, publicly charged them with fomenting slave revolts, the Tappans and the New York Tappanite Negro pastors Theodore Wright
and Sam Cornish were among the American Antislavery Society's
officers signing a denial of the charge. The society issued a statement
in 1835 promising not to give the "slightest aid" to slave insurrection
and saying that if they could reach the slaves, they would advise them
to be "quiet and peaceful." About the same time, a Massachusetts
abolitionist claimed that three-quarters of the abolitionists did "not
believe even in defensive war, much less in the 'sacred right of
insurrection,'" and the moderate Unitarian pastor William E. Channing said that though millions of eyes were watching abolitionists,
there was no evidence that a single one had incited slaves to insurrection.[1]

Despite their strong stand against insurrection, abolitionists took
two positions in regard to it which alarmed the South. First, they
alarmed the South by warning—as Quaker Whittier did as early as

1833—that if the South did not free the slaves voluntarily, the slaves would inevitably seize their freedom by slaughtering their masters. By 1849, Negro antislavery lecturer William Wells Brown said abolitionists had issued such warnings "again and again."[2]

Second, they also alarmed the South by proclaiming—as Garrison did as early as 1831—that slaves had a right to revolt. All through his abolitionist career Garrison, like many nonviolent abolitionists, used a double standard for judging violence. He said that by the patriotic American standard, based on the Declaration of Independence, slaves had a right to revolt for their freedom, but by the standard he followed, the Christian standard, based on the Sermon on the Mount, they did not. The distinction between the two standards was a logical one for a pacifist to make, but the fact that he made the claim that slaves had a right to revolt under any standard infuriated slave owners and gave them convenient quotations to use, out of context, against him.

In 1831, Garrison recognized the right of slaves to revolt when the slave Nat Turner, a Virginia preacher who believed he was called by mysterious voices, led a revolt, killing white men, women, and children. Garrison said Turner and his friends had done no more than "our fathers in slaughtering the British." Yet Garrison insisted, in answering to the absurd charge that he himself was behind the Turner revolt, that his own purpose was to prevent slave revolts by voluntary emancipation.[3] He said that he did not wish to emancipate the slaves at the expense of the planters' safety. Moreover, insurrections would fail and would only bring greater burdens upon Negroes, he told a Negro national convention, adding, "I believe you have stronger reasons for dreading a Southern insurrection than the whites themselves."[4]

As for the slaves, they were so generally denied the rights of human beings—more than slaves in Latin America were—that their natural sense of self-respect was often crushed, and many of them, especially the field hands, seemed to be docile and dependent. Under these circumstances, abolitionists were expecting a great deal if they expected slaves to find effective means of protest, either by violence or nonviolence. Yet many abolitionists did expect slaves to protest, and many slaves did find means to do so.

Slaves experimented with various forms of noncooperation with the slave system—it is difficult to know how often—and some of this action bordered on nonviolent direct action. There is abundant evidence that slaves tried to protect themselves by such devices as lies, thefts, and careless use of tools. Frederick Douglass, from his experience as a Maryland slave, reported that slaves were careful not to do too much work on any one day, because they knew that if they did, their master would then expect the same amount every day. In a Richmond tobacco factory, slave workers slowed down their work for several days to protest the punishment of one of their fellows. Mississippi plantation records indicate that slaves were more often ill on work days than on Sundays, and more often ill in seasons when their labor was most needed than in other seasons. When slaves wished to escape their duties, a Virginia planter said, they pretended to be ignorant. If slaves were afraid that they would be sold away from their families, they might, like some North Carolina Negroes, tie their limbs tightly until they were swollen and purple. If slaves were tired of being forced to work for their "Christian" masters, they might run away to swamps or woods to live or even escape to the North.[5] Such noncooperation with slavery—especially when it was open—could provide Negroes with experience out of which a deliberate nonviolent protest tradition could grow.

As for outright slave revolt, there were three serious revolts during the nineteenth century, but all local in character: the Prosser revolt in Virginia in 1800, the Vesey revolt in South Carolina in 1822, and the Turner revolt in Virginia in 1831. No such serious revolts occurred after the founding of the American Antislavery Society in 1833.

Evidence of slave inclination to revolt in the three decades before the Civil War is difficult to interpret. On the one hand, Southern whites tried to hide evidence of revolt from the outside world; on the other hand, they were so fearful of revolt that they easily exaggerated rumors of them. Fearing revolt, whites developed an elaborate system of control over the movements of blacks, both slave and free. While according to the Southern press, plots for slave revolts were common, evidence for their having been carried out is thin. Certainly slave revolts were more rare in the United States, where slaves were often forced into the role of dependent children, than in Latin America, where slaves were given many of the rights of men.

What usually prevented slaves from revolting was debated among abolitionists. Some abolitionists said the basic docility of the slaves was a factor; some emphasized the slaves' fear of white repression; some emphasized the slaves' hope that abolitionists would free them. Others believed that the deliberate abolitionist policy of discouraging slave revolt was a factor.

The British reformer Harriet Martineau, who visited the United

States in the late 1830's, decided it was largely Garrison who pre-vented slave revolts. "Garrison is as strenuous a 'peace man' as any broad-brimmed Friend in Philadelphia," she wrote, "and this fact, in conjunction with his unlimited influence over the Negro population, is the chief reason why no blood has been shed—why no insurrectionary movement has taken place in the United States from the time when his voice began to be heard over the broad land till now."[6]

Quite differently, some abolitionists attributed the lack of slave revolts to the threat that the North's military power would be used to suppress them; without the North's assistance, they said, Southern whites would be too weak to quiet the slaves' innate desire for liberty. Both the Garrisonians and the Tappanites eventually came to accept much of this view. By the mid-1840's the Garrisonians advocated that the North secede from the Union in part so that the North could escape its Constitutional obligation to help suppress slave revolts; without the North's help, the Garrisonians said, the South could not hold the slaves down.

The Southern abolitionist James Birney admitted in 1835 that the threat to use Northern troops had seemed effective in suppressing slaves so far. But he believed that when serious slave revolts occurred, as they inevitably would as slavery grew more and more oppressive, the Southern whites, after bloody fighting, would call for the help of Northern conscript troops. In a speech to the annual meeting of the American Antislavery Society, Birney presented a remarkable vision of what he believed would then happen. When the Northern troops arrived, the remnants of slaves not already killed would confront them in a massive nonviolent demonstration. The troops would be met by a first line of slave orphans, he said, "whose fathers were cut off in the struggle, and they will hold up a banner with this inscription: 'God is the Father of the Fatherless.' They will be followed by a second line consisting of their widowed mothers, and their ensign will bear upon it this motto: 'God is the Friend of the Widow.' The warriors who survived the contest will meet you next, not with a sword, nor any weapon of war, but with this inscription on their flag: 'All men are created free and equal'; and they will say, 'and now what will you do? You may wash out our inscriptions in blood, and trample us in the dust, but slaves again we will never be. Now execution-ers, strike!'" Birney implied that the Northern troops would find themselves unable to strike against such weaponless lines, and the slaves would be free.[7]

This was probably one of the earliest detailed abolitionist statements of the idea of mass nonviolent action in confronting armed men. It was presented more as a vision than a program. But it is significant as coming from Birney, who was only a limited Tappanite nonresistant and who was a man of affairs who knew the South: he came from an aristocratic, slave-owning planter family in Kentucky and had himself been a planter, lawyer, mayor of Huntsville, Alabama, and a member of the legislatures of both Kentucky and Alabama.

Abolitionists did not pick up Birney's idea and develop it into a substitute for slave revolts. They did not consider such mass nonviolent action within the realm of reality in the South at that time nor at any time in the abolitionist period. But it is significant that such ideas were in the back of their minds. In the early 1850's, when abolitionists were being harried by attempts to enforce a newly severe fugitive slave law, they were to develop similar ideas into proposals for mass action in the North to protect fugitive slaves.

In the 1840's, as abolitionists became less confident that nonviolence could bring emancipation soon, they gradually became more open to the idea of slave revolt.

Probably one of the first Northern abolitionists to propose a specific plan to promote slave revolt was county judge Jabez D. Hammond of Cherry Valley, New York, a former congressman. In 1839 he proposed to the president of the New York State Antislavery Society, Gerrit Smith, that young Negroes be trained in military schools established for the purpose in Canada and Mexico and then sent to the slave states to lead slave revolts; slaveholders would never allow slavery to be abolished peaceably, Hammond argued. But Smith, a strong peace man in touch with both Garrison and the Tappans, rejected the plan.

In the early 1840's there were minor slave revolts, and some abolitionists welcomed them. For example, the slaves on board the slave trader *Creole*, en route from Virginia to New Orleans, seized control of the ship and sailed it to freedom in British Bermuda. Frederick Douglass took pride that it was a black slave, Madison Washington, who brought the ship safely to shore—"a black man, with wooly head, high cheek bones, protruding lip, distended nostril, and retreating forehead, had the mastery of that ship, and under his direction, that brig was brought safely into the port of Nassau." The

Tappanites' American and Foreign Antislavery Society praised the slaves' "great bravery, tempered with great humanity"; they did not kill as many whites as they easily could have, the society said; they engaged only in a "short struggle, in which only one white man lost his life." The Tappanite *Oberlin Evangelist* asked, "who can tell the difference in principle between the conduct of George Washington, the hero of the American Revolution, and Madison Washington, the hero of the *Creole* Revolution?" Abolitionist Congressman Joshua R. Giddings of Ohio argued that once the ship was on the high seas, it was out of the jurisdiction of a slave state, and therefore the slaves were no longer slaves and had a natural right to seize their freedom. Congress censured Giddings for this opinion. Giddings then resigned, ran again for election, and, despite the opposition of his own Whig party, won overwhelmingly, suggesting Northern popular approval of slave revolt at least under these unusual circumstances.[9]

However, in 1842, the Liberty party, the small, recently organized abolitionist party in which many Tappanites were active, advised slaves to resist their masters peacefully. A convention of the party decided to take the unusual step of defying Southern restrictions on freedom of speech by sending an address directly to the slaves—even if few of them could read it. The address was written by the nearly complete nonresistant Gerrit Smith.

Do not revolt, Smith urged the slaves. Some abolitionists oppose taking life under any circumstances, he said, "but the great majority of abolitionists justify their forefather's bloody resistance to oppression." They "can, therefore, dissuade you from such resistance to a ten thousand-fold greater oppression," Smith continued, "not on the high ground of absolute morality, but on the comparatively low one of expediency." We will not continue to work for your freedom unless you continue to be peaceful. While "we rejoice in the strong probability" that your "remarkable forbearance" from insurrection is because of your "reliance on the philanthropic efforts" of abolitionists on your behalf, "we tremble, lest discouraged by the tardy results of these efforts," you "extinguish" your "hopes in bloody despair." While waiting for the abolitionists to free you peacefully, love your masters, Smith advised, and at the same time nonviolently break their laws as necessary—break their laws which forbid you to learn to read, break their laws which forbid you to escape, for the masters are but pirates and pirate victims can violate pirate laws freely.[10]

The next year, 1843, a Negro national convention, meeting in Buffalo, also considered sending an address to the slaves. But this address would be different. Instead of advising them, as the Liberty party had, to resist their masters peacefully, the Buffalo convention would advise them to seize their freedom and then defend it if necessary with violence.

This Buffalo convention was part of the Negro national convention movement which represented, as well as any movement at the time, the Negro antislavery cause, insofar as it was separate from the predominantly white antislavery cause.

At the Buffalo convention, it was Henry Highland Garnet who proposed that the convention distribute a violence-inciting address to the slaves. In making his proposal, the tall, volatile Garnet, who was to be called the best-known Negro clergyman in the country, created a crisis for Negro abolitionists.

To explain the crisis, it is necessary to trace how the Negro national convention movement came to be what it was.

Negroes had organized their own national convention movement in Philadelphia in 1830, and weak though it was, it met in sporadic conventions throughout the three decades of the abolitionist period and into the Civil War. In 1834, a year after the American Antislavery Society had adopted its nonviolent Declaration of Sentiments, the Negro national convention also adopted a nonviolent declaration. Written by the Garrisonian Negro William Whipper of Pennsylvania, this declaration said, the weapons of our revolution for freedom and peace "are not carnal, but spiritual" and the "struggle is not for blood, but for right." In 1835, Whipper and another Pennsylvania Garrisonian Negro, Robert Purvis, a signer of the American Antislavery Society's declaration, persuaded the Negro national convention to decide to disobey the fugitive slave law "peaceably" and to praise the forbearance of Northern Negroes in response to recent rioting against them.[11] Among Negro abolitionists, as among white abolitionists, a nonviolent tradition was growing, but its roots were less deep.

In the mid-1830's the leaders of the Negro convention movement became concerned over the issue of whether Negroes should work to improve their position in society primarily through all-Negro agencies, like Negro national conventions, or through interracial agencies. The nonviolent Pennsylvanians Whipper and Purvis led the faction that favored interracial agencies, and they became strong enough in 1835 to persuade the all-Negro national convention movement, which they themselves had helped to create, to turn itself into the American Moral Reform Society, a new, ostensibly interracial organization with such broad reform purposes as peace and antislavery. For several years after this, the all-Negro national convention movement as such was quiescent.

William Whipper was the son of a white lumber dealer and a Negro house servant. According to family tradition, when William and his white half brother were small children, they were tutored together at home by a Quaker; when they were older and the white brother but not William was sent away to Quaker school, the white brother passed on to William what he learned. As a young man, William Whipper followed his father into the lumber business in Columbia, Lancaster County, Pennsylvania, in partnership with his Negro relative, Stephen Smith. They both prospered, Smith becoming the wealthiest black man in the country.[12] As active abolitionists, Whipper and Smith used their firm's railroad freight cars to transport fugitive slaves. Whipper developed broad reform interests, and he attributed them especially to Garrison: "The key that opened the moral world to my view," he said, was Garrison's motto in the *Liberator*, "My country is the world—my countrymen are all mankind."[13] Whipper became the major Negro spokesman for complete nonresistance in the 1830's.[14] As the leader of the American Moral Reform Society, he tried to make it and its monthly *National Reformer*, which he edited, into engines for nonviolence.[15]

In the late 1830's and early 1840's, the activist Negroes of the Philadelphia and New York areas, the two largest centers of Negro population in the North, competed with each other for control of Negro abolitionism. The Philadelphia Negroes, led by such men as Whipper, Smith, and Purvis, leaned more toward the complete nonviolence of Garrison and were more visionary, less inclined to act through separatist Negro organizations, and more willing to work with whites. The New York Negroes, led by the Reverends Theodore Wright, Charles B. Ray, and Sam Cornish, among others, were more inclined to the limited nonviolence of Lewis Tappan, more willing to work through abolitionist political parties, and, while they shared the Philadelphians' goal of integration and also worked in integrated antislavery societies, they were more willing to work through separatist all-Negro organizations when they felt it practicable to do so. The Philadelphia Negroes tried in vain to make their new Moral Reform Society into a functioning, national, interracial instrument, while the New York City Negroes, using the weekly *Colored American*, which Cornish and Ray edited, as their organ, tried, also in vain, to revive the distinctly Negro national convention movement.

In 1843 the Negro national convention movement finally revived with the Buffalo convention. It did so, however, not as much under the leadership of the moderately nonviolent Tappanite New York City Negroes as under the leadership of upstate New York Negroes who were less closely related to the Tappans and more violent.

At the Buffalo convention the strongly nonviolent Pennsylvania Negroes were conspicuous by their absence; they were boycotting the separatist all-Negro national convention movement, and it would be ten years before they would drop their boycott. The moderately nonviolent Negroes of New York City were well represented by the Tappanite pastors Theodore Wright and Charles B. Ray. But it was the still less nonviolent upstate New York Negroes who had led in calling the convention and who were the best-represented group in terms of numbers. Outstanding among them was Garnet, the one who put to the convention the question of whether it would repudiate its earlier nonviolent position by calling the slaves to revolt.

Henry Highland Garnet, like most abolitionist leaders, had been subjected to some nonviolent influences. His family escaped from slavery in Maryland with the aid of Quaker Thomas Garrett of Delaware, and as a child he attended a New York City school founded by Quakers. He was led toward becoming a minister by his Presbyterian pastor, Tappanite nonresistant Theodore Wright, and for his ministerial education he attended the Tappanite-related Oneida Institute. Garnet was conscious of the claims of nonviolence; he said he preferred peaceful, moral means to end slavery but had no confidence that they would succeed.[16] While he can be called an occasional nonresistant, the role that he often played was to encourage violence.

As a youth Garnet had also been through experiences that might have prepared him to accept violence. He had escaped with his parents from slavery in a terrible ordeal, including hiding in swamps and woods. In New York City, when a slave agent tried unsuccessfully to seize his family and return them to slavery, Garnet's father jumped off a roof, the family household goods were destroyed, and Garnet armed himself with a knife. When Garnet was a student at the abolitionist-supported interracial school in Canaan, New Hampshire, an anti-Negro mob dragged the school building off its foundations by rope and shot at the Negro students; Garnet led a group of students in shooting back.

By the time of the Buffalo convention, Garnet, only twenty-seven years old, was pastor of a black Presbyterian church in Troy, New York, and, despite having only one leg (a crippled leg had recently been amputated), he had developed a powerful body and a brilliant speaking style. When he proposed that his call to the slaves to seize their freedom be distributed in the South, he stirred the convention, it was reported later, more than any other convention speaker in the entire history of the Negro convention movement.[17]

It is sinful to "make voluntary submission" to slavery, Garnet said in his call to the slaves. "It is your solemn and imperative duty to use every means, both moral, intellectual, and physical, that promises success" in attaining freedom.

Stop work, Garnet advised the slaves, suggesting something like a general strike. Tell your masters you are determined to be free, "and forever after cease to toil for the heartless tyrants who give you no other reward but stripes and abuse. If they then commence the work of death, they and not you will be responsible for the consequences." He assumed the consequences would be violent. "If you would be free in this generation . . . there is not much hope of redemption without the shedding of blood," he said, and he praised leaders of slave revolts like Nat Turner and Madison Washington as "noble men."[18]

Garnet was wording his proposal judiciously to appeal to Negro leaders, most of whom he knew had long been committed to some degree of nonviolence. He did not directly ask slaves to revolt. Nor did he suggest, as Birney had in 1835, that slaves reply to white violence by mass nonviolent action. He was proposing that slaves take action which in itself was nonviolent but which would lead whites to respond by violent action, against which blacks in turn would then be justified, he said, in defending themselves with violence. It was only in such an indirect way that he could possibly persuade most of the Negro convention delegates to favor insurrection.

Garnet eloquently urged the convention delegates to support his plan for slave revolt. As the convention chairman, pastor Amos Beman of New Haven, said later, Garnet's speech shook "stern men . . . as the wild storm sways the oaks of the forest," and "every eye" was "suffused with tears."

But another young delegate, the twenty-six-year-old Frederick

Douglass, a more recently escaped slave and only self-educated as he was, did not fear to oppose the more prestigious Garnet. There was "too much physical force" in Garnet's address to the slaves, said Douglass; slave insurrection would be catastrophic. He preferred "trying the moral means a little longer"; he wanted emancipation to come in a "better way," and he expected that it would.[19]

Charles Lenox Remond assisted Douglass in the debate. Remond came from a free Negro family of hairdressers in Salem, Massachusetts. He had already been prominent as a New England antislavery lecturer before the young Douglass came to share the prominence with him. Together the two Massachusetts delegates, according to the *Liberator*, developed as arguments against circulating Garnet's call, "the good already accomplished [by abolitionists]—the example afforded in the abolition of [British] West India slavery without bloodshed—the change in public opinion—enemies giving way— and, in view of these facts, the responsibility involved in putting forth such a document."[20]

Several delegates from Ohio—where recent rioting against Negroes had been severe—also opposed Garnet, predicting that if his call were circulated, it would provoke violence against them when they reached home.

By a close vote of nineteen to eighteen the delegates decided not to circulate Garnet's call. Never before had any major abolitionist organization come so close to endorsing slave revolts, even in an indirect form.

Among those voting with Garnet was Garnet's former pastor in New York City, Theodore Wright, a Tappanite nonresistant. Among those voting with Douglass were the Garrisonian antislavery lecturers Remond of Massachusetts and William Wells Brown of Buffalo.[21]

Several days later the supporters of Garnet insisted on another vote on the same issue. Fearing the convention would approve sending the address this time, the Tappanite chairman of the convention, Beman, who had not voted the first time, stepped down from the chair to oppose it. Though he had been a student of Oneida Institute at the same time as Garnet and maintained cordial relations with him, in a forceful plea of an hour, Beman opposed sending Garnet's address to the slaves. The address "had too much of the physical, and not enough of the moral weapon about it," he said. This time the delegates had recovered from the immediate impact of Garnet's eloquence. This time, too, they had had a chance to consider the relation of Garnet's address to the song they often sang during their sessions:

> *Ours is not the tented field—*
> *We no earthly weapons wield—*
> *Light and love, our sword and shield,*
> *Truth our panoply.*

This time pastor Wright switched to voting with Douglass; two other Tappanite pastors who had not voted the first time, chairman Beman of New Haven and Charles B. Ray of New York City, also voted with Douglass; and to the surprise of Garnet's friends, Douglass' majority was much larger.[22]

An analysis of the two votes suggests that among the four regions represented at the convention, New England, New York State, the Midwest, and the South, nonviolence was strongest in Douglass' New England, weakest in Garnet's New York State; and that distance from the slave states was not a clear factor in greater inclination to either violence or nonviolence. It is probable that if the Pennsylvanians had not boycotted the convention, their usual nonviolent tendencies would have given Douglass a substantial majority on the first vote.

The rejection of Garnet's address to the slaves, wrote the Garrisonian nonresistant Maria Chapman in the *Liberator*, was a sign of "love, forgiveness, and magnanimity," and, she added severely, the man "who imagines that a civil and servile war would ultimately promote freedom" really "knows nothing of nature, human or divine, of character, good or evil."[23]

After his defeat Garnet announced that he would defy the convention by publishing his address to the slaves himself. Several years went by without his doing so.

Meantime the Mexican War, beginning in 1846, temporarily helped to strengthen the abolitionists' opposition to violence because abolitionists opposed the war as being fought to extend slavery. During the war the colored national convention turned down a proposal to recommend to Negroes "the propriety of instructing their sons in the art of war" and unanimously adopted a report, prepared under the lead of Douglass and revised with the help of the adaptable Garnet, expressing its "entire disapprobation of any plan of emancipation involving a resort of bloodshed."[24] Even in the continued absence of the Whipper-led nonviolent Pennsylvanians, the revived Negro national convention movement had roundly reaffirmed its nonviolent tradition.

Since black abolitionists were more likely to be subject to oppression than white abolitionists, it might be expected that black abolitionists would find it harder to develop a nonviolent tradition than white abolitionists would. In fact, the black abolitionists' nonviolence was not as strong as the whites', as the 1843 convention vote suggests. However, three tendencies appeared to influence black abolitionists toward some degree of nonviolence. First, if blacks were violent, whites, because of prejudice, were likely to react with special ferocity against them. Second, there was a tendency for blacks, as a weak minority, to be dependent on whites, a tendency that was difficult even for black abolitionists to escape; so when some white abolitionists were deliberately nonviolent, it was not surprising that some black abolitionists were too. Third, there was a tendency for blacks, both slave and free, subject to oppression as they were, to develop both the techniques and the personal qualities necessary to survive despite suffering. In doing so, some of them developed techniques related to, if not identical with, the techniques of nonviolent direct action, and they developed some of the same personal qualities that nonviolent abolitionists, whether black or white, coveted for themselves, such as meekness, long-suffering, and lack of a vengeful spirit. Thus blacks had a foundation in both experience and personality on which they could build their own tradition of nonviolent protest.

At the end of the 1840's the gradual trend toward abolitionist acceptance of slave revolt resumed, a trend that was to accelerate through the fifties. The trend resumed under the impact of the increasing doubts among abolitionists that they would succeed in ending slavery peacefully—whether by the "moral suasion" of words, by direct action, or by political action. It came particularly under the impact of the victory of the slave interests in the Mexican War, including the resulting acquistion of new territory likely to be open to slavery.

By the end of the 1840's, abolitionists were not urging slaves to be patient as much as they had in the 1830's. Both the Negro national convention meeting in Cleveland and the New England Antislavery Convention meeting in Boston urged slaves to take every favorable opportunity to obtain their freedom, and they did not specify that it should be by nonviolent means. Abolitionist Congressman Giddings now not only defended slave revolts on the seas but also in the slave states; it was the slaves' unquestioned duty, he said, to obtain their liberty "even to the taking of the life of every man who opposed them." The Garrisonian *Liberty Bell* published a moving short story sympathizing with the hero of a slave revolt,[25] and Garnet at last found the time suitable to publish his pro-violent address to the slaves.

Douglass, who had taken Whipper's place as the most prominent Negro champion of complete nonresistance, continued to be disturbed by Garnet. Though Douglass called him "one of our best and most talented men," he lamented that Garnet had "held up moral suasion repeatedly to the scorn and contempt of the colored people, in our presence, and made many speeches in favor of insurrection among the slaves."[26] Despite Douglass' influence, Garnet's ideas were gaining currency. In 1849 the Ohio Negro convention voted to distribute five hundred copies of Garnet's violence-inciting address. When Southern white leaders endorsed the liberal revolts in progress against oppression in Rome and Hungary, the New York City Negro paper, *Ram's Horn*, assured its readers, tongue in cheek, that these Southerners would therefore surely endorse similar revolts of slaves against oppression in the South. Stop work and demand freedom, *Ram's Horn* advised the slaves, much as Garnet had; throw the responsibility for beginning physical violence on the masters; once they begin violence, die rather than bequeath slavery to your posterity.[27]

About the same time, the educational reformer and congressman, Horace Mann, an occasional nonresistant who objected to children being taught that soldiers were heroes, nevertheless was approving the current liberal revolts in Europe and saying he would approve any similar slave revolts in America as well. The once nonviolent Garrisonian Remond, who had supported Douglass in rejecting Garnet's address, now had become so impatient with the progress of abolition that he said he would "welcome any means that will abolish slavery."[28]

A convention of Maine and New Hampshire Negroes debated in 1849 whether it would be their duty if slaves revolted "by physical force . . . to help sustain them." The president of the convention declared "he was not for war, but if need be, he would not be backward in shouldering his musket and girding up his sword that his brethren might be free." A fugitive who had recently escaped from slavery by peaceful means and who still had a wife and children in slavery said if there were an insurrection among the slaves, "he would not be long in joining his brethren in a contest for freedom." Although the vice-president of the convention said he insisted on "moral means" instead of force to free the slaves, the convention, according to his official record,[29] voted unanimously that "it was their duty to assist slave revolts."

Among abolitionists in general—and especially among blacks— there was clearly a new tone of impatience with the apparent inability of nonviolence to abolish slavery.

However, Frederick Douglass, who by this time was editing his own paper in Rohester and was the towering figure among Negroes, was still a Garrisonian nonresistant. In 1849 he agreed with Garrison that slaves had the right to revolt, and he agreed with Whittier that if emancipation did not come voluntarily, it would inevitably come by bloody slave revolt. Like many abolitionists, Douglass had more expectation of slave revolts than the events justified. But he still believed that violence was neither the desirable means nor the likely means for emancipation. The "only well grounded hope of the slave for emancipation," he wrote in his *North Star*, "is the operation of moral force."[30]

Other Negroes supported Douglass. Two fugitive slaves, the Garrisonian antislavery lecturer William Wells Brown and the Tappanite Presbyterian pastor J. W. C. Pennington, were part of a large American delegation to the World Peace Congress in Paris in 1849. Brown and Pennington agreed in telling the Congress that it was the war principle—the threat and use of violence—which kept slaves in slavery. "The dissemination of the principles of peace," Brown said, "would be the means of . . . emancipation."

In the same year peace man Brown edited a book of antislavery songs. One of them warned the South of the horror of slave insurrection:

> *Slaves yet may see their masters cowering,*
> *While whole plantations smoke and blaze!*

But the song advised against freeing the slaves by this method because it would not remove the prejudice in men's hearts:

> *Yet free them not by sword or shield,*
> *For with men's hearts they're unavailing.*[31]

Though under pressure to accept more violence, even at the end of the 1840's most abolitionists, black and white, still encouraged slaves to be peaceful. The abolitionists marveled that in fact slaves made relatively few attempts to revolt. Said the nonviolent Garrisonian H. C. Wright, in regard to all American Negroes, North and South: "There are no instances in the records of man, of more commendable forbearance, and suppression of revenge and its murderous promptings, than are found among the oppressed of this republic."[32]

On each fourth of July, when abolitionists could celebrate the violent freeing of American whites from Britain, and on each first of August, when abolitionists could celebrate the peaceful freeing of West Indian blacks from British slavery, black and white abolitionists often marched, picnicked, and heard speeches together. They heard complete nonresistant Frederick Douglass say that the peaceful evolution of England to greater freedom was a better example for America than the recent violent revolution in France. They heard the complete nonresistant C. C. Burleigh say that peaceful abolitionist agitation was already rocking the nation. They heard the Tappanite Negro pastor Beman of New Haven ask God to free the slaves not by the thunderbolts of vengeance but by energizing the conscience of the slave owners. They heard the occasional nonresistant Wendell Phillips quote Napoleon at St. Helena as saying: "Nothing permanent was ever done by violence." They renewed their dedication to nonviolence by singing songs like this one by the young Garrisonian James Russell Lowell:

> *Friends of Freedom! Ye who stand*
> *With no weapons in your hand*
> *Save a purpose stern and grand*
> *To set all men free. . . .*
> *Though we were but two or three*
> *Sure of triumph we should be. . . .*
> *Tyranny is always weak,*
> *Truth is young and strong!*[33]

6. The Nonresistance Society

◇◇◇◇◇◇◇◇◇◇◇◇

GARRISON AND HIS ASSOCIATES had several reasons for wishing to create a separate agency to promote nonresistance. One was that they had mixed their abolitionism and their nonresistance so much that even some of their friends accused them of confusing the two. Another was that the Lovejoy affair had convinced them that abolitionist dedication to nonviolence needed strengthening. Still another was that they had long considered the American Peace Society to be too timid.

For such reasons as these, in 1838, nearly a year after the Lovejoy murder, Garrison and some of his abolitionist associates led in founding the Nonresistance Society in Boston.

During the eleven years of the Nonresistance Society's life, its members were virtually all abolitionists. One reason nonresistants were likely to be abolitionists was that nonresistants looked on slavery itself as a form of violence. As the nonresistant Henry C. Wright said, the "martial spirit . . . is the same as the spirit of slaveholding, a spirit which leads men to domineer over his brother, to crush and despoil him." Correspondingly, destroying the war spirit would inevitably destroy slavery. As the Nonresistance Society explained in a public statement, if a slaveholder should become a nonresistant, he could "never resort to that law of violence in which the relation of master and slave originated, and by which it must be continually sustained."

A more direct reason for nonresistants being abolitionists was, according to nonresistant leaders, that abolitionists often became nonresistants through the experience of participating in the abolition movement. Explained Garrison, "The cause of nonresistance is gaining new adherents continually through the radical character of the antislavery movement." One of Garrison's close associates, Maria Chapman, suggested that some reformers simply found nonresistance a suitable means for accomplishing their goals: "I never could separate nonresistance from my idea of reform generally," she explained; nonresistance "is the temper of the mind in which all enterprise for humanity should be undertaken rather than a distinct enterprise in itself."[1]

The founders of the Nonresistance Society called themselves "a few obscure, moneyless, uninfluential men and women." They were mostly Garrisonian complete nonresistants; in addition, they also included a few Garrisonian-leaning Quakers—such as Lucretia Mott —who wished to carry their peace testimony further than most Quakers did. The society was too radical for Tappanites or other limited nonresistants to wish to join. The strongest support of the society came from New England, as indicated by the geographical distribution of the society's paper, and the second strongest from Pennsylvania. Most of the members were religious, especially from the "evangelical denominations"; according to one of the society's officers, almost every sect in the land had representatives among nonresistants, but one did not have to be religious to be a nonresistant; even an atheist could be one. Some nonresistants derived their beliefs from "considerations of safety and expediency," H. C. Wright said, "some from [the] nature and constitution of man, some from the Gospel, and some from all these sources."

H. C. Wright was the general agent of the society and next to Garrison the major figure to give the society its character in its most vigorous early years. A former Congregational minister, Wright was a fire eater who traveled the North holding meetings in which he welcomed direct debate with opponents. When he confronted military men, he told them that a Christian might as well be a robber as a soldier. Wright's "style of preaching is blunt and severe," said Garrison, "but . . . in the social circle he is a delightful companion."

Garrison was probably as intimate with Wright as with any American abolitionist. Like Garrison, Wright was New England born and brought up in a poor, Calvinistic family. He had the same Puritan discipline as Garrison: he could do sustained concentrated work, he was frugal, he didn't get angry under provocation. Being an Andover Theological Seminary graduate, Wright had more formal education than Garrison, but his interests were not so much in theology as, like Garrison's, in practical righteousness. From 1835, when they first met, Garrison and Wright so interacted on each other as to develop the same general views on peace, slavery, liquor, and women's rights, the same disdain for ceremony and cant, the same liberal theology, the same bluntness of speech combined with warm enthusiasm for courage in the righteous life. Garrison wrote Wright in 1844: "There is no one on the wide earth, among the great circle of my friends, for whom I entertain greater love and respect. Your views of the nature, spirit and design of Christianity—of the brotherhood of the human race,—of the corruption of existing political, religious, and governmental institutions—are more nearly identical with my own than those of almost any other individual."[2]

Wright had already been a traveling agent for some time before the Nonresistance Society was founded. Since 1833 he had been successively an agent of the American Sunday School Union, the American Peace Society, and the American Antislavery Society. As an agent, Wright was cautioned by his employers not to be too radical. While he was an agent for the American Peace Society, its head, William Ladd, advised him not to mix his private nonresistance views with his public pleas for peace; Ladd wrote him, though you and I believe that national and individual self-defense is a sin, the public isn't ready for the idea yet. While Wright was an agent for the American Antislavery Society, its Tappanite-controlled executive committee requested him to stop advocating noncooperation with war-supporting governments, but Wright insisted on continuing to do so, and in 1837 the committee finally refused to renew his agency. It is probable that Wright pushed Garrison toward the noncooperation with government policy—which Garrison began moving toward about the time he met Wright—and that Wright was a major factor in making it a part of the Nonresistance Society's program.[3]

Garrison himself wrote the Nonresistance Society's constitution, and he boasted that it was radical. It was adopted by a vote of thirty to thirteen, which suggests considerable opposition to it even among peace men who were interested in the formation of the society. Predictably, the constitution provided that members would not perform military service. Less predictably, the constitution also included provisions that made it clear that the Garrisonian nonresistants differed with respect to government from many nonviolent abolitionists—including most Quakers and Tappanites. According to the constitution, nonresistants would acknowledge the authority of divine government only, would not "acknowledge the allegiance to any human government," would not sue any man for redress of grievances, and would not hold any office in which they would come under obligation to execute penal law. While the constitution did not require members not to vote, most members would not vote because by doing so they felt they would participate at least indirectly in the government's penal and war-making powers. In fact, Nonresistance Society members were even more distrustful of government than most eighteenth-century liberals were; they were extreme even in the American tradition of chest-thumping individualism; they were anti-institutional like the New England transcendentalists—some of whom were in the society; they were almost Christian anarchists, like Tolstoy.

With respect to methods for bringing about such social changes as the abolition of slavery, most of the Nonresistance Society members agreed on five principles derived from the New Testament: (1) not resisting evil with evil (hence the misleading term "nonresistant"), (2) positive resistance to evil with good, (3) obedience to government in general but disobedience to specific unjust laws, with meek acceptance of any resulting punishment, (4) not so much inflicting suffering on others, as taking suffering on oneself, (5) not so much changing outward situations—which action through government is likely to do—as fundamentally changing individual motivation.

Immediately after the founding of the Nonresistance Society, Garrison was patient with his peace friends who found the society's position difficult to accept; even pastor May[4] and gentleman scholar Edmund Quincy struggled within themselves for some time before deciding to accept it. "Indeed, we shall not have a great and sudden rush into our ranks," Garrison wrote privately. "There are very few in this land, in this world, who will be able to abide by the principle we have enunciated, though there may be many whose consciences must assent to their correctness."[5] Boston lawyer Phillips, far less of a nonresistant than Garrison, was one of those who attended the founding convention but never joined; so also was American Peace Society leader William Ladd of Maine.

Lydia Maria Child, the urbane novelist who became editor of a Garrisonian paper in New York, also never joined even though she was a complete nonresistant. She attended only one meeting of the Nonresistance Society—she didn't like to attend meetings anyway, she said; she was often aloof, sensitive, critical. For many years, she wrote privately, her mind had been traveling in the same direction as the Nonresistance Society leaders, and they happened to have come to essentially the same views. She believed nonresistance is *"the* idea which distinguishes the gospel of Christ from all other wise and philosophic utterance; it is this which makes it *holy.* " But as a religious liberal influenced by Unitarians and Swedenborgians—she was more liberal in the early 1840's than Garrison or H. C. Wright —she found the Nonresistance Society too dependent on the letter of Scripture.[6]

Quite differently, the Tappanite leaders rejected the Nonresistance Society because it did not sufficiently depend on Scripture as they interpreted it. They were horrified by what they understood to be the society's antigovernment policy. Arthur Tappan returned a sample copy of the Nonresistance Society's paper, saying he refused to be "instrumental in disseminating non-government sentiments." Lewis Tappan, fearing that Gerrit Smith was about to join the Nonresistance Society, fervently urged him not to, explaining "not that I am not a lover of peace" but that Garrison was not a Christian after all and that the Nonresistance Society's doctrines were "part and parcel of a system of innovations that will, so far as they succeed, overturn all that is valuable." Birney charged publicly that the Nonresistance Society was for "destroying all government" and that therefore it was repelling the "intelligent" minds of the country whose cooperation abolitionists needed. Garrison replied, insisting that he was a supporter of government and should not be called a "no government" man; he simply wanted to make earthly government perfect, like the government of heaven. He pointed out that there was some Christian tradition for not voting, as among the Presbyterian sect called Covenanters and among "many" Quakers.[7]

One abolitionist who was enthusiastic about the new society was the Pennsylvania Negro lumber dealer, William Whipper. While Whipper found he could not accept the new society's views on government, he found most of its arguments "irresistible." "We venture to predict," he wrote in his *National Reformer* in 1839, that in ten years the Nonresistance Society "will have awakened the evangelical piety of our land, and that it is ultimately destined to remodel the civil and ecclesiastical codes throughout the entire globe." Another abolitionist who was enthusiastic was Chares Spear, the Boston Universalist minister and prison reformer, who recorded in his diary in 1842 that he had "had no idea that nonresistance would prevail so extensively in so short a time."[8]

For several years the Nonresistance Society published a twice-monthly paper, the *Nonresistant*. Most of the time it was edited by a committee consisting of Garrison, the suave Mrs. Chapman (Garrison said that when she was out of the country it was "as though a hundred of our best men were laid low"),[9] and the young gentleman scholar Edmund Quincy who took the major responsibility.

Quincy, who also served for a time as president of the society, was a merry, exhilarating person, quite unlike what people expected a reformer to be. Like Wendell Phillips, Quincy was from an old established Boston family, Phillips being the son of the first mayor of Boston and Quincy the son of the second. When an English visitor saw Quincy and Phillips walking down a Boston street, he said they were the only Americans he had ever seen who looked like gentlemen. Though close to both Quincy and Phillips in his work, Garrison, not being by any means an aristocrat by birth or taste, was not as intimate with them socially as he was with the blunt, farm-raised Wright.

The Nonresistance Society applied its high standards to many organizations and individuals and found them wanting. It scolded the New York Liberty party's candidate for governor, Gerrit Smith— though he had already given the Nonresistance Society the largest contribution it ever was to receive—for professing to believe that violence and liberty are incompatible and yet running for an office in which, if elected, he would exercise power through violence.[10] It slapped the American Antislavery Society's Tappan-controlled executive committee for having attempted, when Wright was still its agent, to restrict his freedom of speech. By contrast, the Nonresistance Society pointedly instructed Wright that in acting as its agent he fell under no obligation of silence about any reform; "we should be ignorant indeed," the Nonresistance Society said, "not to have learned that every truth strengthens and forms part of every other truth." The *Nonresistant* even warned the Garrisonian-led Massachusetts Antislavery Society that, despite its intentions, its spirit was sometimes violent. "It is extremely difficult," the *Nonresistant* admitted, "to give full scope to a freeman's indignation at the tyranny, cruelty, and insolence of the slave-holding oligarchy, without falling into the spirit of war-like resistance."[11]

The Nonresistance Society sometimes needled the Quakers, too. Though most Quakers had traditionally been voters and officeholders, as in colonial Pennsylvania where they predominated in the government for a time, the Nonresistance Society told them that, by voting and holding office now, they were participating in "governments which are upheld by the sword." Moreover, general agent Wright prodded them by saying that Friends were too much concerned about their denominational machinery; non-Friends, he said, were doing more to sustain Friends' principles than Friends were.[12]

When Quaker William Basset of Lynn, Massachusetts, one of the founders and officers of the Nonresistance Society, was threatened with expulsion from the Society of Friends for his strong peace and antislavery testimony outside of the Society of Friends, the Unitarian-reared Edmund Quincy jabbed Quakers in the *Nonresistant.* The principles of the Society of Friends, "as we understand them, are ours," Quincy wrote. "We feel an interest in it and an affection for it, such as we feel for no other religious denomination. . . . We love it, and would fain have it restored to its original pre-eminence among all religious bodies, as the fearless asserter of human rights and mental freedom, and the strict interpretation of the precepts of the Gospel." But in its present form the Society of Friends was not worthy of Basset, Quincy said. Basset himself protested, in a letter published in the *Nonresistant,* that Friends were being pressured not to associate with non-Friends in making their antislavery and peace testimony, and charged that Friends had so far departed from their tradition that their prejudice against color was "perhaps" as great as that of the country at large. When the Society of Friends did in fact expel Basset, along with others who were similarly active outside of the society, Quincy mourned—a bit prematurely to be sure—that the Society of Friends was dead; "worldly prosperity and the fatal spirit of sectarianism" have killed it, he explained.[13]

The Nonresistance Society also sometimes needled the American Peace Society. Because leading Tappanites—including Lewis Tappan and Judge William Jay—were active members of the American Peace Society, this needling sharpened the difference between the Garrisonians and the Tappanites.

Both Wright and Garrison had long respected the Peace Society's huge, humorous, energetic leader Ladd. As we have seen, Garrison probably became a peace man in part through Ladd's influence. As early as 1835, Wright had tried to push the American Peace Society to the position that war under all conditions was wrong; Ladd told Wright at the time that he agreed with this position himself, "but thought that men were not yet prepared for such strong meat."[14] Nevertheless in 1837, with Ladd's help, Wright and his radical friends captured enough control of the Peace Society's annual meeting to be able to change its constitution. They changed it so that for the first time it condemned not only aggressive war but also defensive war. Within a year, however, it was already clear that in practice the Peace Society was still welcoming as members those who justified defensive wars, as in fact it was to continue to do.

After the Garrisonians founded the Nonresistance Society—in part because they considered the American Peace Society hopelessly insipid—Ladd at first attended the Nonresistance Society meetings, saying that his own principles were the same as those of the new society, though he could not accept all its applications of them.[15] But when Ladd asked the Nonresistance Society to cooperate with his Peace Society in petitioning the United States government for the creation of an intergovernmental congress of nations, the Nonresistance Society declined to do so because this represented too much dependence on governmental rather than individual action. After that, Ladd became aloof from the Nonresistance Society and wrote a public criticism of its members: "I have no doubt of their sincerity and integrity," he wrote. "They mean to do good, and make great sacrifices to do it. There are some minds so ultra, that they will never undertake anything without going beyond the truth." Garrison then retorted that what Ladd had said at Nonresistance Society meetings must have "been remarkably disingenuous and equivocal."[16]

Several years later, political abolitionist Charles Sumner, as a spokesman for the American Peace Society, announced that the society could approve of violence both in personal self-defense and in revolution for freedom. In reply, the *Liberator* said that the Peace Society was "based on expediency instead of principle" and doubted that any such society could "effect any radical moral change in the opinions or practices of mankind."[17] While Garrison could acknowledge the right of self-defense and insurrection in the abolitionist movement so long as it was combined with uncompromising noncooperation with slavery, in the peace movement he insisted on uncompromising noncooperation with war.

As part of his continued execration of the American Peace Society, Garrison explained his theory of nonviolent social reform in one of the most revealing of his statements on methods. Any great radical moral reform, he said, could be successfully pushed only by absolute adherence to the principles inherent in that reform, including noncooperation with the evil against which that reform is directed. Thus, Garrison said, anyone who would expel drunkenness from the world should not be a drinker himself. Nor should anyone who would end slavery be a slaveholder. Nor should anyone who would end war himself "be a warrior, nor swear to sustain an army and navy, nor consent that any body of men shall have power to declare war at their discretion." So when the American Peace Society invited "Colonel" Josiah Quincy, Jr., the mayor of Boston and brother of Nonresistance Society leader Edmund Quincy, to preside at a meeting, Garrison was contemptuous. "Colonel" Quincy was chosen just to present a "respectable front," said Garrison; he was not only a military man himself, but, what was worse, he supported a general—the bloody Mexican War general, Taylor—for President. "The truth is," said Garrison, "the peace movement has been so timidly managed in this country—it has been advocated in such a namby-pamby, milk-and-water, abstract, sentimental, delicate, inoffensive, beg-your-pardon manner—it has sought so assiduously to avoid the reproach of 'ultraism,' and to secure the approbation of politicians and divines—that it has utterly failed to make any impression on the public heart or conscience; it attacks nothing, impeaches nobody, deals in generalities." Since sentimental peace men "engage in politics, vote to uphold a war-endowed government, fill governmental offices, honor military heroes, and consent to all appropriations by Congress for the support of the army and navy, the kingdom of violence is not ruffled by any of their efforts."[18] It was evident that in Garrison's mind, reform could not be achieved without taking uncompromising stands on speciffc issues and being offensive to those in power.

However, as Garrison had already revealed by his stand for the right—but not the wisdom—of both violent slave revolt and violent abolitionist self-defense, there were boundaries beyond which he would not drive his nonviolence. Garrison revealed another of those boundaries when the Nonresistance Society debated the question of paying fines for refusing to serve in the militia.

About the time of the organization of the Nonresistance Society, a wave of refusals to serve in compulsory state militias swept New England, and the society encouraged it. New Hampshire imprisoned nonresistant Amos Wood, once a Congregational deacon, for refusing to serve. Connecticut imprisoned C. M. Burleigh, who was to become an antislavery lecturer, because he refused to train for "human butchery" and would not pay his fine. There were so many refusals to serve in Massachusetts, according to Wright, that the compulsory militia system was crumbling.

A Nonresistance Society meeting unanimously took the position that it was unjust for states to exempt from the militia only "certain classes of Christians," such as Quakers and Shakers, who were "scrupulous" against bearing arms. All who were scrupulous against bearing arms should be treated alike, they said.[19]

However, members of the Nonresistance Society differed on whether, in order to secure exemption from militia service, they should pay militia fines. Some members opposed paying such fines. For example, Charles K. Whipple, the treasurer of the society, opposed on the ground that the fines were used to support the militia system itself.[20] Quaker tradition, too, was that nonresistants should not pay either taxes expressly for war or fines in lieu of military service. Taking a position more strict than the Quakers, the general agent of the Massachusetts Antislavery Society, J. A. Collins, proposed that a meeting of the Nonresistance Society adopt a drastic resolution: "That it is a violation of nonresistance principles to pay military fines, mixed taxes, or to purchase taxed goods." Collins, a virtual anarchist, desired that nonresistants avoid any responsibility for financial support of governments based on violence. Garrison's reply to such arguments was, if government forces nonresistants to pay fines or taxes against their will and then misuses the money, its doing so is not the nonresistants' responsibility.[21] The meeting, doubtless under Garrison's influence, tabled Collins' resolution.[22] As on the question of the right of abolitionists to defend themselves, so also on this issue, Garrison, despite his radical stance among Americans at large, was a moderate among complete nonresistants. Garrison had made clear another boundary beyond which he would not push his nonviolence.

Individuals associated with the Nonresistance Society tried to apply their nonviolent principles in a wide variety of situations.

Nonresistants took positive action to overcome evil with good, said the *Nonresistant*. Many people, it explained, "seem to think that consistency requires of nonresistants to sit calmly by, with their arms folded, and see the evils with which the world is blasted through the violation of God's law without making an effort to resist and remove them. Nothing could be farther from the true genius of nonresistance than such quietism. The true nonresistant has solemnly devoted himself to a life-long conflict. He has assumed the cross of a crusader. He renounces the use of carnal weapons . . . because he wields more excellent weapons."

Garrison put it succinctly: "Passive nonresistance is one thing," he said at a nonresistance meeting; "active nonresistance is another. We mean to apply our principles. We mean to be bold for God. Action! Action!"[23]

In their nonviolent actions, some individuals related to the Nonresistance Society tried to collect debts without violence or even recourse to law. Some tried vegetarianism, a practice that appealed to them because it reduced the bloody slaughter of animals; David Cambell, a signer of the 1833 Declaration of Sentiments who was twice jailed for refusing to do militia service, edited a vegetarian journal and established a vegetarian boarding house at abolitionist Oberlin College.[24] Some stressed the value of being nonviolent in family life; the transcendentalist Bronson Alcott said that nonresistants had to overcome violence in their family life before they could overcome it in the world. Many associated with the society, including Garrison and Lucretia Mott, played major roles in the struggle for women's rights; they believed—as H. C. Wright said—that when women gained influence in church and state, "war and slavery must cease." Many tried to induce people to think in terms of the world rather than merely nations. General agent Wright did so when he was traveling in Europe by calling himself not an American but a man and a brother. Garrison did so too by regularly heading the *Liberator* with the motto, "Our country is the world—our countrymen are all mankind," and by asking the Nonresistance Society to endorse the idea—as it did—that national flags are "symbols of barbarism."

John M. Spear, a member of the Nonresistance Society's executive committee, led a movement to abolish capital punishment. When the state of Massachusetts, despite thousands of petitions asking for mercy, hanged a poor Negro on a charge of murder, Wright supported Spear's campaign, the Nonresistance Society endorsed it, and Garrison said that if the accused had been wealthy and white he probably would not have been executed.

Associates of the Nonresistance Society were also concerned about other forms of punishment of criminals. Edmund Quincy urged that penalties be inflicted not as vengeance but as correction. Adin Ballou, a president of the society, urged that prisons be transformed into moral hospitals. When Whipple, treasurer of the society, was called to jury duty, he refused to serve because doing so might involve his helping to imprison someone; prisons, he said, "improved as they are . . . are still likely to discharge their inmates worse than they entered." Abby Kelley Foster, a member of the society's executive committee, opposed all imprisonment as violent, but said that if it had to be, the ones who should be imprisoned were not so much those who stole money as those, like slave owners, who stole men. Charles Spear represented prisoners in negotiations with prison authorities and established an information center in Boston for discharged prisoners; in his magazine, *Prisoners' Friend*, he circulated the idea that if it was a government responsibility to appoint district attorneys to prosecute accused criminals, it was also its responsibility to appoint other district attorneys to defend them.[25]

Still others associated with the Nonresistance Society tried to apply its principles to education. After pastor May became head of the Massachusetts State Normal School at Lexington (the first state normal school in the country), he spoke at a convention of teachers, using as a motto: "Love the unlovely, and they will put their unloveliness away." Many in the audience responded warmly to this idea, finding it a new one. It was disconcerting, May wrote afterward, to discover that it could be a new idea to teachers "that evil might be overcome with good in schools no less than elsewhere."[26]

May's brother-in-law, the ebullient, improvident Bronson Alcott, founded private schools in which he tried to avoid the customary whipping of children. Alcott tried to learn from his pupils; he did not so much lecture them as ask them questions. He also tried trusting them, in an honor system. He was a disciplinarian, but he said it is better to teach children by example than by demanding obedience.

At an early stage in his teaching, Alcott believed that no punishment was desirable and spent much time reasoning with recalcitrant pupils instead. But he came to believe that reasoning took too long; instead he tried depriving pupils of privileges and using token punishment in the form of one blow of a ruler upon the palm of the hand, always accompanied by explanation.

At another stage, Alcott startled his pupils by asking those who deserved punishment to punish him instead of his punishing them. The children—all under twelve years—balked at his request. "They declared they would never do it," one of the teachers at the school reported. "They said they preferred being punished themselves."

On the first day he tried this method, "the effect was a profound and deep stillness," the teacher wrote. "Boys who had never been affected before, and to whom the bodily punishment was a very small affair, as far as its pain was concerned, were completely sobered." The only exceptions were two boys who deliberately made trouble to see what would happen. Alcott took them out and asked them to strike him on the hand with a ruler."They were very unwilling, and when they did it first, they did it very lightly. He then asked them, if they thought they deserved no more punishment than that? And so they were obliged to give it hard—but it was not without tears which they had never shed when punished themselves." Afterward at home one of the boys said this was the most complete punishment a teacher ever invented. But the children understood the "generosity" of Alcott's method, the teacher reported, and responded by respecting themselves more and being more generous in spirit to one another.

Alcott's Boston school, endorsed as it was by Emerson and William Ellery Channing, at first attracted many pupils. But eventually enrollment dwindled. It did so partly because Alcott seemed to be unfitting children for the world; his concern was more with the development of their inward nature than with what wealthy Boston parents hoped for—their development into efficient lawyers, merchants, or manufacturing agents. It also dwindled partly because Alcott admitted a Negro girl into his school. Alcott knew that doing so would lead some parents to withdraw their children, but on principle he insisted on admitting her anyway. Pastor May honored his brother-in-law for this decision: "If suffering for righteousness sake (as I believe) is the method by which we are to be made perfect," May wrote Alcott, "you and my sister [Mrs. Alcott] are in the way to that desirable end."[27] A few months later, when only five pupils were left—including Alcott's daughter, the future author Louisa May Alcott—the school closed.

Another way some of the persons related to the Nonresistance Society tried to apply their nonresistance principles was by participating in experimental socialist communities. For the nonresistants, participating in these communities was an attempt to reduce some of the basic sources of man's hostility—such as emotional insecurity, economic competition, and racial prejudice—which they believed helped to produce the violence of both slavery and war. Interest in planning communities ran so high in the United States at the time that Emerson said there was "not a reading man but has a draft of a new community in his waistcoat pocket," and especially in the 1840's some sixty communities were formed. As was characteristic of socialism in this pre-Marxian age, these socialist communities were nongovernmental and frequently religious.

Persons active in the Nonresistance Society became leaders in at least five different communities or "associations." These communities ranged from the short-lived (seven months) Fruitlands community that Alcott led at Harvard, Massachusetts, to the long-lived (fourteen years) Hopedale community at Milford, Massachusetts; they ranged from the industrial one at Northampton, Massachusetts, to the intellectual Brook Farm community near Boston, and to the aggressively antigovernmental one that Collins lead at Skaneateles, New York. While the majority of "associationists" in the country were not sufficiently antislavery to suit the nonresistant Mrs. Chapman, and the *National Antislavery Standard* once charged that socialism simply meant "*my* rights—not *yours* or *his,* "[28] in practice at least two of these five communities were interracial, a third boycotted slave-produced goods, and all were at least vaguely inclined to both antislavery and nonviolence.

Early in the fad for communities, Edmund Quincy, the leading editor of the *Nonresistant,* predicted that eventually most nonresistants would be living in communities. As nonresistant principles spread, Quincy wrote a fellow nonresistant, the world will feel more threatened by us, and external pressures may almost compel us into communities; when that happens, our problem will be "to guard our individual liberties," he said. Nonresistant Charles Spear, the prison reformer, regarded communities, however "wild" or "incoherent" they might seem, as valuable experiments. In time society was sure to find a "better way," he wrote with the characteristic optimism of the time, and in its search might have to "try a great many theories."[29] More typical of nonresistants, general agent Wright was not enthusiastic about communities. He thought that nonresistants need have no intrinsic quarrel with private property; they needed only to be concerned with how property was used and defended, he said.

When Collins began to plan his community at Skaneateles, Garrison admitted that Collins had been an efficient antislavery agent but doubted that he had the solid judgment necessary to lead a community successfully. In addition, Garrsion distrusted what he called Collins' Owenite belief that man is largely a creature of circumstances, not responsible for his own actions.[30] Like H. C. Wright, Garrison was not enthusiastic about communities.

Collins' community represented the Nonresistance Society's views on government in caricature. When the community was in the process of formation,[31] the founders denounced "all governments based upon physical force" and promised "therefore we will not vote under such governments, nor petition to them, but demand them to disband; do no militia duty; pay no personal or property taxes; sit upon no juries; refuse to testify in courts of so-called justice; and never appeal to the law for a redress of grievances." None of the other four communities were as hostile to the existence of government as the Skaneateles community, though at least one practiced mild noncooperation with government much as the Nonresistance Society did. The Skaneateles community also favored property being held in common and opposed revealed religion and the organized church.

In practice the life of the community was marked by fierce dissensions. One of the problems was that the community, too trusting at the beginning, accepted participants who turned out to be leeches and who, because of the community's unwillingness to use the agency of government, were difficult to oust. Another problem was conflict over the vegetarian diet. After less than three years Collins became convinced that because of its internal turmoil the community could not succeed, and brought it to an end. The community's theories on government, Collins wrote in a public confession afterward, "might do very well if men were angels, and angels gods; but human nature is too low, too selfish, and too ignorant for relations so exalted." Collins, dropping his association with reformers, returned to conventional views of both government and religion and became the editor of a Whig paper in Ohio.[32]

The most ethereal of the five communities was Fruitlands, led by nonresistant educator Alcott. Located on a splendid site on the side of a mountain, it was essentially a farming community dedicated to plain living and high thinking. To avoid supporting slavery, the members tried to wear linen rather than cotton clothing. To avoid killing animals, they were vegetarians. Similarly, to avoid abusing animals, they refused to use horses for ploughing, and so, fantastically, for a time they worked their fields by hand. Unfortunately, they began community life late in the growing season, and, in addition, when harvest time came, the men of the community sometimes disappeared to attend reform meetings, leaving as harvest hands only the children, who were mostly girls, and poor Mrs. Alcott, who had no enthusiasm for the community anyway. By winter Mrs. Alcott had sold off much of the community's furniture for cash, and there was scarcely any food left. The members drifted away, and the despondent Alcott, realizing himself in the eyes of the world to be a fool, gave up his community, having lost some of the considerable reputation he had acquired as an educator.

Longer lasting than either Fruitlands or the Skaneateles community was Brook Farm. Its leading founder was the patient George Ripley, a former Unitarian minister who participated in at least one Nonresistance Society meeting and called himself an abolitionist, peace man, temperance man, and transcendentalist, all rolled into one. A lesser Brook Farm leader was John Orvis, the son of a Vermont Quaker farmer, who as a student at Oberlin College had helped to form a branch of the Nonresistance Society there. Orvis had assisted general agent Wright on his lecture tours, learning to withstand the furious opposition that Wright's lectures aroused. Orvis had also assisted Collins in founding the Skaneateles community, but, becoming dissatisfied with it, he moved to Brook Farm, for which he became a dependable, hardworking farmer.

Only vaguely related to Unitarianism and transcendentalism, Brook Farm had no set form of worship and included members who toyed with creeds as various as those of Swedenborg and Rome. The participants, not over 120 altogether, dined in common; most lived in one big building; and all did some manual labor—even Ripley did chores in the barn before breakfast. All members were paid at the same rate no matter what their work; Emerson laughingly said one man ploughing all day was paid the same as another who watched him all day from a window. Brook Farm, including many youths as it did—for it had a college preparatory school—encouraged music, picnics, dances, charades, and boating parties on the Charles River. Inclined toward vegetarianism, as were Skaneateles and Fruitlands, the community did not encourage hunting, and one of the members recalled never seeing a gun on the place. Large numbers of Brook Farmers drove by farm wagon to antislavery meetings in Dedham and Boston, and the community itself became a center for the discussion of a wide range of proposals for reform—a center where vivacious visitors like Alcott, Parker, Emerson, and Margaret Fuller kept conversation soaring and crackling. Hawthorne lived there for a time until, too introspective for group living, he decided that shoveling dung was not essential to writing. After five years, lack of capital and a destructive fire so discouraged members that the community dragged to a close, but many participants looked back at their years at Brook Farm as the happiest in their lives.

The most strongly interracial of the five communities and the one with which Garrison was most familiar was the community at Northampton, Massachusetts. It was led, among others, by Garrison's wife's brother, George Benson, who had been for several years a vice-president of the Nonresistance Society. Garrison hoped the Northampton Association would prosper: "Its failure," he wrote his wife, "would cause the enemies of equal rights and radical reform to shout aloud for joy."[33]

The Northampton Association encouraged liberty of thought and speech. It had no religious creed, no antislavery creed, no nonresistance creed; but on one of his visits Garrison told the members that he took it for granted that they were "generally antislavery, anti-war, and temperance men." More than the four other communities, Northampton was basically industrial. Its main enterprise was an already existing silk thread factory. A four-story ugly brick building not only housed the factory, but part of it, which was partitioned, provided Spartan living quarters for many of the association's 130 members. The diet of these associationists "is simple," wrote a nonresistant abolitionist visitor; "their habits [are] frugal, and their expenditures economical. They have a heavy debt resting upon them, a phantom-guest which has ever been present at the feasts of all advocates of community reform."[34]

Among the Negroes in the community was Sojourner Truth, a tall, spare woman of striking presence who was born a slave near Kingston, New York. Though illiterate, before coming to Northampton she had learned to preach in an epigrammatic style, in quaint, broken speech. She had been looking for a "quiet place, where a way-worn traveller might rest." She had heard of Alcott's Fruitlands, but religious friends advised her that Northampton would suit her better, and they took her there. On arrival she was upset by the stark appearance of the place and resolved to stay only one night. By the next day, however, she had become pleased, as a narrator of her life reported later, that "accomplished, literary, and refined persons were living in that plain and simple manner" and decided that if such people could accept privation, she could also. She was soon working in the laundry; as at Brook Farm, everyone in the community did some physical labor and all were paid alike no matter what work they did. Under the stimulus of the community, Sojourner Truth gradually moved toward becoming, in her own simple, picturesque way, an eloquent advocate of antislavery, women's suffrage, and temperance, and by the mid-1840's, Frederick Douglass called her a Garrisonian nonresistant. Several years later, when Douglass was less nonresistant than he once had been, she heard him persuading an audience to believe that slavery could only be destroyed by blood. Disturbed, she waited till he sat down after his speech, and then, when a hush of deep concern had come over the audience, she called out sharply, "Frederick, is God dead?" In a flash, the audience swung to her view.[35]

Another Negro in the Northampton community was David Ruggles who had worn himself out trying to protect fugitive slaves in New York City, including groping through a labyrinth of legal tangles, serving time in jail, and feuding with his co-workers. By the early 1840's, Ruggles, though only in his thirties, was destitute and blind—his physician believed his blindness was due at least in part to the strain of his work—and he found Northampton a refuge. While there Ruggles experimented with water cures for the benefit of his health; his eyesight improved enough so that he could walk without aid, and finally he became so successful in sensitizing his touch as a means of diagnosis that he attracted patients and became a water-cure physician.

Frederick Douglass, who was one of the many fugitives Ruggles had assisted in passing through New York, came with gratitude to Northampton to visit him. Douglass found the people of the community the most democratic he had ever met, and found himself leaning strongly to communities "as a remedy for all social ills."

The community encouraged its Negro members, Sojourner Truth, Ruggles, and others, to share equally in its life. A visiting newsman, representing the conservative New York *Journal of Commerce*, reported that he saw a Negro man sitting at a table with a white girl and felt his stomach turn. Indirectly the community even defied the great American bugaboo of interracial marriage: on Garrison's urging, it accepted as a member a Negro pastor's white widow who had been ostracized from conventional society.[36]

Like Brook Farm, the Northampton community had its own boarding school. Garrison sent a son there; Ruggles called it the best school he knew in the nation and urged Negroes to send their children there too. As directed by William Adam, a former professor of literature at Harvard, the school was unconventional. It forbade corporal punishment and united study and labor. The children cared for the community's silkworms, boys carrying in the mulberry leaves from the orchards and girls distributing the leaves on the shelves. Children learned botany and biology as much as possible outdoors rather than by memorizing what they read; they learned geography by building islands, capes, and other formations in miniature on the banks of the nearby stream.

On Sundays in winter the community met for worship in the big red brick building, in summer outdoors under the trees. They had no set form for their worship, but often had a period of silence, a reading from the Bible, spontaneous singing, and free discussion. One Sunday when Garrison spoke, he told them that he did not consider "himself an unreserved advocate of their principles, but merely expressed his feeling hopes of them as having associated in an experiment to benefit mankind and to retrieve a ruined world."

Northampton community life, like that at Brook Farm, was rather smooth, without reports of significant internal turmoil. But after four years, in 1846, the community as a socialist enterprise broke up, largely because of insufficient capital. For several years afterward Benson stayed on to operate a private cotton mill in what had been part of the community property (he seemed to have no scruples about handling slave-grown cotton). In doing so, Benson took care to employ one of the community's fugitive slaves in charge of the mill's teams, to employ Sojourner Truth in his home as a housekeeper in the style of a guest, and to help Ruggles build a forty-patient water-cure resort near the community grounds—a resort Garrison patronized.

While the members of the other four communities were not necessarily nonresistants, all members of the community at Hopedale, near Worcester, Massachusetts, were. When the Hopedale community was being formed, the *Nonresistant* said warmly, "In this and similar attempts we think we see the germ of the new church and new state which are to supersede the present corrupt institutions of society." Hopedale members—who may have numbered as many as three hundred at one time—were of many sects but all professing Christians. All pledged themselves to return good for evil, to abstain from violence, from vindictive punishment, from military service, from bringing actions at law, from voting, petitioning, oaths, slaveholding, and from caste or color distinctions. They were so anxious to impart their nonviolent concerns to their children that they made it the duty of every member to see to it that children were discouraged from "the use of all war-like, savage-like, or ruffian-like toys, playthings, sports, and amusements, however harmless in themselves."[37]

The head of Hopedale was the large, radiant-faced Adin Ballou, who also served as president of the Nonresistance Society for several years. Before becoming head of Hopedale, he had been first a Universalist and then a Congregational pastor; later he became a Unitarian pastor. Ballou himself called Hopedale "a moral power antislavery society, radical and without compromise . . . a peace society on the only impregnable foundation of Christian nonresistance."

Hopedale, like Northampton, was an interracial community. It welcomed fugitive slaves. Douglass himself brought a fugitive slave girl to Hopedale to live.[38]

The Hopedale community owned its own land and buildings, including some thirty houses, farm buildings, and a church that doubled as a school. On a stream the community built dams for water power for use in its shops—industrial shops for printing, for making boxes, clocks, shoes, and the like. At first, as at Brook Farm and Northampton, they tried paying everyone the same wages no matter how much work they did, but they soon found this system a failure. They experimented with other wage systems, including one in which wage rates varied but no one was paid more than a certain maximum per day and another emphasizing equal division of profits. Finally they settled on a system which first assured that no one suffer for lack of necessities and then in addition, where practicable, paid wages "by the piece or percent" for work actually done.

A report of the Nonresistance Society, read by Garrison at a society meeting in 1844, said that Hopedale was based on nonresistance as no other association or community in the world they knew of was, and added, "Thus far, the experiment has worked in the most satisfactory manner." At another society meeting in 1849, several Hopedale members told of their experiences in the community. After listening to them, Garrison decided that they had shown "that the possession of that spirit which is ever ready to return good for evil, and which utterly repudiates all carnal weapons and all appeals to the magistracy for protection or redress, ensures tranquility of mind, and the safety of property and life, far beyond anything of an opposite nature." Among the five communities, Hopedale at least had exceeded Garrison's expectations.

Others agreed with Garrison in praising Hopedale. Garrisonian editor Oliver Johnson of the Ohio *Antislavery Bugle*, a complete nonresistant, called Hopedale a "truly Christian fraternity." Garrisonian orator Wendell Phillips, only an occasional nonresistant himself, called it "the best and most successful" of the communities in New England "and I suspect anywhere." The contemporary historian of the socialist communities, John Humphrey Noyes, later said that Hopedale lasted longer, was more nearly religious, and was "more scientific and sensible" than any other community of the age.[39] Hopedale retained its socialist character until financial problems came to a crisis in 1856 and retained its nonresistant character throughout the Civil War.

Hopedale, the community that proved to be the longest lasting of the five socialist communities, was neither the most interracial nor the most antireligious and antigovernmental, nor the most industrial. Rather, the longest-lasting community was apparently the one that was moderately interracial, moderately industrial, the most willing to permit wage differentials, the most clearly religious, and the most clearly nonresistant.

Hopedale leader Ballou wrote extensively on nonresistance. As president of the Nonresistance Society, Ballou briefly revived the *Nonresistant* in 1845 as the organ of the society and edited it himself until he merged it with Hopedale's paper. One of Ballou's books, *Christian Nonresistance*, published in 1846, was the most comprehensive statement of the nonresistance position in the abolitionist period. In this book Ballou said that while he disapproved of all *injurious* force to persons, he approved of *noninjurious* force to certain persons, such as children, maniacs, drunkards, and the deliriously sick, to prevent them from injuring themselves or others. Nonresistants developed this distinction into a general distinction between injurious and noninjurious force; Garrisonian editor Oliver Johnson believed that every nonresistant considered Ballou's distinction sound and important and that it was only injurious force that nonresistants rejected.[40]

About 1890 when the Russian nonresistant Tolstoy read some of Ballou's writings, he acknowledged that Ballou had found the true basis of nonresistance, but he criticized two aspects of Ballou's thought. First, Tolstoy questioned Ballou's approval of noninjurious violence to certain persons, saying that Christ made no exception to his insistence on nonviolence. Second, Tolstoy thought that Ballou did not sufficiently reject property, for Tolstoy believed that a Christian can have no property; he must be poor and suffer. Desire for property, he explained, had been the Achilles heel for both the Quakers and the Hopedale community.[41]

While Garrison warmly admired Ballou—he once praised him as "beautifully and powerfully" representing the principles of the Nonresistance Society in both his life and teachings—Garrison disagreed with some details of Ballou's thought. He found Ballou's nonresistance based more completely on Christianity than it needed to be. In regard to property, Garrison did not consider it as much a key to nonresistance as Ballou did; like most nonresistants, Garrison had less personal interest in tying nonresistance to socialist experiment than either Ballou or Tolstoy. In 1844, when there was a convention of "associationists" in Boston in which some nonresistants took a leading part, Garrison said the associationists combined a "good deal of wholesome, robust, world-saving truth" with absurdities, and he was sure that individual Christian regeneration was more significant in human redemption than any plan of community. Moreover, Garrison did not practice quite the degree of noncooperation with government that Ballou did—like Collins, Ballou opposed the typical Garrisonian petitioning of governments on the ground that the resulting government action might be enforced by violence. Despite minor differences, Ballou and Garrison remained in basic agreement on nonviolent methods in the abolitionist movement until close to the Civil War.

By 1850, when liberal revolutions in Europe had increased popular taste for violence and the victory of the slave power in the Mexican War seemed to make nonviolent methods less likely to succeed in abolishing slavery, the peace movement in both America and Europe was in decline, and the Nonresistance Society, destitute of funds, had virtually ceased to exist. Several years before this, however, the Garrisonian nonresistants—though a minority in the American Antislavery Society—had already induced it to adopt the essence of the Nonresistance Society's policy of noncooperation with government. Though the Nonresistance Society itself did not survive, nonresistants continued to apply its principles in a wide range of abolitionist direct actions, and we now turn to the story of those actions.

PART II

Direct Action Against Discrimination

Our measures "shall be . . . the overthrow of prejudice by the power of love."
—William Lloyd Garrison in the *Declaration of Sentiments,* 1833

7. Regardless of Complexion

◇◇◇◇◇◇◇◇◇◇◇

PREJUDICE AGAINST BLACKS was severe in the North. In some ways it was as severe in the North as in the South. Slave owners felt some responsibility for their slaves, and sometimes they even felt an affection for them much as they did for their dogs, while Northerners, feeling no responsibility for blacks, could ignore them coldheartedly.

Prejudice deeply wounded Northern Negroes. As the Tappanite Negro minister Theodore S. Wright of New York said in a classic statement, prejudice often "causes the colored parent as he looks upon his child to wish he had never been born." Yet Negroes were themselves steeped in prejudice—they borrowed it from whites. When Negro parents had children of varying degrees of color of skin, they found it easier, admitted Whipper's *National Reformer*, to love the ones who had whiter skin.[1]

To reduce such prejudice, many leading abolitionists called not just for talk but for nonviolent direct action. "We must eat, walk, travel, and worship with people of color," said Lewis Tappan at an antislavery meeting, "and show to slaveholders and their abettors at the North, that we will recognize them as brethren." Said Negro pastor Wright—whose wife had just died from an illness perhaps induced by her being forced, because of her race, to spend the night without a cabin on the deck of a steamboat—"Let every man take his stand; burn out this prejudice, live it down, talk it down, everywhere consider the colored man as a man, in the church, the stage, the steamboat, the public house, in all places, and the death blow to slavery will be struck." On the proposal of Quaker Sarah Grimké, in 1838 the Antislavery Convention of American Women adopted a comprehensive direct action resolution: "It is . . . the duty of abolitionists to identify themselves with these oppressed Americans, by sitting with them in places of worship, by appearing with them in our streets, by giving them our countenance in steamboats and stages, by visiting with them at their homes and encouraging them to visit us, receiving them as we do our white fellow citizens."[2]

The more cautious white abolitionists were disturbed by such appeals. Some of them tried—without success—to have Sarah Grimké's comprehensive action resolution omitted from the published report of the women's convention, fearing it would lead to violence against abolitionists. James G. Birney doubted it was wise for abolitionists to associate equally with Negroes because popular emotions against social equality were so strong that they would endanger the achievement of the greater goal of the abolition of slavery. Arthur Tappan explained many years later, "Though I advocated the sentiment that as Christians we were bound to treat the colored people, without respect to color, yet I felt that great prudence was required to bring about the desired change in public feeling on the subject; and therefore, though I would willingly, so far as my own feelings were concerned, have publicly associated with a well educated and refined colored person, male or female, I felt that their best good would be prompted by refraining from doing so till the public mind and conscience were more enlightened on the subject." Even more cautious was the *Friend*, a conservative Quaker journal, which advised abolitionists not to try to abolish prejudice at all. "One of the greatest mistakes committed by the antislavery people is the mixing up with the abolition question the warfare against what they are pleased to call prejudices in regard to the colored race," said the *Friend*. "The great object, it is our settled judgment, should be the extirpation of slavery, by striking at the root; leaving those minor appendages to time, and the gradual but certain effects of advancing light and knowledge."[3]

Antislavery agent Theodore Weld was cautious only about certain forms of public association with blacks. Though Weld attended black churches and black parties more often than white ones, he said that he himself would not walk arm in arm with a black woman down a Cincinnati street because of the vengeance that it would bring upon blacks.

The attitude of Negro abolitionists varied widely. Like Weld, editor Cornish of the *Colored American* saw immediate difficulties in public acts of equality, especially if Negroes initiated them, but he did not therefore advise against them. Blacks were acquiring greater militancy from white abolitionists, Cornish said, and he was glad of it. Blacks were learning to demand equal rights rather than just accept favors from whites, he explained. For Negroes to demand equal rights would do much in the long run to destroy prejudice, he added, but in the meantime their doing so would increase white prejudice because whites did not like Negroes to demand equal rights. On the other hand, Sarah Forten, a daughter of the Philadelphia Negro sail manufacturer James Forten, advised Negroes to avoid facing discrimination rather than to seek opportunities to confront it. Her family, she wrote her friend Angelina Grimké in 1837, seldom went to public places unless sure they were open to all, and therefore they did not have to suffer the mortifications that otherwise would have ensued.[4]

Abolitionists were so torn over the issue of associating publicly with persons of a different color that Lewis Tappan was afraid in 1836 that the American Antislavery Society would split apart over it.[5] But an open split was avoided, and in fact a substantial number of the more daring abolitionists—including Quakers, Garrisonians, and Tappanites—made a point of associating as equals with those of another color, believing that it was a significant means of destroying both prejudice and slavery. Abolitionists often associated with those of another color publicly and at some sacrifice. Regardless of their particular degree of nonviolence in other respects, they often took part in this direct action with a deliberate intent to be nonviolent. They associated with blacks over a period of many years, in a great variety of ways, in what altogether was an impressive record of nonviolent direct action.

Some abolitionists walked in public with those of another color in "walk-alongs."

After dining in Philadelphia at the Forten's house in 1833, Samuel J. May walked with one of the Forten daughters to an antislavery meeting. On his return to Boston, a lady asked May if it was true that he had, and he answered that he would be happy to do it again and wished that "all the white young ladies of my acquaintance were as sensible, well educated, refined, and handsome withal as Miss Forten." Thereafter, reported May, some Bostonians thought him "incorrigible."

Philadelphia was said to be the most anti-Negro city of the North.

About 1839, when its mayor was expecting anti-Negro rioting, he implored Lucretia Mott not to offend the white rabble by walking in the streets with colored people. She replied that she had been in the habit of walking with Negroes as the occasion offered and, as it was a matter of principle with her to make no distinction on account of color, she expected to continue to walk with them, and in fact she did.

About 1835, Henry C. Wright walked arm in arm with a Negro woman in the Boston streets. He did so, he explained, "on an errand of kindness and mercy to the poor—never dreaming of what was to be the result." Back at his boarding house he was told that he had lost his standing in all respectable society. This scolding, Wright said, helped to push him to declare himself an abolitionist and join a Garrisonian society.[6]

About 1841, soon after Douglass first became an abolitionist lecturer, Dr. Henry Bowditch, the Boston physician, invited Douglass to walk home to dinner with him after a meeting. Bowditch confessed later that during their walk along Washington Street, one of the main streets of Boston, he was afraid of meeting his friends; the walk was "somewhat like a cold sponge bath," Bowditch recalled. Douglass, however, remembered the walk as the first time a white had treated him as a man.

Several years later Douglass called on two white English ladies at a hotel in New York City and then in broad daylight walked up and down Broadway with them, arm in arm. Passing pedestrians scowled at them, and passing riders in omnibusses swore. But Douglass and the ladies tried to behave as if they knew nothing of the hostility around them. The way for abolitionists to remove prejudice, said Douglass, when he reported the incident in his *North Star*, "is to act as though it didn't exist, and to associate with their fellow creatures irrespective of all complexional differences. We have marked out this path for ourselves," he said, "and we mean to pursue it at all hazards."[7]

A year later, while waiting to board a steamer for Philadelphia, Douglass and two white ladies walked together in Battery Park, New York City. White ruffians assailed them with coarse language and finally struck the ladies on the head, Douglass warded off further blows with an umbrella, nonviolently. "I felt no indignation toward the poor miserable wretches who committed the outrage," he wrote. "They were but executing upon me the behests of the pro-slavery church and the clergy of the land."

Douglass believed, however, that abolitionists were making progress in overcoming prejudice, at least in Boston. In 1849 he told a Boston audience: "The time was, when I walked through the streets of Boston, I was liable to insult if in company with a white person. Today I have passed in company with my white friends, leaning on their arm and they on mine, and yet the first word from any quarter on account of the color of my skin I have not heard. It is all false, this talk about the invincibility of prejudice against color."[8]

Besides insisting that blacks and whites had the right to walk together in public places, abolitionists often insisted that they had the right to eat together in public places as well. To achieve that right, abolitionists practiced various forms of nonviolent direct action, including sit-ins, boycotts, and fasts, with varying degrees of openness or subterfuge and with varying degrees of success.

Once the Tappanite minister Charles B. Ray, the general agent of the *Colored American,* and Philip Bell, its proprietor, took a steamer from New York up the Hudson to Newburgh. They were campaigning for subscriptions to their paper.

When it was time for tea, they asked for it in the dining cabin with other passengers, but a steward said they could only have it in the kitchen.

"We cannot eat in the kitchen, sir," they said, as Ray reported later; "we are willing to wait till the table can be reset, and then have our tea." Evidently they were willing to wait till the whites had finished, if they could eat in the dining cabin. But the steward was adamant.

They spoke to the captain, and he supported the steward: you can have tea in the kitchen, he said.

"No, sir, we do not like to be the agents of our own degradation," they replied.

"You cannot have the tea anywhere else," answered the captain. "The waiters do not like to set a second table."

"Very well, sir," the Negroes answered; "it is not place we are contending for—but principle," and they refused to eat at all.

A year later, when Ray was again traveling for the *Colored American,* he took an even stronger position. This time he was on an Erie Canal packet boat, near Utica, when he was refused a place at the first table with whites. He "protested firmly, but mildly," Ray wrote afterward, "but to no purpose, and finally to prevent noise retired." Later, when another table was ready, the captain invited Ray to come to eat, but he refused. "Of course I could not submit to such a principle," Ray explained, and told the captain that he considered himself his equal.[9]

Once Douglass was traveling on a Hudson River steamer between New York and Albany. When the dinner bell rang, Douglass, accompanied by two English ladies, went downstairs to the dining cabin. "I went below," Douglass recounted later, "forgetting all about my complexion, the curl of my hair, or the flatness of my nose, only remembering I had two elbows and a stomach, and was exceedingly hungry."

They sat at one of the tables, but gradually the other passengers who were sitting at the same table, all whites, rose and moved to another table. In a few minutes a white steward came up to Douglass and asked him to leave the table.

Douglass demanded on what authority he ordered him from the table. "Well," the steward replied, "yer know the rule." Douglass said he knew nothing of the rule.

"Well," said the steward, "yer cannot get dinner on any boat on this river."

Douglass said he had sailed on the *Confidence* on this river and had taken dinner.

"Well," said the steward, "what yer can do on the *Confidence*, yer can't do on the *Alida*. Are yer a going to get up?"

"No, sir," answered Douglass.

"Well," said the steward, "I will have yer up." The steward went to get help and brought back with him the captain, mate, clerk, and two or three others.

"I sat still during the time of his absence," wrote Douglass afterwards, "but finding they were mustering pretty strong, and remembering I had but one coat, and not caring to have it torn, and feeling I had borne a sufficient testimony against their unrighteous treatment, I arose from the table, and walked to the other end of the cabin, in company with my friends. A scene then occurred which I shall never forget. . . . A large number of American ladies and gentlemen, seated around the table at the other side of the cabin, the very moment we walked away, gave three cheers for the captain, and applauded in the most uproarious manner the steward, for having driven two ladies and one gentleman from the table, and deprived them of dinner."[10]

William Wells Brown was more successful in demanding equal rights in an incident in Cleveland, where he went to attend an abolitionist convention. Having seen an advertisement for a Cleveland hotel in the Ohio Garrisonian paper, Brown, upon arrival in the city, looked for that hotel, found it, secured a room, and prepared for dinner. When the call for the first table sounded, he joined some other abolitionist delegates to the convention—including Susan B. Anthony, the woman's suffrage leader from New York State, and Andrew T. Foss, the New Hampshire antislavery lecturer—and moved toward the dining room. At the door Brown was stopped because he was a Negro and was told he must wait for the second table. Since he couldn't go in, Miss Anthony and Mr. Foss and the other delegates refused to go in, and they all went into the sitting room to consider what to do. Hotel officials came to them and proposed a side table for their party, or meals in their rooms, or anything except eating at the regular table. The abolitionists, however, rejected all offers, refusing to eat without equality for Brown. After an hour the hotel officials gave up and allowed Brown to eat with the others at the regular table, as he did during the rest of his stay at the hotel. "I remained three days," said Brown, "and was never better treated."[11]

As the son of a slave mother and a white master, Brown was light complexioned; he was said to be a grandson of Daniel Boone. His light color played a role in an incident on a little steamer on Lake Cayuga in upstate New York. At mealtime Brown went into the cabin dining room at the same time as the other passengers. He had scarcely taken a seat when a white man, who had apparently been darkened by Southern sun, asked the steward, "Is it the custom on this boat to put niggers at the table with white people?"

The steward hesitated, and the Southerner pressed his advantage. "Go tell the captain that I want him," he said, and the steward went out.

Brown was helping himself to the food as fast as he could when he heard the captain on the stairs, and a happy thought struck him. As soon as the captain came in and called, "Who wants me?" the light-skinned Brown replied, "I, sir," and, pointing to the dark Southerner, added, "I want you to take this man from the table." At this unexpected twist in events, the crowd giggled, while the Southerner seemed to choke.

"Why do you want him taken from the table?" asked the captain.

"Is it your custom, captain," asked Brown, "to let niggers sit at table with white folks?"

The company abandoned themselves to laughter, while the dark

Southerner stomped out, exclaiming, "Damn fools." The suave Brown finished his meal in peace.[12]

Occasionally a whole group acted against discrimination in eating places. When Douglass was on his way with a party of delegates to attend the 1852 national convention of the Free Soil party, their train stopped for dinner at Alliance, Ohio. Douglass attempted to enter a hotel dining room but, because he was a Negro, was stopped. Hearing of it, some of the delegates who were already eating in that dining room left their tables without finishing dinner. Several days later, when the delegates were returning from the convention, their train stopped again at Alliance. This time the hotel proprietor had prepared food for three hundred delegates. However, to protest the hotel's previous treatment of Douglass, in a striking example of group action, not one of the delegates would take dinner there and much of the food was left to spoil.

In 1848, when the young Garrisonian Negro William C. Nell was assisting Douglass in publishing the *North Star* in Rochester, they both received invitations from Rochester newsmen to join them in a banquet at a hotel. Douglass and Nell went to the hotel dining room where the banquet was to be held and presented their tickets at the door, but a hotel official stopped them, dubbing them intruders. They replied by calling this an insult and asking for equal treatment. The official threatened to call police. Several banquet guests gathered, protesting. Douglass and Nell "were about entering the hall to test the question," Nell wrote Garrison afterward, when it was decided to put the issue to a vote of the banquet guests. The majority voted to admit the two Negroes, only six or eight objecting, and thereafter they were well treated. "It was a painful as well as triumphant hour for Mr. Douglass and myself," Nell recalled, "for reasons which [white] abolitionists hardly know how to appreciate. None but the colored man, the immediate recipient of American pro-slavery hate, can fully testify to the emotions excited by such a development."[13]

Abolitionists often took nonviolent action to protest discrimination in transportation and other public facilities. Sometimes they protested through direct actions such as boycotts or ride-ins, and sometimes they supplemented such actions by indirect actions such as court suits or petitioning.

In 1834, when Garrison and a party of abolitionists were traveling from Philadelphia to New York, they planned, as travelers often did, to take a steamboat part of the way on the Delaware River. They found that some of the Delaware boats were segregated and some were not.

One of the party was the light-skinned Negro Robert Purvis. The son of a wealthy English merchant, Purvis was so light that as a youth he had often passed as a white and stopped for weeks at a time at fashionable resorts like Saratoga Springs; eventually he had chosen to identify himself as a Negro in the abolitionist cause.

Purvis could easily have traveled with this party as a white without raising the issue of segregation. But the party deliberately chose a steamboat on which Purvis could ride with them openly as a Negro, thus boycotting another steamboat that segregated its passengers. The party made this choice even though it meant they were taking a slower, more circuitous route. Afterward Purvis, Garrison, and the other boycotters, showing their awareness of the economic coercion involved in boycotting, publicly pointed out that the captain of their steamer by not segregating had gained twenty-seven dollars worth of business that otherwise would have gone to a segregating captain. They concluded that if their boycott of segregated transportation was "extensively imitated by antislavery men . . . every barrier of caste will soon be overthrown."[14]

Several years later the Ohio state convention of Negroes was urging a boycott of stagecoaches that would not accommodate Negroes equally. About that time, when Douglass was on his way from Columbus to Zanesville, Ohio, he paid three dollars for a ticket and took a seat inside a stagecoach. Recognizing Douglass as a Negro, an agent of the coach company ordered him to get out and take a seat on the top of the coach, in the open, where Negroes usually sat. Douglass got out but refused to sit on top and asked for his money back. The agent, using insulting language, refused to return the money. In a hurry to reach Zanesville, Douglass was obliged to hire a private conveyance to carry him there, at additional expense. Afterward Douglass brought suit against the coach company to recover the extra expense and won thirteen dollars in damages.

Once Douglass, traveling on a Hudson River steamer from Albany to New York, had a cold. He was afraid that his cold would grow worse if he had to stay on the deck all night as Negroes often were obliged to do. So he used a ruse to get a stateroom: he asked a white friend to pick up a stateroom key for him. When this incident came to light, it brought down a storm on Douglass. Garrison commented that unjust rules could not be conquered "by stealth, which only irritates and hardens the spirit which framed them. They must be conquered openly, and through much suffering," Garrison said.[15]

In New York City when the elderly Quaker Isaac Hopper saw a Negro woman rudely refused a ride in a horse railway car in which he was riding, he protested to the conductor, refused to ride any farther himself, and walked home in the rain. The next day he protested at the office of the railway company.[16]

For many years New York Negroes deliberately tried to ride in street railway cars, and conductors repeatedly ejected them. In 1853 the Negro Tappanite pastor, Dr. J. W. C. Pennington, complained in an open letter that, since his congregation lived scattered about the city and suburbs, his not being able to ride the public horsecars hampered him in his pastoral work. He kept trying to ride in the cars, he said, but was refused. Since he couldn't afford to hire private hacks, he often walked long distances, exposed to all kinds of weather, and sometimes he was late to appointments or arrived at his destination "physically and mentally" in an "uncomfortable state" for his work. "Has the New York public," he asked, "a right to require . . . this unreasonable amount of exposure?" In reply, a colonizationist paper argued that, since Negroes would never conquer the prejudice against them in America, the only solution for Dr. Pennington, although he was American born, was for him to go "home" to Africa.[17]

In 1854 a black organist on her way to church got into a Third Avenue car reserved for whites and sat down; when asked to leave, she clung to her seat until she was dragged out. She took the incident to court, and the court used it as the occasion to rule that Negroes had an equal right to ride in the New York cars. But the decision was not of sufficient force or clarity to prevent all discrimination in the cars. At this time the Sixth Avenue Railroad Company, for example, insisted that the law permitted it to run separate cars for blacks—it was then running such cars every half hour—and to allow blacks to ride only on the outside platform of cars for whites.

One Sunday in 1855, Dr. Pennington—who lived on the Sixth Avenue line himself—decided to do something about its continued discrimination.

Dr. Pennington was pastor of one of the largest churches in New York City. He was known for having a Doctor of Divinity degree from the University of Heidelberg, Germany. Much respected, he had been elected to one of the highest offices among Presbyterians in the city—that of moderator of a presbytery composed, as Lewis

Tappan reported, of influential white Presbyterian ministers. But Dr. Pennington still could not ride inside some of the public streetcars of New York.

On that Sunday Dr. Pennington urged his congregation to assert their equal right to ride. The next day one of the congregation stepped into a Sixth Avenue horsecar intended for whites only; the conductor ordered him to leave, but he refused to do so. The conductor and the driver ejected the Negro. He sued them but lost his case. In the days that followed a number of other members of Dr. Pennington's congregation also rode in "white" cars and were ejected. Finally the very black Dr. Pennington himself stepped into a "white" Sixth Avenue car. A white man in the car said he objected to riding with a Negro and complained to the conductor. The conductor would not take Dr. Pennington's fare and repeatedly asked him to leave the car or stand on the platform. He refused and was arrested. Though Dr. Pennington was known for his nonviolence, the company charged him with resisting violently, and the court censured him for a breach of the peace.[18]

A few months later a tall, confident, Negro businessman, Thomas Downing, climbed into a Sixth Avenue horsecar.

Downing's oyster house on Broad Street near Wall was patronized by some of the principal bankers and merchants of New York, and Downing, of venerable age, had become wealthy. He was not notably nonviolent; he had brought up his son to defend his rights by force when necessary.

Downing stepped into an uptown car at Park Place with a Negro woman. When he did so, the conductor threatened to put them out but did nothing about it. When the car reached Chambers Street, the conductor went over to Downing, put his hand on his shoulder, and requested the couple to leave.

"I told him we had an errand with letters to deliver in haste, and we should not get out," Downing said to a newspaper reporter later. "Then two or three gentlemen, who sat opposite us, told us to sit still, as the conductor had no right to put us out." The conductor ordered the car to go on but threatened to call police to put them out.

"We want you to call the police," Downing told the conductor, "for the police are supposed to keep the peace, and you are disturbing it."

"Well," answered the conductor, "my orders are to put you out."

"My dear sir," said Downing, "I would not take a business, if I had to break the law to carry it out."

At Canal Street the conductor called in several men who said they were employees of the Sixth Avenue line.

The men moved toward Downing, but, as he said afterward, "from the position I occupied, they were afraid to clinch me. I held a brass key, in my hand, which I suppose they thought was a knife, as they exclaimed, 'Don't use your knife!' "

Downing used no violence. "Gentlemen," he said, "if I have violated . . . the law, here is my card, and you know where to find me."

Downing offered his card to the conductor, who refused it, but when Downing offered cards to passengers, they accepted the cards and, recognizing Downing's name, felt more interest on his behalf. One passenger took a seat by his side and said, "I will sit with you. I have known you for the last thirty years in Broad Street."

Outside a crowd had gathered on the sidewalk and around the car. Someone cried out, "Put him out." Others cried, "Stay in, Downing." The conductor and his colleagues, uneasy that Downing had considerable support, abandoned their attempt to oust him. As the car started up again, some of the spectators shouted, "Three cheers for Downing; hurrah, hurrah, hurrah!" Downing and his friend remained in the car until they reached their destination.[19]

By the late 1850's and early 1860's, Negroes in Boston, Chicago, and even New Orleans rode as equals in the horsecars. In Cincinnati, at least Negro women could ride inside the cars with whites, though Negro men were required to ride outside. In Brooklyn and New York, Negroes rode with equality on all except one or two lines. But in Philadelphia no Negroes—even if they were respectably dressed —were allowed to ride inside the cars; they could only stand on the front platform near the driver. Philadelphia had the most segregated local transportation of any major city in the United States. Many prominent white Philadelphians petitioned the railroad companies to stop this discrimination, but in vain.

One day in 1858, Frances Watkins, the best-known Negro poet in the country and an active Garrisonian, entered a Philadelphia horsecar and sat down. Following company policy, the conductor asked her to stand outside on the platform, but she refused. A sympathetic passenger asked the conductor to let her sit in a corner. She refused to move to a corner either, remaining where she was. When the car reached her destination, she offered the money for her fare to the conductor but he refused to take it. Not knowing what else to do, as she left the car she threw the money on the floor.

On a winter night during the Civil War, a Negro businessman and his wife stepped into a Philadelphia horsecar. When the conductor realized they were Negroes, he tried to enforce company orders by asking them to ride outside on the platform in the cold. They refused. To force them out, the conductor had the car run off the tracks. All the passengers then left the car but the Negroes. In exasperation, the conductor opened all the windows to let the cold air in; he even had the horses unhitched, abandoning the car. The Negro couple, kept warm only by their indignation at this exhibition of legal discrimination in the City of Brotherly Love, remained in the cold car for some time and then, having made their testimony, quietly left. Despite such peaceful protests, Philadelphia horsecars continued to be segregated through the Civil War.

Abolitionists also protested discrimination in other public facilities, and they often did so by means involving an element of coercion. When a Philadelphia newspaper advertised that paintings of the Last Supper and the Crucifixion were to be exhibited to whites on certain days and to blacks on others, the Garrisonian Charles Lenox Remond called attention to this advertisement in a Philadelphia Negro meeting. In response, the meeting recommended a boycott, declaring that any Negro who cooperated in this segregation was "consenting to his own degradation."[20]

In New Bedford, a Northern city with an unusually high percentage of Negroes, when Lyceum officials decided to confine Negroes to the gallery, many abolitionists withdrew from the Lyceum, and some of the lecturers—including Emerson and Sumner—refused to appear there. The Massachusetts Antislavery Society said the boycotting lecturers deserved "the warmest thanks of every friend of justice and humanity." The next year New Bedford abolitionists founded a new nonsegregating lecture association to rival the Lyceum, and the Lyceum saw the wisdom of dropping its segregation policy.

Boston abolitionist Henry I. Bowditch, the admitting physician at Massachusetts General Hospital, admitted patients according to need whether they were white or black. When the number of black patients went up, however, the trustees became alarmed and decided to exclude Negroes. Dr. Bowditch resigned in protest. But the trustees, determined to keep Dr. Bowditch, withdrew their order to exclude Negroes, and Bowditch stayed on.[21]

Some abolitionists not only insisted on the Negroes' right to equal use of public facilities, but also more daringly insisted on mixing with them socially. Said editor Cornish of the *Colored American*, the majority of our true friends seek social intercourse with us.

Social mixing could arouse fierce hostility. When Douglass was still unpolished in his manners and the wealthy Garrisonian Francis Jackson welcomed him at his dinner table, Jackson felt what Douglass called the "hot displeasure" of nearly all his neighbors.[22] In 1843 on a lecture tour Douglass stayed in a Quaker doctor's house in Pendleton, Indiana, and in doing so helped incite a mob to drive the doctor out of town.

Despite such hostility, white abolitionists sometimes lived with Negro families. Augustus Wattles did so in Cincinnati when he was teaching Negro children there, and Theodore Weld lived at editor Cornish's in New York when he was working at the American Antislavery Society's office. Similarly traveling white abolitionists sometimes stayed in Negro homes, as Garrison and his wife did at the Remonds' in Salem and as May did at the Fortens' in Philadelphia. Traveling black abolitionists sometimes stayed at white homes too. Traveling blacks dined or stayed overnight in Garrison's simple house in Boston and in Gerrit Smith's mansion in Peterboro, New York. The Negro poet Frances Watkins, who traveled in Maine as an antislavery agent, was entertained by whites so often that she wrote in 1854, "I have not been in one colored person's house since I left Massachusetts," and soon she was invited to have breakfast with the governor. On the other hand, when the white Universalist minister Charles Spear, a member of the Nonresistance Society, was traveling with a very black antislavery lecturer, someone in Harvard, Massachusetts, invited Spear to stay overnight but did not invite his black companion. Spear then declined to stay himself and wrote in his diary: "He who shuts out my brother, shuts me out also."[23]

By 1836, Lewis Tappan had several times entertained Negroes at dinner—including fellow officers of the American Antislavery Society; Christ ate with publicans and Samaritans, said Tappan, and they were the outcasts of that time, as the Negroes were in his time. In 1840 the American Antislavery Society arranged for black and white delegates to dine together during its annual meeting in New York, and a mob made trouble over it. But by 1847 and 1848 the Tappans' American and Foreign Antislavery Society held interracial breakfasts in New York without disturbance.

At abolitionist Oberlin College, black and white students mingled freely in their walks, rides, and parties, and when Douglass visited Oberlin, he was invited to dine with college officials. When an English abolitionist visited Boston, the popular Negro caterer J. B. Smith gave him a "handsome" entertainment at his suburban Cambridge home, to which came, according to the *Liberator,* a "select" party of whites and blacks. When the black schoolgirl Charlotte Forten, a granddaughter of Philadelphia manufacturer Forten, visited an anti-slavery fair in Boston, Wendell Phillips shook her hand, the Garrisons greeted her cordially, and the irresistible Mrs. Chapman walked through the fair with her arm in arm.

What it took to smooth the embarrassments that sometimes arose when blacks and whites mixed together socially is suggested by a story, told among abolitionists, about Quaker Isaac Hopper. When a Friends yearly meeting was in session, a black Friends couple, the David Mapeses of New Jersey, came to stay at the Hoppers'. At dinner time, white Friends were present who, Hopper suspected, might be unwilling to eat with Negroes. The wily Hopper said, "Dinner is now ready. David and his wife will come with me; and as I like that all should be accommodated, those who object to dining with them can wait till they have done." Several of the guests smiled, but none stayed behind.[24] Hopper had provided an example of preferential treatment for Negroes used, ironically, as a device to assure their equality.

Negro participation in abolitionist societies sometimes caused problems within the societies. In the early 1830's, abolitionist practice varied from encouraging Negroes to form separate local abolitionist societies to encouraging them to come into existing societies with whites. In 1835, Lewis Tappan arranged to seat white and colored choirs next to each other at an antislavery convention, and some abolitionists believed the seating arrangement had helped to cause the anti-abolitionist riot that followed. About that time the Boston Unitarian preacher William Ellery Channing, an idol of many abolitionists but not fully an abolitionist himself, advised against permitting Negroes to be members of abolition societies with whites. Even as late as 1836, when Lewis Tappan proposed in the American Antislavery Society's executive committee to invite the Negro minister T. S. Wright, himself a member of the committee, to speak at the society's annual meeting, most of the committee thought it unwise because he was a Negro. But gradually the question of Negro participation was resolved by admitting Negroes into full participation in abolitionist activities, and the number of separate Negro abolition societies declined. In advanced Massachusetts, according to Negro historian Nell, Negro and white abolitionists met together after 1835 as "kindred drops mingle into one."[25] Negroes were major officers

of the American Antislavery Society from its beginning and continued to be so throughout its history, and when the Tappanites split
off and formed the American and Foreign Antislavery Society,
Negroes became major officers of it too. In the 1840's or 1850's for
several years Remond was president of the Essex County, Massachusetts, Antislavery Society, and Purvis was president of the Pennsylvania Antislavery Society. Negroes also came to provide some of the
most prominent lecturers for the antislavery cause; they frequently
drew larger audiences than white lecturers.

Beneath the appearance of equality some racial tensions among
abolitionists persisted. Negro pastor T. S. Wright said in 1837 that it
seemed to him that as abolitionist societies had become more popular, the new members coming into them did not understand that for
slavery to be abolished, prejudice had to be killed; it seemed to him
that even the Quakers, who had done more for the cause of destroying prejudice than any other churchmen, only went half way in
accepting Negroes equally in their own churches and homes. In a
particularly perceptive comment, Negro editor Whipper complained in 1839 that white and colored abolitionists did not really
communicate: "The national prejudice has so complexionally separated the interests of the people of this nation," he said, "that when
those of opposite complexions meet each other, it is for the most part
under a mask, like courtiers, so that it is next to impossible, generally
speaking, to divine their real meaning and intent."[26] Other Negro
abolitionists still maintained in the 1840's and 1850's that white abolitionists accepted them only on sufferance.

A white abolitionist accused of patronizing Negroes was a Brooklyn minister who boasted at an antislavery meeting in 1860 that he
had "never had the consciousness of prejudice against color." He
"had eaten with black men," he said; he "had slept with a black man;
and this, perhaps, is as severe a test as man's antislavery character can
be put to." Robert Purvis, characteristically quick tempered, became
indignant at the minister's tone. Negroes, Purvis replied at the meeting, "ask no favors of any man. . . . A white man may . . . associate
with colored men, without conferring thereby any favor. It is quite
possible that the favor may be on the other side!"[27] All through the
abolitionist period, some blacks continued to bristle at what they felt
to be white abolitionist condescension.

Abolitionist action that brought the two races together equally,
whether in public places or in private homes, inevitably raised questions about interracial marriage.

The New York *Courier and Enquirer* presented the popular view when it expressed its horror that Negroes had been invited into the families of some white abolitionists. "To secure the purity of our families," it said, New York State should have a law against interracial marriages as Massachusetts does; racial mixing is "unnatural, defiling."[28]

In reply to such statements, abolitionists characteristically denied that they favored amalgamation but pointed out that slavery fostered it. The *Emancipator*, like many abolitionist publications, argued that abolition would lead to less amalgamation of the races than slavery, a system that permitted masters to lie with their slaves almost as they wished. The *Liberator* claimed that slavery had promoted the mixing of the races so efficiently that forty-nine out of fifty Negroes had white blood; after all, it explained, a mulatto was worth more on the slave market than a pure Negro. Negro abolitionist Professor William G. Allen predicted that in less than two hundred years Negroes would be almost wholly Anglo-Saxon. The New York City Antislavery Society believed that emancipation would "furnish the only effectual check to the disgraceful amalgamation between the white and colored races, which is now making such rapid progress wherever slavery exists. Restore the blacks to their rights . . . honor the marriage institution among them, permit families to remain together, and there can be no doubt each race will, of choice, seek alliance only among themselves."[29]

During the 1834 riot in New York City, the executive committee of the American Antislavery Society tried to calm the rioters by denying stories in circulation that abolitionists were adopting colored children and that abolitionist ministers were officiating at the marriages of racially mixed couples. Soon afterward William Goodell felt it necessary to deny the rumor that Arthur Tappan had divorced his white wife and married a Negro. The Tappanite abolitionist Judge William Jay tried to refute the charge that abolitionists favored amalgamation by pointing out that no white abolitionist was known to have married a Negro or to have been the father of a mixed-race child. The New York Negro Ruggles denied that abolitionists favored amalgamation and denied that he favored it himself, yet he also denied that amalgamation was repugnant to nature and cited as evidence the common interracial marriages in Latin America and the common suckling of white and black infants at black mothers' breasts in the South; Ruggles insisted that amalgamation seemed repugnant in the United States only because prejudice taught that it was.[30]

At an antislavery meeting, someone asked Gerrit Smith the inevitable question: do you want your daughter to marry a Negro? After admitting that he invited Negroes to visit at his house, Smith said, "I do not suppose God has given me a right to control my daughter by coercion, in her choice of a husband, yet I should feel bound to use all proper persuasiveness to prevent a union with any person of color, because it might injure her usefulness, with that of her parents, or impair her happiness." Yet, he added, he did not consider interracial unions a sin.[31]

Following such attitudes, most abolitionist leaders, while they opposed amalgamation, nevertheless insisted on social equality and on the legal right to marry interracially. They argued that the Massachusetts law forbidding interracial marriage represented an attempt by government to control the affections of its citizens, which it had no right to do any more than to control their consciences. By 1843 abolitionists—including Garrison—had successfully carried through a campaign for the repeal of the Massachusetts law.

There were, of course, some interracial marriages. One rare case was that of a white man in Mississippi who had a free Negro mistress; when Mississippi law forbade free Negroes to remain in the state, he took her and their children to Ohio and married her. There also was the case of a slave who fell in love with an Irish girl in Virginia and, after escaping to Canada, married her there. Because male fugitive slaves were more likely to reach Canada than females, according to Underground Railroader William Still, the young men there "frequently" married whites, especially Irish girls. In New York City during the 1830's, according to the *Courier and Enquirer,* there were some interracial marriages, and at about the same time Lydia Maria Child, the abolitionist novelist, said she knew of two or three in Boston between white women of the laboring class and respectable, industrious Negro men, even though interracial marriage was still illegal then in Massachusetts. One year during the Civil War, Boston officially reported that an extraordinary 16 percent of the Negroes marrying were marrying whites.

A celebrated interracial marriage in which Garrison became involved was that of Nathaniel Paul, the Negro pastor of the African Baptist Church in Albany, New York. Paul, whom Garrison called "a man of fine personal appearance and talents," was in England in the mid-1830's, lecturing against slavery, when he met an Englishwoman whom he wished to marry. Garrison, also in England at the time, warned her that, while in England an interracial marriage would be generally accepted, in America it would not be. Nevertheless they married and sailed for America. On reaching Albany, Mrs. Paul was insulted in the streets, and the only people who would visit her were a few abolitionists. Though Mrs. Paul was "an accomplished, intelligent, amiable and pious woman," according to Garrison, she "was treated, with some noble exceptions, with that scorn and neglect which are meted out to all who dare, in their practice, to assert, that God has made of one blood all nations of men." After Mr. Paul died in about 1841, Garrison wrote privately in regard to Mrs. Paul: "Her case is one that strongly appeals to us as the friends of humanity, and especially as abolitionists. She is indeed a stranger in a strange land, without funds or relatives." The Southwicks, a Massachusetts abolitionist family, took her into their home for a time. Then Garrison arranged for her to stay in the Northampton interracial community where his brother-in-law George Benson lived, and for several years the Garrisons and the Bensons continued to watch out for her welfare there. When Mrs. Paul died in 1853, after suffering a "complete nervous derangement," Wendell Phillips said at her funeral that she was "a martyr to American prejudice."[32]

The abolitionist Negro William G. Allen, a graduate of Beriah Green's Oneida Institute, taught Greek and German at the abolitionist-supported, interracial Central College, in McGrawville, New York. There he met a white student, the daughter of a Fulton, New York, abolitionist minister. When it was rumored in 1853 that he intended to marry the girl, a Fulton mob of several hundred armed men assaulted him. Soon afterward the couple did marry, in New York City, and then fled to England for safety. Garrison gave the Allens a letter of introduction to a British abolitionist, but the English —who had few Negroes among them—received the Allens anyway as a matter of course.

New Haven Negro pastor Amos Beman—one of the major Tappanite Negroes—married an English-born white in 1857. His Negro congregation was shocked. By the next year Beman felt compelled to leave the church that he had served for nineteen years, and he had lost some of his leadership role among Negroes. But the Tappanites did not reject Beman: a Tappanite-controlled antislavery missionary agency soon appointed him as a missionary to serve New England.

After the Civil War two other leading abolitionist Negroes— Douglass and Purvis—were also to marry whites, both from Quaker families.

The broad range of nonviolent direct action against discrimination, as briefly reviewed in this chapter, was usually individual action with little organization or plan, often spontaneous, often not sustained over a long period. It was more likely to be aimed at peripheral discrimination, as in public accommodations, rather than at more fundamental discrimination, as in employment.

Such nonviolent direct action kept occurring in widely separated places. It was led by a considerable variety of activists, including Garrisonians, Quakers, and Tappanites, who were nonviolent largely from principle, and also others who were nonviolent largely from expediency. Individualistic though the actions usually were, and different as the actions were in different situations, they were fundamental expressions of the thrust of the nonviolent abolitionist movement.

Whatever form the direct actions took—including walk-alongs, sit-ins, refusals to eat, boycotts, ride-ins, visiting in homes, or even interracial marriages—insofar as these actions had a social rather than personal purpose, they were usually aimed not so much at changing or enforcing law as at changing custom and attitudes.

The actions were examples of the emphasis of many abolitionists on "moral suasion" rather than governmental coercion—an emphasis especially characteristic of abolitionists in the 1830's but increasingly in dispute among them afterwards. This emphasis was parallel to the emphasis among temperance men—most abolitionists were temperance men, too—who in the 1830's emphasized moral suasion as their method but in the 1840's and 1850's increasingly turned instead toward the legal prohibition of the sale of intoxicants.

In these actions, while abolitionists did not usually employ governmental coercion, they often employed elements of nongovernmental coercion. The sit-inners and ride-inners employed the coercion of nuisance. The New Bedford abolitionists who created a rival lecture association employed the coercion of competition. Dr. Bowditch used the coercion of the withdrawal of his skill from Massachusetts General Hospital. The Free Soil party delegates in their boycott of the Ohio hotel's dining room employed economic coercion; so did Garrison and Purvis in denying business to a segregating steamboat —and they were very conscious that they were doing so. But even in these cases it is not clear that wielding coercion was the participants' primary intention; their coercion was often incidental to their determination not to cooperate with what they regarded as evil. While some nonviolent abolitionists could frankly justify their use of coercion, many nonviolent abolitionists were inclined to be wary of very much dependence on coercion because they doubted that it reached their opponents' consciences. Although they used nonviolent coercion, in some cases they regarded it as a regrettable necessity; usually the interpretation they wished to give to their nonviolent direct action was that they were being "consistent" in their own behavior by avoiding contamination with the sin of discrimination or slavery; they were using the method of "truth," or "moral suasion," or appeal to public opinion. Change primarily by coercion, they were likely to believe, could scarcely be fundamental, permanent change.

Participants in nonviolent direct action, rather than intentionally inflicting suffering on others, often intentionally took suffering on themselves, as the Nonresistance Society expected that nonviolent activists would. Garrison and Purvis chose a steamboat that took them by a slower route. Ray, Bell, and Douglass refused to eat at all unless they could do so with what they regarded as equality. Hopper refused to ride farther in a streetcar that would not pick up Negro passengers, and walked home in the rain. Spear denied himself a place to stay because his Negro companion could not stay there too. The Indiana Quaker doctor was driven out of town partly because he invited a Negro to his house. Many abolitionists took suffering on themselves by losing "respectability" because they treated Negroes publicly as equals. It was in part by taking suffering on themselves that the abolitionists convinced some of their opponents of their sincerity and won a hearing.

In addition to the abolitionists' usually individualistic, brief, nonviolent direct actions presented in this chapter, the abolitionists also developed more concerted, more long-term nonviolent direct action campaigns against discrimination, some of which we shall now examine. Such campaigns had more chance to effect a permanent social change.

8. Railroad Ride-Ins

◇◇◇◇◇◇◇◇◇◇◇◇

Much of the effectiveness of nonviolent direct action was likely to come about when it was concerted rather than individual action, when it was aimed at a limited objective, and when it was combined with other methods.

An example of such action was a desegregation campaign in the early 1840's. It was led—though not rigidly controlled—by Garrisonian nonviolent abolitionists, especially Garrison, John A. Collins, and Frederick Douglass. It was aimed at the limited objective of desegregating seating in New England transportation facilities, particularly Massachusetts railroads. The campaign combined at least five methods: (1) speech and writing, (2) the ride-in, (3) the boycott, (4) court action, and (5) legislative action. Four of these included an element of coercion.

When the campaign began in 1841, the proportion of Negroes in the New England population was small: less than 1 percent in New Hampshire, about 1 percent in Massachusetts, and about 3 percent in Rhode Island. Yet some New England stagecoaches, steamers, and railroads segregated their passengers. On stages Negroes might be required, even in bad weather, to ride on top in the open, or they might not be allowed to ride at all. On steamboats Negroes might be denied cabins and forced to ride on a part of the deck where cattle were carried. Of the railroads—a new form of transportation on which fourteen miles per hour was a high speed—only two in Massachusetts segregated their seating. One, the Eastern Railroad, ran north from Boston to Lynn, Massachusetts, and Portsmouth, New Hampshire. The other, the New Bedford Railroad, ran south from Boston to New Bedford, Massachusetts, and Providence, Rhode Island.

Ironically, the segregated railroads allowed slaves visiting from the South to ride with their masters in the superior cars reserved for whites, while they forced free blacks into the inferior cars. In fact, as the abolitionists delighted to point out, the railroads allowed monkeys and dogs to ride in the white cars, while excluding black-skinned human beings.

The abolitionists' campaign had the advantage that Massachusetts was advanced with respect to Negro rights. Though there were exceptions, in general Negroes in Massachusetts voted, served on juries, and attended the same public schools as whites, all of which they could not do in the majority of Northern states. In addition, most seating in Massachusetts public transportation was already desegregated. To desegregate the remaining stagecoaches, steamers, and railroads, abolitionists argued, would be to bring them into line with usual Massachusetts practice.

In June, 1841, a furiously active New York Negro, the young David Ruggles, was visiting Massachusetts. Though half blind, Ruggles had not let his handicap stop him from being bold to assert his rights and those of his black brothers. He had already made a name for himself in protecting fugitive slaves in New York, and besides he had already ridden in a white railway car and, when asked to leave, had refused and was dragged out.[1] Though not without ambivalence, his stance was generally nonviolent.

In New Bedford, a whaling seaport that had a considerable number of Negroes, Ruggles boarded a steamer for Nantucket, a whaling island that also had a considerable number of Negroes. On the voyage, the captain asked Ruggles to buy a ticket for the second-class accommodations that the steamer customarily set aside for its many Negro passengers, but instead Ruggles insisted on buying a ticket for first-class accommodations or none. On his persisting, the captain attacked Ruggles, forcibly seizing his personal papers.

The next month, back in New Bedford, the insistent Ruggles boarded a white car of the New Bedford Railroad, intending to go to Boston, and took a seat. But when conductors asked him to move to a "Jim Crow" car—as cars for Negroes were already called, the term having originated a few years earlier—he refused, and conductors dragged him out of his seat, tearing his clothes. Ruggles prided himself on his refusal to accept discrimination, saying, "While I advocate the principles of equal liberty, it is my duty to practice what I preach, and claim my rights at all times.[2] Though broadly a Garrisonian, Ruggles did not share Garrison's scruples against appealing to the coercion of law; he brought action against the railroad in a New Bedford court. But the judge, who was a stockholder in the railroad, upheld the railroad's right to seat Negroes as it wished.[3]

The two instances of discrimination against Ruggles stirred New Bedford Negroes. They were accustomed to being well treated; Frederick Douglass said that among them were sailors who commanded the highest wages and navigators capable of taking ships anywhere in the world. They called a protest meeting, and at the meeting they chose as chairman Frederick Douglass who knew and admired Ruggles (it was Ruggles who had hidden Douglass for several days in his own home while he was passing through New York City as a fugitive slave only three years earlier). The meeting resolved that the steamer captain's assault on "our devoted friend" Ruggles was "an open violation of the laws of the Commonwealth." The *Liberator* called the judge's decision against Ruggles in the railroad case "unspeakably atrocious." The Bristol County Antislavery Society, meeting in New Bedford, unanimously adopted a resolution, reported by Garrison for the resolutions committee, that the judge's decision was "a violation of the first principles of humanity."[4] At that meeting Douglass, only twenty-four years old, heard Garrison speak for the first time and was profoundly stirred.

The next day, August 10th, Garrison, Douglass, and a party of about forty abolitionists, white and black, boarded a steamer in New Bedford, on the same steamer route on which one of the Ruggles incidents had recently occurred; the party was headed for an abolitionist convention in Nantucket. But the captain refused to sail from the dock until the Negroes in the party occupied the segregated upper deck set aside for them. Highly conscious of segregation because of the Ruggles incidents, a few of the party refused to accept such an arrangement and left the ship. Most of the party, including Garrison, Douglass, Parker Pillsbury, James N. Buffum, and Massachusetts Antislavery Society general agent John A. Collins, persuaded the captain to let the white and black abolitionists together occupy the Negro upper deck, which, since it was a fine day, was an agreeable place to be, so agreeable that other white passengers joined them there. In fact the abolitionists were carrying off a ride-in, with the captain's permission. As the steamer moved toward Nantucket, the abolitionists cheerfully held a meeting—open to all, as antislavery meetings usually were—to protest the steamship company's already crumbling segregation policy.[5]

A few days later a meeting of the Massachusetts Antislavery Society decided to circulate petitions asking the state legislature for a law requiring equal rights for Negroes in all conveyances chartered by the state.

At the same meeting, however, the Garrisonian nonviolent action-ist Stephen S. Foster, impatient with political methods, proposed a more direct method of desegregating public seating. He recom-mended using the principle involved in the ride-ins—both the rail-road ride-in of Ruggles and the steamer ride-in of Garrison and his party. Foster moved: "We recommend to [white] abolitionists as the most consistent and effectual method of abolishing the 'Negro-pew,' to take their seats in it, wherever it may be found, whether in a gentile synogogue [church], a railroad car, a steamboat, or a stage coach."

The idea in Foster's resolution was not new. As early as 1838, the Antislavery Convention of American Women had adopted a compre-hensive policy in support of sit-ins and ride-ins, but no concerted campaign had followed.

At stake now was the possibility of a sit-in and ride-in campaign sponsored by the Massachusetts Antislavery Society, which, as Dou-glass said, was "the most efficient" antislavery society in the land. In the debate that followed, among the nonviolent leaders who spoke for Foster's resolution were Foster's New Hampshire devotee, Parker Pillsbury, and the Massachusetts Antislavery Society's gen-eral agent Collins, both of whom had been with Garrison on the steamer ride-in. Among the nonviolent leaders who spoke against Foster's resolution were Garrison and the Nonresistance Society's general agent Wright.

The debate grew heated. The New Hampshire radicals, Foster and Pillsbury, "became very much excited," calling Garrison and Wright "recreants to the cause" for not daring to support Foster's resolution. Garrison and Wright, according to the *National Antislav-ery Standard*, "seemed rather amused at the assault." They kept majority opinion with them, however, in support of their position that all abolitionists were not required to go into the place of Negro "proscription" themselves but required merely to protest against such segregation and work in some way to abolish it.[6] As in the debate on Lovejoy's use of arms, Garrison, while personally a radical, organizationally was playing the role of a moderate among the nonresistants. Foster's resolution was defeated. The Massachusetts Antislavery Society had refused to sponsor a ride-in campaign.

However, Ruggles, Garrison, and others had recently provided precedents for ride-ins in Massachusetts. Soon, even without the Massachusetts Antislavery Society's blessing, more individual abolitionists, including some of the most prominent in New England, were riding-in.

When Garrison traveled with his *Liberator* assistant, Negro William C. Nell, they sat together, where Nell was not supposed to sit, in a white railroad car. Conductors ordered Nell to go to a Negro car. Garrison protested and then, when Nell consented to go to the Negro car, went with him. Garrison's fidelity to principle, Nell reported, was not lost on the other passengers.[7]

Editor Rogers of the New Hampshire *Herald of Freedom* also began to ride in Negro cars,[8] the small, dirty cars that were often placed near the smoke of the engine. When whites rode in a Negro car, said Rogers, it "is no longer the place of dishonor. It is the place of honor. . . . It is the only place of honor about the cars. . . . Nobody of any soul will sit anywhere else."[9]

When the wealthy young lawyer Wendell Phillips, of a distinguished Boston family, also began to ride-in, the *National Antislavery Standard*, the official organ of the American Antislavery Society, said that if ten "patricians" like Phillips from each city would ride in the Negro cars, railroad segregation would stop. In the meantime, while ten "patricians" from each city did not ride in the Negro cars, a few whites did, and sometimes the conductors ordered the whites to get out and, if they refused, dragged them out.[10]

More disturbing to railroad officials, however, was that Negroes kept trying to ride in the white cars. At the Lynn depot, Mrs. Mary Green, a young Negro of light complexion who was secretary of the Lynn Female Antislavery Society, stepped into a white car of the Eastern Railroad. Conductors ordered her out, but she refused to go. As the Massachusetts Antislavery Society reported it, "She was dragged out of the car . . . in a very indecent manner, with an infant in her arms, and then struck and thrown to the ground. Her husband [who was called to the scene] was also beaten for daring to interfere for her protection." When the incident was over, her finger was cut, her knee and shoulder "badly hurt" and her husband's face was bloody.

Afterward Mrs. Green wrote the stockholders of the railroad: "I think I have a right, in common with others, to go in any car I choose. When I behave disorderly, it will be time to order me out."[11]

Getting on a train at Taunton, a white minister, Hiram Cummings, invited Boston Negro dentist Dr. Thomas Jennings to sit with him in a white car. The conductor let them sit there until the train came to the Norton station when the conductor ordered Dr. Jennings into a Jim Crow car and, according to Cummings, "at the same time seized him by the collar, and violently began to drag him out." Dr. Jennings and pastor Cummings were both nonviolent. Dr. Jennings refused to move, while pastor Cummings "appealed to the passengers to protect the Doctor from such a violent outrage," as he wrote afterward, "and took hold of the Doctor to prevent them from injuring him. . . . Upon that, I was seized by two of the brakemen, who attempted to drag me out also, but not succeeding. I still holding to Dr. Jennings to protect him instead of myself, they jammed me back against the window and smashed it. . . . We kept our places against the whole force of this band of highwaymen, until our clothes were badly torn and the Doctor said he would go out. When he said that, I let go of him." The railway men then "threw" Dr. Jennings out onto the platform, and struck him. "They care nothing about the standing, professions, or character of the persons they attack," Cummings insisted, "but seem to prefer assaulting those whose religious principles will not allow them to pay them on the spot in their own coin."[12]

The ride-inners were usually, but not always, nonviolent. One who was not was a poor black man, Shadrach Howard, who, discovering there were no seats available in a Negro railway car, went into a white car instead. The conductors asked him to leave, and after protest he reluctantly began to do so when conductors, not satisfied with his speed, shoved him. Howard resisted, and in the fight that followed he drew a knife. While onlookers shouted, "Niggers should know their place," the conductors dragged him out of the car, struck him in the face, kicked him, and tore his coat. Howard was arrested and jailed.

A committee of abolitionists—including Negroes—investigated the case. They announced that actions which most people would laud in a white man as "evincing a . . . liberty-loving spirit" were condemned in a black man as "saucy, brutal, and murderous." However, the committee would not approve of Howard's violence. It urged Negroes "never to exercise that spirit of violence which holds their fellow countrymen in bondage, and sustains the present murderous system of caste."[13] Though Howard did not share Garrison's nonresistance views, the *Liberator* collected a fund to pay Howard's fine and other costs.

On his way to Philadelphia, a Lynn Quaker, Isaac Basset, boarded a train at Lynn with his daughter, her two small children, and a black servant who regularly took care of the children. Soon after the train got under way, the conductor came up to Basset and whispered, "You must not think to take a colored person in with you again— this is the second time—and if you ever do it again, she shall be taken out," evidently meaning taken out to the black car.

"It would be next to impossible to get along without her assistance," Basset replied, as he recorded it afterward; "if she is removed, we must go with her."

"No, you shall not," answered the conductor; Basset protested, but anyway this time the conductor allowed the maid to remain in the white car. The Bassets had no other trouble in keeping their Negro maid with them on their journey to Philadelphia.[14]

The *Liberator*'s general agent, Henry W. Williams, a white complete nonresistant, invited a black man to sit with him in one of the Eastern Railroad's white cars. Another white coming into the car, occasional nonresistant Dr. Daniel Mann,[15] a Boston dentist who employed Negro dentist ride-inner Jennings as an assistant, did not know Williams or his black companion, but he knew that there had been trouble for Negroes who rode in white cars and decided that since they might need help, he would sit near them. When the conductors ordered the Negro out, the Negro and Williams protested mildly, but, as Mann wrote afterward, the conductors rushed on the Negro to drag him out "with a violence which appeared to me highly dangerous to his life." Mann, determined, he said, not to use violence, interposed his body between the black man and the conductor, caught hold of the seat, "and when they were pulling the man out, took hold of his arm, and attempted to hold him back." However, the conductors, amid excitement, did succeed in dragging the Negro out. Then they came back for Dr. Mann and dragged him out too. Once more they came back and this time dragged out two or three other white objectors.

Afterward Dr. Mann brought charges in a police court against the conductors for assaulting him. Williams, being, like many Garrisonian nonresistants, conscientiously opposed to court action, would not testify. The judge decided that the railroad was justified in making rules for seating passengers and hence the conductors were right in preventing Dr. Mann from interfering with the enforcement of those rules.

Once the black Frederick Douglass and the white John A. Collins were on their way together to an antislavery meeting in New Hampshire. By this time Douglass was an agent of the Massachusetts Antislavery Society and was beginning to be a star antislavery exhibit. That a young man of such manly bearing, melodious voice, and ready wit could have been the property of another man—as Douglass had been but three years earlier—was in itself an effective argument against slavery, and the abolitionists enjoyed showing him off. General agent Collins, a graduate of Andover Theological Seminary, was also an impressive young man. Garrison said of him about this time that he had "set at work nearly all the machinery that has kept the cause in motion for the last three years"; he had "almost superhuman energy."[16] As we have seen, Collins was soon to become founder of the utopian socialist community at Skaneateles, New York.

At Newburyport the two agents together boarded a white car of the Eastern Railroad. When the conductor asked Douglass to move to the Jim Crow car, Douglass refused. The conductor brought help. Then he asked Collins, who was sitting next to Douglass by the aisle, to move so he could more easily drag Douglass out. Collins also refused, saying discrimination was a violation of the state constitution, and added: "If you haul him out, it will be over my person." The conductor and several other railroad employees together took hold of Douglass and, as Collins reported it, "snaked him out over me . . . and thrust him into the 'Negro car,' with a 'Go there, that's good enough for you, damn you!'" Afterward one of the conductors went into the Negro car and "consoled" Douglass by telling him that the Eastern Railroad's rule for separate seating could not "be so bad, for the churches, you know, have their 'Negro pews.'"

A few days later, at Lynn, Collins and Douglass again boarded an Eastern train, and this time they were more carefully prepared. Douglass and Collins occupied adjoining seats in a white car, with a white lady friend a seat in front of them and the white Quaker, James N. Buffum, who frequently presided at abolitionist meetings, a seat behind. At once the same conductor who had previously dragged out Douglass came up to them, as Collins reported in the *Liberator*, "greatly enraged. . . . He was pale as death. His lips quivered, his whole frame shook. . . . From my heart I pitied him. He forced up his courage sufficiently to collar Douglass, and ordered him out."

"Can't I ride with him, if he goes into the forward car?" asked Buffum. "I want to have some conversation with him."

"No," answered the conductor. "I'd as soon haul you out of his car, as I'd haul him from this."

"There are but very few in this car," said Douglass, "and why since no objection has been made, do you order me out?"

A passenger proposed a vote. Buffum endorsed the idea. Other passengers did too, but the conductor insisted that the company rules required Negroes to sit in the colored car.

The conductor called eight or ten railroad men to help. He led the lady in front of Douglass to another seat. Five or six men laid hold of Douglass, but this time Douglass, a powerful man, clung to his seat. The men found Collins in the way, but Collins also refused to move and clung to the seat.

"Damn that Collins," cried one of the railroad men; "out with him!" Several men seized Collins. One hit him on the back of the head, another on his face, cutting his lips, but neither Collins nor Douglass retaliated or gave up.

Eventually the men pulled both Douglass and Collins so hard that their seat gave way, and they dragged the two protesters out, head first, and deposited them on the ground.[17]

Such incidents involving Douglass, Collins, Buffum and others occurred often enough at Lynn for Eastern Railroad Superintendent Stephen Chase to order passengers trains not to stop there any more. But the order boomeranged. People coming to the station to take trains were angry. While some Negroes as well as whites protested that the ride-ins were hurting them, large meetings in Lynn—of both abolitionists and non-abolitionists—supported the ride-ins. Those at one of the meetings resolved to "use all the means in their power, consistent with their views of law and Christianity, to defend the colored people who may see fit to take their seats in the long [white] cars." After two days, Superintendent Chase ordered trains to stop at Lynn again.

Superintendent Chase, whom desegregationists dubbed "Bulldog of Prejudice," was, ironically, a Quaker; in fact he was one of a committee responsible for expelling Garrison's associate, William Basset, from the Society of Friends for his too aggressive abolitionism. Chase argued that Negroes ought not to expect railroads to abolish Negro cars before churches abolished Negro pews; railroads, he said, shouldn't be expected to be better than churches. In reply, the local Essex County Antislavery Society—of which erstwhile

Quaker Basset was president and ride-inner Quaker Buffum was treasurer—recommended that railroads and other corporations set the churches a "holier example" by outdoing them in desegregation and praised many railroads for already having done so.[18]

Quaker Buffum believed that the ride-ins were not only helping to end segregation but were stimulating the abolitionist movement generally. "I am convinced," Buffum wrote to the *National Antislavery Standard* in New York, "that the agitation growing out of these incidents will do much good. In Lynn, it has been the means of bringing new converts to our cause; and even in Salem, where it has seemed as if nothing short of Almighty judgments could wake them from their guilty slumbers, the people are roused into active discussion. Indeed," he added, "everywhere I go, I hear men and women talking of these shameful transactions."[19] Even though the number of ride-inners was small—in this campaign possibly as few as fifty different adult ride-inners took part—Buffum believed, as Gandhi did later in South Africa, that a handful of determined people, willing for the sake of conscience to perform just actions despite public distaste and even violence, could make an impact on racial injustice.

To desegregate railroads, abolitionists were not only riding-in but were also using another nonviolent direct action method, the boycott.

As we have seen, Garrison and the Pennsylvania Negro landowner Robert Purvis had boycotted a segregated steamer on the Delaware River as early as 1834. At that time both the New England Antislavery Convention and the Negro national convention[20] were recommending a general boycott of segregated transportation. Even before that time Quakers and others had been promoting the general boycott of slave labor produce as well.

However, a boycott of the segregated Massachusetts railroads had far more chance of succeeding than either the general boycott of slave produce or the general boycott of all segregated transportation in the country. For one reason, the Massachusetts railroad boycott was directed toward a limited objective, as the other boycotts were not. For another, in Massachusetts unsegregated rail or stage service was often available as an alternative to segregated service and without much inconvenience or additional cost, whereas alternatives to slave labor produce and segregated transportation in much of the country were not.

While antislavery societies refused to urge their members to participate in railroad ride-ins, the societies were more favorable to the boycott. Participating in ride-ins perhaps meant subjecting oneself both to public scolding by conductors and to violence; it might also mean breaking the law—all of which, although part of the nonviolent discipline as Garrisonians understood it, could become a heavy burden. On the other hand, participating in the boycott sometimes involved taking on oneself inconvenience and perhaps extra cost— also part of the nonviolent discipline but less likely to become a heavy burden. Of course, most abolitionists found it easier to participate in the boycott than in the ride-ins. Yet it is doubtful that without the drama of the ride-ins, often heightened by the violence of the conductors, a boycott of significant proportions would have developed.

The Garrisonian Negro, Charles Remond, was representative of many dignified middle-class abolitionists, white and black, in his preference for participation in the boycott rather than the ride-ins. Remond was a foppish, very correctly spoken young man of sensibilities who had recently been giving abolitionist lectures in Britain and had been received in high society there. When the ride-ins began, Remond was willing to have whites ride with him in the Negro car if they wished, as they sometimes did, but he himself was not willing to ride in the white cars. "I am unwilling to descend so low," he explained, "as to bandy words with the superintendents, or contest my rights with conductors." Yet this by no means meant that Remond was not deeply wounded by discrimination. Soon after his return from Europe, when asked if he was glad to get home, Remond replied that he had never loathed his American name so much because of the contrast between the discrimination in America and the absence of it in Europe. Later, after the railroad boycott had long been under way, Remond joined in it. Between Boston and Salem, where Remond lived, there happened to be no unsegregated railway service competing with the segregated Eastern Railroad, so for three months Remond went to the expense of hiring private conveyances.[21]

Unlike Remond, actionist Stephen S. Foster supported both the ride-in and boycott methods. In August, 1841, when the ride-in flurry was new, Foster had asked the Massachusetts Antislavery Society to say that in combatting segregated seating anywhere they recommended the sit-in and ride-in method, but the society had refused. Now in December, when the ride-ins had about run their course and when the boycott was well underway, he asked a meeting of the Bristol County Antislavery Society to commit themselves to using either the sit-in and ride-in method on the one hand or the boycott on the other: he asked whites to say, anywhere we meet segregated seating, "we feel it incumbent on us to identify" with "our colored friends" by sitting with them "or to withdraw ourselves wholly from such places." Though this request was milder than his August one, since it offered a choice, and though the experienced ride-inners Douglass and Collins were present, the meeting was unwilling to endorse Foster's statement.[22]

While the Massachusetts Antislavery Society was not willing to support the ride-ins even indirectly, antislavery societies often supported the boycott directly. In Massachusetts, the Essex County Antislavery Society, on the suggestion of Pillsbury and Buffum, urged "the friends of humanity" to patronize only the railroads that were open equally to all. The Middlesex County Antislavery Society decided that for conductors to drag out the white passengers who protested violence to Negro ride-inners should teach whites that "our liberties" are "intimately bound up" with the liberties of Negroes, and they supported the boycott. The Worcester County (North Division) Antislavery Society, with Collins present, urged travelers going from Boston to New York to avoid the discriminatory Boston-Providence-Stonington route, but use the nondiscriminatory Boston-Norwich route instead.[23]

In New York, the American Antislavery Society's official organ, the *National Antislavery Standard,* endorsed the boycott. In New Hampshire, the Dover *Morning Star,* an organ of the Freewill Baptists, an antislavery denomination that had endorsed the nonviolent Declaration of Sentiments of the American Antislavery Society, urged friends of the black man not to "patronize any railroad, stage coach, steamboat, or other conveyance" whose proprietors allowed "outrages" such as Douglass had suffered. The Strafford County, New Hampshire, Antislavery Society, with Garrison, Phillips, Collins, Rogers, Pillsbury, Foster, and Douglass present, unanimously urged "all friends of true democratic principles" not to use the offending Boston-Portsmouth Eastern Railroad route into New Hampshire, but rather the rival nondiscriminatory Boston-Haverhill-Exeter route. In Portland, Maine, a Negro convention decided that "those stages, steamboats, and railroads, that will not treat our people with respect . . . after having taken our money, deserve the frowns of every true philanthropist."[24]

Beginning in April, 1842, every week Garrison's *Liberator* assisted the boycott by publishing a full column of Massachusetts railroad schedules interspersed with editorial comment. Said the column repeatedly, while most railroads treated all races alike, the Eastern Railroad had a "bullying propensity" to force its "odious distinction on account of color," and the New Bedford Railroad made "a vile complexioned distinction, enforced by brutal assaults." The *American Antislavery Almanac* similarly publicized the boycott. Quaker Nathaniel Barney of Nantucket took upon himself a special form of the boycott. Not only did he refuse to ride in any public conveyance from which anyone was excluded on account of color, but as a stockholder in the New Bedford Railroad he refused to accept his dividends in protest against its continued practice of segregation. "Surely," Unitarian pastor May wrote of Barney afterward, "the name of such a man ought to be handed down to our posterity to be duly honored."[25]

Meanwhile abolitionists continued to press for a law to desegregate Massachusetts railroads, as they had been pressing ever since soon after the ride-ins began in 1841. Abolitionists organized their drive for a law more than they organized any other aspect of their railroad desegregation campaign. On the urging of antislavery societies, abolitionists queried candidates for the state legislature on their attitude toward the proposed law, and in 1842 three abolitionists, the Negro lecturer Remond and the white lawyers Phillips and Ellis Gray Loring, appeared before a committee of the legislature to testify in support of it. The Massachusetts Antislavery Society printed petitions in pamphlet form, sent them to abolitionists in nearly every town in the state, and urged them to have them signed and sent in to legislators—most Garrisonian complete nonresistants, though nonvoters, approved of petitioning governments. The general agent of the society, the beaten ride-inner Collins, issued a statement with the petitions, asking what influence Massachusetts could have on Southern slave owners while her railroads "are allowed to proscribe people on account of their complexion, and to beat, maim, and mutilate all who may protest against their inhuman regulations." A meeting of the black citizens of Boston, with Nell serving as secretary, resolved that they viewed "the illegal and oppressive customs of some of the railroad corporations of the state as a more immediate and trying grievance than any other which rests upon us in the Commonwealth; and we pledge to the friends of liberty our most strenuous efforts to cause government to yield to us our constitutional rights in this respect."[26]

In the legislature the course of the railroad desegregation bill was a zigzag. In 1842 the senate turned it down. Early in 1843, however, the senate passed it. Then unexpectedly the house of representatives turned it down. One representative from Boston who voted against the bill urged that the railroads desegregate voluntarily so the legislature would not have to force them to.

By this time the New Bedford Railroad had already shown signs of desegregating voluntarily. In March, 1843, when Collins and Buffum were leading conventions of abolitionists in scheming how to prevent the reelection of representatives who voted against the bill, the Eastern Railroad also quietly moved toward desegregation. Apparently the abolitionists' various devices together brought about sufficient pain of conscience, nuisance, and loss of business to the railroads, as well as threat that the legislature would soon force an end to segregation anyway, so that the railroads chose to desegregate.

By the end of March, 1843, the *Liberator* had dropped its traveler's directory, which had long been promoting the boycott of the offending railroads. By April 20 the Norfolk County Antislavery Society, with Collins, Buffum, Remond, and Douglass participating, felt able to announce in triumph "that we hail, with unfeigned delight, the removal of the colored car, from the Eastern Railroad, viewing it as the quailing of cruel prejudice against color before the indignant rebuke of public opinion—that we congratulate our colored fellow citizens on the fall of this, almost the last shackle from their limbs within our Commonwealth—that we will spread the knowledge of this fact far and wide, that slaveholders may know how rapidly Massachusetts hastens to redeem her escutcheon from every stain, and that meeting-houses [churches] may blush for their infamous preeminence in being the last to give up the Negro seat."[27]

The fact that in Massachusetts public transportation was desegregated before most churches were was a hint of the similarly infamous order of events to come more than a hundred years later in the South, in another movement to abolish segregation.

A few months later, when the new railroad desegregation policy had become fairly fixed in practice, the New Bedford Railroad stockholder, Quaker Barney, asked the company to send his accumulated dividends to Garrison, "in view of his faithful and undeviating advocacy of the rights of humanity."

In 1846 when the Negroes of Boston honored Garrison, their spokesman for the occasion praised him, perhaps too generously:

"Even the stages and steamboats," the spokesman said, "are now opened to us through your instrumentality."[28]

Two years later Douglass happened to be looking for a seat in a crowded Massachusetts railway car in which the governor of the state, George Nixon Briggs, was already seated. Recognizing Douglass, the governor immediately offered him a seat next to him, and Douglass accepted it. Sitting side by side, the governor and the once beaten ride-inner Douglass chatted familiarly about antislavery affairs without the governor showing any condescension or fear of criticism from others, as far as Douglass could tell.

About the same time, Douglass, looking back at the Massachusetts desegregation campaign, wrote that a "few colored men" in New England had "frequently gone into the cars intended only for white passengers and allowed ourselves to be beaten and dragged out." This "conduct on our part," he said, produced "the result" of the desegregation of the railways "because the railroad companies became ashamed of their proscription."[29]

Looking back at the railroad campaign in 1865, ride-inner Nell recalled that the ride-ins "had much to do in so influencing public sentiment that one by one these [color] distinctions have become things of the past, and today, in the Old Bay State, the manifestations of color phobia are only exceptional."[30]

Neither Douglass nor Nell—nor indeed the abolitionists generally—gloried in having wielded the coercion of nuisance or economic damage or political pressure against the railroads. For the abolitionists the desegregation campaign was not so much victorious coercion as victorious appeal to conscience.

9. Pray-Ins and Pray-Outs

◇◇◇◇◇◇◇◇◇◇◇

AMERICAN CHURCHES often kept Negroes in a subordinate position. From colonial times it was customary in the North as in the South for churches to segregate seating by race. Churches set aside seats for Negroes in as inconspicuous places as possible, in the rear or sides or galleries—even Quaker meetings sometimes did so. White pastors often administered communion to whites first, blacks afterward. The gifted black pastor Samuel R. Ward—an unusual figure because he served both white and black congregations—grieved at the effect of such "religious barbarism"; it drove some Negroes to deny all religion, he said.[1]

Abolitionists and others often took direct action against church segregation. They did so essentially by two methods. One was the invasion method: they went into churches to break up the traditional seating pattern by sitting where they were not expected to sit—in "pray-ins." The other was the withdrawal method: they walked out of churches that practiced segregation—in "pray-outs"—and sometimes they created new churches instead.

Abolitionists often encouraged both blacks and whites to use the invasion method. A national women's antislavery convention urged whites to sit in the Negro sections of segregated churches. The *Colored American* told its readers, if you are not allowed to sit where whites do, you should "stand in the aisles and rather worship God upon your feet than become a party to your own degradation. You must shame your oppressors, and wear out prejudice by this holy policy." With characteristic boldness, Frederick Douglass, who at the time opposed separate Negro institutions of almost any kind, urged every Negro to abandon his black church and to attend white ones in a massive pray-in: Negroes "should go in and take seats without regard to their complexion," he said, "and allow themselves to be dragged out by the ministers, elders, and deacons. Such a course would very soon settle the question, and in the right way."[2]

There was no massive pray-in movement of the kind Douglass envisioned, but in accordance with the more usual abolitionist inclination toward individual protest action, a substantial number of individuals—including Quakers, Garrisonians, and Tappanites—did pray-in.

A Negro woman in Philadelphia sat in the part of her church reserved for whites and stayed there despite whites glaring at her and Negroes whispering to her to sit with them. A Negro family in Randolph, Massachusetts, purchased a pew in a Baptist church with a white congregation. They went there one Sunday morning to find their pew removed, but instead of walking out, they sat on the floor where their pew should have been; returning the next Sunday, the family found even the flooring of their pew area removed, and so they stood during the service. In Genessee County, New York, Seth Gates—the only abolitionist congressman from the state in 1840—risked voters' support by inviting a visiting Negro abolitionist to sit with him in his church pew; a local paper denounced Gates as an "amalgamator," but he was re-elected to Congress anyway. In Newark, New Jersey, a white minister walked to church with a black woman who was a servant in his family and seated her in a pew with his wife; for doing so, he was driven out of his pulpit.

In a predominantly white Baptist church in Newport, Rhode Island, a white lady invited a black girl—a member of the church—to sit with her in her pew instead of in the Negro gallery. The church called a meeting to reprimand the lady for doing so and, when the time came to renew the lease for her pew, refused to renew it. Prevented from sitting in her pew, the lady provided herself with a campstool, placed it in the aisle beside her pew, and sat there instead. Said the *Liberator's* report of the incident: "Jesus could not get into many of his churches if he should come this way now, unless he took the gallery."

At a Friends meeting, a young white Friend "deemed it his duty" to take a seat with the black men in the separate pews assigned to them. An older Friend immediately reprimanded him for "sitting in judgment" on those who had assigned the pews, but for several months the young man continued to sit there, and another young Friend joined him. After the Grimké sisters became Friends, they insisted on sitting in their Philadelphia meeting house in the seats where the black women sat, and when scolded by whites for doing so, replied, "While you put this badge of degradation on our sisters, we feel it is our duty to share it with them."[4]

A Negro girl came into the Sunday school of a Boston mission chapel devoted to poor children and sat where she liked among the white children. Some of the teachers proposed setting up a Negro pew for her. But another of the teachers, the prestigious Garrisonian physician Henry I. Bowditch, who was later to become president of the American Medical Association, flatly promised to leave the chapel if they did. He heard no more about it.

In New York one Sunday, merchant Arthur Tappan—despite his general policy of not offending public opinion by openly associating with Negroes as equals—invited Negro Presbyterian minister Cornish, the editor of the *Colored American*, to share his pew in a Presbyterian church; afterward elders protested and at least one occupant of a neighboring pew withdrew from the church. In Farmington, Connecticut, when lawyer John Hooker invited a Negro to share his pew, Hooker reported that "the moral shock was very great. One of the church members said I had done more to break up the church than anything that had happened in its whole history."[5]

Tappanite Negro minister Theodore Wright, visiting in New Rochelle, New York, attended a Presbyterian church and sat with whites. He was asked to move to sit with Negroes. "I did not think it proper, however, to move, and thus sanction my own degradation," he reported to a state antislavery society meeting, and added, "The sufferings of the colored man are fully known only to him who experiences them."

The general agent of the *Colored American*, William P. Johnson, was visiting one Sunday in Coxsackie, New York, a small Hudson River town. In the morning he attended a church and was seated in a corner. In the afternoon he visited another church, and when an usher showed him to a Negro pew this time, Johnson, having already had enough of the humiliation of separate seating, sat in a white pew instead. That day, Johnson said, he suffered more than he ever had since his release from slavery, and, he concluded, this was how Negroes were made infidels.[6]

In 1836, Lewis Tappan led in an attempt to found a new New York church that was predominantly white but welcomed blacks as equals —it even chose the black abolitionist Thomas Van Rensselaer as a trustee. But the evangelist Finney, the great father figure for many Tappanites, thought such racial equality was too extreme, and Finney's opposition quashed the new church. Tappan then decided that since he could not associate equally with Negroes in a predominantly white church, "it seems my duty to unite in a colored church," and for a brief period he thought of joining the Reverand Theodore S. Wright's black Presbyterian church. But as he thought about it further, he asked himself, "Will it not invite insult to my black brethren?"[7] Eventually Tappan abandoned the idea of joining a black church, but he continued to act against church segregation by other means.

During the summer of 1837, Tappan visited his family where they were vacationing on the Hudson above Newburgh. On Sunday he and one of his daughters walked four miles to attend the Marlborough Presbyterian church where he knew the pastor. At communion time he noticed several Negroes come down from the gallery, advance up the aisle to the front, and sit on a narrow bench between the pews and the communion table. "What!" thought Tappan; "have they a 'nigger seat' at the Lord's table?"

At once Tappan decided what to do. Taking his hat, he left his pew walked up the aisle, and sat with the Negroes on their special bench.

The minister, who considered himself to be antislavery, had been accustomed to serving communion to the whites first, then to blacks. Tappan's sitting with the blacks, the minister told him afterward suddenly made him realize for the first time that he had been treating the blacks "in an anti-Christian manner." The minister at once resolved to serve the blacks and whites at the same time.

Seeing him do so, some of the congregation reacted furiously. They refused to eat the bread of communion that day, leaving it in their seats. Afterward they charged their pastor with conniving with a stranger to foist abolitionism on their church.[8]

Tappan's pray-in, like other pray-ins, was agonizing for many of those concerned—for those who violated segregation, for those who tried to preserve it, and for those who merely wished to keep peace within the church.

Not satisfied to protest against church segregation only by the painful method of invasion, abolitionists also protested by another painful method, withdrawal. Though on the surface the invasion and withdrawal methods seemed contradictory, some of the same people —including Douglass—supported both methods.

More abolitionists supported withdrawal than invasion. The Middlesex County (Massachusetts) Antislavery Society urged "all true worshippers" to avoid any church that had Negro pews. Gerrit Smith told an annual meeting of the American Antislavery Society that rather than enter a Negro pew, Negroes "should be willing to go miles, and walk them all, to worship with the disciples of an equal religion"; in 1850, Smith wrote that for fifteen years he himself had shunned "as I would a pest house" all churches where Negroes are not treated equally. A convention of fugitive slaves in upstate New York, presided over by Frederick Douglass, adopted an address to the slaves, saying, if any of you succeed in escaping to the North and go to church there, "it were better that you sacrifice your lives, than that by going into the negro-pew you invade your self-respect —debase your souls—play the traitor to your race—and crucify afresh Him who died for the one brotherhood of man." Garrison said, every black who occupies a segregated pew "dishonors himself, and should shun it, as he would a cage for wild beasts." The Negro national convention, at the urging of Douglass and Remond, called for a mass exodus of Negroes from any church that discriminated in seating or at the communion table.[9]

Following such advice, in Placerville, California, several Negro women went to worship in a white Methodist church and sat among whites. When the pastor and sexton objected, offering them a back seat instead, the ladies refused to accept it and left.

A young Negro Methodist in Gardiner, Maine, who had been a member of his church for eight years and had never been discriminated against, contributed to the building of a new church. After it was built, church officials told him that he could only buy a pew at the rear. Stunned, he asked for his money back, and they gave it to him. Walking out of the new church, he paused on the steps in grief and thought, "This is the first time that I have entered these walls, and possibly it may be the last."[10]

Two Negro brothers stopped attending Friends meetings because, as one said, "I do not like to sit on a back bench and be treated with contempt." So many Negroes stopped attending Friends meetings because of separate seating, reported a Quaker antislavery journal in 1850, that the Negro membership of the Society of Friends had steadily declined since the early 1800's.

In his Unitarian church in Brooklyn, Connecticut, pastor Samuel J. May invited Negroes to sit in the center of the church, but during a period when May was away lecturing on abolition, the church arranged to move the Negroes to the gallery. The church's action was a part of a long hassle over abolition between May and his congregation which finally led him to resign.[11]

In Boston, when Dr. Gannet became pastor of a prominent Unitarian church, a leading lady of the church met the Garrisonian Charles K. Whipple and invited him to hear Dr. Gannet and share her pew.

"Have you room for more than one person?" the white Whipple asked. "I should like to bring a friend with me, if you have an additional seat." Whipple, a graduate of Amherst, was rather suave.

"Oh, yes!" said Mrs. X, as Whipple called the lady in his report of the incident afterward. "There is plenty of room. And come to see us this evening; we have a pleasant little circle of friends, whom I know you will like; bring your friend with you there also. Who is he?"

"His name is Y. He is a very worthy man, well educated, of good principles and good manners. I should mention to you, also, that he is a colored man."

"Oh," said Mrs. X, with a sudden start.

"I am glad you have invited us," continued Whipple evenly, "for I have heard Mr. Gannet's sermons much praised, and we shall both be gratified to hear him."

"Well, you *will* come, won't you?" replied Mrs. X, recovering herself.

"Certainly, it will give us the greatest pleasure. What is the number of your pew?"

"I have quite forgotten it," said Mrs. X with a smile.

"Never mind. I will ask the sexton."

"But Mr. Whipple, you are not in earnest."

"In most serious earnest, I assure you. I tell you sincerely, that we shall be delighted to sit with you."

"Why do you insist upon bringing a black man to our pew?"

"You mistake. I insist upon nothing. You *invited* us to go there, and we accept the invitation with pleasure."

"But cannot you go without him?"

"It is out of the question. He is a brother of mine."

As they parted, Mrs. X promised to ask her husband if there was room in their pew for two guests, but she never let Whipple know, and Whipple never went to hear Dr. Gannet.[12]

Frederick Douglass as a slave in Maryland had become an active member of a segregated Methodist church. Soon after he first settled in New Bedford, he was appalled to discover that a Methodist church there was segregated also; the minister called the white people of the congregation forward first and served them with bread and wine; then he called the black people and served them. "The colored members—poor, slavish souls—went forward as invited," Douglass wrote afterward. "I went out, and have never been in that church since." In fact, Douglass soon joined a New Bedford Negro church and became a local preacher for it—it was a church of the predominantly Negro denomination, the African Methodist Episcopal Zion Church, which had broken off from the predominantly white Methodist denomination largely over the issue of segregation. Explained Douglass later: "Those who are acquainted with the character of the Methodist Church, and have a spark of self-respect, will commend us for our course."[13]

Since at least the late 1700's, Negro churchmen—not necessarily all active abolitionists—had been protesting against segregation, as well as against church acquiescence in slavery, by withdrawing from predominantly white churches and, in group nonviolent direct action, creating predominantly Negro ones. Some of the new churches joined together under the lead of Richard Allen to form the African Methodist Episcopal denomination in 1816, and others under the lead of James Varick to form the African Methodist Episcopal Zion denomination in 1821. All through the abolitionist period Negroes continued to withdraw from white churches and create new Negro churches—usually Methodist or Baptist—especially in the North where whites exercised less pressure than in the South to prevent Negroes from withdrawing. While the Negro population in Northern cities went up only moderately, the number of Negro churches multiplied rapidly, reaching thirteen in New York and nineteen in Philadelphia by about the time of the Civil War.

Whether the withdrawal trend was wise or not was debated among abolitionists, both black and white. It was part of the larger question whether blacks should create a separate life of their own—including separate schools, lodges, political groups, or even whole communities. It ultimately raised the question whether it was necessary to fight white racism with black racism, a basic question that was to return to trouble Negroes at many periods—in Delany's emigration movement in the 1850's, Booker T. Washington's "separate as the fingers" policy in the 1890's, Garveyism in the 1920's, Black

Muslimism in the 1950's, and Black Power in the 1960's.

The American Antislavery Society in 1836 was ambivalent on separatism. "Our colored friends ought to avail themselves at present of their separate institutions," it advised, but separate institutions, it added, strengthen the very white prejudice that created them, and "no time should be lost, on our part, in the work of introducing a better system."

The *Colored American* was also ambivalent on the question. In 1837, while it was edited by Tappenite pastor Cornish—who had been the center of disturbance when he sat in Arthur Tappan's pew—the *Colored American* said it wished there were no separate Negro churches at all, explaining that their existence fanned prejudice against Negroes. But in 1840 and 1841, when the *Colored American* was edited by Tappanite pastor C. B. Ray—the boycotter of segregated dining facilities on passenger boats—it acknowledged the necessity of separate institutions. Said Ray, since the predominantly white churches segregate blacks, can anyone "wonder that where there are a sufficient number of us we should establish worship of our own, however much for other reasons to be lamented?" Moreover, asserted Ray, since the elevation of blacks must come largely through our own action, we must organize separately to accomplish it.[14]

Vehemently opposing Negro separatism was the Garrisonian Negro lumber dealer William Whipper of Columbia, Pennsylvania, whose opposition to the separate Negro national convention movement we have already seen. Whipper—whom Douglass called a "profound thinker"—urged Christians to boycott any church—whether predominantly black or white—which prevented people of differing color from associating as equals at the same altar. Said Whipper, when Negroes demand equal rights among whites, their demand is not likely to be effective if they have separate Negro churches, Negro schools, and Negro benevolent societies which discriminate against whites; moreover, he added, whites are likely to interpret separate Negro institutions as aimed against whites.[15] Supporting this position generally were Whipper's American Moral Reform Society; Dr. James McCune Smith, New York City Negro physician, who argued that for Negroes to organize separately, in the words of the common abolitionist maxim, "does evil that good may come"; Henry Bibb, the Negro orator, who said there was no more sense in black churches than in a black heaven or a black God; and the Boston Negro Garrisonian William C. Nell, who hoped that the day would come when Negro churches would disappear.

Frederick Douglass wavered on this difficult question. Sometimes he seemed to oppose separate black institutions at the same time that he himself was a major leader in the Negro convention movement and edited what he called a "colored newspaper," the *North Star*. At one time he insisted his children should not go to separate Negro schools; at another time he decided that a special industrial school should be created for Negroes because of their great handicaps in finding jobs or even apprenticeships. At one time, as we have seen, Douglass was active in a Negro denomination, but later he withdrew from it because he decided it was not sufficiently antislavery. At one time he said he opposed black churches, giving as a reason that "with few exceptions, colored ministers have not the mental qualifications to instruct and improve their congregations"; at another time he persuaded himself that he could approve predominantly black churches if they were open equally to whites. When a group of Negro Baptists in Rochester purchased a building, Douglass said: "We believe this is not a colored church in an exclusive sense, although most of the persons who attend there are colored; and we have therefore no hesitation in giving the trustees and members our heart's good wishes." Similarly, he approved of a new black cemetery in Philadelphia because in a "noble example"" to whites, the cemetery was to be open to them, too. Douglass was angry if black churches segregated seating, and on this issue he lambasted Negro pastor Samuel R. Ward, who for a time edited a paper that competed with Douglass' paper; when Ward spoke without protest in a Negro church in Philadelphia even though he knew beforehand that, to encourage whites to come to the meeting, seating would be segregated, Douglass published an extra edition of his paper to denounce Ward's action as "the most cowardly, contemptible and servile specimen of self-degradation which has ever come under my notice."[16]

Like Douglass, Connecticut Negro pastor Amos G. Beman admitted that most Negro pastors were poorly educated; there was more intelligence in the pew than in the pulpit, Beman said. But the white Gerrit Smith was also disturbed by the behavior of those who sat in the Negro church pews. When he visited a Western New York Negro church, he found the "unregulated zeal of not a few of my fellow worshippers was loud and frenzied, indecent and disgusting"; he urged that Negroes and Caucasians should worship together if for no other reason than that Negroes could learn more dignity. Similarly, a white writer for the New York *Evangelist*, visiting one of the three black churches in Washington, found the language being used "uncouth," "the hymns so mutilated as to make one smile, and in one or two instances the tones and gestures quite extravagant"; nevertheless he found "Christian simplicity" and "heartiness of faith and love."[17]

Some Negroes took pride in their own church tradition. Seen through friendly eyes, the Negroes' "Christian simplicity" and "heartiness" were highly significant assets. Pastor Ward—who was so black that, according to Wendell Phillips, when he closed his eyes you couldn't see him—claimed that American Negroes were "in feeling" the most religious people in the world, with the possible exception of the Welsh.[18] From the nonviolent point of view, Ward gave considerable substance to his claim—especially considering that he was only moderately nonviolent himself—when he said that no "class of whites, except the Quakers, ever spoke of their oppressors . . . as mildly as we [Negroes] do."[19] At a New York State Negro convention, a delegate proposed a resolution that "under God, the important duty of preserving the Christian church from idolatry" depended on Negroes. An Albany delegate protested that this resolution would be arrogating too much to the black people. But a black Brooklyn pastor, Eli N. Hall, said he "saw clearly the providence of God in preserving the religion of Jesus Christ pure among his persecuted people, and those very persecutions were a means to that end"; he supported the resolution and it passed.[20] Such pride by Negroes in the mission of their churches could grow toward either poisonous Negro racism or a healthy self-respect that would elevate Negro aspirations.

The Negro churches became the strongest institutions of Negro society. While the churches were sometimes dependent on whites financially, at least Negroes were more free of dependence on whites in their churches than they were likely to be in most aspects of their lives. Negro churches provided more opportunity for Negro leaders to develop than white churches could have done—Negro pastors developed into such strong leaders that Nell complained in 1855 that they had come to monopolize leadership among Negroes. The great majority of Negro pastors were not active abolitionists—Douglass said in 1848 that most of them had "little sympathy with the antislavery cause"[21]—but at least among the most active Negro abolitionists were many Negro pastors.

Meanwhile in predominantly white churches, partly because of abolitionist pray-ins and pray-outs, there was some progress in reducing segregation. In 1836 the presbytery of Chillicothe, Ohio, recommended that anyone who wished to segregate Negroes in church ought to be excluded from communion till he repented. In Cleveland, when the First Baptist Church built a new building, the members proposed to their outstanding Negro member, John Malvan, an abolitionist and carpenter who sometimes preached for them, that he select a group of pews anywhere in the church for Negroes to sit in, apart from whites. He refused any such compromise with segregation and continued to protest against any segregation until by 1838 the church gave in, allowing Negroes to sit anywhere they chose. After this victory the other predominantly white churches of Cleveland—a city comparable to Boston in its low degree of prejudice—followed the Baptist example, and Cleveland's Negro churches were left for the most uneducated Negroes and the most recently arrived from slavery. In 1838 at a Methodist antislavery convention one delegate reported that when a new church was built in Charlestown, Massachusetts, "some of the best seats in the house were occupied by colored brethren," and another delegate reported that when "caste" was abolished in a Lowell church, a "refreshing season of revival followed." By the end of the 1840's, William Wells Brown said that "hundreds of churches in the country had abolished the odious Negro-pew system"; and Douglass said that in New England, while to a "large extent" Jim Crow seating in churches persisted, hardly anyone could defend it any more. By 1859 the Boston *Courier* reported that for Negroes to sit in separate pews in New England churches was largely a memory.[22]

However, the trend for whites to desegregate their churches was not fast or thorough; in fact, by the time of the Civil War most churches in the North—even if not in New England—still segregated seating, and of course even overcoming the outer form of segregated seating was not a sure indication of overcoming the inward malaise of prejudice. Some black abolitionists kept urging blacks not to attend black churches but instead to attend the many white churches that were open to them as equals. But even in New England perhaps fewer and fewer Negroes did so. The nonviolent direct action of Negro withdrawal from predominantly white churches had proved too be a stronger force than the nonviolent direct action of invading predominantly white churches to desegregate them. In what was at best a long-term tragic necessity for the development of Negroes' self-respect and ability to organize their own struggle for freedom, the number of Negroes in separate Negro churches continued to go up and the number of Negroes in predominantly white churches continued to go down. Tragic necessity or not, the abolitionists' attempt to solve the old problem of segregation in the white-controlled churches had helped to create a new problem, the segregated black church.

10. Creating Schools

◇◇◇◇◇◇◇◇◇◇◇◇

WITH TRADITIONAL American faith in education, abolitionists were likely to believe that better education would help Negroes overcome the common prejudice against them. Said an address issued by a colored national convention: "Knowledge is power." The Tappanite American and Foreign Antislavery Society agreed: "It is emphatically true" for Negoes "that knowledge is power." With pathetic hope, a black woman attending an antislavery convention said: "We have been brought up in ignorance; our parents were ignorant, they could not teach us. . . . We are blamed for not filling useful places in society; but . . . give us learning, and see then what places we can occupy."[1]

To improve educational opportunity, abolitionists and other humanitarians took nonviolent action in many forms. In the South they violated laws and customs which forbade teaching Negroes to read. In the North they sometimes invited Negroes into white schools; if Negroes were not permitted to enter, abolitionists sometimes created new schools that would accept Negroes; if schools were segregated, Negroes sometimes withdrew their children in protest. Occasionally abolitionists combined such nonviolent direct action methods with nonviolent indirect action, including petitions, court suits, or political maneuvering. Scarcely ever did education-promoting abolitionists combine these methods with violence, although violence was often used against them.

In the South, in the liberal Revolutionary War period and immediately afterward, there had been considerable effort to educate Negroes, but beginning about 1830, Negro education became increasingly limited to oral religious instruction. Both custom and law generally forbade teaching Negroes to read, and slaves who had escaped to the North kept abolitionists well aware of it. The escaped slave J. W. C. Pennington, a blacksmith who later became a minister, said that he could never forget that slavery had robbed him of an education. Frederick Douglass wrote in the story of his life that as a slave boy, when he tried to learn to read, his master's wife would snatch his newspaper out of his hand. According to abolitionist preacher Henry Ward Beecher, the American South was the only region in the world where Christian missionaries were not free to teach reading and writing to all.[2]

When a grand jury in Lexington, Kentucky, moved to break up a school for slaves, it gave a hint about why the South restricted Negro education. The school would enlighten "the minds of those whose happiness obviously depends on their ignorance," the jury said. William Wells Brown, the escaped slave, explained it more directly. "The slaveholders generally do their utmost to perpetuate this mental darkness," he said. "The perpetuation of slavery depends on it."[3]

From the point of view of nonviolent direct action, abolitionist discussion of Southern restrictions on Negro education led to one logical conclusion, and though abolitionists did not often express it openly, both the Garrisonian H. C. Wright and the Quaker Garrisonian Angelina Grimké did: it was the duty of Southerners, they said, to teach Negroes to read, even if against the law.[4] There were in fact thousands of Americans—black and white, abolitionists or not —who defied the Southern way of life by teaching Negroes to read, in nonviolent direct action.

Negro parents who had enough knowledge to do so sometimes secretly taught their own children to read. White masters who fathered mulattoes sometimes taught them themselves or sent them North to school. Regardless of law, an occasional master deliberately educated his slaves so that they could be more useful; for instance, a brother of Jefferson Davis educated a slave to be a plantation accountant. Slaves sometimes educated themselves while assisting printers or clerks.[5]

In Savannah, Georgia, for over thirty years a black woman secretly taught a black school in defiance of law. In South Carolina, the young white Sarah Grimké, the future abolitionist, disobeyed the law by secretly teaching her maid to read, keeping the door of her room closed and even the keyhole covered. Robert Edmond, a Scot who came to South Carolina in order to teach planters' children, was so shocked by the degradation of slaves that he tried to teach some of them to read. But his actions became known, and a band of disguised white men came to his schoolroom, dragged him away, and covered him with a coat of tar and feathers; Edmond fled to the North. In North Carolina the young Friend Levi Coffin, the future Underground Railroader, taught neighborhood slaves to read until their masters threatened him; Coffin eventually migrated to the Midwest, as many Southern Quakers did, to escape such suffocating restrictions.

In Virginia a white family illegally taught a free black girl employed in their household to read; when company came to the house, they took care that she hid her books. In Petersburg a mulatto taught Negroes secretly at night, going from house to house. In Prince William County an old slave taught a free black boy to read in his cabin by the light of burning pine knots; for fear of being discovered, they talked in whispers.[6]

In the upper South, educating Negroes was tolerated a little more than farther south. In Delaware in 1850, Quaker abolitionist Thomas Garrett reported that there were four schools for Negroes in Wilmington, two of which were maintained by Quakers. Elsewhere in the whole state, he said, there was only one other school, near Dover, that Negroes could attend, and it was kept open only three or four months in the year.

In Kentucky in the mid-1830's, Presbyterians had persisted in their eighteenth-century antislavery tradition longer than most denominations. The Presbyterian synod, recommending gradual emancipation, regretted that only "here and there" did white families teach their own slaves. A white Presbyterian, Mrs. Meaux, owned a slave who joined a Presbyterian church and wished to study to become a minister. Trying to help him, she placed him under the teaching of a white Presbyterian minister. Then, deciding that the slave deserved more education, Mrs. Meaux freed him and appealed to the Kentucky Presbyterian Center College for his admittance. He was willing to appease white pride by accepting any necessary seating arrangements, but the college rejected him.[7]

In Kentucky in the late 1850's the Tappanite abolitionist Reverend John G. Fee dared to try to create schools open to both blacks and whites. "It is all important that we be able to demonstrate to the world," he wrote friends, "that true abolitionists can . . . teach . . . schools at the South, and schools in which caste shall be lived down." Within a few months Fee had built a school house in Cummins, Rockcastle County, with the express understanding among the local whites who had helped him build it that both blacks and whites from the neighborhood would be admitted into the school, and in fact the school did open with both white and black pupils. A few months later, however, armed pro-slavery men burned the school building, dragged the nonviolent Fee out of the county, and told him never to return.[8] But the indomitable Fee soon returned, as usual refusing to carry arms to protect himself, and, despite frequent mobbings, continued to create integrated schools.

In Baltimore and Washington there were several schools for free Negroes, some supported by the abolitionist Quakers, some by the nonabolitionist Catholics, many by Negro churches. Once rioters in Washington broke up nearly all the black schools, totally destroying their furniture; at another time they burned the schoolhouses where two Englishmen taught Negroes and drove the Englishmen out of town. In the early 1850's Friends—including the slave-produce boycott leader Samuel Rhoads—helped Myrtilla Miner establish a normal school for Negroes in Washington. The mayor condemned the school for raising the Negroes' standard of education beyond their social and political condition. Boys on the street tormented the students. But when Miss Miner's enemies invaded her schoolroom, threatening her with violence—as the U. S. Commissioner of Education reported later—she "laughed them to shame; and when they threatened to burn her [school] house, she told them that they could not stop her in that way, as another house, better than the old, would immediately rise from its ashes." In 1860 the school was set on fire but was saved.[9]

In Norfolk, Virginia, a white seamstress ran a school for Negro children and refused to run away when the law threatened her. The *Liberator* said that her account of her experience was one that every American should read and ponder.

The seamstress, Mrs. Douglass, had a free Negro boy living in her house as a servant. At a Sunday school that a white church held for black children, the boy was given religious books to read; he brought them home, and Mrs. Douglass and her daughter Rosa helped him to read them. Through this boy, Mrs. Douglass and Rosa gradually gathered about them other free black children who attended the same Sunday school. From this beginning the Douglasses developed a regular school in their house, with eighteen or twenty pupils. It was the only day school open to Negroes in the city. Rosa, aged sixteen, did the teaching in an upstairs room, while Mrs. Douglass kept a general oversight but most of the time was busy sewing in another room.

The school had been proceeding peacefully for nearly a year when one day a policeman arrived at the door, asking to see the black children.

Mrs. Douglass led the policeman upstairs and, without warning, into the schoolroom. According to Mrs. Douglass' account, hysteria broke loose. Rosa "sat paralyzed, covering her face with her hands." Some of the children cried; some clung to Mrs. Douglass in terror. Mrs. Douglass explained afterward that in slave states all Negroes had a terror of police.

After restoring order, Mrs. Douglass asked the policeman and another one who had followed him in, what they wanted with the children. One of the policemen answered that he must take Mrs. Douglass and the children to the mayor as it was against the law to teach Negroes to read and write.

Mrs. Douglass arranged the children in couples and marched them down the street. The two officers followed, carrying great clubs in their hands. It seemed to Mrs. Douglass that the children were little lambs being led to slaughter.

They marched into the mayor's office. The mayor read the law that forbade teaching black persons, whether slave or free, to read and write. Mrs. Douglass replied that she had not known the law applied to free Negroes, and the mayor arranged to give her a trial.

Outside the building again, Mrs. Douglass and Rosa gathered as many of the children as they could and led them back to their schoolroom. There they handed out to the children their books and slates, "and with wounded hearts," as Mrs. Douglass wrote afterward, "took leave of them, one by one. It was a sad parting, and we grieved to think that they must henceforth grow up in darkness and ignorance."

Meanwhile the white people of Norfolk were becoming embarrassed by the Douglass case. This was the first time any case under the Negro anti-education law had been brought to court. Evidently Mrs. Douglass had enemies who had brought the charges against her, but the truth was that some of the most respectable people in the city were occasionally teaching Negroes to read in the Sunday schools,

so the noise over her arrest was annoying to them. "It was the hope
. . . of everyone that she would leave the city," said the Norfolk *Argus*, and then the whole matter could be forgotten. But she refused
to leave. She was willing to face the danger of being punished. She
thought the law unjust and wanted a chance to say so openly.

When the time for her trial came, she appeared in court wearing
a black velvet dress and carrying a pocket Bible. According to her
account, she was calm. Acting as her own lawyer, she called three
witnesses in her defense, all white teachers in the Christ Church
black Sunday school, which nearly all her pupils attended and where
even some of the family of the presiding judge were teachers. By her
questioning she established the fact that the Sunday school taught the
black children to read.

Since the church was teaching blacks to read, she said, she, of
course, supposed it was lawful to do so. She explained that she had
been a slaveowner herself, and added, "I would be again, if I felt so
disposed. . . . I am no abolitionist, neither am I a fanatic, and I am
by education as strongly opposed as you are to the interference of
Northern antislavery men with our institutions." She didn't intend
to disobey the law, she claimed, but added it was "one of the most
inhuman and unjust laws that ever disgraced the statute books of a
civilized community."

According to the Norfolk *Argus*, Mrs. Douglass lost the sympathy
of the whites by refusing to leave town, by bringing her daughter to
court to witness her trial as if she were proud of it, and by her
statement of contempt for the law.

The jury declared her guilty, and then the judge considered how
to sentence her. Negroes could be taught religion and duty verbally,
without being taught to read and write, the judge said. There might
not need to be any law forbidding Negroes to read and write, he
explained, except "as a matter of self-defense against the schemes of
Northern incendiaries"; teaching Negroes to read would mean
slaves would learn to read appeals for them to rise and "cut our
throats." He admitted that Mrs. Douglass was apparently of "respectable standing in the community," but he condemned her opposition to the law as bold and open. He said to her, your teaching of
the children was "the settled and deliberate purpose of your mind,
regardless of consequences, however dangerous to our peace." He ·
sentenced her to prison for one month.

When Mrs. Douglass came out of prison, she moved to Philadelphia, "happy in the consciousness," she said, "that it is here no crime to teach a poor little child, of any color, to read the word of God."[10]

In the North in the 1830's and 1840's the education of Negroes was more advanced than in the South but still far from equal to that of whites. Typical of many Negroes in the extent of their formal education were the Southern-born abolitionists Frederick Douglass and William Wells Brown, who never had any schooling, and the New York State–born abolitionist Sojourner Truth, who never even learned to read and write. At the end of the 1840's according to Garnet, not one hundred Negroes were in the high schools and colleges of the country; according to M. R. Delany, two-thirds of all Negro men in the North could not read, and even when Negroes did go to school, they often didn't learn anything well enough to be able to use it for any practical purpose.[11]

Popular prejudice against Negroes was a major cause for the low Negro educational level, abolitionists believed. Most white parents did not relish having the "inferior" Negroes in school with their children, but public school admission practice varied. In New England, it varied from general acceptance of Negroes in Maine to general exclusion in Connecticut. New York State legally permitted separate public schools for Negroes; areas of the state having more Negroes tended to establish separate schools for them, while those that had fewer tended to accept them into their district schools. On the whole the public schools in the Western states discriminated against Negroes more than the schools in the East.

If Northern city public school systems accepted Negroes at all, they often put them into inevitably inferior separate schools; they did so for at least some portion of the 1830's and 1840's in Boston, Providence, New York, Rochester, Buffalo, Philadelphia, and Pittsburgh. Even when Northern schools admitted Negroes into the same schools with whites, the teachers sometimes subjected the colored children to discrimination and discouragement. When a Negro entered a Wilbraham, Massachusetts, boarding school, he was allowed to eat only after the white pupils had finished. When William Wells Brown brought his daughters to school in Massachusetts, they attended school with whites but occupied segregated seats. In some schools teachers found it convenient to punish white pupils by making them sit with blacks.

Colleges generally excluded Negroes. In the early 1830's, William

C. Munro, a young black minister in Portland, Maine, applied to enter Bowdoin, Amherst, and Dartmouth, but reported that he was either rejected or "was offered admittance only on such degrading terms, as no one who had any sense of the rights of man would accept." Similarly, about the same time Negroes Charles B. Ray and Ames G. Beman tried to study at Wesleyan College in Connecticut; some of the Southern students objected so strenuously to their presence and won such support from other students that they made life miserable for the Negroes, who finally left. Complained Douglass, you whites "close your colleges and seminaries against us, and then ask why we don't know more."[12]

Under these circumstances, Northern abolitionists, black and white, often considered it a part of their purpose to raise Negroes' educational goals, to open up existing white schools to Negroes when they could, and when they could not, to establish new schools that would admit Negroes. In an address to the Negroes of Philadelphia, Lucretia Mott said that she did not wish to see black children educated to be servants, but "would have them aspire to an elevation of character and station in the community." The New York State Antislavery Society announced: "We view the education of the people of color as a most important means of bringing about the abolition of slavery and the removal of that prejudice against color which is at once the fruit and support of the system." Abolitionists in every city and village should establish day schools, evening schools, libraries, and lyceums for blacks, urged Theodore Weld; doing so, he said, would give blacks a "mighty impulse to help themselves."[13]

In attempting to improve the education of Northern Negroes, the three major groups of nonviolent abolitionists moved differently. The Quakers proceeded quietly and steadily, if not very far. The Garrisonians stormed into the problem at first, only later discovering a more constructive role. The Tappanites deliberately marshaled their considerable resources for a daring, difficult goal.

The main contribution of Northern Quakers, like those in the upper South, was establishing separate schools for Negroes. In Philadelphia a visiting abolitionist found the young Quaker, Rebecca Buffum, teaching a private school for black girls. She ran the school as if it were her family, the visitor said. She was affectionate to the children, and they in turn were affectionate to her, delighting to have her tie on a bonnet or adjust a cloak for them. The results were excellent, the visitor decided; the girls were "in no respect" inferior to white girls "of the same opportunities." In the late 1830's, Philadelphia Quakers officially ran seven schools for Negroes, including day schools for children and evening schools for adults, with a total enrollment of over six hundred. In the 1850's the Quakers' Institute for Colored Youth (the future Cheyney State College) was the only high school open to Negroes in the city; it prepared students not only to become mechanics, but also teachers and preachers, and its standards were comparable to those of white schools.[14]

In the Midwest, where Negroes were virtually excluded from public schools, Quakers assisted in sponsoring large numbers of separate schools for them. In doing so, Quakers often worked with Negro churches. If the schools were in town, they often met in Negro churches; if in the country, in log cabins built for the purpose. Friends contributed funds, donated books, and occasionally supplied teachers from their own numbers.[15]

Where Negroes were not numerous enough to justify creating separate schools for them, Quakers—particularly in the Midwest—sometimes quietly let Negroes into the schools intended for their own Quaker children. The number of Negroes they took into their Quaker schools was considerable, but far smaller than the number they assisted in separate schools. For example, in 1852, Friends took eighty-two Negro children into Friends schools under the jurisdiction of Indiana Yearly Meeting, while at about the same time the meeting was helping to support twenty-one separate private schools for Negroes. In 1860, the Western Yearly Meeting, which included large parts of Illinois and Indiana, took into its own schools twenty-six Negro children but at the same time was assisting eighteen private schools for Negroes. Nevertheless the Midwest Quaker pattern of taking a few Negroes into Friends schools became fixed and persisted into the Civil War.[16] It was a pattern little noticed then or since. It was developed not as part of a planned campaign to overcome segregation—as some abolitionist action was—but simply as an acceptable and inexpensive way to meet the needs of Negro children in areas where few Negro children lived. It attained significance for the nation in at least one way: Quakers helped educate in one of their Indiana Quaker schools a Negro who was to be a United States senator from Mississippi during Reconstruction.[17]

It may well have been goading from the minority Yearly Meeting of Antislavery Friends—who seceded from the majority Orthodox Indiana Yearly Meeting in 1843 in protest against their antislavery apathy—that pushed the majority of Friends in the Midwest into their considerable involvement in education for Negroes. It was the minority Antislavery Friends who led in sponsoring the most ambitious Quaker effort—though not exclusively Quaker—for interracial education in the abolitionist period: the founding in 1846 of Union Literary Institute in heavily Quaker Randolph County, Indiana, with four Negroes on its original board of trustees. By 1849, Union Institute had 230 students, of whom 165 were Negro. During the 1850's the total number of Union's students declined and the proportion of Negroes went up until by 1863, when it had a Negro principal, only fifty students remained, probably all Negro. As an interracial enterprise Union did not flourish, but as a school open to Negroes it lasted twenty-eight years.[18]

In general, Friends did not open most of their schools or colleges to Negroes. In the East it was rare even for radical Friends to try to have Negroes admitted into Friends schools. Friends made little protest against segregated education, whether their own or anyone else's;[19] they were usually content to aid the education of Negroes, North and South, by creating or sustaining separate Negro schools, and at least in the North they managed to do so without arousing much antagonism.

The Garrisonians also attempted to assist in creating schools open to Negroes. They did so particularly in two notable projects in which they met a response quite different from the response the Quakers usually met.

In Canterbury, Connecticut, a young *Liberator*-reading teacher, Prudence Crandall, admitted a Negro girl from the neighborhood into her private girls' school. The white girls accepted her easily, but their parents did not, and they withdrew their daughters from the school.

Although Prudence Crandall was a Quaker, it was not so much to Quakers as to Garrisonians that she turned for help. It was with Garrison's encouragement that in early 1833, Miss Crandall turned her school into a school for Negro girls, including girls from out of the state.

The town of Canterbury was horrified. It imagined that the school would bring in hordes of Negroes to ruin it and eventually all New England. The selectmen said, "Open this door, and New England will become the Liberia of America." Led by colonizationists, the town tried to drive the school out, and in doing so they showed that they, as well as abolitionists, were capable of both violent and nonviolent direct action. Merchants refused to sell the school supplies, the town doctor refused to treat its pupils, and the town church refused to admit them. In addition, vandals threw manure into the school well and pelted the school building with stones.

With abolitionist help, Prudence Crandall struggled to keep the school open. Garrisonians in nearby Brooklyn, Connecticut, including Unitarian pastor May and George W. Benson, into whose family Garrison was soon to marry, provided encouragement. Meantime the town had persuaded the state legislature—which was elected by whites only—to require that schools teaching out-of-state pupils have town approval, which, of course, Miss Crandall could not obtain. She defied the law by continuing to hold school, and was arrested. In a sophisticated move, May and Benson advised her to refuse to let her friends provide bail money so that she would be jailed; she accepted the advice. As May explained to the sheriff, "The people generally will not so soon recognize how bad, how unkind, how cruel a law it is, unless we suffer her persecutors to inflict upon her all the penalties it prescribed. She is willing to bear them for the sake of the cause she has so nobly espoused." Miss Crandall was jailed overnight; then, since she had made her witness, May and Benson arranged to pay the required bail money, and she was released. Her jailing inevitably called attention to the barbarous effort to crush her school, and Prudence Crandall became an abolitionist heroine.

She continued to operate the school until, in the summer of 1834, town people tried to set the school building on fire and attacked it with iron bars, smashing many of the windows. May finally advised that it would not be safe for the pupils to continue to live in the building, and the school closed.

Afterward a high court threw out the Crandall case on a technicality. But by 1838 the growth of abolitionism and the reaction against the crude violence to Miss Crandall's school had brought about such a change in Connecticut public opinion that the state legislature, led by some of those who had persecuted the school, repealed the law that had been passed in order to close it.[20]

About the time that Prudence Crandall's school closed, Garrisonians kept the initiative in the New England struggle for Negro educational opportunity by attempting to establish an openly interracial school. The Garrisonians were so sure that they were morally right in trying to establish the school that, despite their experience in Canterbury, they seemed little concerned about whether it was practical or not. The Garrisonians chose to locate Noyes Academy—as their new school was called—in Canaan, New Hampshire, even though they knew that a great part of the town was in opposition.

They did not begin modestly by admitting only one or two neighborhood Negroes into the school. Instead they admitted fourteen
Negroes along with twenty-eight whites, and, as at Canterbury,
many of the Negroes were from out of the state.

During the school's first year, the local town meeting, hysterically
crying that the school would bring in Negroes who would become
paupers for the town to support, voted that the school should be
removed. At the town meeting's call, three hundred farmers gathered and with ropes and oxen dragged the school building from its
foundations into a swamp.[21] Noyes Academy, like Prudence Crandall's school, had come to a violent end.

Although the Garrisonians participated in creating several other
schools open to Negroes, unlike the Quakers they never did directly
create any substantial, viable schools, whether open to Negroes alone
or open to both Negroes and whites.

However, by the 1850's the Garrisonian Negro William C. Nell
believed that the vicious public reaction against the Noyes and Crandall schools had significantly aided Negro education. The reaction
had called attention to the barbaric exclusion of Negroes from
schools, Nell explained, and caused a humanitarian counterreaction
that had opened the doors of many schools to Negroes, so that the
need for separate Negro schools had long since gone.[22] Whether Nell
was correct or not in his explanation, it was certain that schools and
colleges opened their doors to Negroes faster in New England than
in any other part of the country, so that even by the 1840's there was
less need for Garrisonians to establish schools for Negroes in their
home base of New England than there was for Quaters to do so in
Pennsylvania or Tappanites to do so in New York.

The Tappanites, like the Quakers, created separate educational
institutions for Negroes. In New York City they helped Negroes—
including pastors T. S. Wright and Sam E. Cornish—to create and
run a high school, an adult school, a lecture series, and a library for
Negroes; they formed Negro neighborhood groups that loaned
clothes to children if they would attend school but would take them
back if they neglected to attend. In upstate New York the Tappanites
helped Gerrit Smith find pupils and teachers for his manual labor
school for Negroes in Peterboro. In New Haven, led by the mild S.
S. Jocelyn, they tried stimulating Negroes to self-improvement by
"mental feasts," social affairs in which Negroes read to each other
essays or poems they had written and discussed them or other serious
topics; encouraged by the Tappanites, the feasts kept spreading and

thirty years later were still continuing in Pennsylvania and the West. In addition, the Tappanites were not content merely to foster separate schools, as the Quakers usually were. The Tappanites successfully did what the Garrisonians tried but failed to do; they created substantial and enduring interracial schools.

In upstate New York the Tappanites helped to develop Oneida Institute into an interracial school. In 1827, Oneida Institute had opened within sight of the new Erie Canal, in Whitesboro, near Utica, as a Presbyterian school to prepare ministers. It soon came under the influence of abolitionist Charles G. Finney, the Presbyterian evangelist whose fire, sweeping through central and western New York, was burning out old Calvinist theological restraints and freeing churchmen to throw themselves into reform. Finney-enthusiast Lewis Tappan sent his sons to Oneida Institute; Finney-protégé Theodore Weld studied there and helped raise the funds for the school. In 1833, Reverend Beriah Green, who was soon to be one of the founders of the American Antislavery Society, became president of Oneida Institute on the specific condition that he was free to express his abolitionist beliefs. After that Oneida became a center of education for blacks as well as whites, a center of abolitionism, and a center of pacifism—in 1836 students founded a peace society dedicated to complete nonresistance. It was also a center of manual labor education, a reform many abolitionists supported as a means to help equalize educational opportunity for rich and poor and at the same time to help students to learn and respect a variety of skills. Some Oneida students made wagons; others, dubbed "onion grubbers," worked on the Institute's farm; still others printed the New York State Antislavery Society's paper.

With the Tappans marshaling financial support, Oneida flourished for a time. But eventually hostility to it grew. Ridiculed as a "Negro school," it was also criticized for President Green's conspicuous and not always tactful abolitionism. Presbyterian support dropped. In the state assembly in 1836 several senators proposed that the state, in making its usual educational grants, deny a grant to Oneida Institute because its abolitionists were fomenting sedition.

Abolitionists came to Oneida's defense. The New England Antislavery Convention issued a public statement, saying, "Oneida Institute is the only literary institution east of Ohio, where it is officially announced that colored students can enjoy equal privileges with others in a collegiate course of education," and appealed for "abolitionists to bestow on Oneida Institute their patronage and support."[23] A meeting protesting the possibility that the state might not give Oneida its usual grant raised a thumping five thousand dollars for the school.

Oneida Institute held on, but precariously. The New York Tappan brothers, bankrupted in the panic of 1837, could not give as much as they had previously. Finally by 1844, after having helped to educate many abolitionist leaders—including the occasional nonresistant black Henry Highland Garnet, the Tappanite limited nonresistant black Amos Beman, and the complete nonresistant white Amos Dresser—Oneida Institute was closed. The disappointed Green stayed in Whitesboro as pastor of the antislavery Congregational church that he had helped to found, becoming increasingly isolated from reformers.

Meanwhile in 1833 the Tappans led in founding another institution, Lane Theological Seminary, which they located in Cincinnati as an evangelical outpost in the expanding West. Reform oriented, Lane Seminary, like Oneida Institute, followed manual labor principles; Lane also admitted Negroes, but, being more cautious than Union, Noyes, or Oneida, at first it admitted only one. The Tappans persuaded the vaguely antislavery Lyman Beecher, who had been Garrison's pulpit idol in Boston, to become president.

Theodore Weld, like a number of other students, went from Oneida to Lane to continue his education on the graduate level. In 1834 the sharp and glowing Weld led the Lane students in a long series of debates on abolition versus colonization. Cutting deep, the debates helped to convert the majority of the Lane students, including many from the South, to abolition. The converted students then formed an abolition society and began intensive teaching and visiting among Negroes in Cincinnati. However, influential forces in the city, having valuable commercial ties with the nearby South, became alarmed, and mobs threatened violence. The trustees reacted by forbidding students to continue their work with Negroes in the city or even to discuss slavery at all; the students considered this a serious breach of their freedom, and a heated controversy arose between them and the trustees. President Beecher wavered. He admired the courage and piety of Weld and never really quarreled with him; he was proud of all his students. But finally he supported the trustees.

In a historic nonviolent direct action, most of the Lane students —some fifty of them—withdrew from Lane as a protest against the restriction of their freedom. Most of these students were in their late twenties or thirties; they were dead serious; they had taken a momentous decision and they knew it. Many years later Garrison said of their withdrawal: "There is no event . . . more full of moral sublimity, than the exodus of those noble young men . . . in vindication of their right of speech, and the claims of religious duty."[24]

In part through the intense dedication that the withdrawal experience developed in them, the Lane Rebels, as the boycotting students were called in succeeding years, became unusually effective abolitionist leaders. Among them were Theodore Weld, whom the other students warmly admired, Amos Dresser, another former Oneida student, and George Whipple, all nonresistants in various degrees.

Many of the Rebels, after negotiating at length with Oberlin College—a recently founded, weak, manual labor college in the forests of northern Ohio—moved to Oberlin. There, with the help of the Tappans, who transferred their generous donations from Lane to Oberlin, they refounded Oberlin on the principles of free discussion of controversial reforms and the acceptance of Negroes as students.

While Lane survived and continued to accept Negroes as students, it was Oberlin that became the bastion of nonviolent abolition in the West, attracting students from other colleges where conservative forces had clamped down on them. Expressing their concern for peaceful methods, Oberlin students in 1840 founded a branch of the Nonresistance Society, and it became strong enough on campus for the faculty to be disturbed. By 1843, after a long debate between complete nonresistants and those who justified defensive wars, with the help of the most prominent Oberlin professors (including the great evangelist Finney who eventually became Oberlin's president), the Oberlin community established a new peace society that took a nearly complete nonviolent position.[25] In its early years Oberlin produced many evangelical abolitionists who worked for abolition through abolitionist societies. Later, after abolition societies became less significant in the abolition movement, Oberlin, under President Finney's urging, was more likely to produce abolitionist evangelists who, like the Tappans, believed in working for abolition as much as possible through the church.

Oberlin continued to accept Negro students all through the abolitionist period. Frederick Douglass sent one of his children there. Southern slave owners sometimes sent their illegitimate mixed-race offspring there too. Negroes were never more than a modest 5 percent of the students, but they were too numerous for some of the parents, especially because Oberlin—among its many dares—also dared to be coeducational. A girl student felt it necessary to assure her parents that she didn't have to kiss Oberlin "Niggars" or even speak to them if she didn't want to. Any number of Negro students was too many for Delazon Smith, a rare anti-abolitionist Oberlin student who scorned white Oberlin students for doting on Negroes. Said Smith, when students hear of the arrival of a Negro, "there is a great noise, like the rush of many waters, so great is their anxiety to see another of their colored brethren. . . . Parties of pleasure are got up, for the purpose of exhibiting, and glorifying these individuals." To Smith's disgust, one male white student even took a colored girl home to visit his family. "Not satisfied by outraging the feelings of his father's family," Smith reported, "he gallanted her to church and through the neighborhood . . . thus insulting those he knew abhorred the revolting doctrine of amalgamation."[26]

Lewis Tappan expected great things of Oberlin's Negro students, despite their being subjected to occasional scorn. When he heard that a Negro was one of Oberlin's best scholars, he wrote Gerrit Smith that these colored students "are to be the teachers of our children and grandchildren . . . for aught we know."[27] A few Negro students graduated to become teachers, ministers, or lawyers. No other college before the Civil War contributed as much as Oberlin either to the freedom of the slaves or the education of Negroes.

The teaching of Negroes that the Lane Rebels began in Cincinnati they continued and extended elsewhere in the state. Since Ohio did not permit black children to enter public schools at all, by 1837 under Tappanite leadership there were at least one hundred young women, many from Oberlin, teaching in private black schools scattered over the state.

Sometimes these schools taught nonviolence. As one of the teachers reported, when black boys on the way to school were bothered by white boys throwing brickbats at them, their teachers taught them "the gospel method" of putting down their enemies. A thirteen-year-old pupil wrote in a school composition, "when the white boys try to raise a fuss with us, we ought to go along like we do not hear or see them, then they will get quite sick of doing such things."[28]

Teaching in these black schools was not easy. Some of the teachers were paid less then the cost of their food. Though most of the teachers were white, they found that local whites would often have nothing to do with "nigger teachers"; few could find white families willing to rent them a room. Still more disturbing, their relations with Negroes were sometimes strained. The white Tappanite

Augustus Wattles, a former Oneida and Lane student who was supervisor of some of these schools, was anguished to discover that the gulf between the teachers and the Negroes of local communities widened when they knew each other better. Abolitionist committees on which Wattles served reported that most Ohio Negroes were "ignorant—many of them intemperate and vicious," but the teachers associated with them, the committees explained, "on terms of perfect friendship and equality." Yet after doing so for a year, they said, "we . . . find on their part . . . an increased sense of moral and intellectual distance. This to us is sometimes exceedingly painful." By 1854 the faithful Wattles, who had poured much of his energy and fortune into Negro schools, was reporting that Ohio Negro schools were being taught by Negroes. Admitting in a sense the failure of the white teachers to integrate into the black community, he believed that the change from white to black teachers was an improvement.[29]

The Tappanites were adaptable. Like the Garrisonians they preferred interracial education, but like the Quakers they also worked with segregated education. They founded viable black or interracial schools, they helped staff black or interracial schools, and they helped encourage and support these schools whether they were taught by whites or blacks.

As we have seen, particularly in the 1830's and early 1840's the three groups of nonviolent abolitionists contributed to Negro education differently. The Quakers and Tappanites kept at the slow, often discouraging work of educating Negroes in Negro-segregated schools—either schools they themselves established or helped Negroes establish or they simply helped sustain.

The Garrisonians at Canterbury and Canaan had sharpened the issue of the denial of educational opportunity to Negroes by bringing on themselves a hysterical community reaction.

On the level of higher education, Tappanites—along with dissident abolitionist Baptists, as we shall see—provided examples of functioning interracial institutions.

By the 1840's, with Negro education at lower levels improving, with the issue of educational opportunity having been sharply raised, and with examples of functioning interracial colleges before them, a few predominantly white abolitionist institutions were more willing to open their doors to Negroes than they had been. The State Normal School at Lexington, Massachusetts, headed by the Garrisonian Samuel J. May, at his insistence admitted a Negro girl. A

Negro entered Amherst College; another Negro graduated from Middlebury, another from Dartmouth, and two more from Bowdoin. In 1845 the American and Foreign Antislavery Society said that fourteen, or more than half, of the academies, colleges, and theological seminaries in New England—where the most influential educational institutions of the country were located—were known to be open to students of every complexion on the same terms. In the rest of the North, the society reported that, to the extent of its information, the only institutions open were: in New York State, three Free Will Baptist academies; in Ohio, four colleges, including Oberlin and Lane; in Illinois, two colleges modeled after Oneida—Knox College in Galesburg and the Mission Institute in Quincy. That was a total of twenty-three predominantly white institutions open to Negroes, of which six were controlled by the mildly abolitionist Free Will Baptists, four could be said to be Tappanite influenced (Lane, Oberlin, Knox, and Mission), none clearly Garrisonian, and none clearly Quaker.

Concern for desegregating education grew stronger as antislavery opinion spread and as abolitionists achieved at least partial victories over segregation in such areas as transportation and church seating. By 1848, while the national Negro convention admitted that separate Negro institutions would be necessary "for many years," it advised Negroes "to occupy membership and stations among white persons and in white institutions just so fast as our rights are secured to us" and, specifically on schools, advised Negroes to "use every just effort in getting their children into schools in common with others." In 1849 and 1851, Negro state conventions in Ohio and New York flatly opposed schools exclusively for Negroes. In 1850, Lewis Tappan, scarcely less strong for integration than the Garrisonians, said that while in some places it was not yet practicable, "the true policy . . . is to encourage colored youth to enter schools, academies, and colleges where they can associate with white youth, rather than to build up separate institutions, which go toward perpetuating instead of annihilating caste."[30]

By the late 1840's and the 1850's abolitionists were helping to create more interracial colleges. The new Central College at McGrawville, in the Finger Lakes region of New York, was not only interracial in its students but was the only college in the country to have Negro professors—limited to one at a time. It was sponsored by the abolitionist American Baptist Free Mission Society; Gerrit Smith contributed to it heavily, and for several years almost ran it himself to keep it in financial order. When Antioch College was founded in Ohio in 1853, its president, the independent Massachusetts abolitionist Horace Mann, insisted on admitting black students even though doing so led to the withdrawal of a few white students, the resignation of the chairman of the trustees, and the alienation of desperately needed contributors. As we have already seen, in hostile Kentucky the persistent Tappanite, the Reverend John G. Fee, succeeded in founding schools open to both black and white students. Just before the Civil War, Fee was developing these schools into Berea College, an openly interracial, antislavery, anti-rum, and anti-sectarian college modeled after Oberlin. In addition, the number of predominantly white nonabolitionist colleges open to Negroes continued to increase. Abolitionists had made striking progress in opening higher educational opportunities for Negroes.

The Negro national convention recognized this progress but at the same time brought out a serious shortcoming in it: the few Negroes in high school or college were finding that their education was usually "classical" in nature and offered them little preparation for industrial jobs, yet preparation for industrial jobs was what increasing numbers of Negroes desperately needed. About 1850, Douglass, who in many respects shared the Garrisonian horror of separate Negro institutions, startled some abolitionists by favoring a separate institution in the special case of a national industrial school for Negroes. He said Negroes needed such a school because whites denied them a chance for industrial skills by denying them apprenticeships and because existing manual labor schools were not rigorous enough in their training in mechanical skills to make up for the loss. The Negro national convention at first decided to accept Douglass' proposal, voting to create a Negro industrial school. Then the convention faltered. Among the Negro opponents of such a separate school were the Garrisonians William C. Nell and Charles Lenox Remond and also the Tappanite Charles W. Gardiner who said if there were five hundred qualified Negroes looking for opportunities in higher education, he could find places for all of them in predominantly white colleges and academies already open to Negroes. In 1855 the Negro national convention, short of funds for an industrial school and deeply divided both on the need and the principle of separatism involved, decided to abandon the plan.[31]

Other tough problems for Northern Negro education remained. It was disturbing that nonabolitionist denominations believed it necessary to create Negro colleges in the mid-1850's, as the Presbyterians did in Pennsylvania (Lincoln University) and the Methodists did in Ohio (Wilberforce University). Of more concern to the ordinary Negro, whose educational sights were likely to be limited to the public schools, was that if public schools were open to Negroes at all, they were often segregated, and the abolitionists' creation of new schools did not alter that fact.

11. Boycotting Schools

◇◇◇◇◇◇◇◇◇◇◇

WHILE IT WAS the Tappanites and Quakers who proved themselves to have the patience and command of resources necessary to create lasting schools open to Negroes, nevertheless, as historians have scarcely noticed,[1] it was the Garrisonians who proved that their characteristic unwillingness to compromise with segregation lent itself well to improving Negro educational opportunity by boycotting segregated schools.

By the mid-1840's the idea of boycotting schools was a familiar one among abolitionists, as was also the idea of boycotting slave produce, segregated churches, and segregated transportation. There had already been small boycotts of schools. Two Negro students refused to attend the Episcopal General Theological Seminary in New York City when its authorities would not allow them to live with other students as equals. The Garrisonian William Wells Brown would not let his daughter attend school in Buffalo because she was not allowed to attend the same school as whites and sending her to a black school would have meant accepting segregation. The Tappanite minister Sam Cornish, once an agent for Tappanite segregated schools in New York City, later refused to send his children to any black school, public or private; doing so would reinforce prejudice, he said, and provide them with inferior education besides. After trying to enter his children in the "innumerable" white Presbyterian schools of the city and being rebuffed, he announced in his *Colored American:*

"We are . . . making preparation to . . . go from the city, if not from the country, that we may educate our children and hide them from that scorching, withering prejudice." There had already been larger school boycotts, too. The walkout of the Lane students had provided a notable example of a large-scale boycott. Similarly, some fifty students walked out of Phillips Academy in Andover, Massachusetts, when its officials forbade their forming an antislavery society.[2]

Following such precedents, in the 1840's and 1850's concerted Negro boycotts against segregation developed in the public schools of at least five different places—Nantucket, Salem, and Boston, Massachusetts; Newport, Rhode Island; and Rochester, New York. Available evidence indicates that Garrisonians were the major leaders of the boycotts in Boston and Rochester and suggests that they were at least considerably involved in Nantucket and Salem.

By the mid-1840's public schools in New England already had a long history behind them, with roots in early Puritan concern for education for the common man. As a result, New England had by far the highest literacy rates in the nation, while the South, partly because of slavery, had the lowest. Secretary Horace Mann of the Massachusetts Board of Education, the future president of the interracial Antioch College, was emphasizing the democratizing function of public schools in providing a common experience for children of different degrees of wealth and of differing national and religious backgrounds. Mann was improving the quality of public schools in order to reduce the large number of children who missed this democratizing experience by attending private schools, and he was raising the public expectation of what public schools could accomplish with adequate funds. Most Massachusetts public schools were already open equally to Negroes, but there were a few exceptions.

On Nantucket, a whaling island off Cape Cod, in 1844 the school committee expelled Negro children from all the public schools except one which they made into a segregated Negro school. During the next two years, according to a Nantucket resident, the Garrisonian Quaker Nathaniel Barney, who had boycotted segregated Massachusetts railroads, "the colored children generally refused to go back to that school" and were "scattering and roaming" about the island. Nantucket Negroes were boycotting the segregated school in protest.

Aroused by the Negroes' boycott, in 1846, Nantucket voters—including a considerable number of abolitionists—by a narrow margin chose a new school committee that admitted black children to all schools on the same basis as whites and kept the black school open as a primary school for the few Negroes who still wished to attend it. The boycott had helped to bring compulsory segregation to an end.[3]

North of Boston, in Salem, a seaport grown prosperous in the China trade, there was a Negro public school that normally served one hundred pupils. As a protest against the segregated nature of that school, however, many Negro parents kept their children out of it until in 1844 its enrollment dropped to a startling low of twenty to twenty-five. At that time, under pressure from the boycott and with the help of the antislavery Stephen C. Phillips, former mayor of Salem and a generous contributor of funds to the public schools, Salem completely abolished school segregation. The Salem Garrisonian Negro Charles Lenox Remond was so grateful for Phillips' help in ending segregation in Salem schools that when Phillips ran for governor of Massachusetts on the Free Soil ticket in 1848, Remond broke the usual Garrisonian rule of boycotting elections by voting for him.[4]

The desegration of schools worked well in Salem, as it did in Massachusetts generally. In 1854, Charlotte Forten, the sixteen-year-old granddaughter of the wealthy Philadelphia Garrisonian Negro, James Forten, came to study in the desegrated Salem school because her father refused to send her to the segregated Philadelphia schools. She lived in Salem with the Remonds, who were friends of her family, and participated with them in the endless abolitionist activities of Salem and Boston, hearing lectures, attending sewing circles, visiting bazaars, and entertaining traveling abolitionists.

As a Negro, Charlotte felt a compulsion to do well in school to help prove that her people were not inferior; she deliberately tried to improve her mind. In a competition in preparation for high school graduation, fifty pupils, including Charlotte, anonymously submitted words for a farewell song. After the song had been sung at the graduation ceremony without anyone knowing who wrote it, the principal called for the author to stand. Charlotte stood, and, according to William Wells Brown, "thunders of applause greeted her" from the audience, some of whom were "the most aristocratic people in one of the most aristocratic towns in America." Afterwards Charlotte also graduated from the new state normal school in Salem and then became a teacher in a desegrated Salem public school—the first time a Negro had taught whites in a Massachusetts public school. The boycott had helped move conservative Salem onto the road away from caste, and with Salem's acceptance of Charlotte as an indication of how far it had gone down that road, the *National Antislavery Standard* exulted: "Who will say after this, that the prejudice against color is invincible?"[5]

In 1847, Frederick Douglass, then still a Garrisonian, moved from Lynn, Massachusetts, near Salem, to the bustling wheat milling center of Rochester, New York, to begin publishing his own weekly paper. In Rochester, Douglass discovered that the proportion of Negroes was small, much less than Nantucket's 5 percent, a little less than Salem's 2 percent, about the same as Boston's 1.5 percent. Nevertheless, Douglass found that Rochester's public schools were segregated, as schools were more likely to be in New York State than in New England. Deliberately boycotting the one separate Negro school, Douglass searched for a private school that would accept his nine-year-old daughter Rosetta as an equal to whites. Douglass thought he had found such a school in Rochester and sent his daughter there, only to discover later that the school put her in a room all by herself. In a rage, Douglass withdrew the girl, sent her to a private school in Albany instead, and told Rochester's shame in his paper. Douglass had begun his campaign to desegregate the Rochester schools.

About a year later, Negro population trends in Rochester seemed to require the creation of a second separate public school for Negroes, on the east side of town, if the segregated system was to be maintained. After the school board had debated whether to drop segregation in order to save the expense of building a new school, what Douglass called the "pro-slavery Irish faction" in the board won out, and the board decided to create the new separate school.

Instead of constructing a building for the new school, however, the school board contracted with the trustees of the Negro Zion Methodist Church to use its basement for the school. Douglass was furious that a Negro church would thus cooperate in preserving school segregation. The church trustees, he said, "santified . . . the spirit of caste, by which we are constantly haunted and tormented." Douglass promised never to send any of his children "to the miserable cellar under Zion church," and in his *North Star* he promoted a boycott of both the new and the old Negro schools. A meeting of Negro citizens promised to support the boycott. When the new school opened in the Zion Church basement, the *North Star* reported happily that both Negro schools were "almost deserted."

Douglass continued his own boycott for several years. In the early

1850's he was still refusing to send his children to the public schools, having them taught at home instead by a Quaker woman. Meantime, with his participation in the boycott making the depth of his feeling clear, Douglass kept urging the school board to end segregation. It was Douglass who continued to lead the campaign that eventually pressured the school board into integrating the new east-side school; at last Douglass could consent to sending his children to that school. By 1857, Rochester had dropped school segregation completely.[6]

In Newport, Rhode Island, a boycott was briefly tried at the beginning of a school desegregation campaign.

The Newport campaign—which broadened into campaigns also to desegregate the only other two segregated school systems in Rhode Island, those of Bristol and Providence—was led by a Negro of kingly bearing, Thomas Downing. He was the son of the prosperous oyster house proprietor of New York City, George Downing, who sat-in to desegregate horsecars. Somewhat like his father, the younger Downing was first a caterer in New York City, serving upper-class whites; then in 1846 he became a caterer to the upper-class white summer community of Newport. Vigorous and efficient, he became wealthy enough to build a hotel and business block in Newport. As an active abolitionist, he tied himself to neither Tappanites nor Garrisonians nor apparently any other abolitionist group.

Downing began to act against school desegregation when his children were refused admittance to the white schools of Newport, a town with a high 7 percent of Negroes in its population. Assisted by the venerable Tappanite black Charles W. Gardiner, who had become pastor of a black church in Newport, Downing turned to a boycott as a protest. At their private expense, in October, 1853, Downing, Gardiner, and others created a free black private school so that blacks would not have to attend the inferior segregated public school for blacks. According to an account by Amos Beman, they "prepared a place and paid a teacher and opened a free school to all who chose to send, thinking that . . . the parents would hail with joy a place where their children could be taught and their self-respect maintained." But, Beman said, the parents were so deep in prejudice and ignorance that the school soon closed for lack of pupils.

Downing then turned primarily to political means to secure desegregation, and for many years he led in holding public protest meetings, interviewing school committeemen, and petitioning the state legislature.

The boycott idea was never wholly dropped in Rhode Island;

according to Beman, in 1863 a few black children continued to be privately taught or were sent out of the state to receive equal education. But the emphasis of the campaign was on legislative action. Downing continued active in the campaign despite his belief that pro-segregationists had set his buildings on fire for a loss of perhaps as much as $40,000. When the Rhode Island victory finally came in 1866, it came under Downing's leadership and in the form of a state desegregation law.[7] The boycott method seemed of little importance in the victory, but at least according to Beman it had set the campaign in motion. Newport—the last of the five places to desegregate its schools in part through a boycott—was the one with the highest proportion of blacks and the least Garrisonian influence.

In Boston, school desegregationists combined their boycott with state legislative action, as they also did in Rhode Island but not in Rochester, Salem, or Nantucket. In Boston boycotters briefly ran a school of their own to compete with the segregated public schools, as they also did in Newport, but it is notable that the Boston boycotters reached a high point of effectiveness while their own school was functioning. According to the information available, the Boston boycotters received more help from white abolitionists than the boycotters did in any of the other four places where boycotts are known to have occurred, and they kept a concerted boycott going longer—eleven years; they also left more records about what they did, so that a fuller account of their boycott is possible.

Before 1800, Boston public schools were open equally to Negro children, but few of them attended. About 1800 some Boston Negro parents, like Negro parents elsewhere in the North at the time, began petitioning school authorities for separate schools for Negroes so that their children would not have to face the competition and hostility of white school children. By at least 1812 the city was officially supporting a segregated school for Negroes, and segregation was continuous from that time.

In the 1820's school examiners once a year visited all the Boston public schools, both white and black, awarding honors to the students who passed their annual examinations most acceptably. At the black school on Beacon Hill in 1829 the examiners awarded honors to several of the scholars, among them a slight, serious boy, William C. Nell. Afterward, when the mayor invited all the white honor winners from the Boston schools to a dinner at Faneuil Hall but did not invite the black winners, Nell felt the discrimination. He believed he had a right to be at the dinner, and he was enterprising enough to do something about it. He inveigled one of his friends who was to be a waiter at the dinner to let him wait on the table in his place part of the time. At the dinner one of the school examiners recognized Nell and whispered to him, "You ought to be here with the other boys." Nell wanted to reply, if you think so, why didn't you do something about it? In fact Nell said nothing, but, as he explained long afterward, the wound of this incident developed in him the determination to help integrate Boston schools.

Nell, who became a Garrisonian abolitionist by the time he was barely out of school, by the 1840's and 1850's emerged as the major leader in the campaign to integrate Boston's schools. The campaign was led by Negro Garrisonians, especially Nell and the barber John T. Hilton, the most active Boston Negro in the Massachusetts Antislavery Society. The campaign was supported by white Garrisonians such as William Lloyd Garrison and the orator Wendell Phillips. It resulted in Boston becoming the first major American city in the abolitionist period to integrate its schools.

Nell was born on Beacon Hill, and he continued to live there for most of his life. Not impressive as a speaker, Nell was guarded in his manner, and he became known among abolitionists as careful on details. He considered becoming a lawyer, but Phillips dissuaded him from doing so because he would be required to take an oath to support the slavery-protecting United States Constitution, which Nell, as a Garrisonian, was reluctant to do. However, with the help of his experience in a lawyer's office, Nell developed himself into a "business agent" who conducted correspondence, prepared deeds and mortgages, and served as an accountant and collector. He also wrote on the history of Negroes in America and has been called the first American Negro to do so seriously. At various times over many years, Nell also worked for Garrison, assisting in the *Liberator*'s printing office, running its employment bureau for Negroes, and writing on Negro activities in Boston. Briefly Nell also assisted Frederick Douglass in Rochester on the *North Star*, occasionally writing editorials during Douglass' absence. Because of his familiarity with both Boston and Rochester, Nell was able to exchange news about their simultaneous school boycotts.

Like Nell, most Boston Negroes lived on the back slope of Beacon Hill, farthest from Boston Common, where the Negro Smith School was located. Downstairs in the Smith building was one of the city's public primary schools for Negroes. Upstairs was Smith Grammar

School for Negro children of about eight to thirteen years. Since it was the only public Negro grammar school in Boston, all Negro children were required to attend it no matter where they lived in the city. Because there was no Negro high school, Smith Grammar School was also expected to serve as a high school for any Negroes who were persistent enough to push their education that far. It was Smith Grammar School around which the Boston desegregation campaign swirled.

Sporadic protests against Boston school segregation had been made by blacks and whites previously, but in 1844, at about the time Salem school segregation was abolished, the Boston campaign began in earnest. It was thirteen years since Garrison had founded the *Liberator* in Boston, plenty of time for Garrisonian intransigence to have infected Boston Negroes. It was just one year since the last Massachusetts railroads had ended segregated seating, following a Garrisonian-led ride-in, boycott, and legislative campaign.

In 1844 citizens petitioned Boston authorities to end school segregation; in 1845, 1846, and 1848 they did so again.[8]

It was Negroes who led this petition movement, though the opposition often charged that white abolitionists were behind them. In 1844, when Negroes opposed to school segregation organized, they chose the middle-aged barber Hilton as president and two bright young men in their twenties, *Liberator* assistant Nell and law student Robert Morris, as secretaries. The group petitioned school authorities to end segregation. At the same time it also complained against the white principal of the Smith Grammar School, Abner Forbes, charging him with punishing the children cruelly and with having such a lack of confidence in the mental ability of blacks that he was not competent to teach them. After investigation, a school committee recommended that segregation be continued; and, while exonerating Forbes from the charges against him, it recommended that, since the charges had impaired his usefulness at Smith School, he be transferred to another school. For the time being, however, Forbes remained at Smith School. Disappointed, the protesting Negroes announced that they believed Mr. Forbes was "totally unworthy of his present responsible station," that segregation was contrary to "that equality which is the vital principle of the school system of Massachusetts," and that for both these reasons Negro parents should "withdraw their children from the exclusive school." They were urging a boycott.

By this time Hilton had already withdrawn his daughter from the

Smith School, where she had been doing poorly, and moved her into an integrated school in nearby Cambridge, where she soon carried away the honors from the white children. The next year, 1845, a minority report of a committee appointed by Boston school authorities to study segregation reported a general move by Negroes to withdraw their children from the segregated schools; a clergyman had already moved out of Boston to an adjacent town so that his children could attend schools with whites; many Negroes kept their children out of school solely because they would not let them be degraded by segregation; one woman had already kept her children out of school for two years for this reason alone. The boycott campaign was well under way.

In 1846, when Negroes again petitioned school authorities for desegregation, for the first time the major documents in the matter were published. The Negroes' petition was forceful: "All experience teaches that where a small and despised class are . . . confined to separate schools, few or none interest themselves about the schools —neglect ensues, abuses creep in, and the standard of scholarship degenerates." They felt that separate schools were insulting.

The majority of the subcommittee assigned by the Boston Primary School Committee to study the petition—three out of the five members—replied that they believed that the petition did not represent the opinion of most Boston Negroes. They admitted that separate schools cost the city more than desegrated schools would, but they predicted that if schools were desegrated, black pupils, with their irregular attendance record, would hurt the whites' record and that many whites "would vex and insult the colored children" and many would be driven from the schools. They insisted that racial distinction, created by God, "is founded deep in the physical, mental, and moral natures of the two races" and that legislation could not erase it. They warned that desegregation would lead to the horror of intermarriage and advise Negroes not to lean on whites but to "cultivate a respect for themselves."

The minority of the subcommittee was composed of two white Garrisonians. They reported that Bostonians generally considered Negroes to be an inferior race and that the usual effect of this opinion on the school authorities, teachers, and black children was "want of heart and faith" in their work. Boston schools had not yet produced a single Negro scholar for high school, and Boston was the only place in the state where common schools were still segregated. They recommended gradual abolition of the separate schools, at first allowing Negroes to choose, as in the recent desegregation in Nantucket, between entering the white schools or staying in the separate Negro schools.

However, the Primary School Committee followed the advice of the majority report and decided to continue to require segregation. At least the votes of the various school committees were less and less strong for segregation: in 1844 the vote of the Grammar School Committee was 24 to 2, in 1845 the vote of the Primary School Committee was 55 to 12, and in 1846 it was 59 to 16. While the school protesters still had a long way to go, they were making headway with the school committees. If the protesters persisted, said the *Liberator* editorially, "they will at last prevail."

Meanwhile Secretary Horace Mann of the Massachusetts Board of Education was looking for a new master to replace Forbes as head of Smith School.

Mann, who was only vaguely antislavery in the mid-1840's, had been silent during the struggle to desegregate the schools in Nantucket and Salem. So far he had also been silent during the struggle to desegregate the Boston schools. In looking for a new master to replace Forbes at Smith School, Mann's interest was not desegregation but finding someone who would avoid using corporal punishment on the children, as Forbes admittedly did. At this time Mann was flaying the Boston schoolmasters for their reliance on corporal punishment. Perhaps influenced by his friend Samuel J. May, Mann was doggedly insisting that corporal punishment should not be used until all other methods had been tried. Mann was not a complete nonresistant, but as a believer in the perfectibility of man, he held that when schools and society were improved enough, physical punishment would no longer be necessary at all and that schools should already be moving in that direction.[9]

Dr. Samuel Gridley Howe, who was already famous for his pioneering school for the blind and who was a member of the Boston School Committee, advised Mann to ask May to accept the Smith School post. Mann knew that May, both as an abolitionist and as a nonresistant who abhorred physical punishment, would do the job he wanted done, and he wrote May: "Howe has asked me several times whether I thought you to be so devoted to the cause of practically improving the conditions of the colored people, that you would come to Boston and take the Smith School; for the general opinion is that Forbes must go."

It is unlikely that May would have been willing to cooperate in school segregation where Negroes were protesting it; as it was, he was already committed to a new post as Unitarian pastor in Syracuse, and he kept his commitment.

Mann continued to look for someone who was willing to accept the low status of a teacher of Negroes and who also generally opposed corporal punishment. In time he found one in Ambrose Wellington who, as Mann reported to Howe, was "an abolitionist, and a sort of nonresistant." When Wellington finally accepted the post of master of Smith School, the boycotting Negroes were soon forced to admit that they no longer could complain against the master, and so some of the steam was taken out of their boycott.

While Mann was thus making the boycott more difficult, he made no public comment at all about segregation in Boston schools. Disturbed by Mann's silence, Wendell Phillips, the leading Boston Garrisonian orator, decided to do something about it. He publicly charged Secretary Mann with "timid silence" on Boston school segregation. Mann did not reply.

The next year, 1847, Phillips repeated his charge. Mann remained silent, and Phillips said he believed he knew why. Mann was a compromiser, trying to avoid controversy over segregation to ensure that he could accomplish other objectives, said Phillips; he was sacrificing despised Negroes for the sake of obtaining well-ventilated schoolrooms, new books, "physiological seats," and "broad playgrounds." Still Mann was silent.

Phillips repeated his charges in 1848, the year Mann resigned as secretary after twelve years of stormy but illustrious service to Massachusetts public schools, the very year in which he said, in one of his eloquent pleas for public education, that it was "the great equalizer of the conditions of men—the balance-wheel of the social machinery."[10]

It was disturbing that Mann was silent on school segregation because, though never a Garrisonian, he was mildly antislavery and antisegregation, and from the abolitionists' point of view, he, like other silent humanitarian leaders, might have done much to desegregate schools all over the North. As early as 1833, when he was a member of the Massachusetts legislature, Mann had defended the right of Negroes as well as whites to attend Howe's school for the blind. In 1842, Mann had dared to appoint his friend May, even though he was a well-known Garrisonian, to be principal of the Lexington State Normal School. Mann had established the first state normal schools in the nation and later had cooperated with May in opening them to a few black students. But while Mann could be bold up to a point, he avoided offending the public on matters he didn't consider central to his school cause; he did not wish to alienate those whose support he desperately needed to keep his public school mission alive, as it sometimes barely managed to be. When May took some students from his normal school to an abolition meeting, Mann was upset; May offered to resign, but Mann would not accept his resignation. When May was planning to deliver an abolitionist speech in Boston while he was still head of the normal school, Mann wrote him worriedly: "I have further plans for obtaining more aid [for schools], but the moment it is known or supposed that the [school reform] cause is to be perverted to, or connected with, any of the exciting party questions of the day, I shall never get another cent." As the generous May said later, as usual entirely without bitterness, Mann was "at that time, so intent upon his great undertaking for the improvement of our common schools, that he thought it our duty to repress our interest in every other reform that was unpopular."[11]

It was only after Mann had ceased to be responsible for Massachusetts schools and had become first a congressman and later president of Antioch College that he allowed himself to become an outspoken opponent of slavery and segregation.

So the Negro boycotters and their white Garrisonian allies continued their struggle for school desegregation without the direct help of Horace Mann and other well-intentioned humanitarians, doubtless for similar reasons. Few whites were willing to be as uncompromising on segregation as the "fanatical" Garrisonians were.

Despite the competent, new master Mann recommended to Smith Grammar School, Negro parents were making their boycott of the school increasingly effective. Average attendance dropped from more than a hundred before the boycott began in 1844, to sixty-six in 1848, and fifty-three in 1849.

The visiting examiners in the spring of 1849 reported that the school was in a "very low condition," the best scholars were deficient in most of their studies, the tone of the school was disorderly, and "there is no one of our public institutions that more needs reform."

Why Smith School morale was low was a question on which Boston Negroes differed. Those who wished to keep the segregated school open explained it by saying that only white teachers taught at Smith School and they didn't care about black children; black children needed black teachers, the segregationists said. As a matter of fact, for several years some abolitionists, too, had been saying that having black teachers would stimulate black children to do better work.

However, those who wished to close the segregated school explained its low morale differently. They said they had no complaint against the new Mann-recommended master, who was white. The trouble was that the pupils felt the injustice that forced them to attend this school and so the teachers, no matter how competent, could not teach them effectively.

The school authorities, falling in with the wishes of their segregationist Negro allies, decided to appoint a Negro master for Smith School. The boycotting Negroes considered this merely a sop. Insisting that the major issue was segregation, they refused to become part of the segregation system by helping to select Negro teachers. At a meeting they resolved: "We will not in any way attempt to better the condition of the school by recommending any persons as an instructor."

By the fall of 1849, however, a Negro had accepted an appointment as master of Smith School. He was Thomas Paul, son of an earlier pastor of the African Baptist Church on Belknap Street, on the same street as Smith School. When Garrison first published the *Liberator,* young Paul had assisted him as an apprentice; later Paul had been a student at the Garrisonian academy at Canaan, New Hampshire, until its building had been dragged away by farmers protesting its interracial character, and still later he had graduated from Dartmouth.

Paul's arrival at Smith School created a new crisis for the boycotters, and it was during this crisis that Nell began to emerge as their outstanding leader. For Smith School to have a Negro master, one well educated and from a family respected in the Negro community, was an even greater threat to the boycott than the arrival of Mann's protégé had been. The crisis came to a head the day the school opened in September, 1849, Paul's first day as master.

Early in the morning of that day, before the school opened, supporters of the boycott—whether with the approval of such leaders as Hilton and Nell or not is unclear—went to the school with the hope of preventing pupils from entering. As a historian of Boston Negroes described it, they surrounded the school and tried to use "every means, short of actual physical violence, to prevent the children from going in." A school official explained what happened somewhat differently: "A collection of rude boys . . . all of them persons of color . . . beset the doors in a disorderly manner, and sought to intimidate and keep from the school all who repaired to it as pupils. The prompt appearance, however, of a police officer . . . scattered the noisy group; and the school opened with comparative quiet. Still, it was found expedient to keep up a patrol about the place for a day or two more." The first day only twenty-three children registered.

On the evening of the same day Nell and the boycotting Negroes met in the Belknap Street Baptist Church, near Smith School. Outside, doubtless in retaliation for the morning attempt to keep pupils out of the school, opponents threw stones at the church, breaking some of the windows. Inside, Nell spoke contemptuously of those who threw the stones; the stones would be preserved, he said, "as trophies of the prowess of those who resort to such methods of appeal."

Nell was concerned to avoid violence, but he was not a complete nonresistant like Garrison; there is no evidence that he was a conscientious objector to war. As a historian, although he was not as chauvinist as some Negroes, he wrote extensively in praise of Negro soldiers who fought in the American Revolutionary armies. Nell was an occasional nonresistant,[12] like Phillips, whom he much admired.

Within a few days the boycotting Negroes met again and, as Nell reported in the *Liberator*, officially promised to "maintain at all meetings, and in our daily intercourse with the entire public a consistent regard for law and order; . . . no matter what violations of either may be perpetrated during the controversy, others, and not ourselves, shall be responsible therefore."[13]

About the same time the protesting Negroes also decided to continue their boycott—they claimed that they had kept the attendance at Smith School "very small" the previous year—and to make the boycott effective despite Paul's arrival, they planned to do something new—to open "temporary schools" of their own so that the boycotting children would not be deprived of their education. To run these schools, Nell appealed for funds, and many of those who responded were Garrisonians, including both blacks and whites. By October the *Liberator* rejoiced that the boycotters had already created a temporary school and it was "well attended."

Meanwhile legal action to end segregation in Boston schools had reached the state supreme court. It was in the form of a suit by Negro parent Benjamin F. Roberts, a printer, asking the city of Boston for damages because his child Sarah had been excluded from the public school nearest her residence. The suit claimed that exclusion was contrary to the equal protection guarantees of the state constitution. Lawyers for Roberts were the aggressive black Robert Morris, who had already associated himself with Hilton and Nell in the cause, and the white Charles Sumner, the chairman of the state Free Soil party's executive committee who was soon to be United States senator from Massachusetts.

Negroes thronged the courtroom to hear the illustrious Sumner give his argument. Even if the separate schools were as good as the other schools, Sumner said, compulsory segregation should be condemned because it contributes to distrust. "Prejudice . . . is sure to prevail where people do not know each other," he explained. Moreover, school segregation deprives blacks "of those healthful animating influences which would come from a participation in the studies of their white brethren. It adds to their discouragements. It widens their separation from the rest of the community and postpones that great day of reconciliation which is sure to come." It was notable that Sumner's argument was to a considerable degree psychological and social, rather than strictly legal, much as the school desegregation decision of the United States Supreme Court was also to be in 1954.

While the boycotters were hoping for a court decision that would end segregation in all Massachusetts schools, they held "enthusiastic" protest meetings at the Belknap Street Church. The Negro Garrisonian Charles Lenox Remond and the white Garrisonian Phillips spoke, giving their encouragement. The pastor of the antislavery and interracial Wesleyan Methodist Church in Boston came regularly to the meetings, assuring the protesters that they had his church's full support, while others pointed out by contrast that none of the ten clergymen on the general Boston School Committee favored desegregation. Two Negro men told the meeting that to secure "equal school rights" for their children they had moved their families away from Boston, one to Cambridge and the other to Fall River.

Of course, not all Boston Negroes joined in the school protest. There were Negro clergy, for example, who did not support the boycott. And one Negro speaker, the escaped slave, Josiah Henson, then visiting from Canada, pointed out a mundane reason why it was difficult for black businessmen to join the protest: "Few colored men, in their business associations, have independence sufficient to practice" fidelity to principle, Henson said. However, Nell wrote in the *Liberator* that the protest meetings and the sacrifices blacks were

making in the boycott indicated that never before had the blacks of
Boston been "so united and persevering in a progressive movement."

In April, 1850, the state supreme court announced its decision in
the Roberts case: each local school system could decide for itself
whether it wished to have segregation.

Disappointed, Nell and the "Friends of Equal Schools Rights," as
the desegregationist Negroes called themselves, reconsidered their
position. So far they had done well in involving considerable numbers of their own community in their cause; they had won the support of a growing minority in the school committees and the aid of
eminent legal counsel and of many white Garrisonian leaders. Their
boycott had been impressive: the average attendance at Smith School
had dropped from a normal of over a hundred before the boycott
began in 1844 to fifty-three in 1849, and after Master Paul arrived, the
attendance, instead of rising, had dropped even lower by the spring
of 1850, to twenty-five. They had met the crisis of Master Paul's
arrival by bringing the boycott to its most effective point so
far.

But all this protest had not yet accumulated enough power in legal
argument, or in appeal to conscience, or in nuisance, or in popular
outcry to induce the school committees or the state supreme court
to decide against segregation.

The protesters didn't abandon their boycott; they continued it, but
less intensely than in the year of Paul's arrival. They stopped the
extra drain on their time and funds from maintaining their own
"temporary school" and instead encouraged the boycotting parents
to send their children to existing private schools. In addition, they
looked for new forms of protest to reach wider circles of people in
more effective ways.

During the early 1850's, if Nell was correct, the school protesters
developed another form of school boycott, a Negro taxpayers' boycott of Boston. In the *Liberator* in 1852, Nell wrote: "Boston is fast
losing many of her intelligent, worthy, aspiring citizens, who are
becoming taxpayers in adjoining localities, for the sole advantage of
equal rights." Similarly, in the *Liberator* in 1854, Nell wrote: many
Negroes have "within the past few years, removed from Boston to
Cambridge, Charlestown, Roxbury, Salem, New Bedford, and elsewhere, where equal school privileges prevail, rather than submit to
the fiat of colorophobia which school committees in the Athens of

America yet ingloriously thrust upon colored taxpayers." In his 1855 history book, *Colored Patriots,* Nell repeated the theme, explaining that Negroes who had moved out of Boston included "many of the largest taxpayers" and in moving they "withdrew their investments from Boston real estate."

There was in fact a general trend of Negroes to the Boston suburbs in the period 1850–55, part of a long-term trend of both Negroes and whites to the suburbs. Among Negro desegregation leaders who by the early 1850's had moved to the suburbs were hairdresser Hilton, who had moved to Brighton, lawyer Morris, who had moved to Chelsea, and clothier Henry Weeden, who had moved to Cambridge. It is possible that Negroes' desire to avoid paying taxes to support Boston's segregated schools, whether they had children of school age or not, was at least a factor in the Negro trend to the suburbs.

In addition, almost at once after the disappointing state supreme court decision in the Roberts case, the equal-school-righters tried for the first time to persuade the state legislature to prohibit school segregation.

Negroes considered that they were leading this legislative drive. They wished to make it clear that they wanted desegregation themselves and were not being pushed into wanting it by white abolitionists, as opponents often charged. Negroes announced that the school protest movement had begun with them, not with whites, and that even now "on this subject, we are unadvised."

Nevertheless, they knew that they needed white help. In 1850, on behalf of the black school protesters, Nell asked the New England Antislavery Convention for its aid in the political campaign, and the convention promised it. To avoid too much identification with whites, the blacks arranged to petition the legislature separately, as blacks, leaving the whites to petition separately as well. With the *Liberator*'s support, Benjamin Roberts, the black parent who had brought the case of his daughter's exclusion from a Boston school to the courts, undertook touring Massachusetts to secure signatures.

However, the year 1850 was not a fortunate time for a campaign for a desegregation bill. In that year Congress passed a new, harsh, fugitive slave law that led many Massachusetts blacks to become preoccupied with protecting themselves from being seized and sent back into slavery in the South, while it led many Massachusetts whites to become preoccupied with how to punish the renegade Daniel Webster and other Whigs for their share in enacting the harsh law. Abolitionists gave little attention to the petition for a school desegregation bill, and in May, 1851, the legislature rejected it.

But the cruel attempts to enforce the new fugitive slave law led to a gradual rise in antislavery feeling in Massachusetts, and beginning in 1853 another black parent's complaint sharpened the school segregation issue. Boston school officials had excluded from the white schools a child, Edward Pindall, who, though he appeared to be white, was of mixed white, Indian, and Negro ancestry. City officials had ordered him to attend Smith School, but his father refused to allow him to do so and formally complained to the city. By 1854 a city committee, including the mayor and five common councilors, after studying the complaint, reported that in the rest of Massachusetts' schools racial integration was working harmoniously and that racial exclusion in Boston was "doing more injury" to its boasted common schools "than any other influence"; for the first time an official Boston committee had recommended segregation be dropped. The Boston common council at first endorsed this committee's recommendation but later withdrew its endorsement by a vote of 21 to 14.

Even this later withdrawal vote represented a much more favorable proportion of votes for desegregation than the comparable committee votes noted earlier for 1844, 1845, and 1846. Nell was pleased. Boston officials were more inclined to desegregation than ever before, he said. He urged Negro parents to renew their petitioning to Boston school authorities to admit their children to the white schools.

Pindall's father, still dissatisfied, carried his complaint to the courts, suing the city. Robert Morris, the same Negro lawyer who had participated in the Roberts case, represented Pindall, but in the fall of 1854, Pindall lost his case.

The disappointing Pindall decision provided the occasion for Nell to call for a new campaign of petitions to the legislature, which, fortunately, following a popular reaction against the Whig party for its complicity in the fugitive slave law, had just come under the control of the new, mildly antislavery Know Nothing party. The *Liberator* published a suggested form of petition several times, and Nell urged that the petitions be circulated, signed, and returned to him at the *Liberator* office.

For this final victorious round of petitions in 1854–55, Nell was responsible for obtaining 311 names in Boston, and Lewis Hayden, the fugitive slave who ran a fashionable clothing store in Boston, obtained 87 more. In addition, friends in Nantucket and Salem, having had "successful struggles" in desegregating their schools, as Nell said, assisted the Boston boycotters by circulating petitions; the wife of Charles Lenox Remond was one of those who secured signatures in Salem. In several towns white antislavery friends were also active.

This time, while the total number of petitioners was only about 1500, a law prohibiting all distinctions of color and religion in admitting children to Massachusetts public schools easily passed the Know Nothing–controlled house. It passed its third reading with a shout, not more than half-a-dozen voices being heard in opposition. The Know Nothing senate quickly concurred, and the Know Nothing governor signed the bill on April 28, 1855.

Why Nell and his friends were more successful in persuading the legislature to accept desegregation in 1855 than they had been earlier in persuading the school authorities or the courts or the legislature can at least be suggested.

First, the desegregation campaign had been persistent. It had lasted eleven years. One key part of it had been the continuous leadership by the same dedicated men, especially Hilton and Nell. Another key part had been the Smith School boycott, which, though it diminished in its intensity—attendance steadily rising from the low of twenty-five in 1850 to thirty-seven in 1851, forty-four in 1852, fifty-one in 1853, and fifty-four in 1854—nevertheless survived; even in 1854 the boycott kept attendance to almost half what it had been before the boycott started. The boycott, by requiring personal sacrifices of participants over a long period of time, as it often did, inevitably helped to make clear to concerned observers the depth of Negro feeling on segregation and to unite those who participated into a loyal group.

Second, the campaign was comprehensive. It drew blacks into three forms of boycott: refusing to send children to segregated schools, refusing to recommend teachers for appointment to such schools, and moving out of Boston to avoid paying taxes for such schools. It drew blacks and whites into two court suits and seven petition sallies. It drew them into meetings for information, encouragement, policy decisions, and entertainment; into money raising, negotiations, testifying at hearings, publicity, and lobbying.

Third, the party that had swept into overwhelming control of the legislature in the fall of 1854, the nominally anti-immigration Know Nothing party, was, in Massachusetts at least, anti-aristocratic and antislavery. The *Liberator* praised the new legislature for being composed to an unusual degree of the common people—mechanics, farmers, and laborers. It was honest and progressive, the *Liberator* said, and by enacting a state personal liberty law to counteract the federal fugitive slave law, it had put resistance to the slave power first. United States Senator Charles Sumner and most other former Free Soil party supporters—including many Boston Negroes such as Nell —cooperated with the Know Nothing party, though Sumner himself, like the Garrisonians, was uncomfortable with its nativist features. Because Sumner was a senator and was friendly to the Know Nothings, Nell believed that Sumner's earlier argument for desegregation before the state supreme court in the Roberts case had a "potent" effect on the legislature.

Fourth, if the Know Nothings were likely to tolerate any minority group, they were more likely to tolerate the small, Protestant, Negro minority, whose numbers were not noticeably growing in relation to native whites, rather than the rapidly growing Catholic Irish, who by this time were the majority of Boston's population. For the mildly anti-immigration Know Nothings, their natural enemies were the Catholic pro-slavery Irish, who in turn were the natural enemies of the Negroes who competed with them for menial jobs. A Catholic weekly, the Boston *Pilot*, said that the Know Nothings "in their ignorance" (a play on words) probably intended the desegregation law "as an insult" to the large number of Catholics in the public schools.[14] In the debate in the legislature before the desegregation bill passed, a Boston representative who supported the bill hinted how anti-Irish prejudice affected the issue for him when he said that Negroes living on the outskirts of Boston were forced to go a long distance to Smith School, passing other schools on the way, while white children, including the "dirtiest Irish," were allowed to step from their houses into the nearest school.

Fifth, in 1855, Massachusetts abolitionists were stronger than ever. They had just been bolstered by the popular reaction against the federal government's arrogant display of military power in Boston to ensure the return to slavery of the pathetic fugitive slave Anthony Burns.

After the school desegregation law was passed, Nell helped to prepare for the day in September, 1855, when all Boston schools would be open to Negroes.

Boston officials had arranged to keep the Negro schools open for Negroes if they wished to attend them, as Nantucket officials had also arranged when all its schools were first opened to Negroes. But Nell and his friends wanted all the Boston Negro schools closed.

They made strenuous efforts to strengthen their boycott against Smith Grammar School—in fact by June they had succeeded in reducing its attendance from fifty-four in the previous spring to twenty-eight; they hoped that by school opening day in September so few children would be attending any of the Negro schools that school officials would feel obliged to close them all permanently.

As opening day approached, Nell helped to arrange for the smooth entry of the Negro children into formerly all-white schools. With Negro mothers, Nell visited teachers and school committeemen. School authorities, Nell said, cooperated excellently in preparing for the transition. In a meeting with Negro parents, Nell urged them to have their children arrive on time at the new schools, be well dressed and ready to work hard.

The day before the schools were to open, Nell saw a Negro boy walking by Smith School. Raising his hands, the boy exclaimed to his friends: "Good-bye forever, colored school! Tomorrow we are like other Boston boys!"

On the first days of school, residents on Beacon Hill and elsewhere were at their windows watching the Negro children walk through strange streets on their way to strange schools. At one school, reported the Boston *Transcript*, one or two white boys made sport of the new black pupils until the principal quietly asked, "Is that your politeness to strangers?" There was no serious trouble in any part of the city. Soon the Negro desegregation leaders were satisfied that white children were accepting Negro children, and Boston school officials agreed. But the South Boston *Gazette* was contemptuous: some Boston schools now look like puddings with here and there a dark huckleberry in them, it reported. And the Catholic Boston *Pilot* was doubtful that integration would succeed in the long run: mixing the children will test the capacity of blacks to learn in comparison with whites, it said, and blacks may want to return to their separate schools.

Of more immediate concern to Nell was how many children were still attending Negro schools. On the first day not one pupil attended Smith Grammar School; on the second day two appeared, and only slightly larger numbers attended the other Negro primary schools. The boycott had reached its most effective point ever, and the boycotters were delighted. Within a few days the Boston School Committee, believing that the small attendance made keeping the Negro schools open inefficient, had decided to close them all and use the space for new integrated schools.[15] The boycott had proved decisive in the last stage of the desegregation campaign.

Afterward, looking back at the last few months of the boycott, the combative Negro lawyer Morris described them in words that the more restrained Nell would not have used: "We decided on a desperate step," Morris told a Negro state convention, "but it turned out to be a successful one. We went round to every [Negro] parent in the city, and had all the children removed from the caste schools; we made all our people take their children away, and in six months we had it all our own way—and that's the way we always should act. Let us be bold, and they'll have to yield to us." Morris' frank espousal of coercion—whether of Negro parents or of Boston school authorities —was not typical of the school boycott leadership; Morris was not a Garrisonian and was not nonviolent.[16]

In December, 1855, desegregationists held a victory celebration in honor of Nell. Hilton presided. Garrison said that Nell had been indefatigable. Phillips said, if Nell "had not been the nucleus, there would have been no cause." Children presented Nell with flowers; adults presented him a watch.

Nell reviewed the long campaign. When some of us became lukewarm and we were "betrayed by traitors within and beset by foes from without," Nell said, "the women kept the flame alive." He insisted on covering "with the charity of our silence, the names of all who have opposed us." Since the opening of all schools to black pupils, Nell said, despite predictions no star had shot madly from its course, and Faneuil Hall was still standing firm. Garrison claimed that the Boston school victory had been achieved, as were all reform victories, by individual action. All great reform, he said romantically, "begins in the heart of a solitary individual; humble men and humble women, unknown in the community, without means, without power, without station, but perceiving the thing that ought to be done, loving the right above all things, and having faith in the triumph of what is just and true, engage in the work, and by and by, the little leaven leavens the whole lump; and this is the way the world is to be redeemed." And he concluded with naïve but moving faith, "It is impossible to do a right act, and be defeated."

More realistically, the Negro Remond declared that the school victory took "self-sacrifice," "drudgery," and "consistency" on the part of Negroes. But this victory also showed that Negroes needed whites, he said. As the *Liberator* reported it, Remond "had no sympathy with the plea that was now made by some, that the colored people should take their cause into their own hands. He held that the antislavery cause was as much the cause of the white man as of the colored man, for the moment a white man becomes thoroughly identified with the cause, he was subjected to the same odium and the same insults as the colored man."

None of the speakers at the celebration followed Morris in glorying in the coercion they had helped to wield during the campaign.[17]

In the years that followed, the number of Negroes attending Boston schools went up markedly, suggesting the continued workability of integration, and elsewhere in the nation abolitionists took note of the Boston victory. In Rhode Island abolitionists who were petitioning to open all that state's schools to Negroes quoted extensively from Nell and Boston school officials on the harmony in their interracial schools. The Negro national convention, meeting in Philadelphia, rejoiced over the Boston victory; with a number of experienced school boycotters present, including Nell from Boston, Frederick Douglass from Rochester, and Robert Purvis from Byberry, Pennsylvania, the convention resolved that schools, "when open to every class," were "the greatest leveller of all species of prejudice." In New York City, Negro pastor Charles B. Ray, speaking as president of the New York Society for the Promotion of Education Among Colored Children, said that, with the example of Boston before them, they believed "there is no sound reason why colored children shall be excluded from any of the common schools supported by taxes levied alike on whites and blacks."[18] But, while a few small cities desegregated their schools before the Civil War, Boston was the first and only major city in the nation to do so.

The school boycott method was a Garrisonian contribution to nonviolent direct action methods and particularly a Negro Garrisonian contribution. While Quaker and Tappanite abolitionists contributed to improving Negro educational opportunity by other methods—the Quakers particularly through their creation of separate private schools for Negroes and the Tappanites particularly through their creation of interracial private schools—the Garrisonians contributed particularly through their desegregation of public schools by means of the boycott.

PART III

Direct Action Against Slavery

Our measures "shall be . . . the abolition of slavery by the spirit of repentance."
—William Lloyd Garrison in the *Declaration of Sentiments*, 1833

12. Boycotting Slave Produce

◇◇◇◇◇◇◇◇◇◇◇

IN THE STRUGGLE to end slavery, one of the nonviolent methods abolitionists tried was the boycott of slave-produced goods. Though historians have often neglected the boycott, in the 1830's nearly all abolitionists endorsed this direct action, and for many years some outstanding abolitionists practiced it at considerable sacrifice to themselves.

There was already an American tradition for such a boycott. Just before the American Revolution, the New Jersey Quaker tailor John Woolman, in a lonely, agonizing testimony, abstained from using sugar and other slave-produced foods at a time when few others did so. By soon after the Revolution, not only did many Quakers practice the boycott, but the Pennsylvania Society for Promoting the Abolition of Slavery, of which Benjamin Franklin was first president, also encouraged it.

In Britain, too, there was already a tradition for a boycott of slave produce. About 1800 perhaps as many as 300,000 Britons gave up the use of slave-produced West Indian sugar as part of the successful campaign to persuade Parliament to end the British slave trade. Later, in the campaign to abolish slavery in the British West Indies, 800,000 Englishwomen signed a pledge that they would not use slave-grown sugar; in doing so they produced a drop of a penny per pound in the price of sugar, thus alarming the West Indian slave owners, it was claimed, "more than all the alarm that had been produced by moral and legislative action."[1] Such British precedents were likely to have strong weight for Americans in an age in which they regarded Britain as being pre-eminent in benevolence and reform.

In the United States between 1830 and the Civil War it was especially Quakers who led the boycott of slave produce. The boycott—or preference for free produce, as participants often called it, to emphasize its positive aspect—especially appealed to Quakers as a peaceful way to oppose slavery. The Quaker-led American Free Produce Association called the boycott "one of the most efficient means of peacefully abolishing the system of slavery." The boycott was a suitable method for Quakers, said the zealous Quaker Charles Marriott of Hudson, New York, because it avoided dependence on sword-wielding government, and a New York yearly meeting of Friends praised the boycott as "dignified" and "silent."[2] While none of the regular Quaker yearly meetings required their members to participate in the boycott, they encouraged the boycott as much as they did any other major form of direct action against slavery or discrimination.

Among the Quakers who became prominently identified with the boycott was Garrison's mentor, Benjamin Lundy, who for a time dared to keep a free-produce store in slave-owning Baltimore. Another was the Pennsylvania teacher George W. Taylor who, not knowing where to obtain free-labor produce, for years wore linen instead of cotton and simply went without sugar, rice, and coffee; later he was to operate a free-produce wholesale house in Philadelphia. Still another was Lucretia Mott, the women's rights advocate whose Philadelphia home Garrison often visited. She tried to persuade those who would listen to her that opposing slavery but buying the products of slave labor was like opposing theft but buying from the thief what he had stolen, and Lucretia Mott was an effective persuader. Her eyes were brilliant, her erectness regal. What little she said was so clear and wise that people instinctively felt her authority.

In addition to the Quakers, in the 1830's large numbers of other abolitionists endorsed the boycott. The American Antislavery Society endorsed it at its founding in 1833 and did so repeatedly during the 1830's.

Garrison was already supporting the boycott by 1829 when he was helping Lundy edit his paper in Baltimore. After Garrison moved to Boston and created the *Liberator*, its columns often advertised free-labor produce and its office kept on hand samples of free produce that could be ordered from Philadelphia. Garrison warmly urged support of the boycott. "In no other way can our example or influence be exerted so beneficially," he wrote in 1831. When Garrison was married in 1834 and set up housekeeping, he made a point of stocking up with free produce, including half a barrel of rice, half a barrel of brown sugar, and a barrel of molasses. In 1836, when a free-produce store opened in Boston, the *Liberator* urged that the "enterprise be well sustained."[3]

Among Tappanites, in Ohio in 1835, Theodore Weld signed an endorsement of the boycott and soon afterward said that he had already been practicing it for years. In 1836, Lewis Tappan asked Gerrit Smith to lead in creating an association pledged to "total abstinence from the products of slave labor." In 1838, William Goodell, the editor of the New York State Antislavery Society's paper, wrote that he was practicing the boycott and believed it possible that it possessed "powers of vast energy." When the Tappanites split off from the American Antislavery Society in 1840, their new American and Foreign Antislavery Society endorsed the boycott in its constitution; by that time Lewis Tappan had been boycotting slave-grown sugar for years.[4]

Negro abolitionist leaders also often supported the boycott. In 1830, Bishop Richard Allen of the African Methodist Episcopal Church helped to form a Philadelphia association that pledged its members to buy only from merchants who refused to sell slave produce. In the 1830's both the Negro national convention movement and Whipper's Moral Reform Society repeatedly endorsed the boycott, and in 1834, Whipper opened a free-produce store of his own in Philadelphia.[5]

Scattered over the North were opponents of slavery who insisted on shopping for free-labor produce when they could. At a bakery in Bordentown, New Jersey, they bought cakes baked from free-labor-produced sugar. At a shop in Philadelphia, they could buy free-labor-produced boots and shoes. In New York City, two hundred abolitionists regularly bought free produce from a grocer who delivered to them within five miles without charge. In a free-labor grocery in Greensboro, Indiana, they bought Santo Domingo coffee and Sandwich Islands molasses. Here and there in free-produce dry-goods stores abolitionists shopped for ginghams, flannels, or calicoes —in 1850 there were more than sixty different patterns of free-labor-produced yard goods available in the United States. From free-produce wholesalers in Philadelphia, New York, and Cincinnati, abolitionists ordered rice, towels, sheeting, stockings, oil cloth, and lamp wick.

At home abolitionists might make candy from Northern-grown maple syrup instead of Southern-grown cane sugar. If they were smokers (although Tappan claimed that abolitionists usually were not), they might insist on smoking cigars made from Northern-grown tobacco.

At an antislavery meeting in Hingham, Massachusetts, ladies set one of the refreshment tables with free-labor food. At an antislavery meeting in Kennet, Pennsylvania, it was announced that the refreshment stand was selling ice cream made from free-labor produce, and a crowd gathered around to discuss the boycott. In New York City the ladies of the Reverend T. S. Wright's Negro congregation held a fair to raise funds and promised that the refreshments would be the products of free labor.

In upstate New York the teen-age daughter of the ardent boycotter Gerrit Smith was once at her aunt's house helping to bake a cake from slave-produced sugar. By accident getting a little of the abhorred sugar on her fingers, the girl unconsciously licked it. Suddenly she realized what she was doing and spat it out.

When Negro nonviolent abolitionist leader William Whipper was married in 1836 in his home town of Columbia, Pennsylvania, his wedding cake was made of free sugar; afterward a letter to the *Liberator* urged abolitionists to follow this precedent by using free produce at all their weddings, parties, and festivals. When the two abolitionist lecturers, the Garrisonian-Quaker, Angelina Grimké, and the Tappanite Theodore Weld, were married in 1838 in Philadelphia, they followed the Whipper precedent by celebrating with a cake made from free sugar, and in setting up their new household in New Jersey, Angelina insisted on their having a mattress made without the usual slave-grown cotton ticking.

To encourage young people to support the boycott, Lucretia Mott helped offer prizes for the best couplets written about free produce, and 150 couplets were submitted. One of them read:

> *Take this, my friend, you need not fear to eat,*
> *No slave hath toiled to cultivate the sweet.*

Lucretia Mott pushed the boycott further than most boycotters did. She insisted that the paper on which she wrote her letters be the product of free labor. She even carried in her pocket a little bag of free-labor sugar so that wherever she went she could sweeten her tea, knowing that she was not thereby supporting slavery.[6]

Abolitionists differed on what their main purpose in boycotting slave produce was. Their positions ranged from the unworldly belief that the boycott was primarily a means for abolitionists to purify themselves individually from cooperation with the sin of slavery to the frank avowal that the boycott was the wielding of economic power to compel the slave owners to free their slaves.

For such major abolitionists as Garrison, Lucretia Mott, and Gerrit Smith, the purpose of the boycott was essentially to purify themselves from cooperation with the sin of slavery; for them, if the boycott was to perform the secondary function of affecting the slave owners, it would be more nearly by hurting the planters' consciences than their purses. Smith wrote in 1836 that he had long believed that there was nothing "which abolitionists could do, that would contribute so far to the abolition of slavery, as their abstinence from the products of slave labor. Let 100,000 men and women in this nation avow and adhere to their noble determination never to pollute their lips or their persons with that which is wet with the tears and stained with the blood of the 'innocents,' and I believe, that the testimony of such self-denial would carry more conviction to the minds of slaveholders of the truth and power of antislavery doctrines and of the sincerity with which they are held, than all the testimony of types and pens."[7]

Those who supported the boycott for such reasons were likely to be uneasy at the idea that the boycott was economic coercion of slave owners. After all, the main object of abolitionists in the 1830's, as they often thought of it, was to bring all who supported slavery to repentance. Abolitionists who had little taste for using law to coerce slave owners to end slavery, including many Quakers, Garrisonians, and Tappanites, were not likely to think that using a boycott to coerce them was much better. Some of them did not choose to recognize that they were wielding coercive power in their boycott of slave produce any more than they usually did in such other direct actions as ride-ins, speak-ins, sit-ins, boycotts of transportation, or boycotts of schools. Garrison wrote in 1835 that encouraging free produce in order to make slavery unprofitable was not his purpose; his purpose was to persuade everyone that slavery was a sin. About the same time the Tappanite Elizur Wright, editor of the American Antislavery Society's quarterly, said that if the abolitionists forced the slave owners to abolish slavery by making it unprofitable, that would mean planters would not have repented, and any apparent reformation would be more nominal than real. Lewis Tappan, writing about the boycott of slave produce as late as 1853, declared that to abolish slavery, abolitionists believed that "agencies of a moral and religious nature" were "chiefly to be relied upon" rather than "agencies of an economical and commercial character."[8] Yet Garrison, Wright, and Tappan all favored the boycott at the time they made these statements.

In reply, a substantial minority of boycotters—particularly Quakers or Tappanites—defended the boycott's economic coercion. Philadelphia Quaker Lewis C. Gunn did so apologetically. The boycott's economic coercion, he said, was just an unavoidable consequence of the moral act of refusing to buy slave produce. Anyway, Gunn explained, the economic coercion would just remove the slave owners' opportunity to make money out of slavery; with that gone, "moral means" would have a better chance to "convert" the masters. More boldly, Quaker Lundy argued that no reform had ever been accomplished merely by appeals to conscience. Reformers, he said, should seek the aid of all groups of the population, including those who act from ignoble economic motives; so abolitionists were justified in using free produce to compete with slave produce to induce masters to free their slaves for selfish reasons. Charles Stuart, a former British army officer who had settled as a teacher in upstate New York and was close to Tappanites, carried Lundy's argument further. Would abolitionists insist on leaving slaves to "perish" under slavery until their masters repented? That would be like letting their neighbor's house burn until they could persuade those who had set it on fire to be sorry for having done so, said Stuart. He favored destroying slavery by the economic power of the boycott if possible and persuading the slave owners to repent later. Like Stuart, Tappanite editor Cornish of the *Colored American* seemed to have no qualms about using economic coercion to destroy slavery. Cornish believed in 1838 that there was a good chance that Britain would support the abolitionist boycott of slave produce by prohibiting the importation of slave produce into its empire, which, he believed, would kill American slavery. "Nothing short of some measure of the kind will ever reach the hearts of many of our 'slaveholding patriots,'" declared Cornish. "The strong arm of coercion, of some kind, is needed to awaken them to duty."[9]

Taking a middle position, Angelina Grimké Weld accepted the

two major purposes of the boycott, believing they were not inconsistent with each other. The boycott's purposes were both to clear the individual of participation in slavery, Angelina said in 1841—at a time when as a result of her marriage to Weld she was less in the Garrisonian-Quaker orbit and more in the Tappanite orbit—and also to "compel" the slaveholder to free his slaves.

More characteristic of the boycotters was the middle position of the *Nonslaveholder*, a Quaker monthly founded to support the boycott and edited by the free-produce wholesaler George W. Taylor, among others. The *Nonslaveholder* combined a frank acceptence of the boycott as self-purification with only a grudging acceptance of it as an economic force. It avoided frankly calling the boycott an economic weapon against slavery. Instead it claimed that the boycott, by creating a market for free-labor-produced goods, "offers a bounty to the tens of thousands of non-slaveholders at the South to keep heart and hand clear of the unholy system. It will thus raise up and maintain, in the midst of the cotton and sugar plantation and rice swamp, a body of practical abolitionists, such as we firmly believe no other antislavery instrumentality can effect."[10] In this way, the *Nonslaveholder*, in keeping with Quaker tradition, chose to emphasize the boycott's positive economic assistance to the free laborer rather than its negative economic damage to the slave owner. Like most nonviolent abolitionists, the *Nonslaveholder* was inclined to shy away from the idea of wielding naked economic power.

Because abolitionists participated in the boycott more to purify themselves than to coerce the slave owners, they did not spend much effort in trying to make the boycott coerce slave owners more efficiently. If they had, perhaps they would have discovered that a more selective boycott would have had a better chance to coerce slave owners than the general boycott had. A boycott limited to one slave product such as sugar—a product for which substitutes were fairly accessible—would probably not have been as inconvenient and costly as the general boycott of all slave produce. A boycott of one slave product would have been directed not against large numbers of people who were likely to be united by attack, but against limited numbers who were therefore vulnerable. Also a boycott for one specific objective—such as the easily understood, modest objective of securing slaves the legal right to marry—would probably have had more chance to succeed than a boycott with the revolutionary objective of destroying the whole slave system. If a boycott had been limited to the one product, sugar, and to the one objective of securing slaves the legal right to marry, it might have had a substantial impact, such as the British boycott of sugar had with the limited objective of ending the British slave trade. If a boycott of one kind of slave produce for one limited objective had succeeded, another could have been tried.

But it would have been hard to persuade those who boycotted slave produce largely to purify themselves from contact with the slave system to boycott one tainted produce while continuing to buy others. Though few in numbers, the faithful continued to value the consistency of their general boycott, and instead of looking for ways to limit it, often looked for ways to extend it.

One way in which abolitionists tried to extend the boycott was by undertaking to do the obverse of what the boycott tried to do, that is, deliberately encouraging the production of free-labor produce.

Free-produce societies and stores encouraged the production of free produce by calling for it in the press, by sending out agents to buy it even in the South, and sometimes by deliberately offering higher than market prices for it.

Early in the 1830's, Benjamin Lundy persuaded the Colored Free Produce Society of Pennsylvania to contribute funds toward a premium for free-labor-grown rice. Later in the 1830's the New England Antislavery Convention created a committee to inquire into the expediency of the American Antislavery Society's offering a bounty for all rice, cotton, sugar, and molasses for which satisfactory evidence could be given that they had been produced by free labor, and one of the Lane Rebels, Jonathan Blanchard, proposed that abolitionists petition state legislatures to give a bounty to manufacturers if they only used free produce as raw materials. In 1841, to stimulate more free-labor production in the South, the American Free Produce Association offered a cent a pound above the market price for Southern free-labor-grown cotton.

Abolitionists also encouraged experiments to develop new free-labor products as substitutes for slave products—even abolitionists who did not necessarily support the consumers' boycott did so. For example, abolitionists pushed for the growing of sugar beets and sorghum as substitutes for slave-grown sugar cane and the growing of flax and silk as substitutes for slave-grown cotton.

Abolitionists were particularly enthusiastic about sugar beets. As early as 1835 the Negro national convention recommended, with Purvis' encouragement, that since the French had learned how to manufacture sugar from beets, American Negroes should also try learning to do so. By 1836, with the hope of reducing American dependence on slave-grown sugar, Quaker George W. Taylor was collecting funds to assist a group of Philadelphia businessmen in securing advice on how to grow beets and extract sugar from them. Also in 1836 the Garrisonian David Lee Child, with abolitionist blessing, sailed to France to study beet sugar production. In 1837 the Ohio Antislavery Society recommended that abolitionists promote the planting of sugar beets as a substitute for slave-grown sugar cane. Soon afterward Child was raising sugar beets in Northampton, Massachusetts, and the abolitionist community at Oberlin, Ohio, was doing the same. But such experiments usually failed to make a profit. In the 1850's the *Friends Review* was admitting that growing sugar beets was not yet very successful and was increasingly turning its hopes to sorghum, which in fact already produced usuable molasses in quantity.[11] But growing either beets or sorghum as a substitute for cane sugar did not become profitable in the United States on a large scale until after the Civil War.

Abolitionists also encouraged free labor to grow more cotton. Quaker Lundy in the 1820's led groups of emancipated American slaves to settle in Haiti with the hope of developing it as a center of production of free-labor cotton to compete with slave-labor cotton. About 1835, Lundy was promoting the creation of an interracial colony in Texas for a similar purpose; David and Lydia Maria Child decided to join the colony, but violence in Texas prevented its settlement. Abolitionists pushed hard to encourage Britain to increase the production of free-labor cotton in India so that Britain—which bought most of the American cotton crop—could reduce her American purchases. For a time the abolitionists had soaring hopes in this regard. In 1841, Wendell Phillips reported that the increase in Indian cotton production indicated that even in a short time Southern American cotton might be driven from the markets of the world, and then there would be hope for the emancipation of the slaves.[12] By the late 1840's, Indian cotton production was still rising, and even though its quality was not comparable to that of American cotton, abolitionists continued to be hopeful that Indian cotton would be a mighty instrument to destroy American slavery.

In the later years of the abolitionist period, free-produce agents continued to tour the South, looking for free-grown cotton to buy. William Whipper urged American Negro colonists in Africa to grow cotton; the Tappanite American Missionary Association expressed its pleasure at any news that the English were importing cotton from Africa rather than the United States; and the *Friends Review* pushed for growing more cotton in Africa, Hawaii, Mexico, and the West Indies. But in fact not enough free cotton, sugar, rice, or any substitutes for them were grown in the United States or anywhere else to compete on a large scale with American slave produce. Abolitionists were grievously disappointed.

Abolitionists also pushed for extending the boycott idea in other ways. Some of them tried to extend the boycott of slave produce beyond the usual consumer level. A New York yearly meeting of Friends advised manufacturers not to use slave produce. The Grimké sisters urged that merchants not take mortgages on slaves. A Philadelphia yearly meeting warned its members broadly that they should "be willing to forego every prospect of gain" from the "diversified and widely spread channels of commerce and business" between North and South if it blunted their "sensibilities to the cruelties of slavery." More directly, the Negro pastor, Dr. Pennington, urged Northern merchants to cut off their connections with the South.[13]

The head of the Hopedale community, Adin Ballou, while not supporting the consumer boycott of slave produce, favored Northerners ostracizing slaveholders and the South at large. "O for that day," he said at an abolitionist gathering, "when a man shall feel insulted at the bare offer of a political power by slaveholding hands; at the suggestion of going down South to seek a fortune; at the mere idea of making money out of Southern prodigality; at the idea of marrying a slaveholder, or a slaveholder's son or daughter. . . at the idea of being a lawyer, a planter, a familiar associate, consenting in any way to live out of, or tolerate slavery."

Ballou's call to ostracize slaveholders was echoed in a song written by Whittier and sung at antislavery meetings. It told the story of a simple Yankee girl who lived in a "low cottage" and did her own work. When a proud Southern planter wooed her, he urged her to come south with him and let his slaves do her work, but the girl rejected the planter scornfully:

> *Go back, haughty Southern! Thy treasures of gold*
> *Are dim with the blood of the hearts thou hast sold!*
> *Thy home may be lovely, but round it I hear*
> *The crack of the whip and the footsteps of fear!*[14]

John Woolman, the eighteenth-century New Jersey Quaker who boycotted slave produce, had set a precedent for the social ostracism of slave owners. After preaching against slavery in a Pennsylvania Friends meeting, he was invited to dinner at the home of one of the meeting's weighty members. At the home, as soon as Woolman discovered that the servants were slaves, he quietly left. The next day, the weighty Friend decided that since holding slaves prevented him from entertaining a respected Friend, he would free his slaves.

H. C. Wright proposed a more aggressive ostracism of slaveholders. When Gerrit Smith, one of the most persistent boycotters of slave produce, was elected to Congress, Wright advised him not to associate with slaveholders, including slaveholding congressmen. Make a motion to expel slaveholders from Congress, Wright advised, and if they are not expelled, refuse to associate with the pirates and go home.[15]

But Gerrit Smith did not follow Wright's advice. Smith was accustomed to associating with slaveholders. His father had been a wealthy New York slave owner. Smith himself had married a girl from the slaveholding community of Hagerstown, Maryland, and Smith's brother had moved to the South and become a slaveholder. Instead of boycotting slaveholders in Washington, Smith entertained them in his home at the same time that he continued to boycott slave produce. The independent abolitionist Elihu Burritt praised Smith for entertaining slave-owning congressmen. "I honestly think," Burritt wrote him, "that by your social intercourse with these Southern members, you have produced an impression of inestimable value, which will work for years in the best direction."

Tappanite Daniel Worth, when he arrived in North Carolina as a missionary to antislavery churches, was faced with a choice similar to Smith's. Worth was invited by a wealthy slave owner, an acquaintance of many years earlier, to dine. Worth at first was uncertain what to do. He felt that the man's furniture and house were the products of slave labor and worried that while visiting at the house he might suddenly cry aloud that they were stained with the blood of the slaves.[16] But eventually Worth curbed his feelings and accepted invitations to slaveholders' houses; such invitations, he decided, gave him an opportunity to discuss slavery with the slaveholders.

Another Southern Tappanite, James Birney, decided differently. He refused to visit his sister and her family in Kentucky because they owned slaves, and when his sister proposed to visit him, Birney replied that he did not wish to have anything to do with "oppressors of their fellow human beings." Somewhat like Birney, but milder, was Theodore Weld. While John Tyler of Virginia was President and kept slaves in the White House, Weld attended a reception there but deliberately avoided shaking hands with the President.[17]

A Southerner who proposed a comprehensive Southern boycott of slaveholding was Hinton Helper, one of the usually silent yeoman class of whites in the back country of North Carolina. Not personally sensitive to social injustice, Helper wanted Negroes driven out of the United States and was inclined to violence. He opposed slavery not because it was unjust to Negroes but largely because it was unfair competition for white nonslaveholders who were, in fact, the majority of Southern whites. He proposed that Southerners discourage slavery by a drastic boycott: not hiring slaves from slave owners, not buying from slave-owning merchants, not stopping at hotels served by slaves, not consulting slave-owning lawyers or physicians, not listening to slave-owning ministers preach, and not voting slave owners into office.[18]

The book in which Helper proposed this boycott, *Impending Crisis*, was largely an economic argument against slavery. Soon after it was first published in 1857, the *National Antislavery Standard* was promoting it as the most remarkable book of the age. By 1859 the Pennsylvania Antislavery Society was selling more than three hundred copies a week, and by 1860 leading Republican congressmen were circulating it as an aid to their reelection.

Nonviolent abolitionists responded warmly to Helper's book but not necessarily to its boycott idea. The *Friends Review* published a summary of the book, including the boycott idea, but did not comment on it. C. K. Whipple talked to Helper in 1858 and in the *Liberator* called his book "spirited and vigorous," but did not refer to its boycott proposal. Garrison also talked with Helper and wrote privately that he was "evidently in earnest, and will not quail," but he did not pick up the boycott idea. However, Henry C. Wright did so in a pamphlet in 1860, and pushed the idea by writing Garrison early in 1861 that Helper's boycott proposal represented "in a brief formula the secret of your power, and the weapons of your warfare." It was true that Helper's proposal was much like Garrison's policy of noncooperation with slavery-supporting government and slavery-supporting churches and consistent with the Garrisonian slogan, "no union with slaveholders," but so was the boycott of slave produce, which Garrison had by this time long since rejected, and despite Wright's advice, Garrison still did not push Helper's Southern boy-

cott idea.[19] In fact, few Southerners tried to practice Helper's boycott. Southern officials, usually allied to slave owners, made it a crime
even to possess the book. Most of the nonslaveholding white
majority, little conscious of their own interests, allowed themselves
to be controlled by the slaveholding minority and passively waited
for that minority to lead them to catastrophe.

Abolitionists tried to apply the boycott principle in many other
ways. Joshua B. Smith, the well-known Boston Negro caterer,
refused to serve a banquet to honor Daniel Webster, who had recently helped make it easier for masters to catch their fugitive slaves.
Whipper's American Moral Reform Society voted to boycott the
Philadelphia *Public Ledger* and any other newspaper that carried
slave owners' advertisements for help in recovering runaway slaves.
To raise the status of Negroes, conventions of Negroes in New
England and Michigan urged that they boycott white business, giving preference to Negro businesses instead.[20] As we have already
seen in previous chapters, on occasion abolitionists boycotted segregated schools, churches, and transportation facilities. As we shall see
in later chapters, abolitionists boycotted churches that supported
slavery and urged boycotts of voting, office holding, or taking oaths
to support any government that cooperated with slavery; some even
urged refusing to fight or pay taxes for such a government. Abolitionists developed the boycott idea in many ways, with imagination, but
their most widely endorsed, concerted, and sustained boycott was
their boycott of slave produce.

While abolitionists frequently endorsed the boycott of slave produce—especially in the 1830's—they were not united in practicing it.

Many abolitionist families did not practice the boycott, and the
American Free Produce Association scolded them. Consider a
family well known for its interest in benevolent enterprises, said the
Association. "They are clad in the finest of Georgia cotton. The
pudding from which they have just dined is made of the best rice
from our Carolina swamps—sweetened with Louisiana sugar. . . .
The father is solacing himself with the aromatic fumes of a Havana
cigar. That man is an abolitionist, and in his own belief a consistent
one. . . . Yet we hesitate not to say, he is as truly giving his support
to slavery, as the planter who wields the lash, or the trader who first
steals the victim."[21]

Abolitionists gave many reasons for not supporting the boycott,
and some of them were flimsy. Certain abolitionists said the boycott

would deprive Northerners of income that produced money for the antislavery cause, or that to destroy slavery they needed the goodwill of Northern cotton manufacturers who used slave-produced cotton. Others said that if the boycott was successful, it would hurt not only the slave owners but also inevitably their slaves. Still others doubted that some of the goods sold as free produce actually were free produce, or argued that the vaunted "self-denial" of the boycott was a sham if it meant buying more luxurious produce like silk in place of slave-grown cotton, or that most of the value of cotton cloth was contributed not by slave labor but by free labor in the process of manufacturing and distribution.

A more substantial reason for abolitionists not to support the boycott was the inconvenience of locating free products. To many abolitionists free products were simply not available when and where they needed them; many abolitionists lived where they could buy certain free products only by mail. In Boston one abolitionist reported in 1834 that he had looked for free-labor-grown sugar in more than forty stores before finding it. In addition, customers often found the quality of free products poor and the supply uncertain. An Ohio retailer complained that free cotton cloth was "coarser, less durable, and more faidy" than the usual cotton cloth. Even enthusiastic promoters of the boycott admitted that "free umbrellas were hideous to look upon; and free candies, an abomination." Free-produce wholesaler Taylor made strenuous efforts to locate high quality free produce in various parts of the world, but found himself constantly vexed by misunderstandings, inadequate supplies, and delays in shipments, and Taylor was well aware that when his customers found he did not have on hand what they wanted, he sometimes lost them for good.[22]

Still more serious was that the prices of free produce tended to be high; this, said the Free Produce Association of the Ohio Friends Yearly Meeting, was the major reason that few abolitionists boycotted slave produce. Prices were high because not enough capital was invested in free produce and also because the demand for it was not large enough to make handling it economical. In addition, prices were high because of extra costs. For example, there was the extra cost of importing free produce from abroad and paying import duties. In the case of cotton, there was often the extra cost of locating free-grown cotton in the South and keeping it separated from the slave-grown cotton while it was being processed both in Southern gins and Northern mills—mills were reluctant to clear their machines of slave-grown cotton when putting through a run of free-grown cotton.

The Philadelphia Free Produce Association of Friends attempted to reduce prices by commissioning George Taylor to operate a mill in nearby Chester County which handled only free-labor-grown cotton. The mill supplied cloth to Taylor's wholesale house in Philadelphia, which in turn supplied goods to boycotters all over the country. Taylor said in 1859 that he sold a portion of his free produce at the same prices at which slave produce sold on the regular market and that if his patronage were doubled, his prices in general could be as low as those for slave produce. But as it was, Taylor lost money.[23]

By the 1840's the reason many Garrisonians emphasized for their opposition to the boycott was not so much inconvenience or high prices—these were sacrifices that abolitionists should be willing to take on themselves for the cause—as the virtual impossibility of boycotting all slave produce. At an antislavery convention in Syracuse, when a Mr. Pool proposed that abolitionists "pledge to abstain from the production of slave labor," Garrison, Foster, and Abby Kelley objected, "because," the *Liberator* reported them saying, "it would be impossible, unless we should withdraw entirely from the social community." Mr. Pool countered by saying abolitionists could live "on a peck of corn per week" as the slaves did, but the meeting was not willing to advocate such an extreme and turned down Pool's pledge. Garrison had doubtless forgotten that in 1829 in Lundy's paper he himself had argued for just such absolute abstention from slave produce—even if abolitionists had to subsist on roots, he had said, and go half clad and shut down every cotton factory in the country.[24]

Abolitionists had long been aware of the difficulty of complete consistency in avoiding slave produce. Quaker Elias Hicks had once brought into a New York City free-produce store one of his pamphlets opposing the use of slave products, and offered it to the store proprietor. Being something of a wag, the proprietor accepted the pamphlet by taking it up with a pair of tongs and then dropped it into an open fire. "Friend Hicks," he said roguishly, "I can't defile my store with slavery-cursed paper." The truth was that abolitionist literature was often printed on paper made from slave-produced cotton.

The problem of consistency in abstaining from slave produce was aired in the *Liberator* in the 1830's. Judge William Jay, the New York Tappanite, called attention to the embarrassing fact that the *Liberator* itself was printed on paper made from slave-grown cotton. A sharp letter writer argued that if, as boycotters said, it was not proper to use anything that was stolen or produced by stolen labor, then Arthur Tappan should stop selling silks to southern slave masters because he was accepting in payment money that they had stolen from slaves; moreover, it was not even proper to eat anything grown in the American soil because it was stolen from the Indians.[25]

At Oberlin College in the 1830's, after a group of students had voted not to use the products of slave labor except in cases of absolute necessity, one of the students discovered that the sheets on his bed were cotton. He told the family of the house where he was staying that it was contrary to his principles to use cloth that he suspected was polluted with the blood of the slaves. Since no other sheets were available, that night the student slept on a carpet on the floor of his room. In the morning when he boasted how he had carried out his principles, the family told him that the carpet was half cotton, and fellow students laughed at his chagrin.

Garrison explained in the *Liberator* in 1847 tht the impossibility of avoiding the use of all slave produce was a factor in his having come to oppose the boycott, as he said his associates the Phillipses, Quincys, Fosters, Pillsburys, and Jacksons had also. The boycott was a waste of time, Garrison said, though he respected the scruples of those who practiced it. The boycott "has the form of abolitionism but without the power," he said, as the failure of the slaveholders to get excited about it suggested. "We have too many practical measures to carry forward—measures which are causing the slave system to tremble to its foundations—to be willing to have our . . . attention . . . diverted to one of at least such doubtful and inferior character." Anyway, he said, the slave economy was so inextricably mixed with that of the rest of the country that abolitionists could not reject all connection with it.[26] Garrison and a good many of his associates, with their habit of thinking in absolute terms, felt that they should either support a total boycott—which was virtually impossible—or none.

Adin Ballou agreed with Garrison, saying, we can properly buy cloth made from slave grown cotton if we make good use of it; but if to avoid buying slave-grown cotton, we buy wool from a Liverpool merchant who then uses our money to buy cotton from Southern slave owners, indirectly we are helping the slave owners anyway.

A few plucky Garrisonians took issue with the weighty New England Garrisonians for such opposition to the boycott. If the use of slave produce was "unavoidable," then it was not "a violation of principle" to use it, a Garrisonian youth convention in Ohio decided; but "our decided preference should be given to the products of free labor whenever and wherever practicable; and to refuse to do so, under such circumstances, does, in our opinion, countenance and sustain the slave power."

Similarly, Lucretia Mott gently replied to Garrison's argument at an annual meeting of the American Antislavery Society in New York. Abolitionists, she said, are beginning to see "that they must despise the gain of oppression, and deny themselves . . . blood-bought sweets and . . . blood-stained cotton." They feel, she continued in a small, clear voice, which Douglass said so completely riveted attention that she was heard throughout the hall, "that they are called upon not to be partakers of other men's sins . . . except so far as in the general admixture of things, they are necessarily involved. . . . Let them be faithful to their trust, so shall their work be blest."[27]

Altogether through the thirty years of the abolitionist period before the Civil War most abolitionists did not regularly participate in the boycott of slave produce.

Friends persisted in their support of the boycott more than Garrisonians or Tappanites did. In the late 1840's or early 1850,'s four Friends' boarding schools in the East were regularly supplied with free-labor groceries, and a New England yearly meeting called attention to ten localities in its area where free-labor dry goods and groceries could be bought. The Indiana Yearly Meeting of Antislavery Friends, a splinter group, made participation in the boycott a required article of discipline, though it found enforcement difficult. Regular Friends meetings, in the cautious language of Friends, usually were still expressing concern about the use of slave products without pushing it too hard. An Ohio yearly meeting "was not prepared to take any action" on the boycott, but "Friends were encouraged to attend to their individual convictions of duty" in regard to it. Similarly, the North Carolina Yearly Meeting, after a year's study, decided that it could not endorse the boycott, "yet Friends were encouraged to attend, in their individual capacity, to what may appear to be required of them."[28]

During two periods Friends made a special effort to draw non-Friends into more participation in the boycott.

The first such period began in 1838 when Friends led in the formation of an organization open to non-Friends, the American Free

Produce Association. The call to the founding convention, held in Philadelphia, appealed to abolitionists to attend, and twenty-three abolitionist societies—especially in Pennsylvania, New Jersey, and Massachusetts—sent representatives. While most of the officers chosen by the new society were Quakers—as they were to continue to be—the convention chose as president the non-Quaker Gerrit Smith and as one of the vice-presidents the non-Quaker Lewis Tappan, and thereafter the association continued to appeal to non-Quakers for support.[29] The Garrisonian Pennsylvania Antislavery Society allowed the Free Produce Association to use part of its office space and allowed its agent, the non-Quaker J. Miller McKim, to serve also as wholesale agent of the Free Produce Association. In addition, the Pennsylvania Antislavery Society's weekly paper published an extraordinary average of two hundred items a year on the boycott in the period 1838–39 and continued to publish a substantial number through 1845. But for the most part Friends found that involving other abolitionists in the boycott was uphill work. A committee of the association complained in 1842 that "abolitionists are so engaged in performing some mightier labor" that "they have not much time to bestow in promoting consistent action among themselves."[30]

By 1844 the American Free Produce Association's sales of free produce—by no means necessarily all the free produce sold in free-produce stores—had risen to nearly eight thousand dollars a year. While this represented an enormous effort by a few hundred abolitionists, it was scarcely large enough to bring significant pressure on slave owners. Quaker boycott leaders were disappointed with the effort to attract non-Quaker support, and they were disturbed by conservative Quaker criticism of their working for the boycott with radical abolitionists outside the Quaker fold. By 1845 some of the Orthodox Quaker boycotters, like George Taylor and Samuel Rhoads, had decided to return to concentrating on developing the boycott among Friends. They organized the Philadelphia Free Produce Association of Friends, which gradually took over the functions of the American Free Produce Association in locating free produce and supervising the manufacture of free cotton into cloth. Under this renewed emphasis on the boycott among Friends, in the years 1845–49, while the nondenominational American Free Produce Association was allowed to die, the boycott reached a high point.

In the period of 1854–56, when the pacifist crusader, non-Quaker Elihu Burritt, developed a new enthusiasm for the boycott, Taylor and other Friends launched their second special effort to draw non-

Friends into participation in the boycott. Taylor merged his Quaker boycott-promoting periodical, the *Nonslaveholder*, with Burritt's paper and helped to form a new non-Friends free-produce organization. But perhaps partly because Burritt lent his help only from the distance of London and partly because increased sectional tensions reduced hope that peaceful methods could abolish slavery, this revival of the boycott, as measured by the formation of free-produce societies and the opening of free-produce stores, by no means lifted the movement back to the 1845–49 high point, and the revival soon faded.

Despite the continued faith of Pennsylvania Garrisonians in the boycott, most Garrisonians in the country as a whole had probably lost faith in the boycott by 1849, when, under Garrison and Foster's leadership, the American Antislavery Society refused to endorse it. Tappanite interest continued longer than the Garrisonian but was not strong. The Tappanite American and Foreign Antislavery Society continued to endorse the boycott as long as the society survived into the 1850's. The Christian Antislavery Convention, held in Cincinnati in 1852 and presided over by the Tappanite John Fee, despite some objections endorsed it, but in the late 1850's the Tappanite magazine, the *American Missionary*, neglected it. Negro grass-roots support, never widespread, also declined. In 1839, Whipper's Moral Reform Society charged that Negro churches were generally silent on the boycott.[31] In the 1840's and 1850's the Negro national convention movement, which once had endorsed the boycott, neglected it, and state Negro conventions rarely endorsed it. While in the late 1840's and the 1850's the black Garrisonian William Wells Brown and the black Tappanite Dr. Pennington were still supporting it and the black Garrisonian poet Frances Watkins became a convert (she was thankful she could pay a little more for a free-produce dress so that she could not see any stain of blood on it), nevertheless the preeminent black leader Frederick Douglass allowed many opportunities to pass without endorsing the boycott.[32]

From the 1820's into the Civil War, Philadelphia remained the great center for the free-produce movement. It was the seat of the state antislavery society which gave the boycott the greatest long-term support, and the seat of the strongest free-produce associations. Available records indicate that the largest number of free-produce societies were in Pennsylvania and Ohio and the largest number of free-produce stores were in Pennsylvania and Indiana, these three being states in which Quakers were numerous.

No doubt largely because of the inconvenience and high cost of buying free-labor produce, those who insisted on buying it over a long period of time were usually only the most conscientious. One student of the subject says conservatively that the number of people "who made some effort to confine their purchases to free labor goods may have reached five or six thousand." But if the *Nonslaveholder* was right in 1847 in saying that 10 percent of the approximately 100,000 Friends in the country participated,[33] that would be about 10,000 Friends alone, and there were surely also thousands of non-Friends who at least occasionally participated.

Faithful boycotters kept admonishing other abolitionists to be more diligent in testifying against slavery by supporting the boycott. Despite the original pledge of the American Antislavery Society to support the boycott, Gerrit Smith grieved in 1855 that only "a small portion" of abolitionists refused to purchase the produce that was "wet with the tears and sweat and blood of the slave." "Female fanatic" Lucretia Mott was still claiming in 1860, after many years of urging antislavery societies to take the boycott more seriously, that a concerted drive for the boycott would destroy slavery.

The boycott of slave produce was a heroic example of symbolic protest and in a noticeably peaceful form. No doubt it helped to sharpen the concerns of those who participated in it and to focus public attention on the inhumanity of slavery, and it did so in a way not as likely to stir emotional hostility as some other abolitionist direct action. But the economic objectives of the boycott were too general, the inconveniences and cost of free produce too great. While abolitionist boycotts directed at limited objectives helped to produce specific gains, the boycott of all slave produce, for the energy expended on it, as Garrison said, produced but slim results. In its too inclusive form, the boycott had not realized its great potential.

When the Civil War began in 1861, a few free-produce stores were still open, including George Taylor's in Philadelphia. At that time Taylor said—probably accurately—that if a majority of the people who thought they were opposed to slavery had abstained from slave produce, war would not have come.[34]

13. Foster Speaks-In

◇◇◇◇◇◇◇◇◇◇◇

ONE SUNDAY MORNING in 1841, a determined young Garrisonian, Stephen S. Foster, entered a Congregational church in Concord, New Hampshire. In a lull in the service he rose and denounced the church for upholding slavery. The pastor asked Foster to stop speaking, but he continued until some of the congregation took him by the arms and led him out. In the afternoon Foster returned to another service and again spoke without permission. This time some of the congregation threw him down the stairs, and he was arrested for disturbing public worship. Like many protesters more than a century later, Foster refused to cooperate with arrest and so had to be lifted into a carriage and into a courtroom.

Later Foster boasted, much as mid-twentieth-century civil righters were likely to boast, of the number of times he had been subjected to violence or jail. Once he said that in a period of fifteen months he had been twice thrown out of second-story windows, twenty-four times dragged out of churches, and four times jailed. Altogether he was to be jailed ten or twelve times.[1] Despite the violence done to him, Foster and all of his team were deliberately nonviolent.

Foster was a New Hampshire farm boy with large gnarled hands. He studied at Dartmouth College, where he was jailed because as a Christian he refused to perform military duties. He also studied at Union Theological Seminary in New York, where, when war with

Britain threatened over the Maine boundary, he was disturbed that its faculty refused him permission to hold a peace meeting. Briefly he had been a Congregational pastor, but he had soon left the church because of its support of war, he explained, and also because its clergy, through their fellowship with slaveholding Southern churchmen, were a "brotherhood of thieves." Calling them thieves was no worse, he maintained, than Jesus calling the clergy of his day "thieves," "blind guides," and "hypocrites."[2]

Foster and his fellow "speak-inners," as they might have been called in the age of Martin Luther King, believed that physical nonretaliation was not only morally correct but a practical device to protect themselves from serious violence. In Derry, New Hampshire, a mob held back the wheels of a carriage in which Foster and Parker Pillsbury—a tough New Hampshire blacksmith and Congregational minister who often toured with Foster—were riding. Afterward Pillsbury reflected that the mob wanted "to provoke us to resistance. Then they would have taken sweet revenge by violence on our persons. . . . We never doubted that our nonresistance principles saved our lives in many a desperate encounter. And in them and their heroic Author we confidingly reposed our trust."

After one of his church "speak-ins," Foster was jailed in Amherst, New Hampshire, because he refused to pay his fine and would not let anyone else pay it for him. "To one as restless as I am, imprisonment is oppressive," he wrote from jail to New Hampshire abolitionist editor Nathaniel Rogers. "But I can endure it patiently for His sake who died for me." He felt that by being in jail he was identifying with the slaves, and he quoted the line of scripture abolitionists often quoted to indicate their identification: "I can now surely 'remember them that are in bonds, as bound with them.' "[3]

Meanwhile, a member of the New Hampshire legislature, reporting that Foster and his friends had interrupted church services in the state "in many instances" and "very much to the annoyance of the citizens of the state," introduced an emergency bill to control the speak-inners, much as Southern legislators in the next century were to do to control sit-inners. Another member supported the bill, saying, if a house of worship can be "invaded" and new practices forced upon its people, then religious liberty is denied. The bill, permitting anyone in a religious meeting to remove anyone else who interrupted it, passed.

Garrison was furious. The motives of the legislature, he wrote editorially, were the same motives that led to establishing the Inquisition. As Garrison interpreted the bill, "If any person, from the purest of motives and for the best purposes, shall venture, in a professedly Christian Assembly, to pray, speak, or prophesy in order, according to primitive or apostolic usage, every ruffian present, whether pious or profane, who may choose . . . to regard it as an 'interruption' of the worship, is duly authorized to spring with the agility and ferocity of a wildcat upon the daring offender, and eject him from 'the house of God.' "[4]

However, though Garrison trusted Foster's religious motivation, he would not necessarily endorse Foster's methods. When Garrison was speaking with Foster in upstate New York, Garrison wrote his wife: Foster "is remarkably successful in raising the spirit of mobocracy wherever he goes. . . . It is useless to reason with him with any hope of altering his course." Editorially Garrison described Foster's team as "undeniably to be ranked among the most faithful and devoted friends of Christian philanthropy and reform in this or any other country," but on their methods he was noncommital.[5] The truth was that the speak-ins were coercive, and Garrison, like many of his colleagues, believed that abolitionists should avoid coercion when they could.

Like Garrison, Phillips admired Foster personally. He called Foster devoted, single-eyed, and eloquent. But Phillips denied Foster's right to impose himself on people who did not wish to hear him. Foster disrupted church meetings, Phillips pointed out, at the same time that he objected to others disrupting abolitionist meetings. Phillips gave an example of what both he and Foster considered indefensible interruption of antislavery meetings. At a meeting when Phillips was speaking, the well-known crank, Abby Folsom, a large, wild-eyed, pitiful woman who was judged by some doctors to be insane, took over the platform from him and began ranting about free speech and women's rights. Phillips, knowing from previous experience that Abby Folsom could rant indefinitely and that the audience couldn't stop her even with hissing, approached her to escort her out. She sank into a chair. Foster came to help Phillips, and together they carried her out on the chair as Abby bellowed her protest. Phillips believed that for either Abby Folsom or Foster to interrupt meetings was unjustified.

Pillsbury admitted many years later that "scarcely any" of the abolitionists agreed with Foster's methods; it was only because he himself so completely trusted Foster's religious devotion that he could accept Foster's methods. "I knew that he was inspired with the very spirit of the Highest," said Pillsbury, "and I could afford to stand by him. I am proud that I did."[6]

To Negro leader Frederick Douglass, Foster "at times seemed . . . needlessly offensive," yet "he was one of the most impressive advocates the cause of the American slave ever had. No white man ever made the black man's cause more completely his own."

The abolitionist poet James Russell Lowell was impressed by Foster's invective. To him, Foster was:

> *A kind of maddened John the Baptist,*
> *To whom the harshest word comes aptest,*
> *Who, struck by stones or brick ill starred,*
> *Hurl's back an epithet as hard,*
> *Which, deadlier than stone or brick,*
> *Has a propensity to stick.*[7]

Foster himself claimed that in speaking in churches with or without permission he was fulfilling Paul's New Testament direction that "all may prophesy one by one." Foster was careful, Pillsbury reported, to speak in a respectful manner. Moreover, according to Pillsbury, Foster and his team never interrupted a worship service unless they had already tried and failed to win a hearing by permission, including attempting to secure the use of the church building to hold their own meetings.[8] However, churches usually declined permission. Although during the ferment of the American Revolution many churches had denounced slavery as a sin, about this time many no longer did so. The official national Methodist policy was that the church had no right to "interfere in the . . . relation between master and slave." The Congregational Association of Massachusetts maintained that abolitionists should not be permitted to speak anywhere in their parishes without the pastor's consent. The Unitarians, who had a tradition of free inquiry, permitted the subject of slavery to be discussed in only two of their many Boston churches. The antislavery New England Yearly Meeting of Friends feared being torn by disputes over slavery; they also feared too much mixing of Friends with the world, and so—like most Friends yearly meetings —they advised the closing of their meetinghouses to abolitionist speakers. Even Massachusetts Negro churches sometimes barred their doors against antislavery meetings.

On a Saturday in June, 1842, Foster led a team to Lynn, Massachusetts. They appealed to the Lynn churches for use of their buildings for antislavery meetings, as they customarily did, but were turned down. On Sunday the team attended a Congregational service during which Foster, without invitation, spoke against slavery until carried out to the sidewalk. There, when he was released, he said, "This then, is your Christianity, is it?"

Soon afterward Foster walked across the common to a Baptist meetinghouse and sat with its congregation till the service was over. Then he began to speak, without invitation. Baptists dragged him outside, where a Baptist youth said, "You ought to be tarred and feathered." "And cowhided," said another.

"Does your gospel run like that, my friends?" replied Foster. "Is it tar your enemies; feather them that hate you; cowhide them that despitefully use you?"

In the afternoon several of Foster's team visited a Lynn Friends meeting which had already been torn over the issue of allowing its members to mix with the non-Friends in working against slavery. One of the team, Thomas P. Beach, who had been a New Hampshire Congregational minister, was the first to break the usual silence of the meeting by speaking on the Friends' apathy to slavery. After he had spoken for ten or fifteen minutes, several elder Friends broke in to say he was interfering with their worship; Beach replied that he understood that speech was free in Friends meetings and proceeded. Thereupon—though it was not the usual time—the elders shook hands, thus signaling the close of the meeting.

As the meeting broke up, William Bassett—who had already been expelled from the Society of Friends for his aggressive antislavery activity and at whose house in Lynn, Foster was staying—called to the members to hear the truth, not flee from it. Brushing aside the piteous pleas of his mother, Bassett poured out his own testimony against slavery which, he said, he had too long pent up.

Foster rose to speak in support of Bassett, when, as one of Foster's team reported, "the older members near the door, dashed forward, and seizing him with great violence, pulled him down from the seat and started with him for the door. . . . But before Foster had been dragged half way to the door, a brave young Friend had reached him, and called out to the furious crowd, 'Hold! You shan't drag this man out!' He was followed by several others, and Foster was rescued and resumed speaking. . . . He cited [Quakers] George Fox and Edward Burroughs . . . [as] authorities for entering any religious assembly, and demanding the right to be heard. . . . The fact was, Beach and Foster had done exactly what the early Friends both did and . . . taught."

As the team summed up their losses for the day, Methodists had dislocated Beach's thumb, Baptists had torn Foster's sleeve, and Quakers had torn Foster's coat collar.[9]

The local Essex County Antislavery Society, unlike most antislavery societies, then moved to endorse Foster and Beach's speak-in method. The president of the society was the disowned Quaker William Bassett, whose antislavery testimony had precipitated the violence in the Lynn Quaker meeting. The treasurer was Quaker James N. Buffum, an aggressive nonviolent actionist. The society adopted a resolution, including an amendment by Foster, "that so long as any portion of our countrymen are held in slavery, it is the right and, so far as practicable, it is the duty of abolitionists, to enter the religious assemblies of all who are concerned in their enslavement, and there demand their immediate release."

Meanwhile a Foster supporter brought legal action against a Lynn resident for kicking Foster. The court ordered Foster to testify in his own behalf, but Foster declined—as many complete nonresistants would—on the ground that this "was not his way of forgiving an injury." So the court fined Foster for refusing to testify and when he declined to pay the fine, briefly jailed him.

Two Lynn area churches—Baptist and Quaker—brought charges against Beach for his speak-ins. Beach was arrested and sentenced to pay a fine, and since he felt conscientiously opposed to paying it or letting his friends pay it, he was jailed in Newburyport for an indefinite time.[10]

On the news that it was churches that were responsible for jailing Beach, the Nonresistance Society condemned the churches as un-Christian. Garrison told *Liberator* readers that Beach had "all the sympathies of our soul." Protest meetings held in Newburyport and nearby towns adopted resolutions honoring Beach, sang abolitionist songs, and collected funds for the relief of his wife and children. In Milford, New Hampshire, abolitionists preparing for a protest meeting cried, "Our liberty, your liberty, every man's liberty is in jail!" In his New Hampshire *Herald of Freedom*, Editor Rogers wrote, "I want Thomas Beach to know that so long as he suffers there [in jail] for antislavery, abolitionists will turn all eyes . . . to him." From the jail Beach wrote an appeal to abolitionists: "I want company here; I wish every jail in Massachusetts and New Hampshire filled."[11] Beach was pleading for protesters to fill the jails much as the Quakers had in seventeenth-century England, as Gandhi and his followers were to do in twentieth-century India, and as Martin Luther King and his followers were to do in twentieth-century America.

At an antislavery meeting in Boston, Quaker Buffum offered a resolution urging petitions to the governor to pardon Beach. Foster opposed—at the time he carried his noncooperation with government to this extreme—but the resolution passed anyway.

A Worcester County antislavery society considered whether Beach had a right to interrupt worship as he did. After a five-hour debate on the question, it side-stepped the issue by agreeing unanimously to condemn the church at large for having imprisoned him.

However, the board of managers of the Massachusetts Antislavery Society, probably under Garrison's influence, met the issue head on. It refused to endorse the speak-in method because it was coercive. We believe, it announced, that Foster and Beach have a right to speak, but there is another natural right, the right to refuse to listen, which also should be respected. "While these views of our own duty in this matter must prevent us from adopting this method [of Foster and Beach] ourselves, we do not presume to prescribe or dictate to others who have arrived at other conclusions, the course that they shall pursue. . . . To the singleheartedness, zeal, and devotion to duty, of the men who have thus proved their sincerity by their sufferings, we bear our most earnest and affectionate testimony."[12]

Editor Rogers defended Foster and Beach more directly. To Rogers—who Whittier said was "the wittiest and shrewdest of New Englanders"—when anyone dragged Foster or Beach out of a church for speaking for the slave, it was as if they had dragged out a slave panting for his freedom. "The runaway slave has a right to come into any house of worship, and thunder the story of his enslavement in the ears of the congregation," Rogers wrote. "I wish to Heaven the next one that passes a northern meetinghouse would do it. I wish he would rush in, in prayer time, and charge his unutterable wrongs and the wrongs of his people, on the hypocritical wretches that are there mocking God and Humanity, with their abominable and vile oblations. . . . See if they would carry on their mockery in his presence! See if they would drag him out!"[13]

While Beach was in jail, he wrote letters that his friends circulated in a little news sheet called "Voice from the Jail." Beach was discovering that jail could be a suitable place for dissenters to write messages to the world, as St. Paul, Gandhi, and Martin Luther King also discovered.

After Beach had been in jail three months, though he still would not pay his fine, he was released. "How soon brother Beach will be dragged out by another Christian (?) mob, remains yet to be seen," wrote the Massachusetts Antislavery Society's general agent Collins, a fellow nonresistant. "One thing is certain, they will not again imprison him. That was a bad investment for the church. It did not pay. The 'Voice from the Jail' reached the ears of too many of the people."

Meanwhile Foster continued his speak-ins. On two Sundays in 1843 he spoke-in at the Cherry Street Friends meeting in Philadelphia. The second time, according to a newspaper account, when Foster began speaking about abolition, "one of the elders from the gallery ordered him to sit down, and the sexton approaching him at the same time, requested him to be silent. He persisted in speaking; and some persons taking sides with him, the congregation rose in a body, and insisted upon his ejectment from the house. He was forcibly put out, and the consequence was a disposition and show of riot in the churchyard. The disturbance, however, was fortunately at once quelled by the appearance and interference" of a policeman. Foster was arrested.

Asked to give bail for his appearance for examination, Foster as usual refused to do so, expecting to be sent to prison. But someone else insisted on giving bail for him. The two-hour examination was "a very exciting one, and the office was perhaps never more crowded on any previous occasion—a large majority of the spectators being Friends."[14]

Other abolitionists followed the example of Foster and Beach by speaking-in.

After Foster was carried out of a church in Nashua, New Hampshire, for speaking without permission, the nonresistant Lewis Ford rose and also without permission asked the congregation "if the course which they had taken with Mr. Foster was in accord with the spirit and example of Christ." Ford, too, was carried out of the church.

Two mechanics of Littleton, New Hampshire, spoke against slavery in church without permission and were imprisoned for sixteen days. "I forgive and pray God to forgive the church and all who sent us here," wrote one of them in jail, and added, "I was never more happy in mind than at present."[15]

While he was traveling with General Agent Wright of the Nonresistance Society, the youthful John Orvis, who had helped form a nonresistance society among the students at Oberlin College and was soon to join Brook Farm, spoke-in at a Congregational church in Hancock, New Hampshire. At two services there Orvis waited for the pastor to finish speaking and then rose "to speak a word for peace and the slave" but, as Wright reported, was dragged out and kicked by two church members while the pastor "looked approvingly on." The Congregational Church in New England, explained Wright, "cannot endure questions of liberty, peace, and human brotherhood to be introduced into her solemn assemblies."

Another speak-inner was Maria French of Salem, Massachusetts, who had withdrawn her membership from a Congregational church because, she said, by fellowshipping with Southern churches, it shared in upholding slavery. During worship in her church one Sunday a few months later, she stood up and said she wished to speak on slavery. The minister asked her to sit down and be silent, but she continued to speak. The minister then asked constables to remove her and they carried her out.

A woman who took action similar to speaking-in was Mrs. Elmira Swett of Georgetown, Massachusetts. She clicked her knitting needles in church to protest against the "pro-slavery" sermons of her pastor. She was arrested for contempt of worship and, while offering no resistance, refused to cooperate with her arrest and so was carried to a sleigh and into a courtroom. She was sentenced to jail. The jail keeper, however, in an action that suggests the power of nonviolence to act on the individual conscience, refused to receive her, declaring that those responsible for sending her there deserved to be in jail more than she.[16]

Still another speak-inner was the Quaker-reared Abby Kelley, a carnation-cheeked young schoolteacher who was engaged to marry the archpriest of speak-inners, Stephen Foster. "In appearance she is lady-like and prepossessing," admitted an Ohio newspaper reporter after hearing her speak. She had "extraordinary mental powers," he said, and was dextrous and scathing in debate. But as an abolitionist orator and as one of the first women in America, along with the Grimké sisters, to dare to lecture to mixed audiences of men and women, most Americans regarded her as brazen. The vast majority of parents who heard her speak, the reporter said, would prefer their daughters would die rather than follow in the footsteps of Abby Kelley.

In 1844, Abby interrupted a Massachusetts Fast Day address, by speaking without permission, probably against slavery. Her action, as she proudly reported to her fiancé Foster, "shocked the whole assembly." In 1845 at an Ohio Friends yearly meeting, when Abby was scolding Friends for their weakness in antislavery work, she was carried out as an uninvited speaker.[17]

After the main period of the speak-ins was already over, in 1852 the Garrisonian editor Oliver Johnson was speaking-in at a Friends meeting.

The usually quiet Johnson, who had been brought up a Calvinist on a Vermont farm, was a recent convert to Quakerism. One Sunday, Johnson visited the Marlborough Quaker meeting in Chester County, Pennsylvania. The meeting was deeply divided about how to oppose slavery. When Johnson stood up in the meeting to speak, some of the members recognized him as the editor of the Garrisonian *Pennsylvania Freeman*. He was only able to say, "It was the promise of Jesus to his disciples," when an elder asked him to sit down. He was silent a moment and then insisted on continuing to speak. An elder appointed two men to remove him. Some in the congregation cried, "Shame, shame," while others called, "Take him out." The two men "rose and approached me," Johnson reported later in the *Freeman*. "They seized me by the wrists with the apparent intention of executing the order of those whose tools they had consented to be; but power did not seem to be given them to perform the deed of violence and shame. I sat down, and, as I did so, their hands relinquished their hold, and they went back to their seats."

The next day some of the members of the meeting legally charged Johnson with interrupting public worship, and he was arrested along with others in the congregation who had attempted to defend his right to speak.

At the trial Johnson insisted that it was custom at Friends meetings that all may rise and speak in an orderly manner, but he was convicted and fined five dollars and court costs, which he paid. Others arrested with Johnson were also convicted of disturbing public worship. They refused to pay their fines and costs on the ground that the trial was really religious persecution, but a constable paid the money for them, having been given it, Johnson believed, by the Friends who brought the charges in the first place, to avoid the embarassment of being responsible for sending them to prison.[18]

The New Hampshire veteran Parker Pillsbury was still ready to support anyone who nonviolently interrupted religious meetings to preach antislavery. When Christ was preaching, Pillsbury wrote Johnson, tongue in cheek, he so often "lugged" out of his meetings those who interrupted him, "that his Marlborough disciples, of course, could do no less. They are bound to be Christ-like."

When the *Friends Intelligencer* defended the right of Friends to use the law to remove a disturber of a religious meeting, Johnson replied that Christians who try to solve their problems through the legal "arm of violence" rather than the "gospel" have no "genuine faith in that gospel."[19]

Foster and his friends did not consider themselves responsible for the violence used against them—whether the violence of angry churchmen or of law officers. They did not consider themselves responsible any more than they considered Jesus responsible for the violence that nailed him to the cross. Jesus knew his unconventional preaching was likely to lead to violence against him, but he continued it anyway. So did Foster and the other speak-inners. So did the nonviolent abolitionists in general, with their various forms of preaching and political action and direct action.

Characteristically, the American Antislavery Society resolved at its convention of 1853 that nothing should postpone the slave's liberation, not even danger to the "preservation of the Union, nor the safety of the church, nor the peace of society."

The number of speak-inners was small, and their methods were questioned by many nonviolent abolitionists. But as Garrison, Thoreau, and Foster explained the power of nonviolent action, what was especially significant was that even a few honest men, without fear of the suffering they might bring on themselves, were taking action that challenged the consciences of the unjust. Said Garrison: "God does not conquer by numbers." Said Thoreau: "Any man more right than his neighbors constitutes a majority of one already." Said Foster: "If but one honest man should live in the 19th century, he would not live in vain."

Many years later Pillsbury claimed that Foster's method of invading churches had aroused the nation to the danger of slavery like nothing else until John Brown's raid at Harper's Ferry.[20]

14. Churchmen Come Out

◇◇◇◇◇◇◇◇◇◇◇

NONVIOLENT ABOLITIONISTS were finding other direct-action methods to arouse churches against slavery. Some of these methods were as imaginative and disturbing as Foster's speak-ins.

Foster's method was essentially an invasion method: he insisted on going into churches to speak whether he was welcome or not. A more common method for abolitionists to use to arouse the churches against slavery was essentially the withdrawal or boycott method.

The withdrawal or boycott method took many forms, particularly these three: (1) refusing to give fellowship to slave owners as Christians, (2) withdrawing membership from slavery-acquiescing churches, and (3) splitting slavery-acquiescing churches. Sometimes the withdrawal method led on to a more positive fourth form: the creation of new antislavery religious organizations, including local churches, national denominations, and national benevolent societies.

The Garrisonians took a major part not only in Foster's invasions, but also in refusing fellowship and in withdrawing memberships from churches. The Quakers, having gone through the experience of refusing fellowship to slave owners within their own denomination in a previous generation, did not take an active part in this action now, but they did take a minor part in withdrawing memberships and in splitting churches. The Tappanites, however, proved to be the most vigorous of the three nonviolent groups in attempting to abolish slavery by withdrawal action related to churches: they took a major part in all four of these forms of action.

In the generation after 1750, Quakers had already purged themselves of slave owning. They had done so essentially by refusing fellowship to Quaker slave owners within their meetings. First they had refused to give slave-owning Friends positions of leadership in their meetings; later they had threatened to disown (or remove from membership) Friends who bought any more slaves; still later they even insisted that in emancipating slaves Friends must compensate the slaves for the years they had served without pay. In the course of gradually tightening this discipline, Friends patiently exhorted their erring members and, if this proved unsuccessful, did in fact disown a few of them. For example, in 1773, because he would not free his one remaining slave, a Rhode Island meeting even disowned Stephen Hopkins, a former governor of the colony who was soon to be a signer of the Declaration of Independence. Friends' success in thus purging themselves of slave owning, at some cost in both wealth and members, serves to indicate that idealism can overcome the general rule that people will not give up power over others voluntarily.

It was tragic for both the church and the nation that the major denominations did not follow the Friends in purging themselves of slave owning, particularly while the American Revolution's fervor for liberty still lingered to help them do so. The Presbyterians at least moved in the Friends' direction. The Presbyterian General Assembly of 1794 adopted a catechism condemning slaveholders as "man-stealers," but they never actually disciplined any members for slaveholding and dropped the catechism in 1816. The Methodists moved further. In 1784 at the organizing of the Methodist Church in America, the Methodist General Conference adopted a rule allowing all its slaveholding members only a year in which to free their slaves or be expelled. Under this rule, some Methodists—particularly in Maryland—did free their slaves, but on the whole Methodist leaders balked at enforcing it. While some Methodists under church pressure continued to free their slaves until 1804, from that time the Methodist Church largely abandoned its responsibility for slaveholding, sometimes saying conveniently that it was a government responsibility instead. As slavery became more profitable with the development of the cotton gin and the rise of the demand for cotton in English factories, American church concern to abolish slavery dropped, and what concern remained was often absorbed into the movement to colonize Negroes in Africa. Probably it was largely because the Friends were better disciplined and were not at the same time trying to convert large numbers to their church that they found it possible to refuse fellowship to their own slave-owning members while major denominations at about the same time did not. If Methodists and Presbyterians had been willing to remain as small and "peculiar" a people as the Quakers, probably they, too, could have purged themselves of slave owning.

In the 1830's when abolitionists revived the practice of refusing fellowship to slave owners, it was in a somewhat different form from that which the Friends had practiced. While the Friends had usually refused fellowship in steps of gradually increasing severity, the abolitionists now were more likely to try to put the practice into effect all at once. While the Friends had not seriously tried to extend this method beyond their own denomination, the abolitionists now tried to persuade many denominations to adopt it and even to persuade churchmen to extend it to relations among denominations. While the Friends had refused fellowship both in the North and in the South at a time when slavery existed in both sections, the abolitionists in the 1830's found themselves hardly able to practice it in the South, the only part of the country where legal slavery continued.

The aspect of refusing fellowship which abolitionists emphasized in the period 1830 to 1860 was excluding slaveholders from membership or communion. As precedent for the exclusion, by this time abolitionists could cite a number of small denominations, including not only the Quakers but also the very small Reformed Presbyterian Church (Covenanters), which had excluded slave owners from membership by 1800, and the larger United Brethren in Christ Church (strong among people of German extraction in Pennsylvania and the upper South), which had excluded slave owners by 1821.

By 1834 the American Antislavery Society was advocating that all churches exclude slaveholders from communion. Within the next few years the great evangelist Finney had excluded slaveholders from communion in his church in New York City; the Indianapolis Presbytery had recommended its churches not receive slaveholders at communion; and associations of Baptists and Congregationalists in Pennsylvania and Maine had recommended excluding slaveholders from membership. President Mahan of Oberlin College introduced a motion at a convention of the Ohio Antislavery Society urging churches to bar slaveholders, and the convention adopted it unanimously. Wherever Oberlin College graduates gained influence, they were likely to try to persuade churches to bar slaveholders. In 1844, Lewis Tappan claimed that the number of churches denying fellowship to slave owners was constantly on the increase; by the latter 1840's at least twenty-seven presbyteries had excluded slaveholders from membership, and Douglass said that the idea of refusing slaveholders the bread and wine of communion had "become very prevalent in the free states."

Another aspect of refusing fellowship was refusing to accept the preaching of those who held slaves or otherwise supported slavery. As early as 1834 the American Antislavery Society urged churches to refuse to accept slaveholders as ministers, and this policy was put into effect during the next few years by church bodies as far apart as a Congregational church in Winthrop, Maine, the Presbyterian Synod of Cincinnati, and the Illinois Congregational Association. Gerrit Smith was pushing the policy in 1844 when he asked a group of abolitionists dramatically: "Who of you would attend on the ministry of the most admired preacher of your sect, were your own child in slavery, and that preacher refused to plead for it?"[1] Hinton Helper, the North Carolina abolitionist, was urging this policy as late as 1857 as part of his general boycott of slaveholders in the South.

Lewis Tappan cited with approval an instance of refusing to fellowship a preacher who supported slavery. A prominent Philadelphia Presbyterian minister, Albert Barnes, sometimes invited a certain pastor to occupy his pulpit. After this pastor had lived for some time in the South, he said to the Reverend Mr. Barnes that he would as soon buy Negroes as mutton. Shocked, Barnes then declared he would never let this pastor preach in his pulpit again.

Another example of the application of this policy occurred at the Congregational Andover Theological Seminary in Massachusetts, one of the most respected seminaries in the nation. When a prominent Presbyterian missionary to the Negroes in Georgia, the Reverend C. C. Jones, was invited to the seminary to preach, fifty of the students announced that they refused to fellowship him as a Christian because he was a slave owner. "We entertain no disrespect to Mr. Jones, personally," the students said, "but wish simply to manifest our unwillingness to extend the hand of fellowship to those who have not repented of the sin of slaveholding; . . . we consider it more important to take this course, inasmuch as Mr. Jones has been recommended to us as a gentleman of intelligence and high Christian character, deeming the influence of any such slaveholder as more calculated to palliate the wrongs of slavery in the minds of Northern Christians than that of any other."[2]

Abolitionists found other ways of refusing fellowship to slave owners and their abettors as well. Occasionally abolitionists refused to become pastors of churches that included slave owners, as abolitionist John G. Fee did when he was offered the pastorate of a Presbyterian church in Kentucky. Occasionally abolitionist students walked out of church colleges that acquiesced in slavery, as twenty-one students did from Alexander Campbell's Disciples of Christ College at Bethany, in western Virginia, after the college requested students to stop preaching against slavery. Abolitionists often refused to contribute to slavery-acquiescing churches, as Gerrit Smith did when he was asked to contribute to the building of a Methodist church in the slave market capital of New Orleans, explaining: "Suppose I were invited to contribute to the cost of erecting a heathen temple, could I innocently comply with the request?"[3] Lewis Tappan refused to extend to slaveholders the greeting of "brother" which churchmen often used among themselves; for example, he refused to use it in addressing a Virginia slaveholder who was a prominent member of a national missionary board. When Northern church members moved to the South, a Tappanite magazine recommended that churches refuse to give them letters transferring their membership to any church that fellowshiped slave owners as Christians.

Lewis Tappan found a way to refuse fellowship in a direct confrontation. At a prayer meeting in Tappan's New York church, the Broadway Tabernacle, a white Georgian visiting the city rose and testified that he was both a slaveholder and a Christian. As he sat down, Tappan—who was in charge of the meeting—stood and said to him with great emotion, "You are no Christian, you are a man stealer."

"I *am* a Christian," the Georgian replied.

"No," insisted Tappan. "No Christian can make a slave of another."

Feeling rose sharply. "The effect was terrible," a Negro witness reported later. "The audience became highly excited, and finally the Georgian walked hastily out of the meeting."[4]

Both Garrisonians and Tappanites tried to persuade British churchmen to assist them by refusing fellowship to American slave owners and their abettors. Since in matters of religion and reform

Britons had great prestige for Americans, British help could be significant. When the Quaker Garrisonian James N. Buffum was traveling in Britain, he tried to persuade the Free Church of Scotland not to accept "tainted" contributions from American slaveholders. More boldly, the Garrisonian Parker Pillsbury tried to persuade the major British denominations to sever all ties with their American counterpart denominations because of their cooperation with slavery. While such drastic efforts did not succeed, at least more limited abolitionist maneuvers sometimes did. On a speaking tour of Scotland, Frederick Douglass claimed that he was partly responsible for persuading Scotch churchmen to deny a visiting South Carolina cleric any opportunity to preach because of his pro-slavery position. "He is terribly mad with me for it," Douglass crowed.[5] Lewis Tappan assiduously advised his many British correspondents about which American clergymen visiting in Britain were posing as abolitionists while there, where it was convenient to do so, but were not acting as abolitionists at home in America; some Britons responded by snubbing these clergymen. William Wells Brown reported with pleasure that the British and Foreign Bible Society would not allow the editor of the slavery-acquiescing New York *Observer*, a Presbyterian paper, to participate in its anniversary.

However, despite some British assistance, abolitionists by no means persuaded most American churchmen—not even most Northern churchmen—to refuse fellowship to slave owners and their henchmen. Pressure to keep denominational unity was strong. Most American denominations were already quite enough torn over other issues, such as temperance, women's rights, and church doctrine—whether God was essentially one or three and whether Christ was soon coming back to earth as William Miller was predicting. A good many denominational leaders were more concerned with maintaining the unity of their denominations than with freeing the slaves.

Concern for church unity was understandable, said the New England Yearly Meeting of Friends, as they urged other churches to follow the Friends' example in excluding slave owners from fellowship. But, the Friends warned, outward harmony that is gained by sacrifice of principle is "worse than valueless."[6]

Not satisfied with the progress they were making in persuading churches to refuse fellowship to slave owners, by the late 1830's a number of abolitionists were preparing for a more drastic form of nonviolent direct action: that of withdrawing membership from churches. Abolitionists withdrew from churches or "came out"—to use their own biblical expression—because, they said, the churches upheld slavery. In the come-outers' view, sometimes the churches upheld slavery directly by preaching in favor of it, sometimes indirectly by not denouncing it as sin, and sometimes indirectly by being part of national denominations that fellowshiped slave owners, as all the major denominations did.

The Garrisonians were strong come-outers. By 1836, Garrison was no longer a member of a Baptist church or of any church at all, and he soon became personally hostile to church organization as such. But the reason he gave abolitionists at large for urging them to come out of the church was simply the church's support of slavery. Suppose, said Garrison in an argument by analogy, that there was a company of pickpockets. Suppose your church blamed them for pickpocketing "so feebly that it rather encouraged them than otherwise—all the while giving them fellowship and pecuniary aid. Would you remain members of that church?" By 1837 the New England Antislavery Society was endorsing Garrison's position on coming out, and soon among leading Garrisonians this position became common.

In her poem "The Come-Outers," the Garrisonian Anne Warren Weston explained why many abolitionists could not stay in the church:

> *No true communion cans't thou find,—*
> *The helpless slave forgot;*
> *For where no love for Man is found,*
> *Worship of God is not.*[7]

At a meeting of the Nonresistance Society, the transcendentalist and progressive educator, Bronson Alcott, asked, "What guide have I but my conscience? Church and state . . . cease to deserve our veneration from the moment they violate our consciences. We then protest against them. We withdraw ourselves from them."

The Garrisonian Frederick Douglass urged Negroes to come out of any church that accepted slave owners as members. He said his right arm should wither before he would worship at any "bloodstained altar." In a variation of the usual Garrisonian emphasis on individual withdrawal, Douglass urged the members of the Negro St. Thomas Church in Philadelphia to take their church as a unit out of the Episcopal denomination which, he said, because it accepted slaveholding members, was a "den of thieves." Taking your church out,

Douglass said, is "the only means of indicating her own self-respect, and placing herself in harmony with the cause of righteous freedom." However, St. Thomas Church did not withdraw.

Of course, many abolitionists hesitated to separate themselves from the congregation or denomination of their youth. They used many arguments to persuade themselves it wasn't necessary to withdraw. They would argue, if my church is not right on slavery, at least it is on most subjects, so why not stay in? Or, my influence for abolition will be greater if I stay in my church than if I go out. Or, divisions in the church are dangerous, and anyway slavery is more a political than a religious question.

But especially in the early 1840's there was a rash of Garrisonians who overcame any doubts they had and decided to come out. In 1840 abolitionist editor Rogers withdrew from the Congregational Church of Plymouth, New Hampshire, after having urged it to no avail to denounce all fellowship with slaveholding congregations and ministers. By 1840, Congregational deacon Amos Wood, a nonresistant of Concord, New Hampshire, had withdrawn from his church and was attending "a little meeting of independent antislavery worshippers." In 1840 the fire-eating General Agent Wright of the Nonresistance Society, a clergyman himself, "excommunicated" his church in Newbury, Massachusetts, before it had time to excommunicate him. When a woman in Royalton, Vermont, had trouble in getting a dismissal from her Congregational church, Wright advised her and any who wished to withdraw from churches: "Walk out, shaking off the dust of your feet as a testimony against their theft and bloodguiltiness. Renounce them as inhuman, soulless, savage corporations, which tend to crush the love of God and man out of all who belong to them. . . . It is more difficult to reform them of tippling, slavery, and war, than what they call the world."[9]

In 1841 after he had lost his license to preach in a clash over slavery, the independent Pillsbury—whom Emerson called a "tough oak stick of a man"—"excommunicated" his Congregational church. In 1841 the mild Henry W. Williams, an associate of Garrison on the *Liberator*, withdrew from what he called his "pro-slavery, war-supporting" church in Salem, Massachusetts, saying: "I now feel that the existing church, in general, is a serious hindrance to the progress of the gospel of our Savior"; but he insisted he had not withdrawn from the "true church." About the same time speak-inner Foster came out of his church in Hanover, New Hampshire, and Foster's fellow speak-inner, Congregational minister Thomas P. Beach, gave up his church in Campton, New Hampshire, and dissolved any connection with his denomination to avoid "any sanction of slavery"; by the next year there were enough come-outers in Campton for two separate groups of them to be meeting in schoolhouses.[10]

In a letter to an abolitionist friend, Edmund Quincy described the shock caused by a few abolitionist withdrawals from the churches in his home town of Dedham, Massachusetts. "They have done great good," he wrote. "The secession of two men and one woman from one church, and the refusal of another man to go to the other church, has made an excitement . . . such as might surprise one who did not know how sure it is that 'one shall chase a thousand and two put ten thousand to flight.' " If we had "tarred and feathered" one pastor and ridden the other one out of town "on a rail," we "could hardly have stirred up a greater commotion."[11]

After the American Antislavery Society had come under Garrisonian control, it voted in 1844 that all abolitionists should withdraw from slavery-supporting churches. In the mid-fifties Garrison said that, although the American Antislavery Society did not make it a test for membership and he was glad that it did not, nearly all its members saw the rightness of "coming out."

Among the more radical Quakers there was sympathy for the idea of coming out of slavery-supporting churches, and there was also a small movement to come out of the Society of Friends itself.

Lucretia Mott advised abolitionists to leave churches that would not clearly stand against slavery. In an address to the annual meeting of the American Antislavery Society in New York, she said: "When the pulpit cannot be enlisted, nor the church aroused, it is the duty of abolitionists to have no longer fellowship with those unfruitful works of darkness, but rather reprove them, by separating from them and not touching the unclean thing." Lucretia Mott herself remained, though uncomfortably, in the antislavery, but slow-moving Society of Friends.

Other Friends reluctantly withdrew from the society that had helped to nurture their abolitionism. Among them, Abby Kelley, a Massachusetts schoolteacher, disowned the Society of Friends in 1841. She did so especially because it tried to prevent members from joining in antislavery organizations with non-Friends and closed its meetinghouses to non-Friends who were antislavery speakers. Yet she acknowledged that "There are some in the society with whom I have taken sweet counsel, and to whom I still look up as fathers and mothers in Israel."[12] James N. Buffum, the railroad ride-inner, withdrew from the Society of Friends, he explained, after he had learned through the *Liberator* the practical application of Christianity to the woes of humanity. Similarly, after hat manufacturer Arnold Buffum had been disowned by Rhode Island Friends for his active abolitionism (he had been president of the New England Antislavery Society), his daughter, ride-inner Elizabeth Buffum Chace, withdrew from the Society of Friends. In 1841 and 1842, after the Society of Friends had expelled Underground Railroader Isaac T. Hopper and other New Yorkers for their vigorous antislavery activity outside of the society, numbers of Friends in New York and Pennsylvania came out of the society in protest. In the Midwest some of the more rural and more radical abolitionist Quakers, including Underground Railroader Levi Coffin, broke off from the larger, more conservative and more urban Quaker groups that had closed their meetinghouses to non-Quaker abolitionist speakers and in 1843 formed the new Indiana Yearly Meeting of Antislavery Friends. Quaker Historian Rufus Jones long afterward said that this split provided a needed shock to awaken Quakers into more antislavery activity.

Tension among Friends over radical abolitionism continued, and even the tactful Lucretia Mott was hurt by it. In 1848, when she fell ill while attending a Friends meeting in Indiana, one of the prominent members of that meeting, a physician, refused to treat her. He afterwards wrote an address, which was adopted by the Hicksite Indiana Yearly Meeting, scolding Friends of the Lucretia Mott school: "Who are these that are running to and fro in the earth . . . babbling of temperance, and non-resistance, and slavery, and benevolence, and communities . . . and women's rights? These are the thieves that cannot abide the way of humility and the cross, but climb up some other way, and steal the testimonies of Jesus, and are lifted up in their self-sufficiency, and are ready to say in their hearts, 'Is not this the house, not that the Lord has built, but that *we* have built?' " In the late 1840's antislavery Friends in rebellion against restraint by the New York and Ohio yearly meetings (Hicksite) over their reform activities formed a new yearly meeting of Congregational Friends, with each congregration autonomous, dedicated to such reforms as abolition. H. C. Wright, who believed that Friends thought more of their organizational machinery than of their principles, welcomed the "searching of heart, life, and discipline" that accompanied the creating of this new yearly meeting.[13] In 1853 other dissident Friends, especially Hicksites in Pennsylvania, established a loosely organized group called the Progressive Friends, not strictly a Friends yearly meeting but more nearly a religious fellowship for those who inclined to radical reforms; among the Quaker leaders who cooperated with it but did not necessarily leave their regular Friends meetings were Lucretia Mott, abolitionist editor Oliver Johnson, and the Delaware Underground Railroader Thomas Garrett, all of whom had strong ties to the Garrisonians. Garrison himself was to take an intimate part in the life of the Progressive Friends without actually becoming a member.

Usually when Garrisonians came out of churches, they opposed forming any substitute antislavery religious bodies, whether new local churches, regional associations, or denominations. The process of creating new institutions would waste energies, Garrison believed. Rather, he preferred to wait until abolitionist devices, such as withdrawals, had induced the churches to remake themselves into what they should be. Garrisonian come-outers might take part in small unorganized groups of antislavery worshipers, as we have seen, but they often simply remained outside of any organized church. In doing so, Garrisonian leaders were following the same pattern they often followed at about the same time in coming out of the traditional slavery-supporting Whig or Democratic political parties and in refusing to join in forming any substitute antislavery party.

In contrast to most Garrisonian come-outers, some Quaker come-outers did create new religious abolitionist bodies, as we have seen, and Tappanite come-outers were even more likely to do so.

On the question of coming out of churches, Lewis Tappan, ardent as usual, at first seemed to move in several directions almost at once. As we have seen, in 1836 he was willing to come out of his own Presbyterian church in New York City to help form a new interracial one, until that project was quashed. Then he considered coming out of his own church in order to join the Reverend T. S. Wright's Negro church and help make it interracial. But soon afterward he struggled to stay in his own church even when, to keep from being expelled on the charge of slandering the pastor, he was obliged in 1839 to carry an appeal all the way to the highest court of his denomination, the Presbyterian (New School) General Assembly. In 1840, after having won his right to stay in the church only after being chastised by the General Assembly for being insufficiently meek and reverent, Tappan wrote Gerrit Smith that he was doubtful that the abolitionists should refuse to accept the preaching of ministers just because their preaching was not sufficiently antislavery. Explained Tappan: my own minister, who claims that he is an abolitionist, "sometimes prays for the slave, promotes the election of some abolitionists as officers of his church, but still is very far, I think, from doing his duty with reference to the slavery question." But, said Tappan, that is no reason for leaving his church; "let us use all the abolitionism" such ministers have, "and try to make them better."[14] Compared to the Garrisonians, Tappan was being restrained.

By 1841, however, Tappan was himself a leader in establishing a come-outer mission society to rival the slavery-acquiescing mission societies, and he was soon acknowledging that Christians were bound to leave churches "which frown upon antislavery efforts." Yet he was still skeptical that abolitionists of different theology and differing denominational backgrounds could successfully form new churches if their "tie is merely or chiefly abolition principles." He wrote Gerrit Smith, the truth is that abolitionists are not "better Christians than all others," but conceded, "Where we can form churches with a prospect of doing more good, it should be done."[15] Tappan remained more cautious than many of his own associates on forming new churches.

By this time many abolitionists more or less associated with Tappan were coming out of their churches. Indicating their concern, like Tappan, that they work for abolition within some church, after coming out they often created or supported new abolitionist churches. In doing so, many Tappanites were following the same pattern that they followed about the same time in coming out of the traditional slavery-supporting political parties to create or support the new abolitionist Liberty party.

Beriah Green, president of Oneida Institute, led an antislavery group out of his Presbyterian church in Whitesboro, New York, in 1837 when his pastor pledged himself to silence on slavery; said Green, slavery is the "test question" of our time. Green and his group formed a new Congregational church that clearly opposed slavery.[16] Many such new abolitionist churches became Congregational because Congregational polity permitted the congregation to have unlimited control over its own affairs, as Presbyterian polity did not.

Gerrit Smith, after having tried in vain to persuade his presbytery to secede from the "pro-slavery" Presbyterian General Assembly and then having also tried in vain to persuade his local church to secede from the presbytery, came out from his local church in Peterboro, New York, in 1842; national denominations were pro-slavery because they foolishly tried to remain national, Smith explained. He then helped to create a new local nondenominational church that supported abolition—one of the probably hundreds of new local churches that abolitionist come-outers created.

William Goodell, the editor of various antislavery papers, seceded in 1843 from his church in Honoye, in the Finger Lakes region of New York, and helped create a new antislavery nonsectarian church. If doubting abolitionists argued that secessions weakened the church, Goodell replied that secessions from corrupt churches were traditional for Protestants. If they argued that seceders would have less chance to influence their churches for abolition, he replied with a probing question: are you abolitionists who stay inside pro-slavery churches exerting more influence on the churches or are they exerting more influence on you ?

The Liberty party Presidential candidate, James Birney, once a slave owner, withdrew his membership from a Presbyterian church because of its refusal to exclude slave owners. In 1846 he helped to found a new Congregational church in Lower Saginaw, Michigan, which declared its faith in the equality of man.

Similarly, John G. Fee, a Presbyterian pastor in Kentucky, withdrew from his denomination in 1847 because of its "persistent fellowship of slaveholding" and led his church to transform itself into a nondenominational church that excluded slave owners. This church was the forerunner of several such churches that Fee established in Kentucky.

There were also larger-scale withdrawals from churches, especially by abolitionists at least loosely oriented to the Tappanites. In a notable instance, the Tappanite Orange Scott led six thousand Methodist abolitionists, especially in New York State and New England, to come out from the Methodist Church and create a new slavery-prohibiting denomination, the Wesleyan Methodist Church. By coming out, Scott predicted, the Wesleyans would increase their influence. Within eighteen months the Wesleyans had increased to fifteen thousand members. Soon they had spread to the South, and although they suffered from poisoning, imprisonment, and even hanging, they secured a precarious foothold there—in North Carolina their numbers increased from forty in 1846 to five hundred in five years. In the North, the Methodist Church, in its effort to prevent further abolitionist secessions, was forced to bend; it gave its abolitionists more freedom to act and they attained a new fervor.[17]

Scott was right; the few Methodist abolitionists who chose to come out had multiplied the influence of Methodist abolitionists at large.

Lewis Tappan was increasingly impressed with the come-outers' achievements. At an interdenominational Christian antislavery convention in Cincinnati in 1850, Tappanite pastor Fee of Kentucky proposed a resolution that "the friends of a pure Christianity ought to separate themselves from all slaveholding churches and all . . . ecclesiastical bodies . . . that are not fully divorced from slaveholding." The resolution passed without dissent, and Tappan commented that it had taken "the true ground."[18] Tappan had discovered that for abolitionists to work within the major denominational organizations was less rewarding than he had expected. During the 1850's, Tappan was to be outstanding in rallying support for those remarkable outposts of nonviolent abolitionism in the slave states, the come-outer churches that Fee helped establish in Kentucky and the Wesleyans helped establish in North Carolina.

Altogether, up to the Civil War abolitionists helped to create or sustain a considerable number of small church bodies that excluded slave owners; these bodies, when added to others that also excluded slave owners but were isolated from the mainstream of abolitionism, made up a formidable list (see table on p. 230). Yet the members of these slaveholder-excluding churches together were but a small portion of the total number of American church members.

Meanwhile all the pressure the antislavery forces could muster, whether by means of direct action or otherwise, was having little effect on the more hierarchically organized denominations like the Roman Catholic and Episcopal. Their bishops determined to preserve the national unity of their denominations, regardless of the moral issues involved in slavery. Perhaps these churches had a different conception of the function of the church than most churches had. Perhaps these churches were influenced by their strength in certain parts of the South among the wealthy slaveholders. Perhaps the Catholic Church—the largest single denomination in the nation— was also influenced in the North by its being composed largely of immigrants or their families who, having scarcely found their own places in American society, were not very likely to worry about others who also had not found their place. Whatever the reason, both the Episcopal and Catholic Churches refused to allow themselves to be disturbed by the antislavery agitation and did not witness against slavery up to the time of the Civil War.[19]

CHURCHES EXCLUDING SLAVEHOLDERS
FROM MEMBERSHIP BY 1864[*]

METHODISTS	MEMBERS IN 1864
Wesleyan Methodists (founded 1843)	21,000
Evangelical Association or German Methodists (founded 1800 by Jacob Albright in Pa.)	47,000
African Methodist Episcopal (founded 1816)	50,000
African Methodist Episcopal Zion (founded 1820)	6,000
BAPTISTS	
Free Will Baptists (founded 1780 in N.H.)	57,000
Church of God or Winebrennarians (founded 1830 by John Winebrenner among Germans in Pa.)	14,000
Seventh Day Baptists (founded 1671 in R.I.)	7,000
PRESBYTERIANS	
United Presbyterians (formed 1858 of a union between the Associate Reformed Church and the Associate Synod known as Seceders)	58,000
Reformed Presbyterians or Covenanters (founded by 1800)	17,000
PEACE CHURCHES (Complete Nonresistants)	
Quakers or Society of Friends (in America by the 1600's)	94,000
Shakers or United Society of Believers (founded by the 1770's as an offshoot of the Quakers)	5,000
Mennonites (in America by the 1600's)	37,000
River Brethren (founded 1770 in Pa. as an offshoot of the Mennonites)	7,000
OTHERS	
United Brethren in Christ (formed by 1800 in Md. and Pa. among Germans)	103,000

[*] Adapted from *Friends Review*, July 23, 1864, p. 748.

However, the more democratically organized Protestant churches, representing the majority of the church members of the country, were profoundly disturbed by the antislavery agitation. Congregations, committees, and boards clashed over appointing pastors or missionaries who themselves owned slaves or were abolitionists. Pastors and laymen debated whether to accept slave owners at the communion table. Church journals and conferences disputed whether churches should accept money from slaveholders.

From the 1830's, antislavery churchmen of major Protestant denominations felt impelled to take separate action within their own denominations. In 1834 the first Methodist antislavery society was formed. Soon afterward young Methodist abolitionists were being denied entry into the ministry, and Methodist abolitionist pastors were being tried for making false charges against the church for its support of slavery. But the result of this persecution was not to stop the growth of abolitionism among Methodists. While in 1835 there were said to be only twenty-five Methodist abolitionist ministers, by 1838 there were two thousand. In that year antislavery Methodists—both clergy and laymen—held their first national convention. By 1843 the withdrawal of the Wesleyan Methodists aroused Methodists into still greater awareness of the slaves' claim for freedom.

Among Baptists before 1800 there was already, a small antislavery sect, the non-Calvinistic Free Will Baptists, which refused to receive slaveholders as members and even to receive their contributions. In 1839 at their general conference the Free Will Baptists decided to break fellowship with some five thousand Carolina Baptists whose practices were much like theirs except in welcoming slaveholders as members; despite this decision, or perhaps partly because of it, by 1845 the Free Will Baptists claimed that they were growing and had spread all over the Union. Abolitionists of the general Baptist bodies held their first national convention in 1840 in New York City; they sent an address to Baptist slaveholders, urging them to abandon slavery, and they said that they themselves refused to receive bread and wine "at the Lord's table" from any minister who "rivets fetters on the innocent" or "shuts up the Bible from human eyes."[20] Among many denominations antislavery conventions became common and so correspondingly did denominational antislavery journals and mission societies.

However, as Northern churchmen took clearer stands against slavery, Southern churchmen took clearer stands in favor of slavery, and they came more and more into open conflict with each other, just as many churchmen had feared. Eventually the main bodies of several denominations split over slavery. The Methodists split into separate Northern and Southern branches in 1844 over the issue, raised by Southerners, of permitting a Georgia bishop to own slaves as bishops had never been permitted to do previously. Similarly, the Baptists split into Northern and Southern branches in 1845 over the issue of permitting missionaries to own slaves. By 1851 several antislavery Congregational associations had cut themselves off from any connection with slaveholding churchmen, and several antislavery presbyteries and synods had come out from the Presbyterian Church, whether Old School or New School. Presbyterians of the New School split formally into Northern and Southern bodies in 1857.

While some of the earlier splits—which had produced minor church bodies like the Indiana Yearly Meeting of Antislavery Friends and the Wesleyan Methodist Church—were led by outspoken abolitionists, the later major North-South splits were not. None of the new major Northern church bodies excluded slave owners from membership.

Nevertheless, from the point of view of some of the nonviolent abolitionists, the major North-South splits were at least a sign that their agitation was having some effect. In particular, the Garrisonians considered the splits to be a useful preparation for the voluntary dissolution of the Union which would, they believed, help to prevent war and free the slave. But from the point of view of those who hoped that the church could use its institutional power to free the slave, the splits were a disaster—a divided church would have little institutional power to effect change against the will of the dominant planter class of the South.

By the late 1840's abolitionists reported modest signs of improvement in the attitude of most Northern churches. The Massachusetts Antislavery Society claimed that almost every religious denomination in the North, great or small, had become anxious to claim an antislavery character. In 1852, Kentucky Tappanite pastor Fee said he was impressed with the "immense good" that individuals and local churches were doing by seceding from slavery-acquiescing bodies. "They are not only . . . waking public conscience, but they are encouraging and inducing many others to follow their example; so that already the old [church] bodies are beginning to look about for their members. Self-preservation begins to look them earnestly in the face."[21] Fee was frankly welcoming the coercive power of the withdrawal movement.

But the fact that some major Northern denominations were moving slowly toward abolitionism did not make them abolitionist yet. Pillsbury in 1847 was suspicious of how much the "boasted" separation of the Northern Methodists from Southern Methodists meant so long as Northern Methodists still permitted slave owners in the border slave states to be members of their church, and indeed Methodists themselves hotly debated the question. Garrisonians continued to goad the churches in general. Garrison badgered Irish-American Catholics for their "peculiarly bitter" prejudice against Negroes (probably no American Catholic priest ever became known as an abolitionist), and he dramatized the refusal of the visiting Irish priest, temperance advocate Father Mathew, to support the abolition of American slavery while in America, where it was unpopular, as he had while in Ireland, where it was popular. When year after year the convention of the Episcopal diocese of New York refused to admit delegates from a black Episcopal church in New York City, Garrison condemned it for having a "harder than adamant" attitude toward black people. Frederick Douglass was still saying in 1848 that clergy were "the strongest defenders" of slavery. And pastor Theodore Parker could write May in Syracuse in 1853: "The American pulpit is the sworn ally of slavery. . . . I know there are exceptional pulpits. I congratulate you that one of them is in Syracuse . . . but how few they are!—little lamps hung out from windows, here and there, on a country road at night, they only show how deep the darkness is."[22]

Perhaps the Garrisonians—and some non-Garrisonians, too—were tactically unwise to continue their severe denunciations of the churches through the 1850's when abolitionist opinion in the churches was patently growing—when the Northern Methodists officially published antislavery tracts and Sunday School papers, and church buildings were increasingly open to abolitionist speakers. Lewis Tappan thought they were not wise. Instead of enlisting the aid of the churches, Tappan said, the Garrisonians are making war on them; the Garrisonians are "furious in breaking down," he explained, "but at no pains to build up."

However, the Tappanites were obliged to continue to denounce the churches in almost the same terms as the Garrisonians, if less shrilly. The Tappanite American and Foreign Antislavery Society, anxious to work within the churches as it was, was still saying in 1852 that the American church "is at this moment one of the strongest buttresses of American caste and slavery"; it even claimed that Jews and Unitarians—both of whom knew from their own experience something of what it meant to be scorned by society—were merely neutral on slavery.[23]

The Tappanites undertook one notable direct action in relation to churches that was more positive than the direct action the Garrisonians usually took. In protest against the pro-slavery positions of most missionary societies, the Tappanites took the lead in creating a vigorous, distinctly antislavery, national missionary society.

The abolitionists' action in the field of missionary societies was part of their action in the larger field of church benevolent societies. For a long time abolitionists campaigned to abolitionize the leading interdenominational, evangelical benevolent societies, such as the American Bible Society, American Tract Society, American Home Mission Society, and the American Board of Commissioners for Foreign Missions. Abolitionists used indirect methods to do so, such as agitation in the press and at meetings; and they also used direct methods such as withholding contributions, refusing to serve as members, officers, or missionaries, attempting to seize control at annual meetings, splitting local auxiliaries from the parent societies, and creating competing societies.

The American Tract Society published large numbers of books and pamphlets against such "sins" as dancing, the theater, intemperance, and desecration of the Sabbath, but refused to publish any against slavery. When it republished works that in their original form contained any incidental denunciations of slavery, it deliberately omitted these passages. Arthur Tappan, at one time the American Tract Society's largest donor, attempted in vain to change its policy, and the American Antislavery Society urged abolitionists not to contribute to it.[24] By 1854 evangelical abolitionists had established in Cincinnati a rival publication agency, the American Reform Tract and Book Society; this new society, announced the Tappanites, is "the only national tract society that grapples with great and popular sins." By the late 1850's abolitionists had also persuaded the Boston branch of the American Tract Society—long the national society's largest source of revenue—to stop giving funds to the national society and itself to publish antislavery tracts. While the American Tract Society never broke its silence on slavery up to the Civil War, it was at least seriously weakened by the split.[25]

With respect to the two Mission societies—the American Home Mission Society and the American Board of Commissioners for Foreign Missions—the abolitionists protested their silence on slavery, the presence of slave owners on their boards, and their acceptance of contributions of slave owners. Lewis Tappan was deeply interested in missions, as most Tappanites were, but he refused to become a member of the American Board of Commissioners for Foreign Missions, an agency that evangelical Congregationalists and Presbyterians often supported. Tappan attended a meeting of the board to say that he was withholding his contributions from it and to request the board to take such action against slavery as would lead it to enlist more fervent prayers and larger donations.[26] Such abolitionist withholding of contributions, however, was slow to budge the mission boards, which were no doubt fearful that by opposing slavery they would lose more Southern contributions than they would gain abolitionist contributions.

Discouraged, the Tappanites led in 1846 in drawing together several small antislavery groups to form the new antislavery American Missionary Association. The new association was nonsectarian and evangelical, like the established mission societies. But in contrast to them, it insisted that any church it supported must be open to blacks and whites equally and must not permit slave owners to be members. It represented in part a renewal of the effort the American Antislavery Society had begun in the 1830's and drifted away from because it seemed hopeless—the direct conversion of the South to the belief that slaveholding was sin. The new American Missionary Association did stoic antislavery work; it did this work abroad, in the North, and in the South, and it was committed to nonviolence.

The American Missionary Association's preeminent leader was the disciplined New York City merchant, Lewis Tappan. He served as the treasurer of the association from its founding in 1846 through 1865. Among the Association's other officers at various times were Lewis Tappan's taciturn brother Arthur, whose wealth by this time had been reduced through his business failures as well as his benevolences, and the white ministers S. S. Jocelyn, formerly pastor of a Negro church in New Haven, and George Whipple, formerly a professor at Oberlin. Many of its missionaries were Congregational (both Lewis and Arthur Tappan in their early New York years had been Presbyterian but in their later years became Congregational). Many of the missionaries had been students of that center of evangelical, abolitionist, and pacifist ferment, Oberlin College; and many had been dismissed by other mission societies or had resigned because of their abolitionist views.

The American Missionary Association's purpose, according to its charter, was "the propagation of the gospel in its peaceful and anti-slavery character." The Association rejected "all carnal weapons for deliverance from bondage" and expressly affirmed the peace principles adopted by the American Antislavery Society at its founding. Lewis Tappan, like some Garrisonians in this respect, advised the missionaries not to retaliate against violence even by taking court action; "unresisting deportment . . . would multiply . . . friends faster," he wrote.[27] The Association's missionaries in Africa helped to make peace among warring tribes. During the "war" in Kansas, while the Association's missionaries there were not necessarily complete pacifists, they refrained from participation in the fighting between pro-slavery and free-soil men, and one of them, Amos Finch, condemning free-soil men for resorting to violence, asked, "Shall we institute another crying sin, equal in magnitude with slavery, to overthrow it?"[28]

The Association—which had a total of 263 missionaries working in the United States in the pre–Civil War years, in addition to many others abroad—openly agitated for the abolition of slavery and believed that the best way to accomplish it was by ridding the church of any taint of slavery. The Association advocated that slaveholders be turned away from the communion table; it refused to accept contributions that were the "known fruits" of slave labor; and it distributed Bibles to the slaves, as the American Bible Society refused to do.

One of the Association's most impressive missionaries was John G. Fee, who served in Kentucky. Fee worked quietly where he could. He condemned vulgar abuse of slaveholders, believing this method would not succeed. He said that the Association's missionaries in the South should approach the topic of slavery with meekness and prayer. But he was firm. He made it clear to everyone that he was an abolitionist, and in accordance with Association policy he insisted on founding churches open to both blacks and whites equally. Despite his quiet style and the fact that he was a native Kentuckian, Fee was mobbed twenty-two times.[29]

Fee said that he did not believe in defending himself with "carnal weapons." The best way to effect reform, he said, is to endure abuse rather than avenge injury; he believed he was protected by God. He idolized the pacifist crusader Elihu Burritt and named a son after him; he wrote Gerrit Smith that he agreed with him that governments should not even prepare for war.[30]

Slavery-defending ruffians attacked Fee repeatedly. They clubbed him on a highway. They left him for dead twice. They dragged him out of a pulpit in Rockcastle County, took him to another county, and warned him not to return on peril of his life. He returned, only to find the churches where he had preached had been burned. He then preached in a private house, and afterward it was burned too. Still Fee never retaliated by offering physical injury. He never carried weapons. He sometimes helped protect himself by taking amiably with his assailants and praying aloud for them so as to deflate their purpose. He also sometimes appealed to law to defend his freedom of speech; this was not only a wise policy, in his opinion, but was a religious duty. Lewis Tappan, however, advised him not to appeal to law. After a mob had driven Fee from his pulpit in 1855, Tappan, sending him a gift of fifty dollars from himself and Gerrit Smith, advised him to use it for the comfort of his family: "Be careful not to expend any of it in law suits unless you can find some precept in the Gospel authorizing you to go to law," Tappan wrote, and added: "Better rely on moral force. I don't think you have any wrong feeling toward those deluded men [who assailed you], but is it not best to leave them to the hands of God?" Despite Tappan's advice, Fee continued to bring legal charges against those who assailed him.[31]

Because Fee and the other American Missionary Association agents in Kentucky would not defend themselves by violence, some of their friends who did not share their scruples felt that they should do so. Once, to protect one of the missionaries, deacons sat with loaded guns in front of the pulpit. At another time men stood outside a meeting place in a forest with guns in their hands to protect Fee while he was speaking inside. At still another time, Fee's abolitionist friend, the violent Cassius Clay, came into one of his meetings which pro-slavery men were turning into a tumult: Clay stormed to the pulpit carrying a brace of pistols and shouted: "This preacher is going to have a fair hearing." But Fee was embarrassed by such protection. He once told some friends who offered to protect him, "I know retaliation will destroy society." At another time he said that people who win a struggle by violence are praised for their skill in violence, not for their principles; such people do not affect the conscience.[32]

Keeping to nonviolent means themselves, Fee and his missionary associates founded in Kentucky nondenominational, antislavery, interracial churches. By 1856 they had founded six of them, and by 1859 eleven, while at the same time they encouraged the twelve already existing Kentucky churches of the antislavery United Brethren denomination. By about this time they also were operating grade schools in at least five counties, and these schools were so superior that slave owners sometimes sent their children to them. At least three of these schools, despite terrible pressure, were open to blacks equally with whites—the schools in Cummins, Rockcastle County; McKee, Jackson County; and Berea, Madison County. In Berea, Fee and his associates also led in founding Berea College, which they hoped would be to Kentucky what Oberlin College was to Ohio—an interracial college to educate teachers and preachers.[33] In Berea they gathered a colony of brave antislavery people, including teachers, farmers, carpenters, and a saw mill operator; they considered themselves a little outpost of enlightened, industrious enterprise in a region generally benighted by ignorance and slavery.

The American Missionary Association decided in 1858 that Fee and his associates, working in a a slave state as they were, provided a model that should be followed in every slave state. Harriet Beecher Stowe, writing in the *Independent* about the same time, pointed to the grandeur of Fee's achievement. Suppose, she wrote, the missionaries of the regular mission societies had gone into the slave states as Fee went into Kentucky, "founding churches on principles of strict antislavery communion. They would have been driven out, say you? How do we know? Fee is not driven out of Kentucky." Fee is fighting the battle in Kentucky which we should fight everywhere in slave territory. "He is fighting it successfully—necessities, afflictions, distress, only make him stronger. Antislavery churches are rising around him, feeble indeed, in their beginning, but mighty in moral force; and every inch which Christianity seems to gain under such auspices, she really does gain."[34]

By this time another impressive missionary of the American Missionary Association, Daniel Worth, was working in North Carolina. A portly man with a hoary head and a commanding eye, Worth had been a prominent organizer of antislavery Wesleyan Methodist churches in the North and president of the Wesleyan general conference. Like Fee, who worked in his native state of Kentucky, Worth worked in his native state of North Carolina. But in neither case did their Southern birth protect them fundamentally.

When Worth arrived in North Carolina in 1857, he found that the six existing antislavery Wesleyan churches had been enfeebled by many of their members escaping into safer denominations or to the North. Worth preached in these churches and attempted to strengthen them. Soon he was claiming that in the region of central

North Carolina where he worked, more converts were coming into the Wesleyan churches than into any of the many pro-slavery churches.

Worth worked more with whites than with Negroes. He not only knew that for him to communicate with slaves when their masters were not present would leave him open to prosecution under state law, but also believed that his purpose of peaceful emancipation could be accomplished only through the whites. Worth was blunt in condemning slavery but tried to keep communication with slaveholders open. "I am in constant and daily intercourse with slaveholders," he wrote in a public letter in 1858; "sometimes I tarry a night with one, and then I always call in the slaves and pray with them and their masters together; and it is worthy of remark, that in many conversations on the slavery subject, several of which have been with slaveholders, not a man has seemed to take any offense; and yet I have maintained the principles of an ultra school, for I am an abolitionist of the Gerrit Smith type."[35] Worth's preaching drew large congregations, often too large for the size of the churches. But as white leaders in the state understood better what Worth was doing, they stirred up popular fear of him, and presently the usual Southern violence against abolitionists threatened Worth, too.

With Quaker help, Wesleyan ministers in North Carolina had already established a pattern of nonviolence in defending themselves. One of them, James McBride, of Quaker origin, had once overcome a mob that attempted to prevent him from preaching, by praying and singing with them. At another time when a mob came to take McBride out of the state, a group of his followers protected him by blocking a road, without direct violence. At still another time when a friend volunteered to form an armed guard to protect some of the Wesleyan leaders in their abolitionist activity, another Wesleyan minister, Adam Crooks, declined the offer, saying that abolitionist "weapons were peaceful and legal and spiritual, not carnal." Crooks had kept moving from place to place to avoid his enemies,[36] but in time both McBride and Crooks were driven out of the South. Worth—who was also of Quaker origin—also became subject to mobs and yet remained nonviolent. Once armed men protected him, but they were not Wesleyans; they were sympathizers. Wesleyans were taught not to resort to violence, and Worth himself never approved of violence even in self-defense. For a time Worth and his associates managed to continue to flourish under violent persecutions, and by 1858 they had raised the number of Wesleyan churches from six to ten.

Altogether the American Missionary Association had done wonders in the South. By mid-1859 it was working in four slaveholding areas: Kentucky, Missouri, North Carolina, and the District of Columbia. In these areas the association, employing peaceful means, was carrying on a dialogue about abolition with a few slave owners and had created or given major support to at least five antislavery schools and twenty-one antislavery churches. The association was bombarding the South with education and the gospel of love, said popular preacher Henry Ward Beecher, and in doing so it had created a "lever" capable of destroying slavery.

When its missionaries suffered persecution in the South, the American Missionary Association claimed, much as abolitionists had claimed when violence broke up their meetings in the North in the 1830's, that persecution strengthened their cause.[37] While abolitionists in the 1830's had little reason to believe this principle was working in the South as well as the North, the abolitionists of the mid-1850's had reason to believe it was working in both sections.

With respect to the American Missionary Association's effect on the older benevolent societies, Lewis Tappan believed that the association was a "tug" pulling them toward abolitionism. The association hardly succeeded in modifying the slavery-acquiescing policy of the American Bible Society or the American Board of Commissioners for Foreign Missions, but at least by competing with the American Home Mission Society it managed to help induce it to drop its acquiescence in slavery. By 1856 the Home Mission Society had decided to refuse to appoint missionaries who themselves held slaves; it had also decided to refuse to help churches that admitted slave owners unless they could show they were temporarily justified in holding slaves for some special reason. Tappanites considered this new policy to be not yet up to the American Missionary Association's high standard, but at least it was a move in the right direction.

Unfortunately for the peaceful progress Tappanites were making, in the fall of 1859 the violent John Brown tried to seize arms in Harper's Ferry, Virginia, to use in helping slaves escape. Brown's raid shocked the South into new persecution of abolitionists.

In North Carolina, the Brown raid plunged Worth into jail. Worth had made the "mistake" of circulating *The Impending Crisis*—the book, written by the North Carolinian Hinton R. Helper, which advocated a boycott of slaveholders. Earlier such a mistake went unnoticed, but in the hysteria Brown had aroused, Worth was arrested; circulating this book, law officers charged, was in violation of the state law that made it a crime to circulate any publication "the evident tendency whereof is to cause slaves to become discontented with their bondage." Worth was jailed for several months while awaiting trial.

In jail in Greensboro in the winter of 1860—where, without adequate heat, his feet were frozen—Worth wrote his wife: "I can never countenance forcible resistance. O for the meek and lowly spirit that was in Jesus!" Even if Worth did not approve of John Brown's course, he suffered because of it just the same. In the spring he was tried and sentenced to a year in prison.

While other charges were pending against him, Worth appealed the sentence and was released on a high three-thousand-dollar bond. He was persuaded by his friends that he was sure to be put to death if he stayed in North Carolina; as he well knew, mobs were waiting for him, and besides a second offense of circulating incendiary literature was punishable by death. Secretly he took a train for the North.

Arrived in New York, Worth was invited to speak in what had become Lewis Tappan's home church, Plymouth Church, in Brooklyn. The pastor, Henry Ward Beecher, introduced Worth to a packed house, saying, "I do not feel that I am worthy to stoop down and unloose the latchet of dear brother Worth's shoes," and Worth melted to tears. The church people contributed to paying off Worth's bondsmen so that he would not feel obliged, in justice to his bondsmen, to return to North Carolina. Tappan took Worth into his home for a rest, and then Worth toured the North, describing to his eager audiences the desperate struggle of abolitionists to survive in the South.[38]

In Kentucky, after John Brown's raid, pro-slavery whites used head shavings, tarrings, legal maneuvers, and threats of death to expel Fee and the other American Missionary Association agents from the state. In fact, they drove nearly all the association's eleven missionaries and three colporteurs out of the South. Along with them, by pressure of one kind or another Southerners drove out the peaceful antislavery colonists whom Fee had drawn to the site of the new Berea College, Wesleyans from North Carolina, Quakers from North Carolina and Tennessee, and United Brethren from Kentucky and elsewhere. Southerners, said the American Missionary Association, were expelling their own best friends, those who labored and prayed for them and their children. The violence of Brown and a few other abolitionists stopped—at least temporarily—much of the work which years of patient abolitionist nonviolence had constructed.

"I can understand now, why the Savior wept over Jerusalem," Fee wrote in grief at the missionary exodus. "How shall I go away, and give up this work?" he mourned. "Can, oh, can this nation be roused to the work of exterminating this monster, slavery?"[39]

Abolitionism was certainly much stronger in the churches in the late 1850's than it had been twenty or thirty years earlier. Yet none of the abolitionist efforts—whether direct actionist or otherwise—had succeeded in making over any of the major denominations into abolitionist agencies by the standards of Garrison, Lucretia Mott, or Lewis Tappan. The invasion effort had not done so, whether of the Foster speak-in variety or the Grimké sit-in variety. Nor had refusing fellowship done so, whether in the form of refusing to accept the preaching of slaveholders or of excluding them from church membership. Nor had coming-out done so, whether of the Garrisonian coming-out variety that was likely to mean staying out of the organized church or of the Quaker coming-out variety that formed some new Quaker bodies or of the Tappanite coming-out variety that led to forming new local churches, the Wesleyan Methodist Church, and the American Missionary Association.

In the late 1850's the abolitionists continued to goad the churches. After *Uncle Tom's Cabin* was published, Wendell Phillips said that the theater by showing dramatic versions of the novel were doing more than the church to abolish slavery. A group of New York Methodists announced that "thousands of the best of their membership" had left the Northern Methodist Church because in its border state congregations it still permitted slave owners to be members. Arthur Tappan admitted, "We appear to be making no progress" in leading churches "to our views respecting fellowshiping slaveholders and slaveholding churches."[40]

When the Civil War broke out, despite considerable numbers of the more democratically organized local Northern churches being by this time bulwarks of abolition, Charles Whipple, Garrison's editorial associate, was predicting that the secular world would continue to "precede" the church at large in abolitionism, "because the clergy . . . cherish, above all things, the unity of their respective denominations."

Yet, ironically, many of the very abolitionists who during the thirty years before the Civil War were the most acrid in denouncing the church themselves continued to have faith in it. The abolitionists were in the 1830's and through the abolitionist period primarily religious in outlook, whether conservative or liberal in theology and whether part of the organized church or not. A convention of anti-slavery upstate New York Methodist ministers announced in 1857, with characteristic abolitionist faith in the power of the church, that if the Methodist Church alone had continued to insist on prohibiting its members from holding slaves as it had in 1784, not a slave would be left in the country. The abolitionists vehemently denounced the church for its weakness on slavery partly just because they were themselves products of the church. They had been sensitized to the inhumanity of slavery by the church, if not directly, at least indirectly—the Massachusetts Antislavery Society said that the church disowned the very antislavery principles "which have sprung from her bosom."[41] And though greviously disappointed if not embittered by the hesitancy of the church to awaken to its responsibility on slavery, they had moved the church in the direction of abolition.

Looking back at the attempts to free the slaves by nonviolent direct action related to churches, abolitionists often regarded them as significant. In 1853, Wendell Phillips, reviewing the movement to "come out" of the churches and point them out as the "bulwark of slavery," claimed "nothing has ever more strengthened the cause [of abolition] or won it more influence; and it has had the healthiest effect on the church itself." Just after the Civil War, Methodist Bishop Edward Thompson admitted that the Wesleyan withdrawal from the Methodist Church had induced antislavery activity within that church which the Wesleyans "could not have accomplished by remaining members of it."[42] The abolitionists' long-sustained nonviolent confrontation of the churches, while achieving less than abolitionists had hoped, had played a major role in rousing the nation to face the evils of slavery.

15. Noncooperation with Government

◇◇◇◇◇◇◇◇◇◇◇◇

GARRISON LED in developing noncooperation with government as a major pattern of nonviolent direct action for the abolition of slavery.

Using the slogan "No Union with Slaveholders," Garrison advocated noncooperation with the slavery-protecting United States government, much as he advocated noncooperation with slavery-sanctifying churches. For Garrison it came to be a sin to cooperate with the Constitution, which, contrary to the Declaration of Independence, supported slavery; it came to be a sin to cooperate with a government that allowed men who held other men as slaves to be eligible for the highest offices, even the Presidency. It was impossible, said Garrison, to be true to the Unites States and to God at the same time.

The major form of noncooperation with government, toward which Garrison began moving as early as 1835, was refusing to vote —a form that religious sects like Shakers and Covenanters had long used and which the Black Muslims were to use in the next century.

Garrison insisted not only on not voting, but also he early insisted on three corollaries: not participating in political parties, not holding office, and not joining in the mockery of patriotic celebrations of American "liberty" while millions of Americans were still slaves. Later Garrison developed two more corollaries—the revolutionary ones of asking the North to secede from the slavery-ridden Union and asking abolitionists to refuse to fight for it.

When abolitionists refused to cooperate with government, they ran into difficult dilemmas. If they refused to vote for officials, could they hope to influence them against slavery? If they refused to fight for their government, could they ask it to do what they thought was right? How could they both believe in an orderly government in general and also believe that justice to blacks could only come through breaking up the government?

Garrisonians came to their noncooperation with government position by various combinations of three routes: the route of general preference for "moral suasion" rather than political action, the route of conviction that the United States government was hopelessly under the control of slave interests, and the route of complete nonresistance.

In the early 1830's, Garrisonians, like most abolitionists, had been careful to act in accordance with the United States Constitution. The American Antislavery Society's Declaration of Sentiments, written largely by Garrison, had endorsed "political action as prescribed in the Constitution" as a means of freeing the slaves. At about this time the Garrisonians, while essentially "moral suasionists," were likely to be voters, to be willing to hold office, to encourage Negroes to take cases to court to protect their rights, and to insist that they not only did not want dissolution of the Union but in fact believed the abolition of slavery would remove the major danger to dissolution. Gradually, however, Garrisonians came to understand that the slave interests had no intention of permitting the Constitutional guarantees of liberty to be enforced—either for slaves, free Negroes, or abolitionists. Because Southerners were obsessed with fear of slave revolts, they demanded silence on slavery even in the North, tried to stop Congress from receiving antislavery petitions, and tried to close the mails to abolitionist literature; even many Northerners, ignoring the Constitution, tolerated violence against abolitionists. Explained Adin Ballou long afterward, it was not until abolitionists "themselves were outlawed, mobbed and murdered, in shameless violation of every guarantee to liberty contained in the federal and state constitutions that they were gradually driven to denounce the Constitution and Union as hopelessly sold to pro-slavery."[1]

In addition, the few but influential complete nonresistants among the Garrisonians came to their noncooperation-with-government position through their belief, developed gradually in the late 1830's, that human government was evil insofar as it depended on injurious force, whether the injurious force of slavery or any other kind.

"Nonresistance," said Ballou, president of the Nonresistance Society, "cannot be for war, capital punishment, slavery, and all sorts of penal injury. Nor can it be for any government which is fundamentally for these things. . . . Its adherents cannot therefore be voluntary participants in existing governments not because they are opposed to government per se; but because they are utterly opposed to these fundamental evils, with which all that is good in existing governments is inseparably interwoven." Thus nonresistants could not vote, could not hold office or bring actions at law; laying aside all pecuniary, political, and military ambition, said Ballou, they should work to improve society by Christian teaching and example.[2]

Noncooperation with government was one of the issues over which the main body of abolitionists split in 1840—into a nonpolitical wing led by the Garrisonians and a political wing led especially by the more moderate Tappanites. The Garrisonian wing, which was possibly one-tenth of the total number of American abolitionists according to Lewis Tappan,[3] tended to allow women to speak in abolitionist meetings and to stress noncooperation with either pro-slavery churches or pro-slavery governments as a method to free the slaves. The new Tappan-influenced political wing—larger, more orthodox and evangelical in religion, more conventional in manners—wished to follow the custom of the time in keeping women from speaking at meetings and wished to stress, as major means to free the slaves, more conventional action through government and churches where possible. The political wing denounced the Garrisonian non-cooperation with government strategy as threatening to destroy the social order and to stamp all abolitionists as fanatics.

The new American and Foreign Antislavery Society, which the Tappanites formed at the time of the split, survived from 1840 through 1854, but it did not flourish. As Lewis Tappan explained long afterward, though it tried to "adopt such language and measures as Christian men could not reasonably object to, to its disappointment those who had been loudest objectors to the extremism of the Garrisonians kept aloof from the new society as well."[4]

In 1840 the upstate New Yorkers Goodell, Stewart, and Gerrit Smith, all peacemen in varying degrees, led in creating a new third party, the abolitionist Liberty party, and many of the pro-political abolitionists followed them into the new party, including, slowly and reluctantly, "moral suasionist" Lewis Tappan himself.[5] For many political abolitionists, the Liberty party rather than the antislavery societies became the main channel of action in the early 1840's. In the late 1840's much of the Liberty Party merged into the Free Soil party, much of which in turn still later merged into the Republican party.

Though weakened by the split, the American Antislavery Society survived as a Garrisonian agency. By 1844, when the issue of Texas annexation led to increasingly popular threats of Northern secession, the society officially adopted Garrison's slogan, "No Union with Slaveholders," and along with it also adopted the essentials of Garrison's noncooperation-with-government strategy.

Soon afterward Garrison wrote H. C. Wright that he was enthusiastic about the new strategy. "No step has yet been taken in our cause, so trying to those who profess to be abolitionists, or that is destined to make such a commotion in church and state. It will alienate many from our ranks, but their defection will be our gain. . . . Victory shall be achieved not by numerical superiority—not by physical might or power—but by the spirit of truth and the omnipotence of love."[6] For Garrison, noncooperation with government was nonviolence in action.

Wendell Phillips with his legal education was the Garrisonians' natural choice to develop a statement of their new official position that the Constitution was pro-slavery. Phillips, writing in 1844, cited in Article One of the Constitution the provision that representation in Congress would depend on counting persons who were not free as three-fifths of a person. In Article Four, he cited the right to reclaim any person "held in service" in one state who had escaped to another state. In addition, Phillips cited the debates in the Constitutional Convention as indicating that the men who framed the Constitution understood it to represent a compromise between freedom and slavery by which slavery was to be protected. Phillips argued that honest men could not support such a pro-slavery Constitution; to vote or hold office under it meant collaborating with the devil. Furthermore, he believed that, given the carefully equalized number of free and slave states, amending the Constitution to make it antislavery was impossible.[7]

Having these views of the Constitution, Phillips came to believe that he could no longer swear to uphold it and therefore could no longer properly appear in court as a lawyer. He had virtually abandoned his law career. He had come a long way from his days at Harvard when he was a leader of the conservative clique that argued for preserving the traditional social order.

Phillips presented the Garrisonian noncooperation-with-government position in a speech in 1845 in Concord, and Henry David

Thoreau heard him. The independent Thoreau, not given to associating with organized reform movements himself, was nevertheless impressed. It was still four years before Thoreau was to write his famous essay on civil disobedience in which he would propose his own form of noncooperation with government. But already Thoreau, reporting on Phillips' speech for the *Liberator*, valued noncooperation: "We must give Mr. Phillips the credit of being a clean, erect, and what was once called a consistent man," Thoreau wrote. "He at least is not responsible for slavery . . . for the hypocrisy and superstition of the church, nor the timidity and selfishness of the state. . . . In this man the audience might detect a sort of moral principle and integrity."[8] Thoreau and the Garrisonians were alike in putting a high value on individual purification and in being suspicious of dependence on institutions.

But many abolitionists were upset by the Garrisonians' refusal to vote. When Negroes complained that Garrisonians, by not voting, would deprive pro-Negro candidates of needed votes, the nonviolent Negro leader William Whipper answered that by not voting the Garrisonians were identifying themselves more than ever with Negroes who in most states were legally deprived of the vote. When Tappanites similarly charged that not voting might prevent abolitionist candidates from winning, the Garrisonians answered that they urged not voting because it was an essential to their self-respect; voting meant supporting candidates who if elected would have to take an oath to the slavery-upholding Constitution. Even if not voting were to slow emancipation, they still would not vote. But in fact, not voting would help emancipation, they argued, because, instead of wasting time on the details required to win elections, they could concentrate on creating the public sentiment necessary to win emancipation.[9]

Lewis Tappan accused the Garrisonians of being untrue to their pledge in the 1833 Declaration of Sentiments to use political action as a means for abolition. Edmund Quincy replied that it was the Garrisonians' unwillingness to compromise which "maintains in the political antislavery movement the very moderate degree of vitality it possesses." Similarly, Phillips even wrote his friend, United States Senator Sumner, that it was the nonvoters' agitation that kept him in office. To assure that nonvoting was effective agitation, Phillips urged abolitionists not to make their refusal to vote a quiet protest; go to the polls, he advised, and make your refusal to vote conspicuous; "I want every man in your town to ask you why you do not vote."[10]

Garrison also believed that the nonvoting of a few would actually not lose any votes to the slave; instead, the nonvoting of a few would rouse the indifferent to vote, he claimed. In fact, Garrison explained, not voting was "the strongest political influence" Northerners could "wield for the overthrow of slavery." By its moral effect, nonvoting would help make possible the peaceful withdrawal of the North from the Union—withdrawal that the Federalists, as Garrison as an early Federalist himself well knew, had advocated during the War of 1812. Withdrawal of the North in turn would destroy slavery, Garrison believed. He doubted that the slave owners could hold down their slaves one hour after the North ceased to help the South to do so.[11]

Though for years many of the leading Garrisonians joined Garrison and Phillips in deliberately not voting, not many of the rank and file did; not voting seemed to most of them to be throwing their vote away. When not voting first was becoming a big issue among abolitionists in 1839, Maria Chapman estimated that only one percent of the Massachusetts Antislavery Society members deliberately did not vote. According to one critic of the nonvoting policy, in 1841 or 1842 possibly one hundred to two hundred abolitionists in New England deliberately did not vote and probably smaller numbers in other regions. By the mid-1850's, Garrison said that the members of the American Antislavery Society were "generally agreed" on nonparticipation in government—the non-Garrisonian abolitionist William Goodell doubted it[12]—but by that time many abolitionists who strongly favored political action were likely to have withdrawn from the society anyway.

Officially Garrisonian antislavery societies did not insist that their members be nonvoters. In fact, following the open membership policy that the American Antislavery Society had made clear after Lovejoy defended himself with guns, the Garrisonians claimed they had no test for membership except favoring abolition. The American Antislavery Society, as its president Garrison explained, did not insist that its members not vote any more than it insisted that they withdraw from the pro-slavery churches, though it recommended both actions. Similarly, the Massachusetts Antislavery Society claimed it made no test of nonvoting, coming-out, or any other specific action, even though it recommended such actions: "Clergymen and Quakers, church members and come-outers, politicians and nonresistants, all stand on an equal footing upon our platform," the society said. "As abolitionists, we have no test but the fidelity of every man to his own rule of duty; no creed, but the inherent wickedness of slavery and the duty of immediate emancipation."[13]

Nevertheless, some Garrisonian societies took action that seemed intended to make voting abolitionists uncomfortable. The Massachusetts Antislavery Society asked for signatures on a pledge not to vote for any candidates who, if elected, would have to take an oath to the United States Constitution. The Essex County Antislavery Society decided, in a resolution it adopted unanimously, with Foster, Buffum, and Pillsbury present, that even to give support to any clergyman who voted was "treachery to the slave . . . and should deprive every intelligent man or woman who renders it, of the . . . honored name of abolitionist." When the Plymouth County antislavery society was choosing officers for the next year, someone asked if any of those nominated had voted for James K. Polk or Henry Clay in the last election, and when it was decided that one had done so, his name was promptly dropped.

Gentleman scholar Edmund Quincy did his part to make voters uncomfortable. At an 1850 meeting of the Massachusetts Antislavery Society, a recently escaped slave was on the platform—a woman who for four weeks had been hidden in a storage room on a ship sailing from North Carolina to Boston. Quincy asked the audience, would any of you help send this woman back into slavery as the Constitution requires? All answered no. Quincy then asked, "How many of you who have just uttered that no, have, within the past year, sworn to uphold the Constitution of the United States, either directly, or through those you have elected to represent you, and to take the oath [of office] in your name?" Many in the hall, reported the Massachusetts Antislavery Society, winced at the question.[14]

The Garrisonians found an opportunity to test their policy of noncooperation with government when the United States invaded Mexico, a country that had already freed its slaves. At this time the Garrisonians found that many other abolitionists would join them on at least some aspects of their noncooperation policy.

Almost as soon as Texas won her independence by rebellion from Mexico in 1836, abolitionists had begun petitioning against American annexation of Texas. Abolitionists believed that annexing so large an area on the border of the slave states could lead to increasing the number of slave states and so forever make slave interests dominant in the federal government.

In the early 1840's when agitation to annex Texas intensified, the wizened Puritan Congressman John Quincy Adams, the former President, together with nineteen other members of Congress declared that if Texas were annexed to the Union, it would justify the dissolution of the Union because annexation would perpetuate the slavery which the Founding Fathers had wished would soon become extinct. At that time, with the encouragement of Adams, Lewis Tappan visited England to attempt to persuade the British government to make a large loan to Texas on the condition that Texas would abolish slavery. Tappan believed such a loan would prevent American annexation of Texas and thus prevent war. Tappan talked with British cabinet members, but did not succeed in persuading them to arrange the loan.[15]

In 1845 the expected blow fell. The United States admitted Texas into the Union as a slave state. To the disgust of the abolitionists, Adams and his nineteen anti-annexation congressional colleagues, instead of carrying through their threat to try to dissolve the Union, accepted defeat. However, the New York Tappanite Judge William Jay, son of Chief Justice John Jay, asked for dissolution of the Union at once before annexation had time to make the South still stronger; in doing so, Jay advised avoiding "as wholly unnecessary and inexcusable, any resort to physical force." As a substitute for force, Jay proposed at once petitioning for dissolution and backing the petitioning by revolutionary action: whenever Northern citizens were imprisoned in the South simply because they were Negroes, he advised Northern states in retaliation to seize citizens of the state committing the outrage, who happened to be in the North, and hold them as hostages. Abolitionists as a whole did not accept Jay's revolutionary suggestion, but in line with Jay, the Massachusetts Antislavery Society at least urged its state legislature to dissolve the Union.[16]

Following a different tack, at about the same time the Massachusetts society called for citizens to sign a pledge that they would not "countenance or aid the United States government in any war which may be occasioned by the annexation of Texas, or in any other war, foreign or domestic, designed to strengthen or perpetuate slavery." The society pushed this refusal-to-fight pledge. The general agent of the society, the nonresistant Charles K. Whipple, urged circulation of the pledge on West Indian Emancipation Day, August 1, 1845, at abolitionist picnics in nine Massachusetts towns. The Worcester County (South Division) Antislavery Society, with the nonresistants Garrison, Ballou, Foster, and Frederick Douglass present, unanimously endorsed the pledge. Garrison repeatedly published it in the *Liberator*. He wrote his friend May in Syracuse that the outcries of its enemies demonstrated how vital the pledge was, and added in his usual discomforting style: "I should like to look in the face the professed abolitionist or peace man, who is unwilling to sign the peace pledge." The Massachusetts society reported that the pledge was "extensively" signed.[17] The Garrisonians were reinforcing their nonviolent tradition.

After war with Mexico broke out in 1846, as Garrisonians had expected that it would, they denounced the war, and many other abolitionists denounced it too. The New England Yearly Meeting of Friends said that the United States was attempting by violence to "reestablish slavery where it had already been abolished." The First Wesleyan Church in New York City resolved that "it is against the principle of the Word of God, and the law of humanity, for a Christian nation to engage in war, unless it be strictly in self-defense . . . and that every consideration of humanity, justice, and duty, call upon our government . . . to offer peace at once, on terms of the most complete generosity and forbearance." Negro leaders including William Wells Brown and Charles Lenox Remond denounced the war; Frederick Douglass said it was "disgraceful, cruel, and iniquitous" and asked for petitions to Congress to recall troops from Mexico instantly.[18]

The Liberty party in general opposed the war. According to Liberty party leader William Goodell, among the nearly thirty Liberty party papers in the country, only four clearly supported the war. Senator John P. Hale of New Hampshire, who for a time was prominently proposed as the 1848 Liberty party candidate for President, said that the war will mark the nation as infamous. Some of the more radical abolitionists in the Liberty party, declaring they sought a broader platform for the party than abolitionism alone, split off from the main body of the party, creating the Liberty League which called for the abolition not only of slavery but also of the armed forces. The league nominated the nearly complete nonresistant Gerrit Smith for President, and Goodell, Birney, and Beriah Green were among those who supported the pacifist league. Lewis Tappan at first regarded the league as disruptive of the Liberty party, but after the main body of the Liberty party allowed itself to be drawn into the less than absolutely abolitionist Free Soil party, Tappan voted for the league candidate, peaceman Smith, anyway.[19]

Lewis Tappan himself regarded the war as a wicked political war to enlarge the slave territory of the United States. At Tappan-related Oberlin College, Professors Charles Finney and John Morgan served as judges of a contest for the best essay to disprove the traditional church doctrine that it is "lawful for the Christian man to go out to fight at the command of the civil magistrate." The *Oberlin Evangelist*—whose wartime editor was Oberlin Professor Henry Cowles, one of the founders of the nearly completely nonresistant Oberlin Peace Society—repeatedly indicated its horror of the war. While opposing Garrisonian complete nonresistance and defending the right of magistrates to use the sword against evildoers within the nation, the *Oberlin Evangelist* said that all international wars "are wrong as well as ruinous" and condemned this war in particular as disgracing the nation before the world. Like the American Peace Society, the *Oberlin Evangelist* urged the unworldly policy that the American government should withdraw all its soldiers from Mexico first and negotiate with the Mexican government afterward.[20]

The American Peace Society, of which Lewis Tappan as well as Gerrit Smith and Samuel J. May were vice-presidents during the war, called the war "folly and wickedness" and repudiated the idea, so incompatible with individual responsibility, that patriots should support their country, right or wrong. The American Peace Society paid to help circulate Tappanite Judge William Jay's book in opposition to the war; the Tappanite American and Foreign Antislavery Society helped to circulate the book too[21] and insisted that Mexico should retain its original territory. The Tappan-related *New York Evangelist* satirized those who presented the New York volunteer soldiers both bowie knives and Bibles: "What a strange incongruity! What a mixture of piety and depravity!" This war is "one of the foulest, darkest spots upon our national escutcheon."[22]

Among those who were basically only occasional nonresistants, Unitarian Theodore Parker—Garrison's pastor—nevertheless at this time took a position in opposition to all war. "Every man who understands Christianity . . . knows that war is wrong," he said, and he suggested depriving Congress of the power to declare war, reserving that right to the people by direct vote. Charles Sumner neglected his law practice to write letters to the newspapers denouncing the war as "the most wicked act" in American history,[23] and when in 1848 the Whigs nominated Mexican War General Taylor for President,

Sumner withdrew from the Whig party to help form the new Free Soil party.

In fact nearly all abolitionists opposed the war. In doing so they were continuing the tradition of considerable numbers of Americans of open dissent from their government's wars—a tradition begun in the American Revolution and continued in the War of 1812.

As for the Garrisonians, immediately after the war began, the New England Antislavery Convention met amid great excitement. Brook Farm enthusiast William Henry Channing offered a series of resolutions denying the existence any longer of any lawful government for the United States and pledging to work for a new Constitution and "to give no aid or support to the Mexican War." Pastor Theodore Parker of Boston and railroad boycotter Charles Lenox Remond of Salem spoke in support of the resolutions, and they were enthusiastically adopted.

Garrison was ecstatic with the revolutionary quality of such meetings. "Never before have such meetings been held in this Commonwealth, or in this country," he wrote H. C. Wright. "The pillars of government are falling—the foundations of existing institutions are shaking—church and state are tottering to their overthrow. Multitudes are lifting up their voices for a new union and a new government, in which nothing oppressive or unchristian should enter."[24]

When Garrisonians called for the creation of a new government, critics charged they were traitors. Replying to such charges, Joseph C. Hathaway, the Quaker president of the Garrisonians' Western New York Antislavery Society, admitted that abolitionists were traitors to the American Union, but they were so, he said, because they were "true to humanity, to the slave, and to God"; they were "the only conservative power in the nation staying its degeneracy."

When Irish Americans denounced the Garrisonians as traitors, the Ohio Garrisonian paper replied that for abolitionists to threaten to dissolve the American Union for the freedom of the Negroes was as reasonable as for Irish patriots to threaten to dissolve the United Kingdom for the freedom of the Irish.

In Syracuse a group of "patriots" invaded an abolitionist-led antiwar meeting, took over the meeting, and announced that the antiwar men, "under the garb of nonresistance," were traitors who gave their allegiance to Mexico. Garrisonian pastor May led the antiwar men out of the meeting to another place, where he presented this resolution in reply: "The treason most to be . . . abhorred is that which would urge on . . . a government in the horrid work of human butchery."[25]

While most political abolitionists would not join the Garrisonians in asking for secession, Tappanites did join them in asking Congress not to vote for war supplies, and in fact most Massachusetts congressmen voted against a bill providing war supplies. Garrisonians reported with relish that mechanics refused to work on government orders for pontoons to get troops across Mexican rivers. The *Friends Review* reminded Quakers not to accept any profit from preparations for war. Negro pastor Garnet denounced Northerners who said slavery in the abstract was wrong but were still willing to make money out of this pro-slavery war. "Who makes the bullets and the powder cartridges" for the war? he asked in a speech to the American and Foreign Antislavery Society in New York. "The South? No. The Yankees make them, and put the money in their pockets."[26]

Meanwhile the Massachusetts legislature went so far as to agree with many abolitionists that the Mexican War was unconstitutional, was a war of conquest, and would strengthen the slave power. Many Whig leaders opposed the war, including Congressman Abraham Lincoln of Illinois, who, however, as long as the United States was in the war, felt compelled to vote for war supplies. The American Peace Society—whose strength was in New England and New York —reported that it hardly knew one minister who did not abhor the war. Clergy of churches with a strong base in New England, like the Congregationalists and Unitarians, overwhelmingly opposed the war. But the clergy of churches with a strong base near the fighting, like the Methodists and Catholics, usually favored the war.[27] In general, the comparatively land-satisfied Northeast, distant from the territory likely to be seized from Mexico by the war, tended to oppose it, while the South and the trans-Mississippi West, devoted to expansion, tended to favor it.

Nevertheless, to the Garrisonians' disgust, Massachusetts reform Governor Briggs, like many other governors, did call for volunteers to fight in Mexico. Garrisonians and Quakers as well as some Tappanites openly opposed volunteering. Volunteers, said the Garrisonian Frederick Douglass, would help "to establish with fire and sword the man-blasting and soul-damning system of slavery" in Mexico. When a missionary group presented Bibles to the Massachusetts volunteers, Edmund Quincy, writing in the *National Antislavery Standard*, quipped: "If the missionary society would only send a chaplain with them, who knows but their means of grace might be blessed with a revival of religion, which would enable them to cut the Mexicans' throats in the true spirit of Christian love?" A group of young Quakers in Philadelphia issued 10,000 copies of a tract to dissuade men from enlisting. Tappanite Elizur Wright, who by this time had become editor of a Boston daily paper, tried to persuade men not to volunteer and invited anyone in doubt to come to his office to talk about it.

Not long after "recruiting sergeant" Briggs, as Garrisonians dubbed the governor, had issued his call for volunteers, he visited an asylum for the blind led by the not-so-peaceful abolitionist, Dr. Samuel Gridley Howe. There the governor was introduced to a girl who was both blind and a deaf mute, the famous Laura Bridgman whom Howe had taught to talk with her fingers. As soon as the girl understood it was the governor who was talking to her, she, having an innocent's view of the war—perhaps sounder than a more sophisticated one—asked him why he wished to let volunteers "go to Mexico to kill people? . . . Why couldn't he hide their clothes, so that they couldn't pack their trunks?" she asked. The governor, reported Quincy in the *National Antislavery Standard,* "was satisfied with a very short interview."

When Theodore Parker spoke at an antiwar meeting in Faneuil Hall, some of Governor Briggs' volunteers who were present heckled him.

"If God please, we will die a thousand times but never draw blade in this wicked war," said Parker, and the soldiers shouted, "Throw him over."

Parker asked the soldiers what they would do after "throwing him over."

"Drag you out of the hall," the soldiers shouted.

"What good would that do?" replied Parker. "It would not wipe off the infamy of this war—would not make it less wicked!

"I blame not so much the volunteers," continued Parker, "as the famous men who deceive the nation." Some of the soldiers cried, "Kill him, kill him!"[28]

"Kill him!" answered Parker. "I shall walk home unarmed and unattended; and," Parker added, showing his considerable confidence in nonviolence, "not a man of you will hurt one hair of my head."

After some of the young volunteers—some only sixteen years old —deserted, Edmund Quincy wrote in the *National Antislavery*

Standard that he hoped that some of them were among the volunteers who had attended abolitionist antiwar meetings. He added: "I am happy to hear that they are deserting with a very creditable degree of application."

The merry young poet James Russell Lowell, who had not yet become an illustrious Harvard professor, identified himself with Garrisonians during the war. He condemned the Mexican War as part of his classic condemnation of war in general in his satire, *The Biglow Papers.* War, said Lowell, in the words of a Yankee farmer, was contrary to the Gospels:

> *As for war, I call it murder,—*
> *There you have it plain an' flat.*
> *I don't want to go no furder,*
> *Than my Testyment fer that.*

Lowell insisted—as the Nuremburg Tribunal was also to do in the next century—that men are individually responsible for what they do regardless of government orders:

> *Ef you take a sword and dror it,*
> *And go stick a feller thru,*
> *Gov'ment ain't to answer for it.*
> *God'll send the bill to you.*[29]

During the early part of the war, the independent abolitionist Burritt, a complete nonresistant, was a major figure in the American Peace Society, but later, after struggling with Secretary Beckwith over the recurring issue of whether the society opposed all war or only aggressive wars, Burritt gave up the society in disgust as too timid. While still editor of the American Peace Society's journal, as well as afterward, Burritt pushed for the signing of a personal pledge promising both never to fight a war in any form for any purpose and, in more vague language, to help abolish slavery. Among Garrisonians, while Edmund Quincy called Burritt's pledge "humbug," Ballou, Frederick Douglass, and Samuel J. May praised it, and Garrison said it "covers the most ultra ground of nonresistance." Among Tappanites, while Beriah Green considered Burritt's movement a "conspiracy," Lewis Tappan advised a British abolitionist that the "devoted" Burritt was doing "much to bring the custom of war into deserved condemnation,"[30] and the Tappanite *Oberlin Evangelist* encouraged Burritt's drive for signatures. Amos Dresser, the complete nonresistant abolitionist who served as Burritt's agent in Ohio, collected seven hundred signatures in Oberlin alone. The New England Wesleyan synod, generally Tappanite in orientation, urged its ministers to present the pledge to their members. By early 1847, twenty thousand people in Britain and America had signed the anti-war and antislavery pledge, and by the next year, thirty thousand. Among the signers, and subsequently among the officers of the League of Universal Brotherhood which all signers of the pledge automatically joined, were Gerrit Smith, Christian Socialist William Henry Channing, and the Tappanite Oberlin Professor Amasa Walker.

As for blacks, in this war they generally escaped the temptation to participate in war as a means to raise their status in American life. Few Negroes served in the American forces in the Mexican War. The Negro national convention of 1847 voted down a resolution recommending that Negroes "instruct their sons in the art of war."[31] Contemporary accounts of Negro services in American wars in general do not mention Negroes serving in the Mexican War. Federal and state laws had barred Negroes from state militias since soon after the Revolutionary War, and while the United States Navy accepted a limited quota of Negroes, the army had excluded them continuously after the War of 1812.

At a meeting of the Western New York Antislavery Society during the Mexican War, an agent of the society, the generally nonviolent Negro William Wells Brown, proposed a daring resolution. As the *National Antislavery Standard* reported it, he proposed advising blacks, "in case of a demand of their services in the field, to fight against the United States." Evidently Brown's resolution meant that if Negroes had to fight at all, it would be better for them in their own interest to fight for the racially mixed, slavery-free Mexico rather than the race-conscious, slavery-protecting United States. An abolitionist pastor who opposed the American war with Mexico nevertheless objected to Brown's resolution as "belligerent." A Negro said that if the United States drafted him, "he would perish in jail rather than obey." But the Negro antislavery lecturer Remond evidently preferred Brown's advice to perishing in jail. Remond, according to the *Standard,* supported Brown's resolution "in a speech of fervid eloquence, and determined hostility to a quiet subjection to American tyrants." Afterward Brown, apparently convinced his "belligerent" resolution could not pass, withdrew it.[32]

One of the few abolitionists who volunteered for the American forces was the pro-violent Kentuckian Cassius M. Clay. When the

United States annexed Texas, Clay denounced it; when annexation led to war, he admitted that the war might easily have been averted. But once the United States was in war, he said, good citizens must support their government or anarchy would result. He volunteered, and soon a professed abolitionist led a company of soldiers of the slave nation, the United States, to fight against the free nation, Mexico.

Long afterward Clay frankly confessed that his volunteering was a political maneuver. "Kentuckians being exceptionally . . . fond of military glory, I hoped by the Mexican War to strengthen myself" in Kentucky politics, he explained; "the result proved that I was right."[33] As an abolitionist in a slave state, the going was so rough for Clay that naturally he looked for ways in which he could earn popular approval, and volunteering for war seemed to be such a way.

But the nonviolent abolitionists were grieved at Clay. He had a "senseless ambition" in thus joining the "chivalry" of the South, said the American and Foreign Antislavery Society. Clay is "doing evil that good might come," protested Kentucky Tappanite John G. Fee, who often worked with Clay. The Garrisonian Maria Chapman wrote him in an open letter: you are not a patriot—in fact you are "a traitor to freedom." The Mexicans are the ones who are fighting in self-defense, she said; they are the ones who are fighting for freedom. A real patriot is one who refuses to aid any tyrant government "in its detestable purposes—he who defies its will, though alone . . . he who sees and binds himself to what is universal and external —'whose country is the world and whose countrymen are all mankind.' "[34]

Fortunately for the internal calm of the United States, there was no draft to raise troops for the Mexican War; if there had been, there might have been a headlong confrontation between abolitionists and the federal government. As it was, the government left the abolitionists to their jeremiads and frustrations, and fought the war almost completely without them. The government fought the war to a victory that brought the acquisition of vast territory from Mexico, which in turn raised the old question about the extension of slavery in new and dangerous forms.

The nonviolent abolitionists had passed the test of the Mexican War. While they had not been able to stop the war, they had kept alive their witness both against slavery and war, strengthening their nonviolent tradition in doing so. A more severe test for the nonviolent abolitionists was to come in the Civil War. Then, in contrast to the Mexican War, there was to be not only a draft to raise troops but also a likelihood that the war, instead of extending slavery, would abolish it. In the Mexican War, the abolitionists' antiwar and antislavery principles reinforced each other. In the Civil War they were to clash.

In their noncooperation with government, the Garrisonians found themselves especially plagued with the dilemma of wishing to influence government at the same time they wished to remain aloof from it. They sought to meet this dilemma in part by allowing themselves to participate in government in limited, selective ways.

Garrisonians did not object to certain kinds of petitioning of governments, as editor Edmund Quincy said in the *Nonresistant* in 1839. They could ask those in power to do something they thought right, he explained, but there was a limit to what they could petition for; they could not petition for any end, no matter how desirable, which would require "compulsion."[35]

Just as Garrisonians had petitioned the Massachusetts legislature to desegregate the railroads in the early 1840's, so also before, during, and after the Mexican War, they petitioned for the dissolution of the Union, and in 1848 a committee of the legislature took their petitions seriously enough to hold hearings on them. For many years Garrisonians petitioned Congress to end the slave trade in the District of Columbia and continued to do so until 1850 when Congress finally ended it. They petitioned state legislatures for laws preventing any state officer from helping to deliver up fugitive slaves to slave masters, regardless of federal law. Among the vast number of other actions they petitioned for were that all United States territories be free of slavery and that the United States government refuse to employ either slaves or slaveholders.

Garrisonians not only participated in government by petitioning, but some of them also participated by voting in limited ways—that is, ways in which they did not vote for candidates who were obliged if elected to take an oath to the United States Constitution. Thus they could vote, the *Antislavery Standard* decided, for state constitutional amendments. In fact, they should vote for amendments that would give Negroes the equal right to vote—Negroes clearly had the equal right to vote in the 1840's and 1850's only in the five most northeasterly states: Maine, New Hampshire, Vermont, Massachusetts, and Rhode Island—while at the same time Garrisonians advised Negroes who had the right to vote not to use it in most elections.

Despite their general noncooperation with government policy, Garrisonians commented freely on legislation, parties, and elections. Garrisonian editor Rogers, of the New Hampshire *Herald of Freedom*, noted ironically that nonvoting abolitionists sometimes became absorbed in politics: "They do not hold office, or vote—but they will hover about the polls, to watch the balloting of others, and about the State House, where they can enjoy the turmoil of legislation."[36]

Often Garrisonians spoke out their opinions of candidates. Frederick Douglass said in 1848, though he was a nonvoter at the time, that the only qualifications of General Taylor for the Presidency were his skill in butchering Mexicans and his unwavering fidelity to the bloody code of slavery. In 1850 the *Liberator* thrashed Daniel Webster for his support of the fugitive slave law and in general denounced any candidate who supported Webster; instead the *Liberator* preferred the election of such Free Soil candidates for Congress as Charles Sumner and Horace Mann. In 1856, Garrison said that, despite his not voting himself, he preferred the election of Fremont, the first Republican candidate for President.

By about this time, as abolitionism became more popular with politicians, the Garrisonians found that their noncooperation with government policy put them increasingly in anomalous situations. Garrisonian lecturers were allowing Joshua Giddings, the pro-violent Republican congressman, to drive them in his own carriage around his Ohio district to introduce them to audiences. Giddings —whom Garrison considered to be, for a politician, a man of rare integrity—believed that the converts whom the Garrisonian lecturers won to the antislavery cause were not as likely to go all the way to nonvoting as they were to become voting Republicans. In fact, Republican financiers, as the Garrisonian nonresistant Oliver Johnson admitted, were so convinced of this that they often contributed to the expense of Garrisonian lecturers. In turn, Phillips felt that, nonpolitical though he was in one sense, his agitation had done enough to help put Charles Sumner into the United States Senate so that he had a right to ask Sumner to appoint his friends to office.[37] At this point Phillips was approaching an involvement in the spoils of office which compromised his claim that nonvoting kept him above suspicion of mundane motives.

Some of the leading Garrisonians were drawn more and more into politics and correspondingly became less and less enchanted with nonvoting. The Garrisonian Negro Remond said at an antislavery meeting as early as 1848: "My confidence in the system of no-votes is lessening; and I bid God-speed to any party which will abolish slavery. If it can't be done in H. C. Wright's way [nonvoting], then let it be done in Martin Van Buren's way [Free Soil party]."³⁸ By 1851, Douglass, having decided that the Constitution, despite its support of slavery in some passages, should be interpreted on the whole as an antislavery document, had abandoned nonvoting and gradually ceased to be regarded as a Garrisonian. In 1854 educational philosopher Bronson Alcott, who had never yet voted, was appalled by the failure of Massachusetts abolitionists to prevent the courts from returning a fugitive slave to the South and determined to use his vote to try to secure the kind of government that would not let this happen again. Stephen S. Foster—ever fertile in concocting new techniques of nonviolent protest—made a proposal at an 1849 meeting of the Massachusetts Antislavery Society for edging away from nonvoting; he suggested that abolitionists willing to vote should do so only for candidates pledged to refuse to take an oath of office if elected. But both Garrison and Quincy opposed Foster's idea, and it was tabled. By 1858, Foster—who personally was still not willing to vote—proposed that the Massachusetts Antislavery Society encourage the large number of abolitionists who were willing to vote to form a new, thoroughly abolitionist political party such as the Republican party was not, but the majority of the society rejected his proposal.

On the other hand, in 1857, when Chief Justice Taney gave his devastating opinion in the Dred Scott case that Negroes could not be citizens of the United States, many Garrisonians felt this justified them anew in not cooperating with such a government. In 1860, Phillips, Garrison, Foster, Pillsbury, and Oliver Johnson were still refusing to vote.

Perhaps, as the political abolitionists argued, nonvoting weakened the abolitionists at some points. Perhaps the Garrisonians' drive for disunion invited most Northerners to distrust abolitionists, with little compensating gain. But Garrisonian leaders countered that it was political entanglements that seriously weakened the abolitionists by subjecting them to the suspicion of motives endemic in politics, involving them in the game of expediency and compromise that was contrary to their moral stand, narrowing their access to the national conscience, and wasting time that should be given to revolutionizing public opinion. To the Garrisonians, their influence was strengthened even in politics by their nonviolent noncooperation with the slavery-protecting government, and their influence would of course be increased much more, they believed, if they could persuade the North to take the ultimate step of withdrawing from its union with the slave-ridden South.

Like the Garrisonians, the arch-individualist Henry Thoreau advocated noncooperation with slavery-protecting government, but the form of noncooperation he emphasized was different.

Like the Garrisonians, Thoreau defied the fugitive slave law; he hid a fugitive in his house. Like the Garrisonians, Thoreau advocated the secession of the North from the South. Also like the Garrisonians, Thoreau did not vote. In his early years he did not vote largely from indifference to politics, but even when he became concerned about the folly of the Mexican War and the corruption of slavery, he remained a nonvoter; in fact he remained a nonvoter all his life. At an abolitionist meeting Thoreau explained tersely: "The fate of the country does not depend . . . on what kind of paper you drop into the ballot-box once a year, but on what kind of man you drop from your chamber into the street every morning."[39] All the Concord individualists, including Emerson, were likely to be nonvoters—they were likely to be willing to take but little responsibility for government, the economic order, education, or the church; they were anti-institutional and anti-establishment.

But Thoreau went beyond the Garrisonians by practicing one form of noncooperation with government that the Garrisonians seldom practiced. "Some are petitioning the state to dissolve the Union," Thoreau wrote. "Why do they not dissolve it themselves—the union between themselves and the state—and refuse to pay their quota into its treasury?" For six years Thoreau did refuse to pay poll taxes, and accordingly in 1846, during the Mexican War, he was imprisoned in Concord for one night until a friend paid his fine. Prison, said Thoreau provocatively, "is the only house in a slave state in which a free man can abide with honor."[40]

The idea of tax refusals as a means of social protest was not new. There was considerable tradition among Quakers both in England and America to refuse to pay war taxes, and when they did refuse, the government sometimes confiscated their property. Just before the American Revolution, Americans resisting British encroachments often refused to pay stamp taxes. During the Revolution the young Quaker-raised sailor, Paul Cuffee, the son of a Negro father and an Indian mother, refused to pay his Massachusetts taxes because as a nonwhite he was not allowed to vote. He was jailed, but he continued to agitate the question, using the popular slogan, no taxation without representation, and by 1783 Massachusetts Negroes had won the right to vote.

In the early years of the Nonresistance Society, it considered the question of refusing to pay taxes. For example, the society's treasurer, Charles K. Whipple, argued in 1839 that the American Revolution could have been won more speedily and under more favorable circumstances for the later development of America if the Revolutionists' tax refusals had been entirely nonviolent and on a larger scale. The result would have been widespread suffering for Americans, Whipple admitted; their property would have been confiscated to pay the taxes. But if they had patiently submitted to this and continued their noncooperation, the prisons would have been "filled to overflowing" with nonviolent rebels, the British could have accomplished nothing, and their power would have come to a stop without blood.

In the 1840's and 1850's Negro leaders became well aware of circumstances in which they felt it was unjust for them to be required to pay taxes. Charles Lenox Remond, writing from England—where he was lecturing with one of the Nonresistance Society's tax-refusal advocates, John A. Collins—urged Negroes to be more radical in their demands, and added: "Let every colored man, called upon to pay taxes to any institution in which he is deprived or denied its privileges and advantages, withhold his taxes, although it costs imprisonment or confiscation. Let our motto be—no privileges, no pay." In Ohio a ladies' abolitionist society, which helped support private schools for blacks, protested that it was "the greatest injustice" for Ohio Negroes to be taxed for public schools when their children were excluded from them. In Michigan a state convention of Negroes protested similarly, and in Indiana the Yearly Meeting of Antislavery Friends did so also. In Rochester, New York, after Negroes protested against paying school taxes when their children were excluded from all the schools, the school board exempted Negroes from taxes until the board could establish schools for Negroes. In Massachusetts, as we have seen, some Negroes avoided paying taxes to the segregated Boston schools by moving to suburbs where schools were not segregated. The 1848 black national convention, meeting in Cleveland, adopted a resolution that came close to being an endorsement for Negroes refusing to pay taxes wherever they could not vote: "Whereas we firmly believe with the Fathers of '76, that taxation and representation ought to go together; therefore, resolved, that we are very much in doubt as to the propriety of our paying any tax . . . until we are permitted to be represented."[41]

Garrisonians usually recommended paying taxes even if the taxes seemed unjust. When the tax question came up during the Mexican War, the Negro antislavery lecturer W. W. Brown gave the stock Garrisonian answer: we are coerced to pay taxes; we are not to blame for what the government does with the money it seizes from us.[42] As usual with the Garrisonians, when they discussed whether they should pay taxes, they discussed it more in moralistic than in pragmatic terms. They were more likely to ask whether paying taxes was consistent with nonvoting and disunion than to ask whether it would be an effective form of protest, and, if so, under what circumstances and at what cost.

Despite the usual Garrisonian opposition, there were a few abolitionists, in addition to Thoreau, who helped to strengthen the slender thread of tax-refusal tradition by deliberately refusing to pay taxes.

Before Thoreau refused to pay taxes, his Concord friend, nonresistant Bronson Alcott, had already refused. Alcott had acted as a general protest against government interference with individual liberty, including government support of slavery. Three years before Thoreau was sentenced to jail for tax refusal, Alcott had already been sentenced to jail for the same reason, but Alcott was released before being actually jailed because someone quickly paid his tax.

A Negro storekeeper in Bath, in upstate New York, stopped paying taxes for a new school building in 1848 when he discovered that his children as Negroes were to be excluded from it. The tax collector insisted on his paying, and when the storekeeper still refused, the collector auctioned off some of his goods in his store. The storekeeper was noble, said Douglass' *North Star*.[43]

In 1853, Garrisonian leader Purvis protested the new policy that segregated his children in the public schools of Byberry, Pennsylvania, by refusing to pay school taxes; the *Liberator* called it a "manly protest." Purvis also protested at the same time by boycotting the segregated schools, having his children privately tutored.

Purvis' influence was weighty. He was the highest-ranking Negro in the antislavery societies; he had served as one of the vice-presidents of the American Antislavery Society and for at least five years as president of one of its strongest auxiliaries, the Pennsylvania Antislavery Society. In addition, gentlemen farmer Purvis was the second largest taxpayer in his township. Purvis' weight made itself felt. He succeeded in having the Byberry schools reopened equally to white and black children.[44]

In the struggle for the control of Kansas in the mid-1850's, free-soil settlers sometimes refused to pay taxes to the pro-Southern Kansas government because they did not recognize it as legitimate. John Brown was a guerrilla abolitionist who supported such refusal, and his brother-in-law, American Missionary Association agent Samuel Adair, was a Tappanite nonviolent abolitionist who also supported it. Adair joined his Kansas community in an open decision to refuse to pay taxes, for which pro-Southerners punished the community with violence.[45]

However, there was no general move by abolitionists to refuse to pay taxes. Perhaps a major campaign of tax refusals would have been at least as effective a form of noncooperation with a racist government as nonvoting or refusals to hold office or refusals to volunteer for military duty or asking for the dissolution of the Union. In the 1850's the *Liberator* was already reporting that a few women suffragists were refusing to pay their taxes until they could vote, and by the 1870's women's tax refusals—in which Abby Kelley Foster was a leader—were to become a significant element of the nonviolent direct-action program of the women's suffrage movement.[46] Later in India, Gandhi was to find salt-tax refusals a powerful form of protest against British colonialism.

As for Thoreau, he was too much of an individualist to lead any movement, for tax refusal or anything else. His devotion to abolition and his experience of jail were pallid compared to those of Garrison or Foster, or Beach or Charles Torrey or Captain Walker or many other abolitionists, and his faith in nonviolence was not to survive the terrible dilemmas of the next decade.

Nevertheless, in conjunction with his tax-refusal experience, Thoreau developed a theory of the power of nonviolence which was to influence not so much those of his own generation as those of later times like Tolstoy, Gandhi, and Martin Luther King.

Thoreau's theory was like the Garrisonians' in its absolute morality and in its argument that those who take suffering on themselves as a protest against injustice have a stronger voice than those who do not take it. Said Thoreau, if anyone thinks that those who disobey an unjust law and are imprisoned for it lose their influence, "they do not know by how much truth is stronger than error, nor how much more eloquently and effectively he can combat injustice who had experienced a little in his own person."

Thoreau's theory, however, emphasized one element in non-violence that the Garrisonians did not emphasize but which Foster with his speak-ins, the Grimké sisters with their sit-ins, Frederick Douglass with his ride-ins, and Garrison with his refusal to vote or cooperate in war employed: the nuisance of which a righteous and unafraid minority is capable. "A minority is powerless while it conforms to the majority," Thoreau said, ". . . but it is irresistible when it clogs by its whole weight. If the alternative is to keep all just men in prison, or give up war and slavery, the state will not hesitate which to choose. . . . This is, in fact, the definition of a peaceable revolution, if any such is possible."[47]

16. Underground Railroad

◇◇◇◇◇◇◇◇◇◇◇

ONE OF THE abolitionists' most daring forms of noncooperation with government was helping slaves escape. In the South, helping slaves escape was against state law. Both in the North and in the South, beginning soon after the federal government was created, helping slaves escape was against federal law. Sometimes the abolitionists' defiance of these laws was violent, but sometimes it was nonviolent, and deliberately so.

For slaves, running away was dangerous. Slave owners commonly chased runaways with guns and dogs. If they were caught, slave owners might punish them by putting them in leg irons or by selling the husbands apart from their wives and the parents apart from their children.

Helping slaves escape was also dangerous. Those in the South who did so were often caught and punished. A free Negro woman in South Carolina who hid two fugitive slave children was sold into slavery herself with her own children. The young minister Charles T. Torrey, who had studied at Yale and Andover Theological Seminary, was caught after having helped some two hundred slaves to escape and was sentenced to six years of hard labor in prison, where he died. A Yankee sea captain, Jonathan Walker, was living in Florida when several slaves begged him to help them escape. He tried to carry them in his ship to freedom in the Bahamas, but was caught. On the order of a federal court he was branded by a red hot iron on one hand with the letters SS, intended to mean "Slave Stealer"; but Wendell Phillips, who declared that Walker had the noblest hand in America, interpreted the letters to mean "Slave Savior."

With good reason to be terrified, some of the slaves who tried to escape armed themselves with knives, pistols, clubs, or whatever they could find. In Nebraska territory a group of escaping slaves killed their pursuers, seized their horses, and fled. In New England an escaping slave fled from one Quaker home to another, disguised as a Quaker lady wearing a thick veil; as the Quakers sent him on his way, he told them that he carried a revolver in his pocket, and if his master ever caught up with him, he would shoot him or be shot, for he would never be a slave again.

On the other hand, a slave who prided himself on having escaped without arms was blacksmith James W. C. Pennington, later an outstanding Tappanite pastor. "I had provided no weapon whatever," he said; "not so much as a penknife—it never once entered my mind."[1]

In New York State a convention of escaped slaves and their friends, presided over by Frederick Douglass, urged slaves to escape but declined to send them any weapons. The convention announced to the slaves we are too poor to send you weapons; moreover, "some of us have become nonresistants, and have discarded the use of these weapons, and would say to you 'love your enemies.'"

Nonviolent abolitionists could regret the readiness of many fugitives for violence at the same time that they tried to interpret it sympathetically. Traveling in central Pennsylvania, nonviolent antislavery agent J. Miller McKim reported that seven fugitives had just passed through the region, each carrying a "pistol and a dirk," and expressing "their determination to die, rather than to be taken back. It is not difficult to understand," he wrote, "how they could be 'sincerely religious' [as they were reported to be], and at the same time, under the popular error that violence in self-defense and for the sake of liberty is justifiable."[2]

Many fugitive slaves were not vengeful toward their masters. Some of them explained that their masters had treated them kindly; they had fled from them simply because they wished to be free. Even some of the fugitives whose masters had treated them cruelly did not therefore seem to hate them. The fugitive Henry Bibb, who became a leading abolitionist orator, wrote from Detroit to his master in Kentucky inviting him for a friendly visit and forgiving him for his whipping of his wife and infant. "As it was the custom of your country," Bibb wrote, "to treat your fellowmen as you did me and my little family, I can freely forgive you." An escaped Maryland slave, aged twenty, when he passed through Philadelphia, told Negro abolitionist William Still that he imagined his former mistress "in a fit of perplexity, such as he might enjoy, could he peep at her from Canada or some safe place. He however did not wish her any evil." Thomas Van Rensselaer, who ran away from his Mohawk valley, New York, slave master in 1819 and became a restaurateur and leading abolitionist in New York City, made a friendly visit to his former master in the 1830's and dined at his table. The remarkable evangelist Sojourner Truth, who ran away from her Ulster County, New York, slave master, nevertheless said many years later that "her home should be open to the man who had held her as a slave and had so much wronged her; she would feed him and take care of him if he was hungry or poor." Garrison, perhaps influenced by his wishes, reported extravagantly as late as 1853 that, though he had talked "with hundreds of fugitive slaves, some of them with backs scarred all over with the lash," he had "never yet seen one whose talk was of revenge, or who wished for an opportunity to shed the blood of his oppressor."[3]

On the other hand, there were reports that some fugitives were vengeful toward their masters. A nineteen-year-old fugitive boy who was staying at speak-inner Foster's farm near Worcester—where Foster's daughter was teaching him to read—said that his master "ought to dance in a fiery furnace" for depriving him of an education. A fugitive who had escaped to Canada wrote his former master inviting him to come to Toronto to try to seize him, just because he wished to have a chance to wreak vengeance on him.[4]

Fugitives who were ready for violence were not always rational in directing it. A group of fugitives escaping through Delaware came across a noisy group of Irish whom they believed, in their fear, to be slave catchers. They fought the Irish, killing one of them, and only afterward discovered that the Irish were merely having a party to celebrate Halloween. Sometimes fugitives' readiness for violence seemed to represent a general rage at whites. Reported the Tappan-led American Missionary Association, which often helped escapees with food and clothing, some fugitives, "goaded to madness by the wrongs they had endured, are ready . . . to seek redress on all whom they meet, even those who would do them good."[5]

While nonviolent direct action at its best was usually open, abolitionists debated whether their aid to fugitive slaves should be open or secret. It was partly a choice between making aid to fugitives a public protest demonstration against slavery in general or making it private aid to individuals trying to escape.

Wendell Phillips seemed to sense that aiding fugitives in the open was more effective protest. "I go against Underground Railroads," he told an abolitionist gathering in 1849. "I would not, of preference . . . even adopt the plan of old [Quaker] William Rotch, of New Bedford, of blessed memory, who kept a hiding place always in his cellar or garret for the fugitive. . . . I would, at least, be at liberty to place him in my parlor, and set the door open, and bid the thousands passing in the street look in, if they chose." But in fact, a few years later, Phillips found that he himself was forced to secrecy in aiding fugitives. As he described his Boston Vigilance Committee work, it included "debates about secret escapes—plans to evade where we can't resist—the door watched that no spy may enter—the whispered consultations of the morning—some putting property out of their hands, planning to incur penalties, and planning also that, in case of conviction, the government may get nothing from them."

Frederick Douglass, who assisted fugitives passing through Rochester, emphasized the value of secrecy. He was thinking primarily of the greater help secrecy could be to the fugitive slaves as individuals, not the effect on public opinion. Douglass chided the abolitionists, especially in the West, who made their operations public. "I . . . applaud them for willingly subjecting themselves to bloody persecution, by openly avowing their participation in the escape of slaves," Douglass wrote. "I, however, can see very little good resulting from such a course, either to themselves or the slaves escaping; while, upon the other hand, I see and feel assured that those open declarations are a positive evil to the slaves remaining, who are seeking to escape. They do nothing towards enlightening the slave, whilst they do much toward enlightening the master." Douglass suggested that if a secret threat of violence hung over slave hunters, it would contribute to the success of the Underground Railroad, whether the aid given to fugitives in a particular case was in itself violent or nonviolent. He would have the slave hunter "imagine himself surrounded by myriads of invisible tormentors, ever ready to snatch from his infernal grasp his trembling prey," Douglass said. "Let him feel that at every step he takes, in pursuit of the flying bondmen, he is running the frightful risk of having his hot brains dashed out by an invisible agency."[6]

Despite Douglass' advice, much aid to fugitives was open at least to some degree. Fugitives on their arrival in the North sometimes appeared in person on the platform at antislavery meetings. Garrisonian pastor Samuel J. May openly said in 1855 that he had helped at least a hundred fugitives pass through Syracuse in the past year, and recently had a fugitive and his wife seated at his table. The Tappanite Negro pastor Amos Beman boasted in print that his New Haven church welcomed fugitives arriving by Underground Railroad and gave them material aid, though at the same time he explicitly refused to say by what route they had arrived because the route would be used again. A Providence church of the abolitionist Free Will Baptist denomination published an open letter in local papers in 1849 saying it operated a branch of the Underground Railroad which had helped over sixteen Negroes escape in the past few months, and appealed for funds to help it continue. The *Liberator* publicly announced the arrival of a fugitive at Foster's farm near Worcester and even ididentified the fugitive's master as the owner of a boat on the James River in Virginia, as if defying him to come to Massachusetts to try to recover his slave. An Illinois abolitionist recorded in his diary in 1848 that he had transported a fugitive on a highway by daylight, and said this indicated that the Railroad had nearly risen to the surface.

In Ohio, the abolitionist Oberlin professor, James A. Thome, got into trouble for telling a small antislavery meeting in 1839 that he had helped a slave escape from his home town of Augusta, Kentucky. Someone in the meeting, unknown to Thome, had the story published, and when it became known in Augusta, the town burst into "a blaze of excitement." Fearing that if Kentuckians could have him arrested in Oberlin, they would persuade the state of Ohio to extradite him to Kentucky for trial, Thome fled for a time to hiding in Connecticut.

Learning from such experiences, abolitionists were in fact often secret about some aspects of their aid to fugitives. Abolitionists at times covered windows, used secret hiding places in their houses, barns, or woods, kept their children from knowing what was happening as well as they could, and transported fugitives at night. Often they did not ask the names of the fugitives they helped or tell their own names to the fugitives. In rural areas, to operate the Underground Railroad effectively, each participating family only needed to know the Undergrounders to the immediate south who sent them fugitives and the Undergrounders to the immediate north to whom they passed the fugitives on. As some Undergrounders emphasized, if you were caught, the less you knew about the whole Underground system the better; the fewer other people you could get into trouble. In 1852, Theodore Parker concealed the names of Bostonians helping fugitives escape. In 1858, J. Miller McKim said he couldn't publicly describe the details of the operation of the Underground Railroad. Even in 1872, when McKim's Philadelphia colleague, Negro William Still, published his detailed account of the Railroad, he still did not dare to publish some of the names of the Maryland and Delaware operators for fear that doing so would bring them punishment.[7]

Because Negroes often knew where fugitives were hiding among them, they were tempted to turn into informers. William Still claimed that Negroes in general were loyal to fugitives, "but now and then some unprincipled individuals, under various pretences, would cause us great anxiety." To prevent informing, the Negroes of New Bedford threatened to kill anyone among them who informed a slave owner where his slaves were hiding. In Burlington, New Jersey, at a meeting in a Negro church, a number of Negroes suspected one of those at the meeting was a spy for slave catchers and stabbed him. In Chester County, Pennsylvania, near the border of the slave states, when a group of Negroes discovered a Negro telling slave agents where fugitives were hiding, they gave him a beating from which he was believed to have died. In Cincinnati a group of young Negroes caught a Negro who for money had betrayed two fugitives into being returned to slavery. The young Negroes "tried" the betrayer and, according to pastor Garnet, who was present, would have torn him limb from limb if it had not been for Garnet's intercession; instead Garnet allowed them to give the betrayer three hundred blows with a paddle.

It was partly because the aid to fugitives was sometimes secret that abolitionist societies and churches—even Quaker churches—did not themselves usually organize the aid. It was also partly because abolitionist societies and churches themselves had doubts about the wisdom of the aid that they usually did not organize it. While Quakers pioneered in the Underground Railroad, some conservative Quakers, though participating in other antislavery direct action, opposed taking part in the Underground Railroad because it was illegal. In fact, a few of the most zealous Quaker Undergrounders were disowned by Friends, as was Isaac Hopper of New York, or made so uncomfortable that they left the regular Quaker meetings and helped create new ones, as Levi Coffin of Indiana did. Non-Quaker abolitionists followed Quakers into the Underground Railroad only slowly. Many abolitionist societies, especially in the 1830's, were afraid of reprisals if they officially took part in such illegal activities. A considerable number of Garrisonians felt it would be a mistake to make aid to fugitives a central part of their work. Aiding fugitives was no substitute for attacking the slave system directly, they believed. In its great expenditure of time and money for the benefit of individuals, it was not as efficient in abolition of slavery as other means; according to Maria Chapman, it was a retail rather than a wholesale measure. In addition, some lukewarm abolitionists, while they were loud in meetings about their devotion to fugitives, when they knew fugitives were being pursued would make excuses and refuse to shelter them. Others naturally suspected that some who posed as fugitives were imposters and also that some who posed as Underground Railroaders were too—as indeed a few of both were.

The abolitionists' aid to fugitives may not have reached most fugitives at all. The nonresistant leader Adin Ballou estimated in 1861 that three-quarters of the fugitives had escaped essentially by their own effort, without significant conscious aid either by whites or blacks, and a recent student of the subject tends to support this view.[8] Many fugitives probably received little if any aid partly because the somewhat secret nature of the Railroad made it difficult for the fugitives, distrustful of most people as they had reason to be, to know how to find it.

Despite abolitionists' doubts, by the 1840's the major abolitionist societies endorsed aiding slaves to escape. The national colored convention meeting in Cleveland, with Douglass presiding, openly pledged themselves "to use all necessary means in aiding our enslaved brethren in escaping." The Garrisonian American Antislavery Society meeting in New York, with Garrison presiding, in biblical language openly instructed abolitionists that it was their duty to God—regardless of human law—to "hide out the outcast, and betray not him that wandereth." The Tappanite American and Foreign Antislavery Society resolved: we welcome fugitives, and "we consider it a privilege and a duty to shield them from assault, arrest, and annoyance, and to aid them in securing an asylum." Even some church bodies made similar pledges; for example, the Presbyterian Synod of Peoria, Illinois, declared that regardless of man-made laws, God's law required Christians to "feed the hungry and clothe the naked," including fugitive slaves.[9]

In rural regions, abolitionists developed a loose network of Underground Railroad routes connecting households willing to shelter fugitives. In the East the Railroad routes seemed to center in cities, among them Philadelphia, New York, and Boston.

In each of these three cities at various times abolitionists organized vigilance committees—sometimes composed of Negroes alone, sometimes of both Negroes and whites—to aid the fugitives. The vigilance committees worked with Underground conductors farther south who brought or sent fugitives to them. The Philadelphia committee in the 1850's had ties with three Underground conductors in Maryland and Delaware who used horses for transportation, who carried more than a hundred fugitives a year, and who were in constant fear of being betrayed. The committee also had ties with two or three sea captains who, for a fee, brought passengers hidden in their ships from more southerly ports to Wilmington or Philadelphia. The various committees hid fugitives, usually in the Negro sections of their cities, provided them necessary clothes, and if they wished to seek more security farther north, paid their expenses to move on by carriage, wagon, train, or ship.

Most of the fugitives settled in the free states rather than in Canada. By 1839 it was already possible that five thousand out of the twenty thousand blacks settled in New York City were fugitive slaves. But slave catchers sometimes seized even these settled fugitives and returned them to slavery. In addition, slave catchers sometimes kidnapped free blacks and sent them South to become slaves; in 1838 the New York Vigilance Committee reported that free Negroes were being kidnapped in New York and sent South "almost daily."[10] The vigilance committees tried to keep track of the arrival of slave catchers from the South and, if possible, warn their intended victims. When Negroes were seized without adequate proof that they were slaves, the committees tried to obtain court orders to free them.

Many of those who led in the vigilance committees were abolitionists dedicated to some degree of nonviolence, but in their attempt to protect fugitives they often found their nonviolence under strain.

In the Philadelphia Underground complete nonresistants included Quaker merchant Thomas Shipley, Quaker lawyer Passmore Williamson, Unitarian pastor William H. Furness, and the general agent of the Garrisonian Pennsylvania Antislavery Society, J. Miller McKim, who signed the 1833 nonviolent Declaration of Sentiments and married a Quaker girl. Apparently neutral was the Negro William Still, office clerk of the Pennsylvania Antislavery Society, who hid fugitives in his own home; Still, as his later book on the Underground Railroad indicates, respected Undergrounders whether they used violence or nonviolence.

One of the Philadelphia Undergrounders who praised nonviolence but found it difficult to practice in protecting fugitives was Robert Purvis, the Garrisonian Negro. Purvis was president of the Philadelphia Vigilance Committee during the late 1830's and early 1840's—at the time it was all Negro—and he hid fugitives in his house in a room entered by a trap door. A public meeting in a Negro church in support of this committee resolved that it was their duty to aid the fugitives "by all moral and peaceable means." Like Garrison, Purvis himself had originally been moved toward abolition by Quaker Lundy. As we have seen, in the national Negro convention of 1835, Purvis joined Whipper in supporting resolutions for nonviolence. In 1836 when one of the Quaker signers of the nonviolent Declaration of Sentiments died, Purvis, himself a signer, delivered a eulogy of him, declaring the declaration was "immortal" and saying that Negroes did not desire to achieve their natural rights by "blood and carnage." However, within a few years, when slave catchers came to his estate near Philadelphia to seize a fugitive slave whom he had befriended, Purvis, according to his own admission, handed the fugitive a gun with which he drove the slave catcher off.[11]

Among leaders in assisting fugitives in New York City were several who were strongly nonviolent, including Lewis Tappan, the Tappanite Negro pastor T. S. Wright, and the Quaker Isaac T. Hopper.

Hopper—of whom it was said, "fugitive slaves know him as well as they know the North Star"—was nearly always successful in employing nonviolence to protect fugitives. He foiled slave catchers, kidnappers, and police, reported Charles K. Whipple, "by the use of their own weapons, strength, courage, confidence, stratagem, [but] without the use of their auxiliary weapons of death."

Lewis Tappan taught nonviolence as a principle that applied to fugitives the same as it did to everyone else. When a New York Negro was "kidnapped" with the approval of a court and sent South to slavery, Tappan attended a Negro protest meeting. "There was considerable heat," Tappan wrote in his journal. "I endeavored to ally it and inculcated peace sentiments; and got them to adopt a pacific resolution respecting the recorder [judge], against whom the colored people are much, and with reason, incensed." Once when Tappan was teaching "peace principles" in a New York Sunday school for Negroes, he asked the question: "If one of you were taking your freedom, and should be pursued by a slaveholder, from whom

you could not escape except by taking his life, what would you do?"
No one answered.

Tappan then asked a Negro man who had once been kidnapped
in the North and carried off to slavery, "What would you do, Jesse?"
"I would kill him," Jesse replied, but a smile came over his
face as he added, "with the sword of the spirit!" Commented Tappan: "There was a general smile of approbation throughout the
school."[12]

Less certain of his nonviolence than Hopper or Lewis Tappan was
the Negro Tappanite editor, Sam E. Cornish, who found that his
desire to protect Negroes from being kidnapped clashed with his
desire to be nonviolent. Cornish, a Presbyterian minister, called the
measures of the American Antislavery Society "peaceful and holy";
"they are the measures of God and the Bible," he said, "and will
surely prevail." After Lovejoy had used violence to defend his press,
Cornish praised the society's nonviolent Declaration of Sentiments
and said that the only weapon he would countenance in the struggle
for "civil rights" was "civil agitation," not "physical resort." When
Cornish was refused a cup of tea at a hotel on the ground that
customers would not like to have Negroes served there, in an
editorial in the *Colored American* he protested the discrimination but
assured the hotel proprietor that "we would not for the world injure
a hair of his head. We have long since learned to do good for evil;
to pray for our enemies, and for those who persecute and despitefully
use us."[13]

However, in 1837 in presenting his readers an essay by Whipper in
favor of complete nonresistance, Cornish wrote that he rejected it
in toto and suggested that his major reason was the necessity for
Negroes to protect their own liberty and property: "We honestly
confess that we have yet to learn what virtue there would be in using
moral weapons . . . against a kidnapper or a midnight incendiary with
a lighted torch in his hand." In 1839, Cornish was still saying in the
Colored American that the "self-defense which wards off the kidnapper or an incendiary's torch should be held sacred," and he even
believed that "offensive aggression" could be "indispensable to . . .
personal liberty and rights." About the same time, in reply to a
nonresistant's letter, Cornish wrote bitterly, "If most of our 'peace
men' were colored men, in the State of Delaware, where we were
raised and where it was not an uncommon thing for kidnappers to
go at night and rob colored parents of all their children, we think
they would forget the principles of 'peace' and observe the first law

of God and nature—taking care of themselves and family."[14]

More nonviolent than Cornish was the major agent of the New York Vigilance Committee for several years, David Ruggles, a young black Garrisonian. Furiously active in protecting Negroes from slave catchers, Ruggles was in such danger himself that he often wore disguises and kept changing his residence. Whipper said of Ruggles that he was like Quaker Thomas Shipley in Philadelphia, "ready at all times, in dangers and perils, to wrest his brethren from the hyenas of the South." Yet there was at least a hint of ambivalence in Ruggles' attitude toward nonviolence. After a free Negro was seized in New York and sent South on the claim he was a slave, Ruggles wrote in 1836: "We must no longer depend on the interposition of . . . antislavery societies, in the hope of peaceable and just protection; where such outrages are committed, peace and justice cannot dwell. . . . We must look to our own safety and protection from kidnappers, remembering that 'self-defense is the first law of nature.' " Perhaps the self-defense he meant was merely the defense of Negroes by Negroes rather than by whites and not necessarily violent defense. For, though he himself had been subjected to violence and jailed, Ruggles, in giving a long report in 1837 to the New York Vigilance Committee of his hectic experiences in protecting fugitives, avoided saying that he was willing to use violence, explaining that he employed "every legal and proper means in our courts of law" to let the slaves go free; specifically he denied that he went on board a vessel in the harbor to free fugitives "by force." About the same time he evidently defended nonresistance in a debate.[15] Also, on the question of how to abolish slavery, while he rejected the "moral suasion of suffering patience" as ineffective, he seemed to favor more impatient forms of nonviolence, for he said in 1838, "Unless we stab slavery through the conscience of the slaveholder, hope of its removal would be chimerical."[16]

In Boston in the 1850's the vigilance committee members ranged widely on the nonviolence-violence spectrum. Members included the complete nonresistant Garrisonian Charles K. Whipple; the slightly more moderate Garrisonian nonresistant merchant, Francis Jackson, who said he believed the doctrine of nonresistance was true but was fearful that he might not always be able to practice it; the occasional nonresistant Garrisonian Wendell Phillips; and the pro-violent Free-Soiler, Dr. Samuel G. Howe. In 1851, after the committee had tried unsuccessfully to use nonviolent means to prevent authorities from returning a fugitive to the South, complete nonresistant Foster charged that the committee had avoided violence in this case not from principle but merely out of fear of public reprisal against Free-Soilers at the polls. Wendell Phillips replied that the committee had simply made the best resistance in its power, pragmatically, without any doctrinal stand on violence or nonviolence.[17]

In sum, in these three Eastern cities, as well as elsewhere, the leaders in protecting fugitives were a mixture of those who clearly believed in violence, those who clearly believed in nonviolence, and many who represented gradations in between.

Despite terrible pressures to use violence to protect Negroes from being returned to slavery, a considerable measure of nonviolence persisted in the Underground Railroad. Perhaps in the thirty years preceding the Civil War the majority of both escaping slaves and abolitionists assisting them were in fact not violent. In William Still's book on the Underground Railroad, which was based largely on his records of the fugitives passing through Philadelphia, in eleven cases the fugitives or their protectors were violent, in ten more cases they possessed arms, though Still gives no evidence that they used them, and in the other approximately four hundred cases Still does not indicate that they possessed arms or used violence. Similarly, even in the comparatively violent 1850's, according to an American Antislavery Society report on the enforcement of the fugitive slave law, in forty-three cases the fugitives and their friends used violence, in five more cases they possessed arms, though the report does not say that they used them, and in the other approximately two hundred cases the report does not indicate that they possessed arms or used violence.[18]

The following accounts of slave escapes or abolitionist efforts to assist slaves escape were selected because they include some element of nonviolence. They were selected almost entirely from the records of the abolitionists. Most of them undoubtedly are substantially true; if a few of them are not wholly so because they were recounted years after they happened, they are at any rate what the abolitionists told each other as true. These accounts, in addition to those previously mentioned in this chapter, suggest that the Quakers, despite their small numbers, played a stronger role in the Underground Railroad than the Tappanites or Garrisonians. The accounts suggest that occasionally the success of nonviolent Railroaders depended on court action or threats of court action or even on the use of violence by others. The accounts also indicate that nonviolent Railroad activities varied in their degree of openness or secrecy and in whether they resulted in suffering for the fugitives and those who protected them.

Quaker Levi Coffin, one of the major figures of the Underground Railroad in the Midwest, harbored more than one hundred fugitives a year over a twenty-year period in his house in Newport, near Richmond, Indiana. At night when Coffin heard one of the frequent knocks on his door, he would open it to let fugitives in, cover the windows for secrecy, and light a fire while his wife would prepare food. Often the fugitives were so frightened, Coffin found, that at first they would not give their names or explain from where they had escaped. They often had been sleeping in the woods, were without adequate clothes, and, having eaten only what they could find in the field for some time, were ill and hungry. Coffin, protected to some extent by his postion as a prosperous merchant, made it known that he harbored fugitive slaves. He was always nonviolent, but he threatened to arrest anyone who entered his house for an illegal search, and no one ever did.[19]

Underground Railroaders were well aware of what punishment they might receive if caught. Nevertheless the Chaces, a Rhode Island Quaker family, were prepared to resist, by all means "consistent with our peace principles," the officers of the law who might come to their house to seize fugitives. Once, as Elizabeth Buffum Chace recalled, they were "in hourly fear and expectation of the arrival of the slave-catcher; our doors and windows fastened by day as well as by night, not daring to let our neighbors know who were our guests, lest some one should betray them. We told our children, all at that time under fourteen years of age, of the fine of one thousand dollars, and the imprisonment of six months that awaited us, in case the officer should come, and we should refuse to give these poor people up; and they heroically planned, how, in such an event, they would take care of everything . . . during our absence."[20] However, the Chaces were never punished, except like many abolitionists by the ostracism of their neighbors.

Quaker Thomas Whitson of Lancaster County, Pennsylvania, was a boycotter of slave produce and a nonvoting Garrisonian. Garrison said of him, "If there be one human being on earth whom we love and respect, and upon whose unfaltering adhesion to the antislavery cause we rely, it is Thomas Whitson." Quaker Whitson protected hundreds of fugitives. They generally came to his house at night, passed to him from neighboring Undergrounders to the south, and he in turn passed them on north the next night. His children were not allowed to ask questions about black visitors at their house; Whitson was very secretive about the details of his Underground activities. Perhaps this was a reason that, while many other abolitionist whites and blacks in the area had their houses searched for fugitives and his neighbors knew he was an abolitionist, his house was never searched.

Once when a group of deputies carried off one of his Negro employees on the charge that he had helped fugitives escape, Whitson pursued the deputies, caught up with them, and asked them to release the Negro. They refused. One of the deputies advanced on Whitson, "with a volley of Billingsgate," and, pointing a pistol at him, asked if he were not an abolitionist.

"I am," said Whitson, "and I am not afraid of thy shooting me. So thee may as well put thy pistol down."

The deputy continued to rail and asked another deputy, "Shall I shoot him?"

"No," the other answered, "let the old Quaker go," and they left, still guarding the Negro.

But Whitson persisted. He located the place where the deputies held the Negro under guard, and this time convinced them the Negro was not the man they were looking for.[21]

A case in which rescuers used both violence and nonviolence occurred in Cass County, Michigan, where a number of slaves who had fled from Kentucky had settled. Their owners found out where they were and sent agents to recover them. The agents broke into their cabins, tied them up, and prepared to rush them back to Kentucky. Meanwhile their Negro friends had seized stakes from a fence and prepared to charge the slave agents. In turn the slave agents prepared to defend themselves with revolvers and bowie knives. But several Quakers lived in the area. They stepped between the two parties, reminding the slave agents that the law required them to go to the county seat to prove that the Negroes were slaves. Under the circumstances, the slave agents felt persuaded to release their captives. Once released, the Negroes fled to Canada.

In Boston abolitionists tried to rescue two Negro women, on trial as alleged runaway slaves, by deliberately nonviolent means. Abolitionists were aware that if the court were to free them, the slave agent who claimed them might well seize them again on some other charge, such as theft, before they had a chance to go into hiding. Abolitionists attended the trial. As soon as the judge freed the two defendants, everyone in court rose, and the slave agent tried to seize the two again on another charge, but abolitionists—most of them Negro women—had already formed a lane through which the two defendants escaped.[22]

Abolitionist Seth Concklin was daring enough to go as far as Alabama to help a slave family escape. In this mission Concklin was deliberately nonviolent. Possibly he was predisposed to nonviolence because of his earlier connections with the nonviolent Shaker community in Watervliet, New York. But at other times in his life Concklin had been a soldier, and once, when an anti-Negro mob in Rochester put a rope around a Negro, Concklin, having a ready sympathy for the underdog, "levelled" the mob's leader.

In his Alabama rescue mission, Concklin said that he decided not to use violence because violence would not work. According to an account of the rescue which Pastor Furness of Philadelphia helped to prepare, Concklin took with him "neither pistol nor bowie-knife." He explained, if I took weapons with me, I would "be tempted to use them," and then I would "be sure to be overborne."

After careful preparation, Concklin invaded slave citadel Alabama. Using subterfuge to conceal what he was doing from the slaveholders, he brought the slave family to a skiff on the banks of the Tennessee River. They shoved off into the water, Concklin standing at the helm of the skiff, playing the role of a white master, while the slave boys, aged about nineteen and twenty, rowed, and the slave mother and daughter hid under blankets on the skiff's bottom. Soon after starting, observers on the shore hailed the boat, but Concklin did not respond in any way. When they fired guns at him, still he did not stop. A wind was blowing, and he supposed it was blowing so hard that those on shore must have decided he simply could not hear them. Under constant fear of being discovered, Concklin and the slaves rowed perhaps three hundred miles down the Tennessee River, then one hundred miles up the Ohio, and finally fifty miles up the Wabash. After rowing seven days and seven nights, they left their skiff near New Harmony, Indiana. Exhausted, they rested occasionally in friendly homes and moved north, walking or riding in wagons.

A few days later they were still slowly moving north in Indiana when police seized them. They did not resist. The police started them back toward Alabama by putting them on an Ohio River steamer—the Negroes to go back into slavery, Concklin in chains for trial. Shortly before the steamer was to land at Paducah, Concklin was found in the river, still in chains, with his skull broken. He may have died accidentally in attempting to escape; he may have been murdered.

"Poor Seth," wrote Indiana Undergrounder Levi Coffin, who had assisted Concklin in his planning. "After all his toil . . . shrewd and wise management, and almost unheard of adventures . . . to be given up to Indianians, to these fiendish tyrants, to be sacrificed. O! Shame!"[23]

Another sad sequel to nonviolent action occurred in Chester County, Pennsylvania, where Quaker Solomon Fussell employed two fugitives as farm hands. One day, as the children on the farm recalled it afterward, slave agents suddenly arrived to seize the slaves and return them to slavery. One of the slaves, Henry, whom the children loved for his gentleness to them, took up an ax and lifted it to strike the agents, but in doing so he cried out in anguish to his Quaker mentor, "Solomon, shall I strike?"

The Quaker was compelled in an instant to decide what to answer. "The awful solemnity of the struggle brought a look into his face impossible even for these children to forget," as they recalled afterward. "It imprinted itself forever, but he answered in accordance with his life-long principles, 'No.' The upraised ax dropped and Henry and his friend went, passive victims, into the abyss of slavery. They were never heard of more on earth."

Another tragedy occurred following the nonviolent action of the young Richard Dillingham, the son of Ohio Quaker parents, who taught Negro pupils in Cincinnati. Some of his pupils had relatives in Tennessee who were slaves who wished to be free. When Dillingham went to Tennessee to see if he could help free them nonviolently, he was caught paying the hack fare for three slaves, and both he and the slaves were arrested. The blacks were soon released, but Dillingham was held in jail for trial. At the trial in Nashville, he said openly that he knew he had violated Tennessee law by helping slaves escape, but he had done so from feelings of humanity. Many spectators in the courtroom appreciated his honesty and his peaceful methods; as they wept, Dillingham was sentenced to the shortest prison term the law allowed for such an offense, three years. In prison he tormented himself over the question whether he should try to escape but decided it would be dishonorable. A sensitive person, he was often low spirited. He wrote his family and friends that he was determined to love his enemies yet found it hard to do so. While working in the prison hospital during an outbreak of cholera, he was worn out by waiting on the ill day and night, and himself became ill and died.[24]

More fortunate was Quaker shoe merchant Thomas Garrett of Wilmington, in the slave state of Delaware, whom Garrison called "one of the grandest men of the ages." Garrett, a big, confident man, gathered around him a small band of people, black and white, violent and nonviolent, who aided fugitives. One of those who worked with him was Harriet Tubman, the violent Negro guide to fugitives. One morning when Harriet Tubman sent word that she had a party of fugitives waiting to cross a guarded bridge near Wilmington, Garrett sent across the bridge two wagons of bricklayers. On their return at night, the bricklayers brought the fugitives back with them, concealed in the bottom of the wagons, unsuspected by the guards. By such methods Garrett was said to have helped nearly three thousand slaves escape, nearly all successfully.

Garrett worked openly to the extent that he publicly admitted that he was aiding fugitives. As a result, police watched his house, and irate slave owners called on him, demanding to know where their slaves were. When they did so, "he met them placidly," his antislavery friends explained, "never denied having helped the fugitives on their way, positively refused to give them any information, and when they flourished pistols, or bowie knives, to enforce their demands, he calmly pushed their weapons aside, and told them that none but cowards resorted to such means to carry their ends."[25]

If slave owners could not stop Thomas Garrett with pistols or knives, they were willing to try court action. In 1848 in a suit against him for having helped slaves escape, at the age of sixty he lost all his property, including his business property and household goods.

"Thomas," said the sheriff who had just finished selling all of Garrett's goods at auction, "I hope you'll never be caught at this again."

"Friend," replied Garrett, "I haven't a dollar in the world, but if thee knows a fugitive who needs a breakfast, send him to me."

Garrett worked at restoring his business and continued to assist fugitives. Several years later, he entered a train in Wilmington to try to rescue a free black woman being carried to the South. According to Garrett's account, "Two or three Southerners took hold of me to throw me off the car. . . . I was then slightly bruised by the railing of the cars, but well in a few days." Garrett tried to explain why such physical assaults did not happen to him more often. Perhaps it was because of his Quaker garb, he wrote, or his age—he was sixty-four at the time—or perhaps because of his coolness, "I cannot tell."[26]

Like Garrett, some Undergrounders, while concerned to be non-violent themselves, tolerated the violence of other Undergrounders with whom they worked. Some nonviolent abolitionists assisted the Canadian, Alexander M. Ross, who helped run off slaves from the South by giving them weapons; Southern Quakers entertained him in their homes and made contact for him with slaves who wished to escape; Lewis Tappan is said to have aided him. In an instance in Salem, Iowa, a group of Quaker Undergrounders allowed them-selves to be protected by the violence of others, though whether they did so willingly or not is not apparent. The Quakers had been help-ing slaves escape from nearby Missouri, and a band of Missourians descended on them to punish them, invading their homes and forc-ing their leaders into hiding. A company of Congregationalist Yan-kees from a nearby settlement, who also assisted fugitives but were not averse to violence, came to the rescue of the Quakers with rifles, dispersing the invaders.[27]

The youth Frederick Douglass, while not a believer in nonviolence at the time, was one of the many slaves who escaped nonviolently. In Baltimore he borrowed a sailor's identification papers, disguised himself with a sailor's shirt, cap, and black cravat, and with great anxiety boarded a train in Baltimore. In twenty-four hours he was in New York City. There Underground Railroaders, including the Tappans, Theodore Wright, and David Ruggles, helped him and sent him on his way to New Bedford to settle. His successful experience with nonviolent escape may have helped Douglass to grow into one of the leading advocates of nonviolent action in the 1840's.

It was also in disguise that a young slave couple tried to escape from Georgia. Ellen Craft, twenty-two, who was nearly white, had the nerve to pose as a wealthy white man traveling north for medical treatment. Knowing that on the journey she would be asked to sign her name in hotels, but not being able to write, she gave herself an excuse for not writing by tying her right hand in a sling. Her hus-band, William Craft, aged twenty-four, was darker, and he dressed as her slave servant. On the trip they boldly stayed at the best hotels —in Charleston they stayed at the hotel where J. C. Calhoun stayed —and while William rode in the Jim Crow railroad cars, Ellen rode in the white cars. Not averse to employing violence if necessary, the Crafts nevertheless reached Philadelphia safely without using or re-ceiving violence. Exhausted from the danger to which they had constantly been exposed on their trip, they rested several weeks in a Quaker home and then went on to Boston to settle. In Boston their story soon became known, and Wendell Phillips told an abolitionist meeting that the Crafts' dramatic escape would lead millions of people in the future to "wish that they could have lived to take part in the glorious struggle" against slavery.[28]

A slave who tried to escape by another kind of nonviolent deception was Jim Conner, who lived on a large Louisiana sugar plantation. He had already attempted to escape several times, and in one escape he was armed with an ax, a tomahawk, and a knife—he was not deliberately nonviolent—but each time he had been recaptured. However, once his master and mistress traveled to Maryland to purchase slaves and took him along. In Maryland they talked of traveling farther north to Pennsylvania. Going with them to a free state, Conner knew, would give him a good chance to escape. "I let on to them that I had no wish to go North," he explained afterward; "that Baltimore was as far North as I wished to see, and that I had rather to be going home than going North. . . . They hated the North, and I made believe that I did too." Convinced that he wouldn't run away, his master and mistress decided to take him along to Philadelphia. In a Philadelphia hotel Conner talked to a black man who told him about the vigilance committee and at the right time led him to the committee's office. The committee arranged to send him to Canada.

Other slaves escaped nonviolently by hiding in ocean ships. One Richmond slave hid in the coal hold of a ship for five days in darkness. On landing in Philadelphia he "could scarcely see or walk," Still reported, but after finding fresh air and freedom, in a few hours he "was soon one of the most joyful mortals living." Another slave, the nineteen-year-old Betsey Blakely, was escaping from a Carolina master who, she said, whipped her to force her to submit to his lust; she hid in a ship's hold used to store cordage. Once the ship reached Boston, abolitionists gave her clothing and tried to find her work. Although Betsey's escape was nonviolent, she, like Douglass, the Crafts, and Conner, was not committed to nonviolence. She said that she had left behind in Carolina a baby boy, but she wished she had killed him so that he could not grow up to be a slave.[29]

A slave girl worked as a maid on a line of packet steamers that sailed between New Orleans and Galveston. Beautiful, she learned good manners and was well treated. The passengers whom she attended befriended her with gifts of money and clothing and helped her to learn to read—she read both French and English. She might have continued to accept slavery, much as she chafed against it, if her master, the owner of the steamer, who was also, she believed, her father, had not decided to sell her "to a dissolute young man for the vilest of purposes."

She looked for a way of escape. She sought out an English ship in New Orleans, confided her plight to the captain's wife, offered to pay for her passage to New York with the money she had saved from gifts, and finally persuaded her to take her on board. On arrival in New York, the girl was frightened to discover in a newspaper that her master was advertising for her capture. The English captain, however, inquired for the abolitionists and took the girl to Lewis Tappan. At once Tappan arranged for her safety in the city overnight, and the next day sent her to a friend in Albany, who in turn sent her on by train to Pastor May in Syracuse. On the train two men watched her sharply. "One had seated himself by her side and tried to engage her in conversation and look through her veil," as pastor May reported afterward. "At length he asked her to take off the glove on her left hand. By this she knew he must have seen the advertisement, stating that, among other marks by which she might be identified, one finger on her left hand was minus a joint. She at once called to the conductor and asked him to protect her from the impertinent liberties the man was taking with her." The conductor gave her another seat, and she reached Syracuse without any further trouble, but in great fright.

Pastor May hid her in Syracuse several days till he supposed any pursuers must have gone on, and then gave her to the care of one of his parishioners who was traveling to Oswego. There the parishioner saw her safely on a ship for Kingston, Canada, and after a few days she wrote May that she had found a position in Kingston as a children's maid.[30]

If slaves were brought into Pennsylvania by their masters, according to state law they were legally free. The young Philadelphia Railroaders, Negro clerk William Still and Quaker lawyer Passmore Williamson, heard from local Negroes that a slave mother and her children had been visiting the city with their master and that the mother desired to be free. Hurrying to the Delaware River, they found the mother and her children on board a ship that was about to sail for New York. At once they informed the mother of her rights. Her master, however, urged her not to take her freedom, reminding her that she still had a child in the South and that she was on her way to New York to visit friends. As the bell tolled for the boat to leave, the mother and her children moved to a stairway to go ashore. The slaveholder, whose name was Wheeler, took hold of her, trying to stop her. Quaker Williamson, as he explained at the trial that followed, "took Wheeler by the collar, and held him to one side; the whole company passed down and left the boat, proceeding peacefully and quietly." William Still said later, "There were no violence or threatenings as I saw or heard." Evidently Still, in keeping with the usual Garrisonian tolerance of noninjurious restraint, did not consider Williamson's restraint of Wheeler to be violent. Still drove the women and children by carriage to a hiding place, after dark took them to his own home, and later sent them on East.

But Pennsylvania officials often sympathized with the South. They brought Quaker Williamson to court on a charge of forcible abduction and assault, and when he said he did not know where the mother was, they imprisoned him for contempt of court for three months. Williamson became an abolitionist hero.[31]

A slave who chose a desperate method of attempting to escape was one who had himself sealed in a box and shipped by boat on the Ohio River toward Cincinnati. While still on the boat, for lack of drinking water, he was forced to call to be let out, and he was arrested. Another slave tried essentially the same method, having himself shipped in a box by express. According to Frederick Douglass' paper, when the box arrived at its destination, and it was opened, the slave was found dead, "his countenance horribly contorted, and his body drawn into a knot. It appeared on examination that the box had no air-holes."[32]

A similiar but more carefully planned attempt at escape was that of Henry Brown, a slave in Richmond, Virginia, who was brokenhearted that his wife and children had been sold away from him. Brown saved enough money to pay a white shoe dealer who had been long aiding slaves to escape, to make a box and ship him in it by express to Philadelphia. Brown weighed nearly two hundred pounds, but he folded himself into an incredibly small box only two feet long, three feet high, and twenty-three inches wide. In the box he took crackers, a small auger, and drinking water in a bladder that couldn't be broken.

On the twenty-four-hour journey, the box was sometimes turned upside down so that Brown was upside down in it for long periods, and it seemed to him that his veins would burst. His head became sore. When he could, he bathed it with water; doing so provided him so much relief that he saved all the water for this purpose. He ate none of the crackers because he was afraid they would make him thirsty. To keep fresh air coming into his box, he bored holes in the box with his auger.

Meanwhile someone from Richmond had come into the Pennsylvania Antislavery Society's office in Philadelphia and told Miller McKim that a slave was likely to arrive by box. Later a telegram came to McKim saying a box had arrived at a Philadelphia train depot. McKim, who expected the slave to be dead, nevertheless had the box brought, with care, to the office. The men in the office, including clerk Still, made sure they were alone in the office, and locked the door. Then McKim, trembling with excitement, tapped the box and asked, "All right?"

"All right, sir!" came the answer from inside. Quickly the men loosened the hoops around the box and lifted the lid. Up stood Brown, saying, "Good morning, gentlemen!" He stretched himself, walked stiffly about the room, and then burst into a hymn—the one he had long been planning to sing if he ever arrived alive: "I waited patiently for the Lord, and he inclined unto me and heard my cry."

McKim told Lucretia Mott afterward, as she reported it, that she could "hardly conceive the relief and excitement" that the men in the office felt on finding the fugitive alive. McKim took Brown home, gave him breakfast and a bath, and then took him to the Motts'. After plenty of exercise in the Motts' yard to loosen up his limbs, the Motts sent him on to the Stills for two days, and the Stills sent him on to Francis Jackson in Boston by the Underground Railroad—without his box.

On the news of Brown's escape, Garrison said, "What a country is this . . . that such expedients should be necessary to obtain liberty!" Brown, said pastor May, would "be remembered as long as the history of the struggles of humanity for her rights shall be remembered." When Wendell Phillips introduced Henry "Box" Brown, as abolitionists came to call him, to a cheering Faneuil Hall audience in Boston, Phillips reminded them that Brown's escape was illegal: "We say on behalf of this man, whom God created . . . that they may pass their little laws in Washington, but that Faneuil Hall repeals them, in the name of the humanity of Massachusetts."

Richmond shoe dealer Samuel A. Smith, who had made the box for Brown, was pleased with his success in shipping Brown. He made boxes for two other slaves who asked his help, and shipped them off in their boxes too. But rumors about Smith's boxes had spread; a warning was sent ahead by Morse's new "lightning line" telegraph, and the boxes were intercepted. The slaves were forced back into slavery, while box-maker Smith went to prison for seven years.[33]

These examples indicate that nonviolence in Underground Railroad action was of various kinds. Sometimes it was the deliberate principled nonviolence that the Quakers, the Garrisonians, and the Tappanites had developed. Sometimes it was deliberate pragmatic nonviolence, like Concklin's. Sometimes it was fortuitous nonviolence, such as the Crafts' or Jim Conner's appeared to be—action that turned out to be nonviolent merely because the circumstances to bring out violence did not happen to occur.

These examples of nonviolence, of whatever kind, provide an impressive record of the resourcefulness of men in developing nonviolent methods in the cause of freedom. They indicate that by employing varying patterns of deception, legal action, bravado, physical restraint, or moral authority, nonviolent Undergrounders often succeeded.

They often succeeded at a cost. One cannot easily forget that the Chaces, successful in protecting fugitives as they were, were ostracized, or that Thomas Garrett, successful as he was too, lost his property, or that box-maker Smith was sent to prison. One cannot easily forget the heroic failures: the fugitive Henry, who held back his ax and was forced to return to slavery, and Concklin, who drowned in chains.

17. Resisting the Fugitive Slave Law

◇◇◇◇◇◇◇◇◇◇

As PART OF a compromise over the question of extending slavery into the vast territory conquered from Mexico, in September, 1850, the South pushed Congress into enacting a more severe fugitive slave law. By the new law, if a master claimed any man as his runaway slave, the man was not entitled to traditional Anglo-Saxon rights, such as a jury trial or testifying in his own behalf; all citizens were required to help catch fugitives if asked by officers to do so; and judges in effect were offered a bribe: they were to be paid twice as large a fee if they sent a suspected runaway into slavery than if they freed him. Henry Clay and Daniel Webster hoped this law would help quiet the slavery controversy and hold the nation together.

However, in response to this law, according to Frederick Douglass, the nation was never so agitated. Many shades of abolitionists, violent and nonviolent, political and nonpolitical, agreed to defy the law. The Garrisonian-led Massachusetts Antislavery Society urged that the new law be "resisted, disobeyed, and trampled under foot, at all hazards." The Tappan-led American Missionary Association asked Christians to refuse to obey this "atrocious" law but to "submit to the penalty." Quaker Whittier said he would die rather than aid in enforcing "that wicked law." President Finney of Oberlin College said that the law was unconstitutional and besides, no law of man could set aside the law of God.[1] Even some rather moderate Northerners who till then had only been vaguely antislavery—including

Emerson—decided that the law showed that the slave power was interfering with the liberty of all Americans, and became committed abolitionists for the first time.

With regard to Northern Negroes, the new law led many of them to feel that they were as likely to be carried off from their homes as if they were living on the slave coast of Africa. In some Northern towns abolitionists reported that nearly the entire Negro population, both fugitives and freemen, were frantically trying to sell their property in order to be ready to flee, if necessary. Within three months of the passage of the law at least three thousand Negroes entered Canada and within another year perhaps ten thousand.

Cruel whites played on the Negroes' fears. In Trenton, New Jersey, white boys frightened a fugitive by crying out that a slave hunter was after him. He ran, the boys ran after him, and he died from the exertion. The fiendish crew of an Erie Canal boat, knowing that a Negro couple on board was trying to escape to Canada, told them for amusement that slave hunters had just arrived on board to seize them. Believing them, the mother jumped into the canal with her child in her arms and the child drowned.

At the same time many Negroes were arming themselves. In the log cabins of Indiana, traveling nonresident abolitionist H. C. Wright met armed fugitives every day; if a claimant or a marshal were to come after them, said Wright, he would get a "rifle ball through his heart." According to Philadelphia Underground Railroader William Still, fugitives were "generally armed." According to the *Liberator*, Boston Negroes, whether fugitives or not, were also generally armed.[2] One day in Pittsburgh one store sold over thirty revolvers and sixty bowie knives to Negroes and their friends.

With Negroes increasingly willing to use violence on the one hand and the federal government being pushed by the South to enforce the new law strictly on the other, nonviolent abolitionists were on the spot: they were forced to face the question whether in this crisis they were capable of developing forms of nonviolent action that could in fact protect fugitives.

The 1850–54 crisis over the use of violence to defend the liberty of fugitive slaves is comparable to the 1837–38 Lovejoy crisis over the use of violence to defend the free speech of abolitionists. In both cases many abolitionists were tempted to use defensive violence. However, there were two major differences. First, in the fugitive slave law crisis, since abolitionists had become more numerous and more acceptable to the public, their chance to use violence successfully was greater. Second, in the fugitive slave law crisis it was blacks more than whites whose immediate safety was at stake.

Understandably, black meetings protesting the law tended to be more violent in tone than white meetings protesting the law, and, following the tradition already long apparent, those in New York State tended to be more violent than those in Pennsylvania or Massachusetts. In New York City when the chairman of a black protest meeting, occasional nonresistant William P. Powell, whom Garrison knew and admired as the manager of a black seaman's home,[3] asked the audience if they would "submit peaceably" to the new law, they shouted "No, no." The speakers who followed seemed to outdo each other in urging violence. A South Carolina fugitive insisted that even women should keep knives ready. Another speaker said that while not all blacks knew how to read, they did know how to fight: "If you want to . . . command respect, you must fight," he added, amid cries of "We will, that we will." The Negro Presbyterian pastor Charles W. Gardiner, an associate of the Tappans and once a leader in Whipper's nonviolent American Moral Reform Society, advised blacks to "take the life of every man that attempted to deprive them of their liberty." The only speaker in the crowd who took anything like a nonviolent position, according to the report of the meeting in the American Antislavery Society's paper, was black jeweler Edward V. Clark, who remarked adroitly: "The principle of dying before your time . . . [is] much better in theory than in practice. . . . I don't know what I might do with a bowie knife or revolver. I am greatly averse to taking life. Suppose, in defending one, we lose the lives of seven. You see it would be a losing game. . . . Now, I go for secreting the [fugitive] slaves; keep them private, shift them about. . . . However odious this law may be, still it is the law, and all the lives we lose in opposing it, will be a dead loss to us. (Laughter)." The meeting, however, resolved that fugitive slaves in the city should "arm themselves with the surest and most deadly weapons" and "resist unto death"; if not prepared to do so, they should escape to Canada.[4]

Negroes who maintained their right to use violence to protect themselves from being carried off into slavery could claim abolitionist leaders had provided them with some precedent to do so. In the Lovejoy crisis many nonviolent abolitionists, including Garrison and Lewis Tappan, recognized the right of violent self-defense in abolitionist actions, while advising against the use of the right, and by that time some abolitionist leaders, including Arthur Tappan, Alvan Stewart, and Birney, had quietly used violence to defend their property or families against anti-abolitionists. Before the 1850 fugitive slave law was passed, under such pressure as the continuous effort to operate the Underground Railroad and the victory of slave interests in the Mexican War, other abolitionists—particularly Negroes—had come to favor using some forms of defensive violence. These included Underground Railroaders such as the Garrisonian Purvis and the Tappanite Cornish; the Garrisonian lecturer Remond; the Massachusetts educator and congressman Horace Mann; the Midwestern antislavery lecturer Henry Bibb; and the upstate New York Negro pastors Garnet, Loguen, and Ward. Naturally, in the crisis over the new fugitive slave law, these leaders were likely to justify Negroes in using violence to protect themselves from being seized under the new law and forced into slavery, some of them, however, still suggesting a preference for peaceful methods when they believed such methods would work.

Frederick Douglass, the towering figure among Negroes in the 1850's, allowed the fugitive slave law to be the occasion for his abandoning complete nonviolence. In the 1841 ride-ins Douglass had suffered physical violence without retaliating. In 1843 he had led the opposition to the violent proposal of Garnet in the national Negro convention. In 1846 he had been such a nonresistant that, though believing war between Britain and the United States, which then threatened, would incidentally free the slaves, he opposed such a war, explaining, "Were I asked the question whether I would have my emancipation by the shedding of one single drop of blood, my answer would be in the negative." In 1848, Douglass compared the advantages of the recent peaceful social reforms in Britain to the disadvantages of the bloody revolution then going on in France. In 1849 while edging toward the right to use defensive violence, he still said, "the only well grounded hope of the slave for emancipation is the operation of moral force." Meanwhile, however, Douglass had moved out of the Garrisonian orbit in Massachusetts to Rochester, New York, and was being influenced by guerrilla fighter John Brown. Within scarcely a month of the passage of the fugitive slave law, Douglass had become an advocate of violence to protect fugitives. At a meeting of the Rhode Island Antislavery Society, Douglass admitted that he rejected the society's nonviolent policy and favored "forcible resistance" to the law. "There are some things for which men deserve to die," he explained. "Tyrants and despots have no right to live. Slaveholders, being such, have no right to live." Two years later he was saying bluntly, "The only way to make the fugitive slave law a dead letter is to make half a dozen or more dead kidnappers.''[5] While Douglass still could support nonviolence in certain circumstances, he had become only an occasional nonresistant, like Wendell Phillips, and was leading Negroes toward greater tolerance of violence.

Among Garrisonians, too, the trend toward greater tolerance of violence was apparent. In the Lovejoy crisis the Garrisonian-led antislavery society of Plymouth County, Massachusetts, had categorically pledged themselves to use nonviolence alone; in the fugitive slave law crisis, however, they merely promised to disobey the new law by giving fugitives "the same protection which we would give to our own families under like circumstances," without specifying whether this would be violent or nonviolent. In the Lovejoy crisis the Garrisonian-led Massachusetts Antislavery Society had recognized the right of self-defense but had urged the specific advantages of nonviolence; in the fugitive slave law crisis, instead, it merely urged disobedience to the law without indicating whether the disobedience should be violent or not.[6]

At the same time some Garrisonian leaders as individuals were slipping from the high position on nonviolence which they had once taken. Garrison revealed his stand in a tense meeting of Negroes in Boston. At the meeting the popular Negro caterer, Joshua B. Smith, advised every fugitive to arm himself with a revolver. A committee headed by Nell, the Garrisonian school boycotter, urged blacks to follow the example of Crispus Attucks and other blacks who had fought for the American Revolution and, like them, "die men rather than live slaves." One of Nell's school-boycott associates, Negro Robert Johnson, was pleased that many Boston stevedores were present "who could do heavy work in the house of difficulty"; he advised them not to be aggressors, but said if a slave hunter "rushes" on us, "kill him." In response, Garrison said that he was a nonresistant himself, "and determined with the help of God, to live and die such," yet he urged those who were not nonresistants "to be consistent with their own principles, reminding them that William Tell and George Washington were among the glorious names . . . at the shrines of liberty." However, he insisted, "the fugitives in this city and elsewhere would be more indebted to the moral power of public sentiment than to any display of physical resistance."[7] Garrison in the Lovejoy crisis had acknowledged the right of self-defense but urged that nonviolence would be wise, but in this crisis, while still urging that nonviolence would be wise, he was giving a little more emphasis to the right of self-defense.

Pastor Samuel J. May, who in the Lovejoy crisis had out-Garrisoned Garrison by crusading for all abolitionists to be nonviolent, now in the fugitive slave law crisis was not insistent on it. Speaking in his Syracuse pulpit, the usually gentle May urged those who believed in violence to be consistent by using violence for the benefit of fugitive slaves. "If you are fully persuaded that it would be right for you to maim or kill the kidnapper who had laid hands upon your wife, son, or daughter," he said, "I see not how you can excuse yourself from helping, by the same degree of violence, to rescue the fugitive slave from the like outrage." But May was using a double standard, much as Garrison was. He insisted that he was still an absolute nonresistant himself. "It is known that I have been and am a preacher of the 'doctrine of nonresistance,' " he said. "I believe it to be one of the distinctive doctrines of Christianity. . . . There is not a doubt in my heart, that, if I should be enabled to speak and act as Jesus would, I should produce a far greater and better effect than could be brought by clubs, or swords, or any deadly weapon. . . . I shall go to the rescue of any one I may hear is in danger, not intending to harm the cruel men who may be attempting to kidnap him. I shall take no weapons of violence along with me, not even the cane that I usually wear. I shall go, praying that I may say and do what will smite the hearts rather than the bodies of the impious claimants of property in human beings."[8]

Somewhat more tolerant of violence than either Garrison or May was H. C. Wright. Though just before the new law was passed, Wright had been lecturing on nonresistance much as he had been when he was a moving spirit in the Nonresistance Society, after the law was passed he was anxious for abolitionists to understand why Negroes were increasingly violent. He spent his time on his speaking tours not so much as he had in the Lovejoy crisis in urging the advantages of nonviolence under all circumstances, as in arguing that if it was right for Joshua to kill the Canaanites and for Washington to kill the British, then it was right for fugitive slaves to kill those who would deprive them of their freedom. Evidently Wright thought it was hopeless at this time to insist on nonviolence. Wright even went so far toward violence as to say that it was the duty of the Northern people to incite the slaves of the South to rebel against their masters. He advocated, somewhat as Garnet had in 1843, that slaves refuse obedience to their masters and attempt to escape. "Such rebellion, and such alone, I advocate," he said. "Then if the masters attempt to enforce obedience and prevent escape, I would not blame the slaves if they cut their oppressors down. They know no higher nor holier rule, and can act on none other," he added.[9] It was clear that Wright—essentially like Garrison, May, Foster, and Edmund Quincy—had become only a personal pacifist; he followed a high standard himself, but was not pushing it for others.

The long years of frustration in their attempt to abolish slavery were eroding the confidence of some of the Garrisonian leaders in nonviolence. Perceiving this trend, an Ohio Quaker wrote a letter protesting it, which the *Liberator* published under the heading, "Nonresistants, Where Are You?" Said the letter, "since the enactment of the fugitive law, it seems that nonresistants have almost laid their armor down." Well, not quite.

On the whole abolitionist leadership still maintained a nonviolent posture. In fact, Lewis Tappan at the 1851 annual meeting of the American and Foreign Antislavery Society said, "The antislavery men of the United States, as a body, are men of peace, and they have neither counseled nor practiced any violent resistance to unjust and unconstitutional enactments. They claim the right of disobeying them and taking the penalty." He added that his society still promised to maintain the 1833 nonviolent Declaration of Sentiments. At about the same time, Garrison, presiding at the rival American Antislavery Society, asked May to read the same declaration, and then said—with exaggeration—that the American Society had "never swerved in the least degree" from the declaration's principles.[10]

Despite Tappan's and Garrison's claims, the abolitionist stand on nonviolence had been frankly ambiguous ever since the Lovejoy crisis, when the American Society, with the aid of Tappan and Garrison, had adopted the policy of tolerating defensive violence. It was sure to continue ambiguous as long as some major abolitionist leaders—including Garrison—apologized for defensive violence to protect fugitives.

Yet many abolitionists reasserted their nonviolence in some degree during this crisis, some of them much as Garrison did largely as a matter of private commitment, others more strongly. Their reasons—when they gave any—varied from the principled to the pragmatic. The New Hampshire Garrisonian veteran, Parker Pillsbury, admitted that fugitives would of course decide for themselves about violence, but wrote: "I can counsel no violence. Instead of counselling it, I disapprove it, both from principle and policy." The Garrisonian and Quaker, Oliver Johnson, editor of the *Pennsylvania Freeman,* told his readers that while nonresistant heroes—"those godlike men who will suffer any injury but inflict none"—are "very rare," nevertheless "in the long run, violent resistance to oppression does more harm than good." Editor Gay of the *National Antislavery Standard* accepted the use of violence by an individual fugitive to preserve his freedom as both right and expedient, but observed shrewdly that general community violence in resistance to the new law would transform the issue before the country from "liberty versus slavery" into "rebellion versus order," and the result would be to "fasten upon a suffering people the very gigantic wrong which it was intended to remove." In Massachusetts the Garrisonian Captain Jonathan Walker, of branded hand fame, wrote that in protecting fugitive slaves he rejected the use of "bowie knives, dirks, revolvers, or any other 'shooting iron' " but recommended instead "the use of all physical and mental means that can be sanctioned by sound morality and reasonable philosophy"; he urged the creation of vigilance committees to protect the fugitives in every town. Connecticut Garrisonian C .C. Burleigh objected to talk among abolitionists about killing slave hunters. "We ought not to do or say anything to encourage a bloodthirsty spirit," he said. "We could not be too careful to keep the cause from all suspicion of relying upon such methods."[11]

The New York Tappanite judge, William Jay, called the new law unconstitutional, but urged "no forcible resistance" as it would tend to increase the hardships of the Negroes and would give excuse for violence on the part of the slave hunters. In Newark, New Jersey, preacher Charles Beecher, brother of Henry Ward Beecher, in a widely quoted sermon for which he was expelled from his ministerial association, said that he could not cooperate with the fugitive slave law because to do so would be a sin. But, he explained, "I incite no man to deeds of blood. I speak as a minister of the Prince of Peace. . . . If a fugitive claims your help on his journey, break the law and give it to him. . . . Feed him, clothe him, harbor him, by day and by night, and conceal him from his pursuers and from the officers of the law. . . . If they fine you, and imprison you, take joyfully the spoiling of your goods, wear gladly your chain, and in the last day you shall be rewarded for your fidelity to God." The long-time nonresistant, Negro lumber dealer Whipper—who in cooperation with a Quaker was shipping fugitives from Columbia, Pennsylvania, in the false end of one of his railway boxcars—counseled nonviolence at this time, as he explained it afterward, in part to preserve his property. "My self-interest was mingled with a sense of humanity," he said. He exhorted blacks "to peace and patience for our own sakes as well as others" to prevent riots that he expected would destroy his own lumberyard as well as the whole town. Also in Pennsylvania the state antislavery society, with many Quakers present, decided that, while according to the doctrine of the Declaration of Independence, Negroes were "fully justified" in resisting the law by arms, they should use Christian means instead.[12]

Better evidence that abolitionists continued to believe nonviolence to be relevant was that they were making specific proposals for using nonviolent means to thwart the fugitive slave law.

Some proposed action through government. They proposed harassing slave catchers with suits against them. They proposed that if fugitives were seized, they would assist them with legal aid. They called for enacting or strengthening state personal liberty laws to make enforcing the new federal law more difficult—as by insisting on a jury trial and forbidding state officials to assist federal officers. They asked Northern state governments to detain slave catchers in the North until Southern state governments released a corresponding number of Northern Negroes—such as seaman who had been seized there on the false claim they were fugitive slaves. Or they called for outright repeal of the law.

Other abolitionists urged that public opinion be marshaled to nullify the law. A meeting of Philadelphia Negroes asked the American people "to create, by all lawful means, such a public sentiment as shall render its operation upon us powerless." The Michigan Yearly Meeting of Friends asked Christians everywhere to "create such a state of public sentiment that none shall be found so base, so fallen, as to assist" in enforcing this "cruel" law. Senator Charles Sumner said the fugitive slave law must be nullified "not by violence, not by any unconstitutional activity or intervention . . . but by an aroused public opinion, which . . . shall blast with contempt . . . all who consent to be its agents. Thus did our fathers blast all who became the agents of the Stamp Act." When a United States Commissioner in Philadelphia resigned as soon as he heard that his office would require him to enforce the fugitive law, the *National Antislavery Standard* called his resignation "manly" and hoped many other officials would imitate him. H. C. Wright suggested publishing the names of all officials appointed to enforce the law and that the people be "taught in the school, in the pulpit, in all circles, to scorn and execrate them." Lewis Tappan promoted the posting of pledges not to obey the law in every house, store, shop, and factory throughout the land. In upstate New York, Tappanite William Goodell believed that two-thirds of the people opposed enforcement of the law and that this opposition was so strong that it would even prevent Buffalo, President Fillmore's home city, from thrusting any victim into slavery.[13]

Many abolitionists proposed disobeying the law by what can be called nonviolent direct action. In these proposals the Garrisonians —whose considerable experience in noncooperation with government prepared them for this role—made more fundamental, creative contributions than the Tappanites or Quakers.

Some abolitionists proposed employing the boycott method. Pastor Henry Ward Beecher proposed a social boycott: anyone who obeyed this law, he said, "were he brother, son or father—shall never pollute my hand with grasp of hideous friendship, or cast his swarthy shadow across my threshold." The Garrisonian Charles K. Whipple recommended not only snubbing those who enforced the law but also that grocers should refuse to sell them food. O. B. Frothingham, Unitarian pastor in Salem, Massachusetts, developed the boycott idea further: he recommended denying food, shelter, or other services to slave hunters, and that owners of carriages or ships refuse to let them be used to help enforce the law. The president of the Sycracuse and Utica Railroad, who often listened to pastor May's sermons, gave orders to his men that if any fugitive slave in irons were put into their cars to be returned to slavery, they should "stop the train, take off his irons, and set him at liberty."[14]

If slave hunters came to seize a fugitive, some abolitionists said that they as individuals would try to protect the fugitive with nonviolence. Timothy Gilbert, chairman of the Boston Vigilance Committee, said that if a slave hunter came to seize a fugitive hiding at his house, if necessary he would plant his body to protect the fugitive until the slave hunter trampled him under his feet. Similarly, the Garrisonian Abby Kelley Foster, insisting that only moral weapons would succeed in this moral contest, said that no fugitive slave would be taken anywhere "if throwing her body in the way of kidnappers, and sacrificing her life, could prevent it."

For larger-scale nonviolent protection of fugitives, abolitionists made impressive proposals. The Rhode Island Antislavery Society decided that when warrants were issued for seizing fugitives, if it was not possible to hide the fugitives or help them escape, "they shall be surrounded by a sufficiently numerous and influential Peace Committee to protect them from assault and capture." The Garrisonian Wendell Phillips suggested that if a fugitive were held in a courthouse, "hundreds of thousands" of people should nonviolently surround the courthouse so that to carry the fugitive off to the South, the officials "would be obliged . . . to walk over our heads." In a particularly daring and explicit proposal, the Garrisonian *National Antislavery Standard* urged that a phalanx of peaceful men, willing to give their lives, could protect a fugitive even from military forces: it called for men "unarmed but determined that no slave shall be taken . . . except over their bodies." Such a "revolution" would be "the noblest the world ever saw, and it would, we cannot doubt, be effectual. We can hardly believe that armed citizen-soldiers would ride over and cut down their fellow-citizens standing and braving death with calm but desperate resolution lest a man should be taken among them and made a slave."[15] Here were proposals for large-scale, death-defying, frankly coercive, organized nonviolent resistance—proposals more explicit and down to earth than Birney's visionary one of 1835—yet they were far ahead of the time when Gandhi made such action well known as a means to struggle for freedom.

Proposing an additional kind of nonviolent direct action, some abolitionists offered to make nuisances of themselves to the slave hunters. Garrison hinted at this when he proposed that abolitionists "resist and baffle the slavehunter who shall dare to make his appearance on our soil." Wendell Phillips hinted at it too when he told a great meeting in Faneuil Hall: "By peaceful resistance, we must interrupt the slaveholder, and make it not worth his while to attempt reclamations." More explicitly, a Worcester County antislavery society urged abolitionists to "throw every lawful cost and other obstacle in the way of the claimants" so their costs would become "ruinous." The Rhode Island Antislavery Society resolved: "Every peaceful instrumentality shall be energetically used to make the slave hunters aware that the atmosphere of the free states is unfavorable for their health, so that they shall be exceedingly glad to go home." The one who developed this idea of nonviolent harassment of slave hunters to a fine point was Charles K. Whipple, who had been the treasurer of the Nonresistance Society and who often wrote for the *Liberator.* As Whipple presented his plan, which was debated and partially adopted by the Boston Vigilance Committee, its essence was as follows:

As soon as the kidnappers arrive in any town, large handbills should be posted in all the public places, containing their names, with a description of their persons and the business on which they come.

An attempt should be made to induce the landlord of any hotel or boarding-house to which they may go, to refuse them entertainment, on the ground of their being persons infamous by profession, like pick-pockets, gamblers, or horse-stealers.

If this proves unsuccessful, some of the committee of attendance should take lodging in the same house with the kidnappers, and take, if possible, sleeping rooms and seats at table directly opposite to them.

The doors of the house should be watched carefully, day and night, and whenever they go out, two resolute, unarmed men should follow each of them wherever he goes, pointing him out from time to time with the word SLAVE-HUNTER. They should follow him into every shop, office, or place of public business into which he may go, and if he enters a private dwelling, wait outside, watching all the avenues, and ready to renew the attendance when he comes out. If he takes a coach, they should follow in another; if he drives out of town, they should follow; if he takes a seat in a railroad car, they should go with him, and make him known as a slave-hunter to the passengers in the car, and to the people of the town where he stops. He should have not one moment's relief from the feeling that his object is understood, that he cannot act in secret, that he is surrounded by men who loathe his person and detest his purpose, and who have means always at hand to prevent the possibility of success.[16]

Following such proposals as these, nonviolent attempts to protect fugitive slaves in the North continued to be made all the way through the increasingly violent 1850's.

Soon after the passage of the new fugitive slave law, two slave hunters arrived in Boston to seize William and Ellen Craft, the celebrated couple who had escaped from Georgia in disguise. The Crafts had lived in Boston for two years and were members of Theodore Parker's Unitarian Church. Parker hid Mrs. Craft at first in his house, later elsewhere. With Parker's encouragement, Craft kept a pistol and dirks ready at his furniture shop and promised to shoot anyone, law officer or not, who tried to force him into slavery. The Boston Vigilance Committee, in which Parker was a prime mover, filed suits against the two slave agents to harass them and in accordance with Whipple's plan, they posted placards describing the agents, followed them in the streets, pointing them out publicly as slave hunters, and at the same time protected them from violence. Finally when the committee told the slave agents that they would no longer protect them from violence, the agents saw the wisdom of leaving Boston. The vigilance committee had succeeded in protecting the Crafts with a combination of violence and nonviolence. Nonresistant Whipple regretted that his plan had not been more thoroughly put into practice against the slave agents, but claimed that "even the moderate degree of it which was practiced . . . so disconcerted and annoyed them, that they . . . felt unable to stay in Boston." Pastor Parker boasted that his actions rested on the "higher law," that is, the principle that moral law is higher than man-made law such as the Constitution. In carrying out the moral law, Parker believed violence was seldom justified. "I deplore violence," he wrote soon after the Crafts affair; "let us do without it while we can, forever if we can. I am no nonresistant; yet I am glad the leading antislavery men are so—that, great as is the right of liberty, they would not shed a drop of blood to achieve it for all mankind; for though I think their doctrines extreme, they are yet nearer right, I think, than the common notions."[17]

In an incident in Philadelphia, abolitionists used Whipple's harassment method even more successfully. By chance J. Miller McKim, the nonviolent agent in charge of the Pennsylvania Antislavery Society's office, heard that a Maryland slaveowner, a Miss Wilson, was in Philadelphia to recover a runaway slave of hers and was trying to locate a local slave catcher to help her. McKim arranged for an abolitionist, posing as a slave catcher, to call on Miss Wilson at her boarding house and offer his services. Miss Wilson accepted his offer, and told him the name of the fugitive she was hunting. The abolitionist then reported the name to McKim, who notified the fugitive, who immediately went into hiding. McKim prepared posters, each about three feet square, and had them posted about the city:

Beware of Slave-Catchers

Miss Wilson, of Georgetown Cross Roads, Kent County, Md., is now in the city in pursuit of her alleged slave man, Butler. . . .

It is requested that all parties to whom a copy of this may be sent will post it in a public place, and that the friends of Freedom and Humanity will have the facts herein contained openly read in their respective churches.

"Hide the outcast; betray not him that wandereth." Isaiah xvi:3

On learning that her name had been posted about the city, Miss Wilson promptly packed her baggage and returned to Maryland, abandoning her slave hunt.

In a similar incident in Boston, when Virginia slave owner Charles Hobson came to Boston to hunt Henry Langhorn, his escaped slave, Langhorn happened to see him in the street without Hobson seeing him. Langhorn at once reported to the Massachusetts Antislavery office that he was afraid Hobson had come to seize him. The office checked local hotels to see if such a man actually was in Boston, and found that he was. At once the office arranged to hide Langhorn in the house of Francis Jackson, the Garrisonian merchant. When Hobson advertised in the papers offering a reward for catching the fugitive, and describing his appearance, abolitionists replied with an advertisement mimicking his own and making known Hobson's purpose. It began: "Charles L. Hobson, twenty-two years of age, six feet high, with a slouched hat on, mixed coat, black pants, with a goatee, is stopping at the Tremont Hotel." Abolitionists also posted one hundred placards about the streets, warning that Hobson was in town to catch his slave. The exposure so unnerved Hobson that he hurriedly returned to Virginia, without Henry Langhorn.[18]

In Christiana, Lancaster County, Pennsylvania, near the Maryland border, Negroes used violence to prevent the seizure of fugitive slaves. William Parker, a fugitive from Maryland, had experience as a leader in such violence. When he heard that a Maryland master was on his way to seize a number of his fugitive slaves in Christiana, Parker told his Quaker landlady, and she advised him not to lead the fugitives to resist by violence. He replied that if the law protected blacks as it did whites, he, too, would be nonviolent and would appeal to the law to protect him. Whites, he said, "have a country and may obey the laws. But we have no country."

When the slave master, Edward Gorsuch, arrived in Christiana, he was accompanied by his son and a federal marshal, and they were armed. Gorsuch's party found the house where Parker and the slaves belonging to Gorsuch were hiding, and called them out. A crowd of some hundred Negroes, armed with axes, corn cutters, and guns, gradually gathered to protect the fugitives. The two parties threatened each other.

Two Quakers living in the neighborhood, Castner Hanway and Elijah Lewis, arrived. The marshal showed the Quakers his warrants and requested them to assist in the seizure of the fugitives as the law required. The Quakers refused. They asked the Negroes not to do violence, but warned the slave catchers that they were likely to be hurt.

A fight began. Parker and the fugitives came out of the house and killed Gorsuch. Then they fled by the Underground Railroad to Rochester, where Douglass sheltered them and helped them to board a boat for Toronto. On the dock the fugitives gratefully presented the once complete nonresistant Douglass with the revolver that fell from Gorsuch's hand when he died, and Douglass accepted it.[19]

The *Liberator* used its usual double standard to comment on the Gorsuch murder. Using the standard of the patriot, it said: "The blacks are fully justified in what they did, by the Declaration of Independence, and the teaching and example of Washington, Warren, and Kossuth." But using the standard of the Christian, the *Liberator* also said soon afterward: "No man, bearing arms, enters into the Kingdom of Heaven. . . . A truly brave man never yet took up the sword." Not being encumbered by the complications of a double standard, Robert Purvis declared that the Negroes in using violence to protect themselves had been true to themselves, to liberty, and to God.[20]

Meanwhile many of those said to be present at the Gorsuch murder had been arrested for treason, among them the Quakers Hanway and Lewis and thirty-seven Negroes, and they were imprisoned. A few weeks later, when Hanway and Lewis had been freed—eventually all the prisoners were freed by the courts—at a meeting of the Pennsylvania Antislavery Society, Quaker James Mott, presiding, said that he saw in the audience "two of the Christiana traitors," Hanway and Lewis. The audience called for them to come to the platform. As they came forward, Congressman Giddings of Ohio, who had just spoken of his admiration for the blacks who had used violence to protect themselves against Gorsuch, took the Quakers' hands and stood between them, saying, "I declare to you, my friends, that I am far prouder of being permitted to grasp the hands of these brave men, than I should to receive the applause of the mightiest prince." The meeting gave tremendous cheers. But the meeting was more discriminating than Giddings on what it approved and what it did not approve. On the motion of McKim, it voted to reaffirm the passage from the 1833 Declaration of Sentiments which insisted on nonviolent methods.[21]

Near where the Gorsuch murder occurred, Negro leader Whipper was still trying to be nonviolent. Whipper lived in Columbia, Pennsylvania, at a major junction of the Underground Railroad—his house was at the end of a bridge over the Susquehanna River. He had long aided fugitives; he claimed he had aided hundreds in the years 1847 to 1850 alone. He believed that it was because he aided fugitives that his lumberyard had been twice set on fire.

After the new fugitive slave law was passed, a fugitive being chased in Columbia was shot to death. Columbia's Negroes—20 percent of the town's total population—were upset. They held heated meetings in which, as Whipper reported it, some proposed that if other fugitives were attacked, they should slaughter all whites within reach and burn the whole town. Whipper's tendencies had long been nonviolent, and these tendencies were reinforced, he explained, by his own desire to preserve his lumberyard. He urged all Negroes to "peace and patience" and urged any fugitives in special danger of being seized to flee to Canada.

Soon afterward slave agents came to Columbia to seize a prominent fugitive, Methodist preacher Dorsey. Whipper, hearing of it, went to Dorsey's house in the dark. As Whipper recalled later, he was refused admittance until those inside ascertained who he was.

Once admitted, Whipper found in the house several men who were armed and ready to massacre any slave hunters who arrived. "I advised Dorsey to leave [town], but he very pointedly refused, saying he had been taken up once before alive, but never would be again. The men told him to stand his ground, and they would stand by him and defend him; they had lived together, and would die together. I told them that they knew the strength of the pro-slavery feeling that surrounded them, and that they would be overpowered, and perhaps many lives lost, which might be saved by his changing his place of residence."

Dorsey said he had no money and would rather die at home with his family than be killed on the road. Whipper asked, "How much money do you want to start with?" and offered one hundred dollars.

"That is not enough," Dorsey replied

"Will two hundred dollars do?" Whipper asked.

"Yes."

"I shall bring it to you tomorrow."

The next morning Whipper brought the money, promised to look after Dorsey's family andproperty in Columbia, and Dorsey promptly left town.

Whipper continued to assist fugitives to escape to Canada. In the five years following the passage of the new fugitive law, the Negro population of Columbia dropped by nearly half.[22]

Abolitionists were not always as successful as Whipper in preventing fugitives from being seized under the new law. When they could not prevent fugitives being seized, the abolitionists were faced with what to do next, if anything.

In New York City officers seized Henry Long as a fugitive slave. After abolitionists had tried to free him unsuccessfully through the courts, two hundred policemen led him through the streets on his way back to slavery. Despite the fervid promises of New York Negroes that they would not submit to the law, no one interfered to save him. Douglass was unhappy. "I had rather have heard," he said in a speech in Rochester, "that colored men had been beaten down by the two hundred policemen employed on that occasion, than that there should have been no manifestation of physical resistance to the reenslavement of poor Long."[23]

By contrast, a group of Boston Negroes, unarmed but not averse to shoving, rescued a fugitive from officers without anyone being injured. Officers had arrested Shadrach, a waiter in a Boston coffeehouse, on the claim that he was an escaped Virginia slave, and took him to a courtroom. Negroes entered the courtroom and, moving about in a hubbub of laughter and jostling, hid Shadrach from the view of the officers long enough to rush him out of the room and start him on his way to Canada. Secretary of State Daniel Webster called the rescue treason, and Senator Henry Clay said it showed that the fugitive slave law should be made even more severe. But an address by the Tappanite American and Foreign Antislavery Society proudly said of the rescue: "Not a weapon had been provided, not a wound was given," and Garrison praised it as "a sudden rush of a score or two of unarmed friends of equal liberty—an uninjurious deliverance of the oppressed out of the hands of the oppressor."[24]

In Syracuse the Underground Railroader Samuel J. May helped plan the rescue of Jerry McHenry, a cooper who had lived several years in Syracuse and who had been seized by police on a Southerner's claim that he was his slave. Others in the planning included the nonviolent Gerrit Smith and the black pastors S. R. Ward and J. W. Loguen who justified defensive violence. The plan was to force open the doors and windows of the police station where McHenry was being held, overpower the police by numbers rather than blows, and take McHenry off by buggy. According to May, during the planning, "I declared [that] I had no confidence in the use of deadly weapons; that I would not carry even my cane to the rescue of one who should be seized under the [fugitive slave] law. I would hold a man who was attempting to execute it if I could; overpower him if I had the strength so to do; but not intentionally harm a hair of his head."

According to plan, a crowd of antislavery men forced their way into the police station with axes and iron rods. Inside, some of them evidently grappled with police in hand-to-hand fighting. At any rate, the only policeman even slightly hurt was one who in panic jumped out of a window. McHenry drove off in a buggy and he eventually reached Kingston, Canada, in safety. More than twenty-five men, white and black, were indicted for the rescue, including May and Smith, but no one was convicted.

Immediately after the rescue, when May and Smith asked if anyone were injured and received the answer no, May said, we "lifted our hearts in thanksgiving." They both often boasted afterward that the rescue occurred without bloodshed. The Jerry McHenry rescue, said the *Liberator*, "was the act of a few unarmed individuals . . . wishing and intending to injure no one. . . . It was designed [in] the spirit of love even to the guilty." However, it may have been a sign of the decreasing concern of the Garrisonians for nonviolence that in recounting the rescue, as well as similar incidents about the same time, the Massachusetts Antislavery Society's annual report omitted any direct comment on the issue of violence.[25]

By 1854, perhaps fifty or sixty slaves had already been forced to return to the South under the new fugitive slave law, and partly in response, antislavery sentiment had grown more powerful than ever. In that year a Virginia slave master tried to force into slavery a young Boston Negro, Anthony Burns, a tailor and ministerial student whom the slave master claimed he owned. Officials held Burns in a courthouse. In attempting to rescue Burns from the courthouse so that he could not be returned to slavery, Massachusetts abolitionists clearly revealed their differences over violence.

Garrison was holding to nonviolence, as sixteen-year-old school-girl Charlotte Forten, the granddaughter of James Forten, reported. When she dined at Garrison's during the Burns excitement, though she herself believed in forcible resistance to tyranny, she was deeply stirred by Garrison's continued faith in nonresistance. She watched the expression on his noble face, she wrote afterward, as he spoke beautifully for his nonresistance principles; he had, she said, the highest Christian spirit. But Garrison remained aloof from the Boston Vigilance Committee as it debated how to rescue Burns.

From nearby Amesbury, Whittier wrote a member of the vigilance committee, proposing that the people from the countryside descend on Boston in nonviolent protest. "If you want the country to march into Boston, say so at once," he wrote.[26]

The vigilance committee, about sixty men at the time, were split on what to do. Half of them decided for complete nonviolence. They chose not Whittier's plan but, for the time being, Whipple's device which they had used previously, that is, following Burns' ostensible master about the Boston streets, pointing fingers of scorn at him, so everyone would know who he was and what he was doing. But the young Worcester Free Church pastor, Thomas Wentworth Higginson, who earlier had admitted that their "most reliable men" were nonresistants, was contemptuous of this nonviolent action as a means to rescue Burns. Instead Higginson led as many of the other half of the committee as he could in getting up an antislavery mob. Higginson did so without the authority of the vigilance committee. He did so against the will of the occasional nonresistants Wendell Phillips and Theodore Parker, who urged a mass demonstration more like what Whittier proposed, not necessarily strictly nonviolent but without guns and disciplined—a demonstration to block the entrances to the courthouse so that the guards would be overawed into surrendering Burns by the great numbers and cool purpose involved. Whittier was too ill to come to Boston; there was inadequate time for Higginson, Phillips, and Parker to consult, and it is not certain they would have agreed on a common plan if they had. With only hurried planning, Higginson led a small group to a door of the courthouse and battered it down with a beam. In the process a guard was killed, probably by one of Higginson's mob. Frightened by the killing, the mob decided its numbers were insufficient, and retreated.[27]

Afterward, an official statement by the American Antislavery Society considered the mob's attack "gallant and generous" but ill advised because not well planned; it did not condemn the violence. Frederick Douglass regarded the killing as being as innocent in the sight of God as the slaughter of a wolf that was throttling an infant.

While state and federal governments poured troops into Boston to prevent another attempt to rescue Burns, crowds milled about the courthouse. One day three hundred friends of liberty came from Worcester. Garrison addressed them, and they marched about the courthouse square, two by two, carrying freedom placards. The police seized the placards, creating great excitement.[28]

At a New England antislavery convention in Boston, abolitionists continued their disagreement on how to save Burns. Garrison on principle opposed any secret plan, he said; he favored adjourning the convention and reassembling it in an open protest demonstration in front of the courthouse, somewhat like the demonstration that had already occurred. H. C. Wright favored all members of the convention taking a pledge to resist the slaveholders, "each by such means as he shall deem right and expedient." A nonresistant pastor, S. S. Griswold, of Mystic, Connecticut, said that Christian means could not in fact always rescue a man from his enemies, as they could not rescue Jesus, but delivering a man from his enemies was "not always the most essential thing." Pastor May of Syracuse said that while he was a lover of peace, forcible rescue without injury would be better than submission. The convention, however, was unable to reach agreement on any plan of action at all.

As it became more and more likely that Burns was to be sent back to slavery regardless of any violent or nonviolent action that could be taken, protesting citizens draped their stores and offices in black and hung their American flags upside down. All day and all night Negroes stood on the sidewalk before the hotel where Burns' master was staying, in a nonviolent protest vigil, like many vigils to come in the next century. When officials finally were ready to usher Burns from the courthouse to a government cutter in harbor, they had gathered a large military force—said to be the largest in Boston since the American Revolution—to prevent citizens from interfering. The vigilance committee, able under this threat of overwhelming force to agree to be nonviolent, advised the people in a broadside: "Let there be no armed resistance; but let the whole people turn out, and line the streets, and look upon the shame and disgrace of Boston, and then go away and take measures to elect men to office who will better guard the honor of the state."[29] The youthful Burns, his head high, walked through troop-lined streets, without interference, to his ship, and returned to slavery. Massachusetts abolitionists had failed in their promises to protect fugitives.

However, there followed a series of nonviolent acts that took the bitterness out of the Burns defeat, if not quite turning it into victory. In Framingham at a protest meeting Garrison held up a copy of the fugitive slave law and burned it, saying, "And let all the people say Amen." They did. Then he held up a copy of the slavery-protecting United States Constitution under which Burns had been returned to slavery, and he denounced it as "a covenant with death, and an agreement with hell" and he burned it, saying, "So perish all compromises with tyranny! And let the people say Amen." Most of them did. In Boston, police captain Joseph K. Hayes resigned so that he would never have to take part in hunting a fugitive slave, and Harriet Beecher Stowe praised him for his "noble example."[30] In Worcester, the American flag flew on the common at half mast, upside down, and draped in black. In Fall River, Pawtucket, and Natick, bells were tolled. In Watertown, Weymouth, and Haverhill, effigies of the judge who sent Burns back into slavery were burned. In Cambridge, Harvard law students boycotted the judge's lectures. Over a period of time, antislavery citizens, urged on by Garrison and others, brought political pressure until they ousted the judge from his state judgeship. Abolitionists even paid Burns' master for his freedom and sent Burns to Oberlin College to complete his study for the ministry. Never again was a runaway returned from Massachusetts to slavery.

Soon after the Burns affair, in a parallel incident in Worcester, speak-inner Foster led an organized nonviolent action.

When the notorious slave catcher, United States Deputy Marshal Asa Butman—who had arrested Burns in Boston—came to Worcester, apparently looking for more fugitive slaves to arrest, Worcester abolitionists were divided about what to do, somewhat as Boston abolitionists had been in the Burns case. Three different Worcester groups planned to oust Butman from the city. One group planned to oust him by tarring and feathering him. Another, a Negro group, planned to beat him. Still another group, led by Foster, planned to use nonviolence. Foster's group chose essentially Whipple's method. As Foster explained it afterward, "Our plan was to present ourselves in as large numbers as possible in the presence of the man, and, fastening upon him an indignant gaze, to follow him wherever he went, by night and by day, till he should leave the town."

The tar-and-feather group, after making preparations, failed to find anyone who dared to tar and feather Butman, and gave up. Foster's group, about sixty men, in carrying out their plan, took posts around the hotel where Butman was staying. One of the group got inside the hotel, unexpectedly discovered that Butman was carrying a pistol, and heard him threaten to use it to kill. Foster's group then charged Butman with carrying a concealed weapon and, after a vigil of eight hours at the hotel, saw Butman arrested. At Butman's trial the judge postponed the proceedings, meanwhile placing Butman under bond.

While Butman was still under the protection of the city marshal, the Negro group invaded the marshal's office and beat Butman on the head, knocking him to the ground. A mob gathered. Frightened for his life, Butman then promised Foster that he would forfeit bond, leave town, and never return. To get the slave catcher safely out of town, Foster's group offered its nonviolent protection against what had become a vicious antislavery mob yelling for Butman's blood. Butman, according to Foster, "joyfully accepted" nonviolent protection.

Butman's acceptance thrust a dramatic responsibility on Foster. "I did not expect the privilege of standing between him and certain death," Foster afterward wrote to his wife, "and taking upon my own person the blows which were aimed at his . . . head."

Foster's group formed themselves into a ring around Butman to protect him as he walked to the railroad depot. The mob, which gradually increased to a thousand, surrounded the ring, slowing its progress. The mob threw eggs and rocks and tried to strike Butman and tear him from his protectors. At the center of the ring, Worcester pastor Higginson, who had led the violent Boston mob to free Burns but was now part of a nonviolent group protecting one of those who had sent Burns back to slavery, warded off Butman's assailants. Foster placed himself behind Butman and, as he wrote—in words that could be interpreted as representing a departure from complete nonviolence but which, according to the traditional Garrisonian distinction between injurious and noninjurious force, probably were not so interpreted at the time—"with my left hand firm upon his shoulder that I might not be separated from him, with my right hand I incessantly thrust back those whose aim seemed to be to tear him limb from limb."

When Butman and the mob reached the depot, they discovered that the train Butman was expected to take had already left. At this crisis Foster and his group put Butman into the depot's privy and placed a guard around it to protect him. Foster pled with the mob to disperse, saying Butman's promise never to return was a victory for freedom and hoping, as a Worcester paper reported it, "that no one would mar the triumph by any further act of violence."

Finally, with the help of police, Foster's antislavery men succeeded in guiding their enemy, the trembling slave catcher Butman, into a hack in which he rode out of Worcester to safety.

Afterward Foster, the veteran of many mobs, wrote his wife: "Never did I feel half the anxiety for my own life which I felt for his, or make half the effort to save it. . . . I felt that the honor of our cause was at stake, and for the moment my heart yearned almost with an agony for a bloodless victory. And when the scene was past and my prayer was fully answered, I felt a lightness of heart such as I never felt before."

The abolitionists' protection of Butman, said Quincy in the *Liberator*, was a "striking example of practical Christianity."[31]

Near the Tappanite center of Oberlin, Ohio, when an attempt was made in 1858 to enforce the fugitive slave law, abolitionists tried to foil it by largely nonviolent methods. A Kentucky slave catcher and a federal marshal seized a Negro boy, John Price, under false pretenses and took him to a hotel as their prisoner; later they charged he was a fugitive slave. An Oberlin townsman, having seen the boy being taken away, sounded an alarm. Oberlin townsmen, students, and Oberlin Professor Peck hurried off by buggy and horseback to his rescue. A few of them were armed. At the hotel they blocked entrances so that the young Price could not be carried out. They tried in vain to negotiate for his release on such grounds as that a proper warrant had not been shown to a magistrate. While some of the crowd distracted officials at the front of the hotel, at the back others placed a ladder against the hotel building, climbed to an upper story, and quickly carried Price out to freedom. The rescue was "without violence," reported the Tappanite *American Missionary* in triumph. "No one was hurt," explained the American Antislavery Society, "not a shilling's damage was done, not a shot was fired, and the boy saved."

However, a federal grand jury indicted at least twenty people for using force to rescue John Price from lawful arrest, and they were jailed in Cleveland. Much of the Ohio public sympathized with the rescuers. The Cleveland jailer, in letting them into his jail, said, "Gentlemen, I open my doors to you not as criminals, but as guests." While they were imprisoned, several thousand people came to the jailyard to hear Professor Peck preach from his cell, and four hundred Oberlin Sunday school children came to visit. The Oberlin *Evangelist* said of the rescuers: "It would not be easy to find twenty truer, better men, or more law abiding and virtuous citizens." Marchers filed through the streets with bands and banners, protesting the arrests. Responding to the protests, Ohio state officials sued the federal marshal and the Kentucky slave catcher for kidnapping, and eventually federal officials, in exchange for Ohio officials promising to drop their suits, dropped the remaining charges against the rescuers. Among the results of the Oberlin affair were a stronger antislavery plank in the Ohio Republican party platform and Ohio's election of more strongly antislavery congressmen.[32]

A nonviolent rescue occurred in Pennsylvania as late as 1859. Officers picked up a Negro, Donald Dangerfield, wearing a ragged coat and hat, on the charge that he was a fugitive slave. A large number of persons attended his trial in Philadelphia, including both supporters and opponents of slavery. Among them was Lucretia Mott, a frail little woman in simple dress, who sat in silence next to the prisoner. She so fixed her eyes on the slaveholder's chief lawyer, the future United States Attorney General Benjamin Brewster, as he spoke, that he was shaken and asked that she be moved; many years later he could still remember the censure on her face so well that he said that having dared to face Lucretia Mott he could dare to face anything.

When Mrs. Mott had an opportunity, she whispered to the presiding commissioner that she earnestly hoped that his conscience would not allow him to return the poor black to slavery. When he replied that he must be bound by his oath of office, she quoted these lines:

The traitor to humanity,
Is the traitor most accursed.

The commissioner thereafter looked pale, as Lucretia Mott remembered later, and it was evident that he wished to favor Dangerfield if he could. After the trial had lasted into the second day, the commissioner finally decided to free the prisoner since the slaveholder's testimony about the slave's height did not tally with Dangerfield's.

Supporters of the South in the courtroom were furious. They threatened to seize Dangerfield when he came out into the street and return him to his alleged master. But the abolitionist young men in the courtroom—most of them Quakers—carried out a nonviolent ruse. They escorted another Negro who looked like Dangerfield out into the street to draw off the crowd, allowing the real Dangerfield to walk out, without harm, to a waiting carriage, in which he soon found his way onto the Underground Railroad and so to Canada.[33]

Altogether the slaves' efforts to escape and the abolitionists' aid to them were impressive. In the generation before the Civil War perhaps as many as 100,000 slaves successfully escaped from the South. It is probable that even with the new fugitive slave law, more slaves escaped in the 1850's than ever before, and that in the North by 1857, as J. Miller McKim claimed, abolitionists had made the law ineffective. Despite the increasing violence in the aid to fugitives, a significant element of nonviolence had persisted up to the eve of the war.

Among the three schools of nonviolent abolitionists, it was the Quakers who led in the Underground Railroad, but if any one of the three schools may be said to have led during the fugitive slave law crisis in protecting the fugitives who had already reached the North, it was the Garrisonians.

Though nonviolence had become weaker during the 1850's, particularly among blacks, nonviolent abolitionists of all three schools, both black and white, had developed a wide range of nonviolent methods to thwart the law. Nonviolent abolitionists had refused to assist officers in enforcing the law, as the law required, and in fact had harassed both officials and slave hunters nonviolently. They had illegally hid fugitives, fed them, given them money, rushed them out of the hands of law officers, and helped them reach Canada. While abolitionists did not, as far as we know, ever form a phalanx of peaceful, unarmed men to place their bodies between military forces and a fugitive slave, which the *National Antislavery Standard* had called for, nevertheless, in action that was perhaps just as impressive, in Boston and Worcester they had formed bodies of unarmed men to protect their enemy slave hunters from antislavery violence until they could get them out of town. They had helped develop public opposition to the law by such nonviolent means as court actions, pressure on officials not to cooperate or else to resign, voting, boycotts, burning effigies, burning copies of the Constitution, hanging flags upside down, meetings, placards, marches, and vigils.

Because violent action may appear more exciting than nonviolent action, it is likely that violent action was more often recorded than nonviolent action was. Probably thousands of nonviolent acts in aid of fugitives remain unrecorded—many of them simple acts of hospitality, like providing a fugitive a place to sleep overnight, a gift of clothing, or a ride in a wagon.

Particularly when aid to fugitives was nonviolent, it gained allies for the abolitionists among those who were humanitarian enough to feel the immediate suffering of a hunted fugitive, if not to feel the injustice of the more remote and abstract slave system. When a Philadelphia newspaper editor who was inclined to apologize for slavery saw a fugitive slave arrive by Underground Railroad for the first time, he became a supporter of the Railroad. When a conservative Baptist deacon who was inclined to intone about the "majesty of the law" by chance met Shadrach on his flight from Boston to Canada and heard his story, the deacon found himself breaking the law by contributing funds to help him on his way. It was easier to raise money for fugitives, Wendell Phillips reported, than for the general antislavery cause. According to a Pennsylvania abolitionist agent, many Pennsylvanians who were hostile to abolition were sympathetic enough to individual fugitive slaves to give them food. When a fugitive hid in a New England village on his way to Canada, many of the villagers, realizing how the law threatened him, became so anxious to demonstrate their willingness to break the law by aiding a fugitive that they deliberately broke bread into small pieces so each person could give him a piece. After the Crafts escaped, when they spoke in a small Massachusetts town, at the end of the meeting the audience rushed to shake their hands. Involving thousands of conscientious citizens in aiding fugitives in some small way such as giving funds, giving food, or just shaking their hands was, in fact, enticing them into acts of defiance of the slave system which psychologically were significant strides toward commitment to abolition.

Aid to fugitives also encouraged commitment to abolition by providing young idealists with freedom heroes—including the kind of heroes, rather rare in American tradition, who were without blood on their hands. Protecting fugitives in the North created heroes like Quaker Hanway, who went to prison for refusing to assist a slave-hunting officer, and Foster, who helped protect a slave hunter while hustling him out of town. Escaping from slavery created heroes who took great risks to become free themselves, like Henry "Box" Brown, while operating the Underground Railroad created heroes who took great risks to help free others, like Quaker Garrett, who lost all his property. All honest Northerners admired Garrett, said Theodore Parker, and "young lads say, 'I wish that heaven would make me such a man.' "

By bringing escaping slaves into Northern families, the Underground Railroad made slavery real to the Northerners. The nonresistant educator Alcott said that having a fugitive slave in his house gave "image and a name to the dire entity of slavery, and was an impressive lesson to my children, bringing before them the wrongs of the black man and his tale of woes." It is difficult to suppose that children, once having helped to hide a fugitive in their household, could easily be callous about the slave system thereafter—as indeed Alcott's daughter Louisa May was not. As the Massachusetts Antislavery Society said, aiding fugitive slaves was part of the process by which the nation was being educated up to abolition.

Participating in this direct action, like participating in sit-ins, vigils, or ride-ins then or a century later, offered both blacks and whites something adventurous to do for the cause of freedom. It gave them close association in action with others who were willing to suffer if necessary for their beliefs. It gave them personal knowledge of the terror implicit in the slave system. And it did much to alert the American people to the abolitionists' determination that slavery must end.

18. John Brown's Raid

◇◇◇◇◇◇◇◇◇◇◇

IN THE 1850's abolitionists increasingly tended not only to accept small-scale, defensive violence, as in protecting fugitive slaves, but also to accept larger scale, more offensive violence.

When Congress gave Kansas the right to decide whether it was to be free or slave territory and pro-slavery Southerners threatened to force Kansas to choose slavery, abolitionists found themselves tempted to use violence to aid the free-soil settlers. Pastor Higginson, who had organized the Boston mob to rescue fugitive slave Burns, went to Kansas to help organize the free-soil guerrilla fighters. Both Lewis Tappan's pastor, Henry Ward Beecher of Brooklyn, and Garrison's pastor, Theodore Parker of Boston, raised funds to send the free-soilers rifles. Others who did the same were Garrison's close associate Phillips, though he was still hopeful that disunion would come nonviolently, and Ralph Waldo Emerson, who once had advocated nonresistance, saying that it was time for history to pass from the state of beasts to the state of man. Still another was Gerrit Smith. "Hitherto I have opposed the bloody abolition of slavery," Smith wrote. But when the slave power "begins to march its conquering bands into [Kansas] . . . I and ten thousand other peace men are not only ready to have it repulsed with violence, but pursued even unto death with violence."[1]

In Lawrence, Kansas, abolitionist storekeeper Charles Stearns, who had once been in a Connecticut prison for conscientious objection to serving in the state militia, by the summer of 1855 was still a nonresistant. Though Stearns had lost a large portion of his property by robbery, he still said that he felt safest among his enemies unarmed; when attacked by a mob, he said it was the mob's knowledge that he was a nonresistant that had saved his life. A few months later, however, with his town expecting attack from pro-slavery men, Stearns had decided to abandon nonviolence. "The cold-blooded murder, last night, of one of our best citizens, has decided me," he wrote Garrison in explanation. "I am sorry to deny the principles of Jesus Christ, after contending for them so long, but it is not for myself that I am going to fight. It is for God and the slaves. . . . I have always said I would shoot a wild beast. If I shoot these infernal Missourians, it will be on the same principle." The *Liberator* grieved over Stearns: we hope he will learn, like Peter, to repent his apostasy, it said.[2]

Higginson, visiting Kansas soon after Stearns abandoned nonviolence, wrote that he could find only one remaining "theoretical nonresistant"—he probably meant only one complete, nonvoting, Garrisonian nonresistant. Higginson, by no means a nonresistant himself, nevertheless went out of his way to call upon this unnamed man "and express my respect, a feeling I could not quite entertain for those who had backslidden, and could then give as an excuse that they 'never imagined there could be such people in the world as the Border Ruffians.' "

However, there were other practicing nonresistants in Kansas. For instance, there were several nonresistant agents of the Tappanite American Missionary Association. One of them, the Oberlin graduate Samuel Adair, was a brother-in-law of Kansas guerrilla fighter John Brown. Adair preached to the free-soilers in their log cabins. He found that their reform interests were shallow: many of them wanted not only to keep slavery out of Kansas, but to keep Negroes out too. Adair preached to them on behalf of Negroes, against slavery, and against war. "People cannot have the spirit of Christ and the spirit of war in their hearts at the same time," he said. After John Brown and his sons dragged several unsuspecting pro-slavery men from their homes at Pottawatomie and slaughtered them, Adair sheltered two of the Brown sons who were not implicated in the murders, but refused to shelter another son who was implicated; he believed in sheltering only the innocent, not the guilty. Two of Adair's relatives were murdered before his eyes. Three times he and his family fled their home because of violence. But he never sanctioned the use of force. At a free-soilers' meeting when John Brown argued for armed resistance, Adair advised disobeying the unjust laws of the Southern-controlled Kansas legislature and accepting any consequent penalties, but not taking up arms. He never carried any weapons. "In all ordinary cases I feel much safer without them," he explained.[3]

Garrison would not aid the Kansas free-soilers in their violence. If rifles were to be sent to the free-soilers, he said, why not send rifles also to the Southern slaves? The injustice to the slaves, he argued, was much greater than that to the free-soilers.

Neither would Lewis Tappan nor Pastor May aid the free-soilers in their violence. When John Brown visited an antislavery meeting in Syracuse to appeal for funds for the Kansas "war," both May and Tappan refused to help send arms, offering relief supplies instead.

Garrison encouraged loyal peace man May: "You see that such men as Gerrit Smith, Ward Beecher, and Theodore Parker are finding in Sharp's rifles more than in the peaceful Gospel of Christ to aid the cause of right and freedom!" Garrison wrote him. "They will cause many professed friends of peace to apostatize from their principles, and give a fresh stimulus to the war spirit. I think this is the time for radical peace men to renew their testimonies, dealing as tenderly as possible with the settlers in Kansas (whose situation is undeniably a trying one), but repudiating a resort to carnal weapons as wrong *per se.*" Much like Garrison, about the same time Lewis Tappan scolded erstwhile peace man Smith: the talk about sending Sharp's rifles to Kansas "has done more injury to the cause of freedom in Kansas than it has done good." A better weapon is the "sword of the spirit. . . . The Queen of Scots feared John Knox's prayers more than she did an army of 50,000 men."[4]

Despite the advice of Garrison and Tappan, as the 1850's advanced, abolitionist faith in nonviolence continued to erode. Too often prayer, politics, speeches, boycotts, civil disobedience—all nonviolent methods—seemed inadequate. The nonviolent editor Lydia Maria Child wrote that her peace principles were shivering in the wind. Theodore Parker and Gerrit Smith spoke of war as inevitable. Adin Ballou of the Christian nonresistant community of Hopedale said there were "precious few" complete nonresistants left, and another member of the same community, William H. Fish, charged that "the spirit of violence . . . manifests itself in the antislavery movement." Negro antislavery leaders—including Remond of Mas-

sachusetts and John M. Langston of Ohio—openly called for slave
insurrection.⁵

In 1859, John Brown—the zealous, independent Puritan soldier, a
veteran of the guerrilla fighting in Kansas—led a small band of men
in seizing the federal arsenal of Harper's Ferry, Virginia. His immediate plan was to use the arsenal's arms to help a continuous
stream of slaves escape into nearby mountains. Both to many abolitionists and to many Southern political leaders, Brown's raid—
though quickly snuffed out, with most of Brown's men killed—was
a deliberate Northern attempt to foment slave insurrection.

Abolitionists were torn over Brown's raid. Predictably, abolitionists without significant scruples against violence, like Harriet Tubman, Pastor Higginson, and Dr. Samuel Gridley Howe, endorsed
the raid; in fact, Higginson and Howe had contributed funds to
support it. Also predictably, the once nonviolent Frederick Douglass, who had in fact advised Brown against the raid simply for the
reason that he believed it could not succeed, endorsed it in principle.
As early as 1847, Douglass had learned to admire Brown, and was
listening sympathetically to Brown's telling him that Negroes
should carry guns. "No people," said Brown, "could have self-
respect, or be respected, who would not fight for their freedom."
Brown's influence, Douglass explained later, convinced him more
and more that slavery could only be abolished by blood. After
Brown's raid, Douglass wrote publicly that if it was right to kill a wild
beast in the act of devouring a man, it was right for slaves and their
friends to kill slaveholders. Also predictably, the once nonviolent
Purvis called Brown extravagantly "the Jesus Christ of the 19th century." Also predictably, Wendell Phillips applauded Brown, saying
that he was the impersonation of God's law at work to mold a better
future;⁶ the once strongly nonviolent Gerrit Smith contributed funds
to Brown for his raid, and so did Theodore Parker, who as recently
as 1854 had been concerned that violence, if necessary at all, should
be only with the hands.

Even Thoreau insisted on calling Brown "the bravest and human-
ist man in all the country." As the crisis over slavery deepened,
Thoreau, too, the man who had stated the positive philosophy of
nonviolent action as sharply as any American of his time, had abandoned what he had called "peaceable revolution." Thoreau explained
that he agreed with Brown that "a man has a perfect right to interfere

by force with the slaveholders, in order to rescue the slave." Thoreau now believed that circumstances would occur in which he himself could kill, much as he wished to avoid doing so. Similarly, Thoreau's Concord friend Alcott, who had been active in the Nonresistance Society and in applying nonviolence to education, succumbed to the simplicity, religious earnestness, and manliness of Brown: Alcott considered that Brown's violence did not prevent him from being worthy of Christ's cross, and on the day of Brown's execution joined Thoreau and Emerson in leading a memorial service in Concord for him. The peace-minded young disciple of Emerson, Cincinnati Unitarian pastor Moncure Conway, at first condemned Brown's violence as "worse than a crime" and then later, swept off his feet by the praise for Brown among some of his abolitionist friends, set aside any questioning of Brown's methods as being as irrelevant as questioning "the moral propriety of a streak of lightning."

The once nonviolent Tappanite Elizur Wright, a signer of the 1833 Declaration of Sentiments and by this time a Massachusetts state insurance commissioner, said governments were supposed to defend individual liberty; if they did not, slaves had a right to do it for themselves, and John Brown had a right to help them. "If anybody got killed by resisting John Brown," said Elizur Wright, "it was his own fault."[7]

Even among those who still considered themselves nonviolent Garrisonians, Brown's raid brought excited speculation that slave revolts might sharply increase if abolitionists encouraged them. Becoming uneasy over this speculation and the acceptance of violence it implied, Adin Ballou, once president of the Nonresistance Society and still the leader of the nonresistant community at Hopedale, Massachusetts, brought the issue out into the open.

While Brown was still in a Virginia jail, at a meeting of a Garrisonian Worcester County antislavery society Ballou proposed a resolution reaffirming the Declaration of Sentiments, which had been adopted at the founding of the American Antislavery Society, including the words, "Our principles forbid the doing of evil that good may come." Ballou interpreted the declaration as a nonresistance pledge.

The Salem Negro Charles Remond—who at the 1843 Negro national convention opposed Garnet's calling for slave insurrection but recently had been calling for it himself—grew excited. "I never supposed on becoming a member of this society," Remond told Ballou, "that I committed myself to the nonresistant sentiments to which you have referred. For whenever I have heard the question asked, 'What constitutes a member of the American Antislavery Society?' the only answer I have heard given was this: that a man who believed that the immediate, unconditional emancipation of the slave was right . . . is a member of this society." And then Remond made clear the extent to which he had become willing to accept violence: "I should be glad if a National Vigilance Committee was formed," he said, "to hang upon every tree and lamppost every slaveholder. They would be doing a glorious work!"

"I am not contending," replied Ballou evenly, "that . . . a man cannot be a member of this society unless he is a nonresistant. . . . What the society should be, as a society, is one thing, and what its individual members should be outside of the society is another thing. In respect to the measures of the society, as a society, it is bound by its declarations. . . . As a society we are pledged not to resort to . . . violence."

The Quaker come-outer, Abby Kelley Foster, put Ballou on the spot. She said she would rejoice if the North had gone so far up the moral scale as to point its guns not at slaves, as was then the case, but at slaveholders instead. Would you? she asked Ballou bluntly.

Ballou was cautious. "I should rejoice with trembling and sorrow," he replied.

Abby's husband, the doughty Stephen S. Foster, spoke up. "I claim to a be nonresistant," he said, "but not to be a fool." The audience laughed. "Every man is bound to use the most formidable weapons in his power," Foster continued. "Why should I use the sword when I can do better without it? But," he admitted, "Brown has shown himself a man in comparison with the nonresistants." Foster explained, I want to act more like a man myself. Since slave insurrections are coming in the South, "I want to go down South and guide an insurrection, to preserve it from those excesses which Brother Ballou so much deprecates." Evidently Foster considered that slave revolt by nonviolent methods—such as Birney had hinted at in 1835—was hopeless. He was proposing to be an adviser to slave insurrectionists with the hope of keeping them from the excesses of violence only.

Ballou ridiculed Foster's notion that he could guide an insurrection. "How pretty he would look," said Ballou, "undertaking to regulate myriads of raging insurrectionists scattered over the Southern country! A rebellion once started would involve all the outrages in the calendar of crime." Besides, if the slaves were freed by rebellion, Ballou added with prescience, "what is to be done with them for the next hundred years? It would take at least a century to educate them out of the ferocity engendered by such conflict. How are they to be employed, trained for liberty, and organized into well ordered communities? And above all how is this work to be accomplished with the great mass of the whites in the country full of horror, loathing, and revenge toward them? ... Can't we wait the operations of a more peaceful process? Can't we content ourselves with holy efforts to bring about a change of public sentiment, so that this thing may be accomplished, without resorting to such horrible measures? It may seem hard to wait, but if we do not wait, we shall do worse."

The New Hampshire abolitionist agent, Andrew T. Foss, a long-time Baptist minister, said that he had held to the nonviolent principles of Garrison and Ballou as recently as when he took part in the attempt to rescue Burns in the streets of Boston. But since then he had ceased to be a nonresistant. Indicating Ballou, Foss said, "I do not say that he is not higher than I am. I have an impression, a sort of instinct, that he is. [But] I ask the privilege of working on this platform in my own way. . . . I don't undertake to justify rebellion [by slaves], but when it comes, God knows, I will pray that the slave may be victorious." The crowd cheered. "Men will come to see," added Foss, "that if our fathers had a right to strike for their liberty, then John Brown had a right to strike for the liberty of the slave."

Why did so many abolitionists forget, Ballou replied later in a prophetic statement, "the vast differences between a people trained for liberty and self-government through a century and a half, and millions of long crushed slaves, schooled to servility and studiously kept in ignorance? Such a people need all the help and benefit of a peaceful emancipation."

But the meeting accepted the Remond-Foss view. It voted down Ballou's resolution reaffirming the American Society's tradition of nonviolence.[8] Even among Garrisonians, John Brown was reducing faith in nonresistance.

To say, however—as recent students of violence among the abolitionists have said—that in the late 1850's peaceful abolitionism completely collapsed[9] is at least misleading.

As we have seen, Ballou and Foster clung to their nonviolent position—Ballou absolutely, Foster less absolutely; they would not accept Brown's methods. Neither would others who had been leading Garrisonian nonresistants: neither Henry C. Wright, once general agent of the since defunct Nonresistance Society; nor Syracuse

Unitarian pastor Samuel J. May; nor the popular writer Lydia Maria Child, though she offered to nurse Brown in prison and did visit him there. Nor would the Garrisonian Pennsylvania Antislavery Society. When an antislavery convention in Utica argued that Brown was justified in forcible resistance to slaveholders because slaveholders were outlaws against humanity, the society's executive committee, after lengthy discussion, united in agreeing to issue a public disapproval of this attempt to justify violence.[10]

Nor would Garrison endorse Brown. Quite consistently with the double standard he had long maintained, Garrison explained in the *Liberator* his inability to endorse Brown at the same time that he respected him. "Judging him by the code of Bunker Hill, we think he is as deserving of high wrought eulogy as any who ever wielded sword or battle ax in the cause of liberty, but we do not and cannot approve of any indulgence in the war spirit. John Brown has, perhaps, a right to a place by the side of Moses, Joshua, Gideon, and David, but he is not on the same plane with Jesus, Paul, Peter, and John, the weapons of whose warfare were not carnal."

Nor would Garrison's close associate Charles K. Whipple endorse Brown. In explaining his position, Whipple made a carefully reasoned, detailed proposal for positive nonviolent direct action. Slaves should stop work, Whipple said, somewhat as Garnet had once advised, but, unlike Garnet, Whipple specified that they should not defend their right to stop work with violence. Since slaveholders were what they were, they were not likely to allow slaves to stop work without violence, Whipple admitted, so he recommended that the slaves escape. If necessary for their escape, they could properly "seize and put under restraint, by uninjurious means, the persons of any slaveholders, until the departure of the slaves is safely effected." The slaves could escape to the Appalachian Mountains, Whipple said, and there he proposed that the slaves follow a program similar to Brown's, but without violence. "If places of secure resort, well stored with provisions, could be established among the mountains of the slaveholding states, to which the slaves could repair and hold themselves safely entrenched, giving shelter to all fugitives," in a short time they might drain "the whole region of the entire laboring population" and leave "it so deserted until the proprietors of the land were willing to obtain laborers by treating them justly and paying them fair wages." If in this process, advised Whipple, the slaves and their friends are attacked with violence, they should do what they can by noninjurious means, leave undone what they cannot do by

noninjurious means, and bear with fortitude whatever evil may be-
fall. Whipple was not sure this method would succeed—nonresistants "must often receive the cross before the crown," he admitted
—but he insisted nevertheless it was the duty of Christians to act in
some such way against the injustice of slavery and not merely acquiesce in it like Uncle Tom.[11]

Many Quakers also refused to endorse Brown's methods. Among
them was Lucretia Mott, although she took Mrs. Brown into her
home to comfort her while she waited for Brown's trial. Quaker
Whittier pointed out the weakness of Brown's method succinctly:

> *Perish with him the folly*
> *That seeks through evil, good.*

The *Friends Review* said that the inevitable effect of Brown's raid on
the slaveholders would be to interfere with "the pleadings of their
conscience" against slavery. Of the two Iowa Quaker brothers who
fought with John Brown at Harper's Ferry, one escaped to return to
Iowa, where his Quaker meeting disowned him; the other was
caught, and while he was awaiting execution, he wrote his mother
that he wished he had never raised a gun.[12]

Tappanite nonresistants condemned Brown's raid too. The Tappanite American Missionary Association's magazine did so, explaining
that the 1833 nonviolent Declaration of Sentiments was the opinion
"of all Christian abolitionists," and adding: "We approve no act that
is contrary to the principles of the gospel. The gospel has power to
overthrow slavery, and properly applied, will do it." Lewis Tappan
invited the often mobbed Kentucky missionary Fee to speak in
Brooklyn, and Fee said: "We need more John Browns—not in the
manner of his action, but in his spirit of consecration—men who
could go out not to entice away a few slaves, for that would not
remove the difficulty—men who would go, not with carnal weapons,
but with the 'sword of the spirit,' the Bible; and who in love would
appeal to the slaveholders and nonslaveholders—to be ready, if need
be, to give up property and life."[13]

Despite the fact that many nonviolent abolitionists publicly denounced Brown's raid, in fact the raid hampered their work. It
provided a dramatic example of how a violent act by a few who
protest an injustice can disturb the nonviolent acts of many others
who protest the same injustice.

Brown's raid was approved, Ballou said, by only "a few hundred"
abolitionists, and condemned by 99 percent of Northerners. It was

small and unsuccessful. But coming as it did after many years of sectional suspicion, fear, and political jockeying, the South's reaction to it understandably was hysterical. As we have already seen, the hysteria stopped most of the abolitionist work of the American Missionary Association in the South. It also stopped much of the work of the nonviolent Burritt. Since 1856 he had been concentrating on a campaign to persuade the whole nation to share the responsibility of the abolition of slavery by compensating the slaveholders for freeing their slaves. He urged the sale of public lands to help provide the necessary funds. He had won some eminent support, including that of President Mark Hopkins of Williams College, President Eliphalet Nott of Union College, and the Brown accomplice, Gerrit Smith. But Brown's raid, Burritt said, created a climate in which it was useless to continue the campaign, and he abandoned it. Similarly, Cassius Clay reported that the Republican party had fine prospects in Kentucky until the Brown raid dashed its hopes. According to David Lee Child, in the increasing excitement following Brown's raid, in 1860 alone, 16 Northerners were murdered in the South, 120 were turned back as they arrived in the South by steamer, and 603 were violently expelled.

The complete nonresistant William H. Furness, Philadelphia Underground Railroader and Unitarian pastor, summarized the damage Brown's raid did to abolitionism. "In resorting to force," said Furness, Brown "tended to hurt the cause which it was in his great heart to serve. . . . He did not take into account the undeviating law that violence produces violence, and that the force, which he intended to employ very guardedly . . . would look, in the eyes of those against whom it was directed, like nothing but . . . pure, untempered, brute force, and so would be sure to arouse a force in them which would regard no restraints. . . . Revolutions effected by force," he added prophetically, "always end, sooner or later, in reestablishing the tyranny they undertake to overthrow."[14]

Perhaps the crisis over Brown's raid should have been the time for abolitionists to redirect and intensify their nonviolent campaign. Perhaps it should have been the time for more creative, better organized, or more widespread nonviolent action—perhaps the American Missionary Association's preaching and teaching multiplied a hundred times. Or Burritt's drive for compensated emancipation much expanded. Or a selective boycott of economic activity related to slavery, a modification of the boycotts Lucretia Mott was promoting for the North and Hinton Helper for the South. Or perhaps a combination of what Birney had suggested much earlier by way of nonviolent slave revolt with what Foster was groping for when he proposed going South to guide an insurrection and with what Whipple proposed by way of slaves refusing to work and escaping to the mountains.

But perhaps it was too late. Maybe the accumulation of fear and bitterness between the North and South, intensified by Brown's raid, was just too great to permit any nonviolent movement to work, much less one that was weak and tired.

The truth was that "moral suasion" was not doing its main task and Garrison knew it. Just as for twentieth-century India nonviolence was to succeed only in part—as in winning independence for India —so for nineteenth-century America nonviolence had succeeded only in part—in revolutionizing Northern opinion about slavery. But for neither the Indian nationalists nor the American abolitionists did nonviolence succeed in the most difficult task they assigned to it: for India, nonviolence, tragically, was not to succeed in persuading Moslems and Hindus to live together peacefully in the same independent state. For America, nonviolence, tragically, did not succeed in persuading the slave owners to free their slaves voluntarily.

Soon after Brown's raid, Garrison, recognizing the weakness of the nonviolent movement, took a position that Gandhi also took— that violence is wrong but cowardice is wrong too and that to do violence to overcome injustice is better than to do nothing about it because of cowardice. Though Garrison had long opposed slave insurrections and in a sense still did, at a Boston meeting in commemoration of Brown's hanging he now said, somewhat as Foss and Abby Kelley Foster had said: " 'Success to every slave insurrection at the South and in every slave country.' And I do not see how I compromise or stain my peace profession in making that declaration. Whenever there is a contest between the oppressed and the oppressor—the weapons being equal between the parties—God knows that my heart must be with the oppressed and always against the oppressor. Therefore, whenever commenced, I cannot but wish success to all slave insurrections. I thank God when men who believe in the right and duty of wielding carnal weapons, are so far advanced that they will take those weapons out of the scale of despotism, and throw them into the scale of freedom. It is an indication of progress, and a positive moral growth; it is one way to get up to the sublime platform of nonresistance; and it is God's method of dealing retribution upon the head of the tyrant. Rather than see men wearing their chains in a cowardly and servile spirit, I would, as an advocate of peace, much rather see them breaking the head of the tyrant with their chains. Give me, as a nonresistant, Bunker Hill, and Lexington, and Concord, rather than the cowardice and servility of a Southern slave plantation."[15]

As early as 1831, Garrison had used the argument—the same that had been used by Foss and had disturbed Ballou—that Negroes had at least as much right to revolt against oppression as the Revolutionary Fathers had. Garrison had long believed that unless slave owners freed their slaves voluntarily, slave insurrections might be God's instrument for freeing the slaves, and he had hinted that a separation of the North and South might provide occasion for an increasing number of insurrections. But after Brown's raid the tired Garrison was giving the Negro's right to revolt more emphasis and nonviolence less.

However, when Southern states began to secede from the Union, Garrison reasserted his nonviolence. He opposed compromise that might hold the tottering Union together; disunion was coming in a form in which he had not expected it or wanted it, but still he was willing to let the Southern states go peacefully. So also was Whittier, who wrote tersely:

> *They break the links of Union: shall we light*
> *The fires of hell to weld anew the chain?*[16]

So also was an impressive number of abolitionist leaders—suggesting there was still considerable influence for nonviolence among the abolitionists. In favor of letting the South go peacefully were the complete nonresistant Garrisonians Henry C. Wright, Samuel J. May, Parker Pillsbury, Stephen and Abby Kelley Foster and Adin Ballou; so also were other complete nonresistants such as the independent Elihu Burritt, the young Philadelphia Quaker wool merchant, Alfred H. Love, and *Friends Review* editor Samuel Rhoads; so also were Lewis Tappan and the Tappan-related American Peace Society. Even the occasional nonresistants Wendell Phillips, Senator Sumner, Emerson, and Emerson's disciple, the Virginia-born Cincinnati Unitarian pastor, Moncure Conway, favored letting the South go peacefully; in fact, most abolitionists did.

Garrison preferred to let the South secede—unjustified as he believed the secession was—and freely take all the federal military installations in its territory. Civil war would be a folly, Garrison said, expressing the basic insight of the nonresistant he still was: the North could conquer the South, of course, he said, but could not "conquer her spirit, or change her determination."[17] He still believed so, when, tragically, South Carolina tried to seize federal Fort Sumter, Lincoln chose to defend the fort, and war began.

As many of the nonviolent abolitionists saw before it began, the war was unnecessary. As fewer of them were able to see once the war swept over them, the war as a means to end the oppression of Negroes was to be little more than tragic futility.

PART IV

Tragic Denouement

"Freedom, in any proper sense of the inspiring word, is not the child of violence."   —Beriah Green, 1861

19. Peace Men Face War

◇◇◇◇◇◇◇◇◇◇◇◇

DURING THE MEXICAN WAR, the abolitionists' traditional antiwar and antislavery positions reinforced each other; nearly all abolitionists, believing the war was being fought to extend slavery, opposed it. During the Civil War, however, when nearly all abolitionists believed the war would end slavery, they found themselves under tremendous pressure to favor their antislavery position and shunt their antiwar position aside.

Soon after the war began, many traditionally nonviolent abolitionists dropped their plea to let the South go peacefully. As passionate enthusiasm for the Union swept over the North, they chose to regard the war as the government's effort to suppress a wicked slaveholders' rebellion and hence justified. If they were complete nonresistants, believing participation in violence was sin, they said they themselves could not fight, but some of them, including Garrison, also said, using much the same double standard he had long used, that those whose beliefs permitted them to fight should enlist in the Union forces in the name of God.

A few black abolitionists, including William Wells Brown, discouraged black enlistments until blacks had won equality of treatment in the armed forces; a somewhat larger group of white abolitionists, including Foster, Pillsbury, Whipple, and Goodell, discouraged any enlistments—white or black—until the government abolished slavery. Neither of these moves was essentially antiwar;

they were more nearly abolitionist strategies, in line with the long Garrisonian tradition of noncooperation with slavery-supporting government, to pressure the government into being more equalitarian and antislavery, and as the government gradually increased its commitment to these ideals, the movements to discourage enlistment largely dropped away. Though a few Garrisonian leaders continued to refuse to encourage anyone to enlist even after the Emancipation Proclamation was issued, there was no major abolitionist movement to persuade Americans at large not to enlist, such as there had been in the Mexican War; there was no such movement among Tappanites, Garrisonians, or Quakers.

Many abolitionists who had once been strong peace men found themselves scornfully rejecting any peace compromise with the South, such as slavery-sympathizing Copperhead Democrats kept proposing. Rather, since the Confederates upheld slavery, the logic of events maneuvered many abolitionists—including Garrison and Tappan—into hoping that the war would continue on year after year, despite its horror, until the Confederacy and slavery together were completely destroyed.

Among once nonviolent abolitionists there was such a tendency to support the Union in the war that the remnant of peace men often grieved over it. Nearly all peace men were allowing themselves to drift into support of the war, mourned peace crusader Burritt. Peace men were fewer than ever, admitted Garrisonian nonresistant Charles K. Whipple, and they were making no converts. It was sad, confessed the *Friends Review*, to see "professed advocates of peace plead the necessity of war." The venerable abolitionist merchant, Joshua P. Blanchard, who had been an officer of the American Peace Society for twenty years, charged that while abolitionist peace men had been scrupulous to avoid compromise with slavery, in this war they were not being comparably scrupulous to avoid compromise with war. The London *Herald of Peace* even accused once peace-conscious abolitionists of providing much of the inspiration that kept the Union fighting.[1]

Americans at large often held the abolitionists responsible for the war. They argued that the abolitionists' long agitation, strident as it often was, had antagonized the South into secession, thus beginning the war, and that the abolitionists' insistence that the war should not end until all slavery had been abolished kept the war going. In 1863 the widely read New York *Herald* made the charge devastatingly personal. It specified that by being responsible for the war, each abolitionist had in effect already killed one man and permanently disabled four others.

In reply to such charges, nonviolent abolitionists stoutly denied that they were responsible for the war. They had tried to abolish slavery peacefully, they said. They regretted they had failed, but their failure was not their fault; it was the fault of the whole nation, North and South, for not responding to their peaceful persuasion that slavery was wrong, for not following their peaceful example of non-cooperation with the unclean thing. The war, they said, was God's punishment of the nation for its acquiescence in slavery.

The abolitionists' nonviolent tradition—though severely bent by the cyclone of the war—still showed itself. Some abolitionists not only regretted that they had not succeeded in ending slavery without war, but also all through the war continued to question whether war was an effective means of destroying slavery. While many individual abolitionists encouraged enlistment in the armed forces, Quaker meetings opposed enlistment of their members, and Garrisonian societies at least avoided directly calling for enlistments. Many conscientious objectors to military service appeared among young Quakers, of course, and a few in Garrisonian and Tappanite circles as well.

Early in the war a number of nonviolent abolitionists were disturbed by the prospect that slavery would be abolished by the method of war. In the midst of the war, when Lincoln expressly stated in his Emancipation Proclamation that "military necessity" was his reason for freeing slaves and he freed them only in limited areas, the concern of these abolitionists was confirmed. For nonviolent abolitionists, the issue was essentially one of abolition by expediency and coercion on the one hand or by a sense of justice and voluntary choice on the other—an issue that in various forms had long concerned them.

While Garrison preferred voluntary emancipation, during the war he come to look with tolerance on the abolition of slavery by military necessity, saying that from seeming evil good may come. Similarly, the Garrisonian-Quaker editor, Oliver Johnson, while also preferring voluntary emancipation, pointed out that no reform ever triumphed except through mixed motives. But the Garrisonian lecturer Pillsbury was contemptuous of such attitudes. Freeing the slaves by military necessity would be of no benefit to the slave, he said in 1862, and the next year when the Emancipation Proclamation was already being put into effect, he said that freeing the slaves by military necessity could not create permanent peace. Pillsbury won considerable support for his view from abolitionist meetings and from abolitionist leaders as well. Veteran *Liberator* writer Whipple insisted that "true welfare" could come to the American people "only through a *willing* promotion of justice and freedom." H. C. Wright repeatedly said that only ideas, not bullets, could permanently settle the question of slavery. The recent Garrisonian convert, the young orator Ezra H. Heywood, pointed out that a government that could abolish slavery as a military necessity had no antislavery principles and could therefore re-establish slavery if circumstances required it. The Virginia aristocrat-turned-abolitionist, Moncure D. Conway, had misgivings that if emancipation did not come before it became a fierce necessity, it would not reflect true benevolence and hence could not produce true peace. The Philadelphia wool merchant, Quaker Alfred H. Love, asked, "Can so sublime a virtue as . . . freedom . . . be the offspring of so corrupt a parentage as war?" The long-time abolitionist Abby Kelley Foster—the speak-inner and Underground Railroader—predicted flatly, if the slave is freed only out of consideration for the safety of the Union, "the hate of the colored race will still continue, and the poison of that wickedness will destroy us as a nation."[2]

Amid the searing impact of the war—the burning cities, the mangled bodies, the blood-spattered hills and fields—a few abolitionists had not forgotten their fundamental belief that to achieve humanitarian reform, particularly if it was to be thorough and permanent reform, the methods used to achieve it must be consistent with the nature of the reform.

During the Civil War abolitionists who had seldom seriously scrupled about the use of violence in the past were likely to support the Union war effort as a means to free the slaves. Worcester pastor Higginson, once leader of the attempt to rescue fugitive Burns by battering down the Boston courthouse doors, became colonel of the first regiment of freed slaves in the Union forces. Dr. Samuel Gridley Howe, a contributor to John Brown, served as an inspector of army camp sanitation, and his wife Julia wrote the "Battle Hymn of the Republic" while accompanying him on one of his inspection trips. The knife-carrying Kentuckian, Cassius Clay, was commissioned a major general of United States Volunteers. Garrisonian Dr. Henry I. Bowditch, who carried a pistol to defend the fugitive Crafts, served as a physician with the Union forces; once Bowditch used nitric acid to mark a "D" on the back of a deserter from the Union army. Pastor Henry Ward Beecher, who had helped send rifles to Kansas, told his son he would disown him if he didn't enlist.

Abolitionists who had been only occasional nonresistants were also likely to support the war. United States Senator Sumner, who remained a vice-president of the American Peace Society through the war, addressed Northern troops on their way South, inspiring them to do their duty. The Garrisonian Phillips encouraged enlistments and visited Massachusetts troops in the field in Virginia to cheer them. But Phillips remained critical of the United States as long as it continued to uphold slavery; he remained a nonvoter, as Garrison, Foster, and Pillsbury also did; he still could not take an oath to support the United States Constitution, he said, until the slavery it protected was totally destroyed.

Negro abolitionists, no matter what their degree of violence or nonviolence had previously been, usually welcomed the war. While in the Mexican War some Negroes—including Remond and Brown —had talked of refusing to fight for a government that supported slavery and was even trying to extend it, at the beginning of this war most Negroes did not emphasize that the Union still upheld slavery. Nor later in the war did most Negroes emphasize that they had to struggle for the privilege of serving in the Union army and, even when granted the privilege, often served in segregated units, under white officers, at less than equal pay. Though Brown and a few other Negroes temporarily protested against Negro enlistments until Negroes were treated equally in the armed forces,[3] most Negroes chose to emphasize the hope that the war would lead to ending slavery and making Negroes equal citizens.

Many Negro abolitionists supported the Union war effort in some way. Bishop Daniel Payne of the African Methodist Episcopal Church, who once had been active in Whipper's nonviolent American Moral Reform Society, prayed for Washington to grow stronger and Richmond to grow weaker. The once nonresistant preacher Sojourner Truth visited Washington to plead with Lincoln to let Negroes enlist, and she herself nursed wounded soldiers. When Negroes at last were allowed to enlist, Boston school boycotter Nell was delighted, saying that for Negroes to fight in this war would "conquer" Northern prejudice. Frederick Douglass, in the 1840's the leading complete nonresistant among Negroes, recruited Negroes for the Union forces at the same time that he doubted that the war could do much more than impose physical control on the South; it could not reform the national heart, he said.[4] Remond and Garnet, who in the 1850's had been finding it increasingly difficult to see advantages in nonviolence, also recruited for the Union, and so did the once nonresistant Tappanite pastors Ray and Pennington. After the United States Attorney General had ruled, contrary to Chief Justice Taney's opinion in the Dred Scott case, that Negroes were American citizens, the long-time Garrisonian Robert Purvis said at a meeting of the American Antislavery Society that at last a black man could feel it was an honor to be an American; Purvis, too, promoted Negro enlistments. The Garrisonian William Still, a frequent associate of Quakers in the Underground Railroad in Pennsylvania, secured a commission as a sutler at a Negro army camp. Garrison's friend, the occasional nonresistant William P. Powell, director of the Colored Sailors' Home in New York City and an experienced sailor himself, received a naval commission. Tappanite pastor Beman, who once had opposed Garnet's call for violent slave revolt, came to believe that the war, despite its "many sad evils and afflictions . . . will prove an unspeakable blessing to . . . the colored race, to the country, and to the world"; visiting a regiment of Connecticut Negroes in training, he said he "felt a glow of honest pride and joy which never filled our hearts before." The Negro national convention, which in the 1830's and 1840's had stood for nonviolent means to free the slaves, met during the war to glorify the Union's colored soldiers without a murmur of antiwar protest.[5]

Negroes gave so much aid to the Union cause that it is a question whether the Union could have won without them. Southern Negroes escaped from slavery to dig Union fortifications, and, knowing the South as they did, they became Union spies, guides to the Union army, pilots to the Union navy. Northern Negroes worked for the Union forces as teamsters, cooks, and hostlers, and after Negro enlistments in the army were allowed, the rate of Negro army enlistments was high. In the Union navy—which had long permitted Negro enlistment—one-fourth of all personnel was estimated to be Negro.

It is doubtful that one leading Negro abolitionist—no matter how nonviolent he once had been—did not in one way or another support the Union in the war. Lumber dealer William Whipper, an outstanding Garrisonian nonresistant in the 1830's and still advising fugitive slaves to be nonviolent in the 1850's, urged Negroes to enlist and proudly claimed that he contributed a thousand dollars a year "to put down the rebellion." Even the elderly Philadelphia Negro abolitionist, David Bustill—the son of a Quaker and himself enough of a Quaker to wear the Quaker garb, to write in Quaker style, and during the war to lend William Still a copy of a Quaker journal—favored Negroes enlisting.[6] Despite the considerable exposure of Negroes in the abolitionist movement to the idea of nonviolence and despite their preparation for nonviolence in their experience of learning how to suffer and survive, the Negroes' inclination to nonviolence could not withstand their flood of hope that by participating in the war they could help end slavery in the South and raise their status throughout the nation.

Even white abolitionists who still considered themselves essentially peace men often encouraged Negroes to participate in the war. As a Philadelphia correspondent of the *National Antislavery Standard* wrote, "Barbarous as it may seem, it is the fact nevertheless, that from the beginning of the world till now individuals and races have been judged—in regard to their fitness for freedom—by their behavior in the battlefield. This is the reason why we abolitionists all—peace men and war men—take so lively an interest in the work now happily commenced of incorporating the blacks into the army of the country."[7]

What abolitionists often chose to brush aside was that after the war most blacks would still be living in the South, among the same Confederates whom they were now trying to kill.

Among Tappanites, some of those who had once been quite peace conscious easily acquiesced in the war. As we have seen, the Negro Tappanite leaders Pennington, Beman, and Ray apparently did. The Massachusetts insurance commissioner, Tappanite Elizur Wright, who in the Mexican War had actively opposed enlistments and just before the Civil War had said that war would be almost as bad as slavery itself, once the war began hoped it would end slavery and offered his services as a mathematician to the Union while it was in peril. The Tappanite John Fee, who had insisted on not carrying weapons to protect himself as an American Missionary Association agent in Kentucky, allowed himself during the war to judge the success of the work he continued in Kentucky not only by how antislavery the people with whom he worked had become, but also by how many soldiers they sent into the Union army. Fee's missionary associate, J. A. R. Rogers, reported proudly that almost all householders in the Berea area kept muskets and were sworn to use them to "protect law-abiding Union men."[8] President Finney of

Oberlin College, which had long provided much of the American Missionary Association's personnel, believed the Union represented the cause of God and the Confederacy that of Satan, and the college encouraged students to volunteer for military service.

Other Tappanites found it more difficult to determine what their relation to the war should be. Early in the war Lewis Tappan spoke at a meeting of the American Peace Society, of which he was still a member. He said he had agreed with the members of the society that "all war was contrary to the Gospel, unnecessary, and wicked" and yet, since the war had come under "singular circumstances," he was perplexed what he ought to do. To help him he had read and reread the Sermon on the Mount and the essays of the British Quaker Jonathan Dymond, but he was still not sure. "This war upon the North is the most unprovoked and wanton that has ever occurred," he said. He wanted to uphold the government at Washington, and he saw no other way to do it but "peaceably, if we can; forcibly, if we must." The perpetual enslavement of four million of our countrymen would be a greater evil than war, he explained. But he could not say he would use violence himself. He could not say, as a Quaker had lately said to him, that he would obtain a revolver because the best way to show his love for Southerners was to put down the rebellion. "But he could say that he felt bound to afford all the aid he consistently could to the government of his country, to sustain them and the interests committed to them, even if he had to lay down his life as a sacrifice. Shall we give up this contest, and thus perpetuate human bondage, the chief cause of the war?" Never clearly a conscientious objector to war, Tappan was not clearly holding out against supporting a war-making government, and neither was his brother Arthur.

The Massachusetts Tappanite banker and merchant, Amasa Walker, who had been a political economy professor at Oberlin and a signer of the Burritt pledge not to support any war, continued to be a major officer of the American Peace Society during the war. Walker insisted that the war was not necessary in itself; people just would not think of other methods of adjusting relations with the South such as letting the South secede, he said. He opposed the conquest of the South; subjugation would not work, he explained. But he could not see how he could avoid acquiescing in the war. Early in the war when President Lincoln issued a call for volunteers, Walker told the American Peace Society that he was pleased that the free states responded well. "Who does not rejoice in this," Walker asked, "if we must have war?" In 1862, Walker was elected a Republican Congressman, thus basically upholding the war-making Republican administration, but he continued skeptical of what the war would accomplish. In 1863, in the midst of the war, he told the American Peace Society: "I have no faith in war. I had none at the commencement of our own contest, and if it were possible, I have less now. I expect nothing good from this war or any war, that might not be obtained in a better way."[9]

The Tappanite-related American Peace Society itself acquiesced in the war. In doing so, it indulged in the sophistry of considering the war not to be a war in the usual international sense, but merely the attempt of a government to punish its own subjects for breaking the law. Indirectly the peace society may have intended to allow for conscientious objectors to war when it urged peace men to "lend their moral, if they cannot their active support, to the government over them;"[10] it said it continued to welcome the help of all shades of peace men—including complete nonresistants—in its campaign to end all international war. At the same time, however, it supported the federal conscription law as necessary without indicating concern to secure exemption for conscientious objectors.[11]

The Tappanites' American Missionary Association, which had condemned the violence of John Brown's raid, regarded the Civil War as God's punishment to both North and South for their having sustained slavery; the association supported the federal government, ordained as it was by God, in suppressing the wicked rebellion. "The rebellion . . . must be put down," said the association's magazine, and it gave passive support to enlistments: "Thousands . . . of our young men are flocking to the standard of their country. . . . This is all as it should be."[12] However, Lewis Tappan led the American Missionary Association to concentrate during the war on the peaceful work of relief and education for the freed Negroes, increasing the association's budget by five times in doing so—this was much the kind of work to relieve war suffering and remove the causes of future wars which many Quakers also emphasized.

William Goodell, who had once said that his peace principles were like those of Friends, was then editing a Tappanite-oriented weekly paper in New York City. Early in the war Goodell discouraged young men from volunteering for the armed forces while it was not yet clear that the war was being fought to end slavery; but after the Emancipation Proclamation was issued, he became a supporter of the government, justified the draft as constitutional, and rejoiced in Un-

ion military victories. Goodell retained at least traces of his formerly
strong antiwar position. He acknowledged that Quakers could oppose the draft without suspicion that they favored the rebellion, and
like other traditionally nonviolent abolitionists he preferred that slavery be abolished by voluntary decision, as an act of justice, rather
than by military necessity.[13]

Not only many Tappanites, but also many Garrisonians, Quakers,
and others who had once taken a complete or nearly complete nonresistant position found themselves cooperating in considerable degree
in the Union's war. Among them, as we have seen, were such
Negroes as Douglass, Whipper, and Sojourner Truth. Among them
also were whites. The once Quaker Sarah Grimké prayed for the
army to sustain President Lincoln; "this war," she wrote Garrison,
is "the holiest ever waged." The disowned Quaker J. N. Buffum, the
promoter of railroad ride-ins, urged army enlistments. One of the
prominent signers of Burritt's peace pledge, Christian socialist William H. Channing, now a Unitarian pastor in Washington, urged his
congregation to sacrifice "everything on the altar of the country"
and offered to lead them then and there in enrolling for service in
the field. Gerrit Smith, while remaining a vice-president of the
American Peace Society, believed that putting down the rebellion
was "our highest and holiest work"; he applauded the enlistment of
his only son and gave thousands of dollars to promote the enlistment
of others, both black and white. The Garrisonian J. Miller McKim,
who had been an agent of the Pennsylvania Antislavery Society for
twenty-two years, promoted enlistment and, as a relief worker for
freedmen in South Carolina, praised the Union generals who cooperated in his relief work as "philanthropists" and "patriots."[14] The
poet James Russell Lowell, who as a Garrisonian during the Mexican
War had rejected war as murder, now as a prominent Harvard
professor and the editor of the *Atlantic*, supported the war to save the
Union and free the Negro: "Freedom ain't a gift thet tarries long in
han's o' cowards," Lowell wrote in one of his colloquial poems.[15]
Among the Concord transcendentalists, Thoreau, who had once
advocated going to prison to shame the state into giving up both war
and slavery, in a sharp reversal now believed that suffering in this war
was regenerating the nation. Similarly, the once anti-institutional,
individualistic Emerson now argued that government must have
dictatorial powers during wartime and that participation in war
taught self-reliance—surely not the same kind of nonconformist self-

reliance that he had once valued. To the disillusionment of Moncure D. Conway, one of Emerson's individualistic, antiwar, antislavery disciples, Emerson even accepted an appointment as an official visitor at West Point.[16]

A number of Quakers abandoned their peace principles even though Quaker discipline on the subject was rather severe: if Friends did military service and repented later, Friends meetings generally retained them as members; but if they did not repent, the meetings disowned them. Burritt suspected early in the war that forty-nine out of one hundred Quakers were abandoning their peace principles. In the fall of 1861, Garrison, visiting the Philadelphia area, reported that his Quaker friends were troubled that there was scarcely a household among them from which at least one son had not enlisted. In the midst of the war, an Iowa yearly meeting admitted that a "few" of their number were entering the army, an Indiana yearly meeting reported a "considerable number" were, while the *Friends Review* claimed that fewer Friends were becoming soldiers in this war than had in the Revolutionary War.[17]

Garrison, just before the war began, in February, 1861, was saying, let the South secede peacefully; the North can then reorganize itself on the principles of freedom. Such a separation would effect the disunion he had long pled for. But soon after April, 1861, when the Union decided not to let the South go peacefully, Garrison dropped his plea.

The South had no right to secede, Garrison said. While he had once argued for Northern secession, he had done so on the basis that the Declaration of Independence recognized the right of revolution for liberty. The South, however, was not revolting for liberty but to preserve slavery; hence the Union was constitutionally obliged to suppress the South's revolt. Garrison soon waxed intensely emotional for the Union cause, at the same time keeping his own personal pacifism. A month after the war began, he was saying, much like Lewis Tappan, that the slaveholders' rebellion was "the foulest conspiracy the world has ever seen."[18]

Garrison no longer emphasized the role of the nonresistants in the abolitionist movement as much as he once had, but he did not forget that role or that he was a nonresistant himself.

During the war Garrison frequently published antiwar statements in the *Liberator*. For example, he published a reminder from the Peace Society of London that war "bequeaths to posterity a sinister legacy of hatreds, jealousies, and rivalries, which poison the blood of nations for ages." He published a protest against the American Peace Society's supine acceptance of the war written by one of the society's long-time leaders, Joshua P. Blanchard. He published the prediction of Dr. Abraham Brooke, a prominent Ohio Garrisonian, that the war would overthrow slavery but that the country would be worse off afterward than before because mankind will be "demoralized" by the means used to overthrow it. In reply to the common charge that nonresistants were not doing their part to abolish slavery if they did not support the war, Garrison published a letter by Samuel Keese, a Quaker of Peru, New York, arguing that nonresistants would be "worth more to the nation" if they lived up to their principles during the war; only if they did so, could they after the war again lift up their "moral and Christian standard." Garrison published a letter of Henry H. Brigham, an abolitionist church come-outer of Abington, Massachusetts, who argued, contrary to Garrison, that wartime was the right time to agitate against the sin of war. "It appears to us," said Brigham, "that the time to rebuke sin . . . is while sin abounds."[19] Garrison published an article from the London *Herald of Peace* charging that Garrison and Lewis Tappan were recreant to their peace principles: they could not see, the article said, that war was as great an evil as slavery, if not greater.[20]

While during the war the *Liberator* published far more items acquiescing in or supporting the war, it published at least seventy-seven items, whether short or long, whether endorsed by the editor or not, condemning war as such. From the content of the *Liberator,* one cannot justly say—as a recent biographer of Garrison does—that Garrison closed the *Liberator* to his old peace friends.[21]

During the war in both his speeches and his writing Garrison often restated that he was a nonresistant. If nonresistant principles had been followed by the nation, he maintained, slavery would have been abolished long ago, and there would be no war now. But while he wished the nation would adopt nonresistant principles, he knew that in the present "whirlwind" this was impracticable; he did not urge abolitionists, unless they were already nonresistants, to follow those principles during the war. It was not the appropriate time to agitate nonresistance, he said, especially because doing so might give "aid and comfort" to Southern traitors and "their copperhead sympathizers" in the North. Instead, taking a weak position for a nonresistant but one consistent with his policy in the crises over the fugitive slave law and John Brown, he reminded abolitionists who did not share his peace principles that they had a duty to offer "all they have of blood and treasure, until this band of [Southern] conspirators shall be put down, and slavery utterly obliterated." He sometimes even allowed himself to delight in the existence of the war because he believed it would lead to the end of slavery. He advocated—as Lewis Tappan did also—that the government abolish slavery under its war power,[22] and this became a common theme in the *Liberator*. The major effect of Garrison's wartime efforts was opposition to slavery rather than either opposition or support to the war.

As a whole the Garrisonians, as pro-war Higginson said, took little direct part in raising troops for war. When they called for support of the Union—which they increasingly did as it became more anti-slavery—they sometimes did so in such a way as to allow for both the abolitionists who could participate in the fighting and those who because of their peace principles could not. H. C. Wright, much like Garrison, said that each abolitionist must oppose slavery by all the means he considered to be right; nonvoting nonresistants could not become soldiers, he insisted, but other abolitionists should. Ballou persuaded his local Worcester County antislavery society to agree unanimously that abolitionists who refused to fight could be as efficient abolitionists as those who did fight, if not more so. The Garrisonian Pennsylvania Antislavery Society—of which Quaker James Mott remained president—adopted a statement worded expressly to meet the requirements of the peace men in the society, saying, "No true friend of freedom and the right, whatever may be his horror of bloodshed, or his aversion to war in itself considered, can fail to sympathize, in this contest, with the champions of the government, and to wish for defeat to those who are battling for its overthrow." The American Antislavery Society, of which Garrison remained president, reminded its members that it had been founded to abolish slavery by "peaceful and moral" means and claimed it had "used no others"; it said that the national government should crush the wicked rebellion, but it did not add that it was the society's function to help it do so. The splinter Progressive Friends—in which Garrisonians often took an active part—were careful to say, in a statement prepared by Garrison, that each man should bear his share of burden for the nation in its time of peril in whatever way he conscientiously could, either by bearing arms or by such nonmilitary service as relieving war suffering.[23]

When Congress was considering a conscription law, the chairman of the House of Representatives committee responsible for drawing up the law estimated there were half a million nonresistants in the country and, he said, if it became known that nonresistants were to be exempted from the draft, there would soon be many more. In contrast, William H. Fish, once a member of the nonresistant Hopedale community, estimated that there were not a hundred nonresistants left in the world. Obviously definitions of nonresistants differed. While Fish was probably thinking of the complete nonvoting nonresistants like the radical Garrisonians he knew, the congressman was thinking, he said of the nonresistant sects, including the Quakers, Shakers, and Mennonites, as well as the clergy of many denominations and even—he added facetiously—some pro-slavery "peace Democrats."

During the war Garrisonian leaders frankly admitted that there were only a few abolitionists whom they counted as nonresistants by their strict definition. H. C. Wright said that not one in a hundred abolitionists would be nonresistants if a highway robber stopped them and demanded, "Your money or your life"; and Garrison explained, while abolitionists have been "largely imbued with the spirit of peace, they have never adopted the doctrine of nonresistance, with a few exceptional cases."[24]

Like most abolitionists, Garrison supported the general right of government to draft men for military service. He had no patience with the murderous riots against the draft, led by Irish Democrats in New York and elsewhere. While a statement he had once written for the Nonresistance Society rejected "every edict of government requiring of its subjects military service," Garrison now considered the draft "indispensable to the maintenance of the federal government and the suppression of the rebellion." By contrast, another nonresistant, the fervent young Garrisonian Ezra Heywood, declared that the government had no more right to draft men than to enslave them. Speaking like an old-time Garrisonian, Heywood said that the draft law, like the fugitive slave law, should "be disobeyed and trod under foot" because it was "plainly in conflict with the divine law"; any military draft was utterly incompatible with free institutions, he said.[25] But Heywood's outspoken opposition to the draft was extreme among wartime abolitionists, whether they were Tappanites, Quakers, or Garrisonians.

Though Garrison considered a general draft justified, he asked in 1862, before any federal draft law was enacted, that nonvoting conscientious objectors, whether church members or not, be exempted, and H. C. Wright and Gerrit Smith endorsed his request. If conscientious objectors were not in fact exempted, Garrison urged those who were drafted to "possess their souls in patience and serenity" in the face of whatever penalties might be imposed on them.[26]

Later Garrison again asked for exemption for conscientious objectors. This time—perhaps because of his greater experience with conscientious objectors or perhaps because the meeting of Progressive Friends for whom he drew up the statement induced him to take a broader view—he did not specify that those exempted must be nonvoters; he asked for exemption simply for "nonresistants or conscientious peace men," and the Progressive Friends unanimously adopted his statement.[27]

The draft law of 1863—providing for the first federal draft in United States history—did not exempt conscientious objectors, but did provide that anyone could avoid military service by hiring a substitute or by paying a $300 "commutation" fee with which the government would hire a substitute.

When drafted, some conscientious objectors were willing to avoid being forced into military service by paying the $300 fee. Mennonites usually paid such fees. Garrison approved of conscientious objectors paying the fee, much as he himself had once paid a fine to escape militia duty. He approved of paying the fee on the same principle that he had long approved of paying unjust taxes or fines: you are forced to pay the fee, he pointed out in the *Liberator;* if the government uses the money for war, that is the government's responsibility, not yours.[28]

Long-time nonresistant Ballou agreed with Garrison in recommending that nonresistants pay the fee. Ballou's nonresistant Hopedale community, though divided on the issue, voted to approve their own draftees paying the fee if they accompanied it with a protest statement. Ballou helped one of them, John L. Heywood, prepare such a statement in which he pointed out that, while as a member of the Hopedale community he respected government and would meekly accept any penalties it imposed on him, he did not vote, enter suits at law, or appeal for government protection against violence. He protested, on behalf of all such nonvoting conscientious objectors, against government forcing them either to kill or to pay for anyone else to kill in their place.[29]

By contrast, if Quakers avoided military service by paying the fee —as a good many Quakers did—Quaker meetings, following traditional Quaker discipline, rebuked them. Either paying military fines or procuring substitutes was a compromise with the war principles, they said. Shaker meetings took a similar position.

Theodore and Angelina Grimké Weld were disturbed that their son Charles, a Harvard student, was a conscientious objector— Charles refused, if drafted, to hire a substitute or pay the fee for a substitute or even let his father pay it for him. This was disturbing to his mother Angelina because, though once a Quaker and Garrisonian complete nonresistant, totally rejecting war, she had become convinced that temporary war was better than permanent slavery. It was also disturbing to his father because, even in the period when abolitionists were most strongly nonviolent, he had been only a limited Tappanite nonresistant, expressly not opposed to military service in itself, and now he was fervently imploring abolitionists to help put down the rebellion. Theodore Weld became so distressed by his son's attitude that the subject spoiled the pleasure of their seeing each other, and the father came to question whether his son was in his right mind. On his part, Charles felt that, believing as he did that this particular war was "unjust," his course was the "only honorable one" possible, and that since he was an "independent man," his father need not consider himself responsible for it. Charles realized that he might be arrested, but, as he wrote his father, he awaited what might happen to him with "some degree of Stoicism." It is "only on account of yourself and mother," he added, "that I have any solicitude for the future."[30]

On the other hand, Garrison regretted that his son George was not a conscientious objector. When George became an officer in a black regiment—an especially dangerous post because the Confederacy had announced that if white officers of black regiments were captured they would be killed—Garrison grudgingly praised him for being loyal to his own beliefs. "True," Garrison wrote him, "I could have wished you could ascend to what I believe a higher plane of moral heroism and a nobler method of self-sacrifice; but as you are true to yourself, I am glad of your fidelity, and proud of your willingness to run any risk in a cause that is undeniably just and good."[31]

Biographers and other writers on Garrison have often reported that his son George enlisted and that Garrison respected him for doing so; they have often presented this information as a sign of Garrison's weakness as a nonresistant. But they have often either not known or chosen to obscure the additional information that Garrison had two other sons who were conscientious objectors and that Garrison made clear that he agreed with them rather than with George.

During the war his son Francis, aged about sixteen, was a student in the Boston Latin School when the school instituted military drill. Garrison wrote the school authorities, requesting that his son "be excused from participating in the drill," explaining, "This I do on the ground of conscientious scruples on my part, as well as in accordance with his own wishes."[32]

His son Wendell was twenty-three years old when he was drafted. Wendell Phillips, after whom he had been named, considered him to be the brightest and most independent of Garrison's four surviving sons. Since the Garrisons were chronically poor and Wendell Phillips had no children of his own, Phillips had financed his namesake through Harvard. While there, Wendell had written for a Harvard magazine, worked for the abolition of compulsory prayers, helped his father by reading *Liberator* proof, and at the same time maintained a high class standing. By the time he was drafted, Wendell, just two years out of Harvard, was often writing for the *Liberator* on broad matters of interpretation of politics, the war, and proposals for post-war reconstruction. He was soon to become an editor of the newly founded *Nation* magazine in New York, remaining one of its editors all his active life.

When Wendell was drafted—by lot, as all draftees were—he wrote a letter to draft officials explaining why he could not perform military service. The *Liberator* published his letter on its editorial page where his articles usually appeared; it was signed with Wendell's initials, just as his articles usually were, so that a number of readers probably knew who the author was. In his letter, Wendell admitted that the Union's attempt to crush the rebellion was just. "No juster war was ever undertaken by any community," he said, and "the cause of liberty and of national unity is as dear to me as to any American." But his principles, he said, forbade his fighting—principles which, if universally applied, would prevent any need for war. He believed in the inviolability of human life. Therefore, he said— in accord with his father's well-known position—he could not kill or vote for any government official who would kill. Since he himself could not fight, he also could not hire a substitute to fight for him, he said. However—still in accord with his father's position—he said he could pay the $300 commutation fee. He could pay it without violating his principles, he said, because he could yield to this requirement as to "superior force," the same as he did in paying his taxes even when part of them was to support war. The responsibility for what the government did with the money that he paid, he explained, was the government's, not his. He enclosed the $300 fee and signed his letter, "Yours for the suppression of the slaveholders' rebellion, and the overthrow of its cause." Wendell's stand was completely in accord with his father's, and Garrison endorsed it in the *Liberator*.[33] At about the same time in Philadelphia, the name of Alfred H. Love, another conscientious objector who often wrote for the *Liberator*, was also drawn for the draft. In facing the draft, Love was to take a stand quite different from Wendell Garrison's.

Alfred Love had believed all his life that war was wrong and became a convert to Quakerism. He also became so active in Garrisonian circles that, like Lucretia Mott, he may be called both a Quaker and a Garrisonian. He participated in the Pennsylvania Antislavery Society, the American Antislavery Society, and Progressive Friends; he arranged for Garrison to lecture in Philadelphia, he entertained a Garrisonian speaker in his home, and he was a nonvoter.

When the war broke out, Love was thirty years old and a partner in a woolen firm in Philadelphia. He made it clear that he could not permit his business to supply cloth for the war in any way, and this led to the dissolution of his firm, at his loss.

A few months after the war began, when a Baptist minister who had been an officer of a peace society succumbed to the war by becoming an army chaplain, Love wrote him his disappointment and asked, what are the principles of the church worth if, when a time of testing comes, the church lays them aside? Love described to the chaplain how he believed nonviolence could both stop the South's rebellion and free the slaves. Somewhat as Birney had proposed in 1835 and the *National Antislavery Standard* in 1851, Love proposed a mass nonviolent confrontation: all the Union soldiers should present themselves in civilian clothes, without weapons, to the Southerners as friends, saying, "We will not fight; if blood is to be shed . . . it will have to be ours. . . . We appeal to your best natures for . . . the welfare of the whole human family. . . . We can make no compromise with injustice." Such a course, Love admitted, was not feasible without a revolution in public sentiment, but if such a course were followed, he believed that few would be hurt and the South would eventually grant all that could be won by the sword.

At the time he was drafted, Love found that he could not accept any of the choices the draft law offered him. He could not accept military service—that would be contrary to divine principles, he believed. He could not furnish a substitute, he wrote in the *Liberator*, "because I hold it wrong to ask a brother to do for us that which we will not do for ourselves." He also could not pay the $300 fee because it would be giving government "the means with which to buy flesh and blood to take my place"; besides, he said, it would mean paying for the right to follow his conscience, a right that he believed was already inherently his by divine law.

Love was willing to cooperate with the government as much as he conscientiously could. He agreed to appear at a hearing before his board of enrollment, as requested, and submit to any penalties for his refusal to serve.

At the hearing, one of the board officials scoffed at him: "There is a law to make every man fight," he said, and conscientious scruples would "avail nothing."

Love's father, who stood anxiously by, pointed out that his son was nearsighted.

Love replied that for him to plead defective eyesight would be dishonest. He had only one reason to offer for his not being able to serve, he said, and that was that he was opposed to all war.

The board's physician examined his eyes on the spot, unsympathetically. He reported that Love was nearsighted, but not sufficiently so to warrant exempting him.

The unhappy father—proving his parental affection if not his understanding—asked if some other physical disability could not be found.

"Only by his consenting to an examination," replied the doctor. But Love refused, saying he was physically sound.

Beginning to sense Love's sincerity, several of the officials sought to help him find a way out. They offered to help him locate a substitute, but Love declined their help. Several even offered money to help him pay the commutation fee, but Love declined such offers too —he had already exacted a promise from his father not to pay the fee for him.

Baffled, some of the officials returned to threats. They told him that he might be "dragged from his home" to an army camp, and then if he still refused to serve, his name might be published as a deserter; this might "kill" his mother, they said. They gave him three days to change his mind.

It was the board officials, however, rather than Love, who changed their minds. Within a few days, another physician examined Love's eyes and decided there was doubt whether his eyesight was good enough to meet draft requirements. The board then decided to exempt Love from the draft, and some of them gave him "kind and encouraging words," Love reported, "which showed the testimony of nonresistance was not entirely unappreciated."

Reflecting on his experience with his draft board, in one of his many letters to the *Liberator*, Love wrote that if at any stage of his "trial" he had paid the commutation fee—as Garrison recommended —or allowed anyone else to pay it for him, it would have weakened his testimony. "The principle would not have been tested," he wrote; "the effect would not have been produced; the seed would not have been planted."

Garrison replied editorially. Despite the fact that Love was censuring the course his son Wendell had followed, Garrison replied gently: "All peacemen liable to be drafted" should "carefully consider" Love's report of his experience; it was in a "sweet and excellent spirit."[34] Once again Garrison was demonstrating his support for conscientious objectors, mild support though it was, without the crusading fire of which he was capable. Garrison was also demonstrating that, while his own position on how conscientious objectors should respond to the draft was moderate, he respected those whose position was more radical.

Another war objector whose draft experience Garrison also published in detail was not a Quaker, not a church member at all. He was a nonvoting Garrisonian abolitionist, like Garrison, his son Wendell, and Alfred Love, but his language was less restrained than theirs and he fell into more trouble.

When John Wesley Pratt was drafted, he wrote draft officials that the draft law "commends itself to the autocrat of Russia and the sultan of Turkey" and was contrary to the doctrines of Jesus. "I repudiate, I denounce such infidelity, such practical atheism. I will obey none of its requirements. . . . I loathe, I detest war. I shall neither evade nor obstruct the government except in the performance of my duty to humanity; but I cannot fight." Officials seized Pratt at his home in Quincy, Massachusetts, and took him, with his cooperation, to the district draft office in Taunton.

There the provost marshal asked him if he would find a substitute or pay the $300 fee. He refused to do either. The marshal asked him to take an oath to support the government. Again he refused and argued at length with the marshal about what the New Testament taught on war.

The next day officers ordered Pratt to put on a uniform, and when he refused, they themselves put it on him. He offered no resistance, but refused to sign a receipt for his uniform. Officers then took him to an army camp on an island in Boston harbor, warning him on the way that if he persisted in his refusal to serve, his wife would lose government financial support, and he could be court-martialed and shot. "Well, let them shoot," he replied.

At the camp Pratt wrote a letter to officers in charge, asking that, since he could not do military service, he be allowed to work in an army hospital. He received no reply. When he was asked to drill, he refused and in punishment was ordered to dig a large hole and fill it up again.

He tried to persuade a lieutenant to help him get an assignment to work in army hospitals. The lieutenant asked him if he voted. When he answered no, the Lieutenant said, "Ah! You are then a Garrisonian—no government, no church, no Bible, no Sabbath, no Christianity!"

Pratt did not deny that he was a Garrisonian. "You are mistaken, sir," Pratt said, "in your estimate of Mr. Garrison."

"But he don't believe in the Bible," said the lieutenant.

"Do you, sir," asked Pratt, "believe in it as a work of plenary inspiration?"

"Certainly. I must believe in all, or reject the whole. Don't you believe in miracles?"

"I don't believe a miracle was ever performed," replied Pratt.

"Oh, I can't talk with you," said the lieutenant, disgusted, and he turned away, leaving Pratt to his own problems.

Soon afterward Pratt was sent with his regiment by ship to Alexandria, Virginia. There the conscripts were issued guns, and when Pratt refused to accept one, an officer strapped it on his back. His major finally sent for him and asked him to what church he belonged. "I belong to no church," he said. The major then stood him up beside a wagon and tied him to it, allowing him only two feet of play and saying, "I'll see if you will refuse to do your duty." For eight hours he was left standing in this position, without food.

The next day Pratt again refused to drill. Again he was tied to the wagon, this time with his hands behind his back, "and drawn up between my shoulders till I could bear the weight of my body only on the forepart of my feet, my heels not touching the ground, a position in which first my fingers, and then my hands, and at last, in about an hour, my arms became perfectly numb; and the pain was so great as to cause the sweat to start from every pore in my body."

The major came to see him and this time asked if there was any duty he was willing to do. He replied that he had offered to do hospital work and said there were cases of other conscientious objectors like him that were awaiting the decision of the War Department.

The major said this was news to him; he didn't know there was another case of the kind in the country. Becoming more sympathetic, he offered to help arrange for Pratt to work in a hospital and in the meantime to let him work for the regiment without carrying a gun. Pratt said he was willing to try, and the major had him untied.

For several days Pratt marched about Virginia with his fellow conscripts without carrying a gun. But it began to seem to him that his regiment and other regiments that were supposed to be defending Washington were in fact desolating Virginia, turning its fruitful fields into barren wastes. He questioned his own contribution to the desolation. He became convinced that by doing any kind of duty in his army unit, "I was assisting directly in the war by taking the place of another," and so he wrote his major refusing to continue his work. The major then put him in irons, holding him with other prisoners. For six weeks as a prisoner Pratt kept asking for a trial, but in vain, and he heard nothing about being assigned to hospital duty.

During this time Pratt was often without regular food. When the regiment marched, it dragged its prisoners along with it, and Pratt was sometimes so hungry as he marched that here and there he picked up acorns to eat and kernels of corn that the horses had left and bones that he found on the ground, covered with dirt. He became ill and weak.

Meantime a number of abolitionists and peace men had interested themselves in Pratt's case. The young antidraft Garrisonian, Ezra Heywood, reported at an abolitionist meeting that Pratt's family was destitute—Pratt had refused to accept any army pay—and abolitionists made up a purse for them; a member of the Hopedale community was especially generous in contributing. Other abolitionists had appealed to Washington for Pratt's release. Among those assisting him in some way, as Pratt reported later, were fellow war-objector Love of Philadelphia; a Rhode Island Quaker who had experience in visiting Washington to appeal on behalf of Quaker draftees; Bostonian J. P. Blanchard, the old-time complete nonresistant and leader in the American Peace Society; Boston abolitionist lawyer Samuel E. Sewall, only an occasional nonresistant himself; and Republican governor John Andrew of Massachusetts, who had been a director of the American Peace Society in the 1850's.

Just over three months after Pratt had been drafted, his officers received an order from Secretary of War Stanton releasing him from the army on his giving his "parole" to return when called for. By mistake the order called Pratt a Friend. As soon as Pratt realized the error, he pointed it out, but his officers, doubtless thoroughly weary of his presence, were willing to waive the error; Pratt gave his "parole" and was released.

Garrison, commenting on the Pratt case in the *Liberator*, again honored a war objector who took a position on the draft that in itself could be interpreted as a rebuke to his own and his son Wendell's: "We honor" Pratt, said Garrison, "for his fidelity to his conscience, in circumstances of severe trial."[35]

A number of peace men thanked Secretary of War Stanton for his charity in administering the draft law with respect to war objectors, as in the case of Pratt; among them were Garrison and *Friends Review* editor Samuel Rhoads. Committees of Friends visited Washington to thank Stanton personally. Stanton, who was of Quaker descent himself, replied to one of these committees by saying that he and Lincoln "felt that unless we recognized conscientious scruples, we could not expect the blessing of Heaven."[36]

At the same time peace men protested that the draft law did not provide adequately for the conscientious objector—it should allow him to serve society in ways that his principles permitted, they said. Garrison called attention to the folly of not allowing Pratt to serve in an army hospital when he offered to do so. The Progressive Friends—that irregular collection of dissident Quakers, Garrisonians, and others—adopted a resolution prepared by Garrison (with Alfred Love also on the resolutions committee), asking that drafted war objectors be assigned to "attending upon the sick or dying upon the battlefields or in the hospitals, or performing some other service equally unobjectionable to their conscience and necessary to the state."[37] Quakers of the regular yearly meetings petitioned Congress for a change in the law, and committees of Quakers visited congressmen in considerable numbers, asking that Quakers be allowed under the law to discharge their duty as citizens in ways that they could conscientiously accept, such as providing relief to war victims.

In 1864, Congress, having become by this time well aware of the existence of conscientious objectors, debated whether to exempt them from military service. In both houses proposals were made to exempt all religious conscientious objectors, whether they belonged to nonresistant denominations or not. In the upper house, Republican Senator Anthony of Rhode Island, a Quaker who reluctantly voted for war measures, made the proposal, and Republican Senator

Sumner of Massachusetts, also a peace-conscious abolitionist, endorsed it, referring to Pratt's persecution as an example of why the change was needed. In the lower house, Republican Congressman Josiah B. Grinnell of Iowa, a graduate of the Tappanite nonviolent abolitionist center, Oneida Institute, favored exempting only those war objectors "who have no new-born creed." As adopted, the new law for the first time exempted conscientious objectors, but only if they were members of the nonresistant denominations and only if they accepted substitute assignments, made by the Secretary of War, to work in military hospitals or for the relief of the newly freed Negroes. Still anyone could avoid the draft by paying the $300 fee.[38]

Some conscientious objectors accepted assignments to military medical work, much as Gandhi was to do during the Boer War. But the *Friends Review,* maintaining a rather severe standard, advised them not to accept such assignments because they would be aiding soldiers to recover so that they could return as soon as possible "to the business of destroying the lives of others"; instead it advised them to accept assignments to relief work for freed Negroes. Even more severely, a Philadelphia Friends yearly meeting advised Friends not to accept any government work assignments at all, because doing so was accepting the right of government to punish them for obeying God rather than man.

During the Civil War as a whole, while most conscientious objectors who were drafted into the Union army were fairly well treated, some were not, and it didn't seem to make much difference whether they were willing to do army medical work. Even Quakers, who were the conscientious objectors the public could most readily tolerate, could be roughly treated. Three New York Quakers, on being drafted and refusing to bear arms, were forced by their army officers to march under heavy loads, without food or water, and then were tied in painful positions. A shy Vermont farm boy, Cyrus Pringle, who had joined the Society of Friends only after the Civil War began, refused to wear a uniform, carry a gun, or accept pay, but was taken with his regiment to Virginia where he was tied by officers and his limbs stretched. An Iowa Quaker, Jesse Macy, who accepted an assignment to army medical work under the 1864 law, was pressured to carry a gun or serve as an army telegrapher. Only after some of his fellow soldiers insisted, did his officers reluctantly recognize his function as a medical aide, and from then on, as he accompanied his regiment on its march with Sherman through Georgia, he was able to do his medical chores without persecution. Massachusetts Quaker

Henry D. Swift willingly worked in army hospitals, but when he refused to take part in military drills, he was tortured and ordered to be shot; just before the order was to be carried out, he was saved by the intervention of President Lincoln.[39]

In the Confederate South the position of abolitionist conscientious objectors was worse than in the North. While in the North they usually suffered only for opposing war, in the South they usually suffered for opposing both war and slavery.

When they could, nonviolent abolitionists fled the South even after the war began. Some Wesleyans—abolitionists whom the American Missionary Association had assisted and who were taught to defend themselves nonviolently—fled from North Carolina; so also did about five hundred Friends during the first year and a half of the war alone. When abolitionists fled, the property they left behind was sometimes confiscated.

The Confederate draft law, like the 1864 Union law, exempted conscientious objectors only if they belonged to the recognized peace churches: the "Friends, Dunkards [Brethren], Nazarenes, and Mennonites." Accordingly, members of other churches or of no church, as in the North, found their position especially difficult. Micajah McPherson, for example, a trustee of a Wesleyan church in Chatham County, North Carolina, opposed both war and slavery, and refused to fight; many of his fellow Wesleyans encouraged him in his refusal. When local supporters of the Confederacy warned him to renounce his view or suffer, he continued to refuse. Eventually a mob hung him up by a rope, and it was only when he was near death that someone cut the rope to let him down. In Montgomery County two Wesleyans, the Hulen brothers, also opposed both war and slavery, and would not fight for the Confederacy; a mob shot them to death and then, before the eyes of their parents, hung up their twelve-year-old brother till he also died.

The Confederate draft law provided that conscientious objectors would be exempt only if they furnished substitutes or paid a fine of $500. While Mennonites and Brethren often paid the fine, and some Friends did also, Southern Friends meetings, following Friends' tradition the same as Northern Friends meetings did, urged their members not to pay it.

Four Quaker farmers who would not pay the fine were drafted into the Confederate army. When they refused to work as wagon drivers, cooks, or hospital aides, officers ordered soldiers to force them to work at bayonet point. Some of the soldiers refused to hurt them at all, while others used the bayonets so as not to hurt them "much." When another Friend—one of a group of twelve North Carolina Friends forced into the army—would not join a foraging party, a colonel ordered some of his men to shoot him; as the firing squad lined up, the Friend lifted his arms, saying, "Father, forgive them for they know not what they do," and the men refused to shoot. Enraged, the officer then struck him on the head and rode his horse over him, but the horse's feet did not touch him. After his army unit dragged him all the way to Gettysburg, he was captured by Union forces and released. Other Quakers forced into the Confederate army—including some newly converted to Quakerism and hence suspected of being insincere—were denied sleep, denied water, kicked, forced to carry logs on their backs, or hung up by their thumbs. One Friend, while tied in a helpless crouching position, had a bayonet thrust into his mouth. Another under torture became temporarily deranged. Another, denied adequate food, died. A non-Friend who refused to guard Confederate stores was tied to a post where crowds gathered to taunt him.

To avoid the draft, some Virginia Mennonites hid in the woods and mountains, visiting their families only at night. Fourteen Tennessee Friends hid in a cave for nearly a year. Another group of Friends, tortured in the army, escaped and hid in the woods; soldiers, attempting to force their families to tell where they were, squeezed their hands in fence rails and hung a woman to a tree until she died.[40]

Altogether during the Civil War, in both the North and the South, among the three groups of nonviolent abolitionists, the Quakers produced by far the greatest number of conscientious objectors, the Garrisonians a few (such as Pratt, J. L. Heywood of Hopedale, and Francis and Wendell Garrison), and the Tappanites a few (if the Welds' son and the Wesleyans of North Carolina may be considered Tappanite produced). Quaker leaders gave conscientious objectors strong support, Garrisonian leaders gave moderate support, while evidence of support from Tappanite leaders is negligible.

Abolitionist leaders who agreed in refusing to participate personally in the violence of the war nevertheless fell into three different groups with regard to their general attitude toward the war: (1) the acquiescent, (2) the skeptics, and (3) the outspoken opponents.

The first group, the abolitionists like Garrison, acquiesced in the war and hoped the Union would win it. While they did not urge their antiwar views on others at this time, they quietly continued to make them known. Among those taking essentially this position were the Quakers Whittier and Lucretia Mott and the Garrisonians Samuel J. May, Lydia Maria Child, Charles K. Whipple, and H. C. Wright.

Like Garrison, Whittier considered himself loyal to the Union at the same time that he remained aloof from the war except to mitigate the suffering it caused. Whittier counseled his fellow Friends:

> *Our path is plain: the war-net draws*
> *   round us in vain . . .*
> *The levelled gun, the battle brand,*
> *   we may not take:*
> *But calmly loyal, we can stand*
> *And suffer with our suffering land,*
> *   for conscience sake.*[41]

Similarly, Lucretia Mott insisted that the fact that the Northern cause was "glorious" did not sanctify the means of war. After a visit from Sanuel J. May, she wrote a friend that she agreed with May "that this terrible war will furnish ample illustration for the advocates of moral warfare, as against carnal weapons." As the war advanced, she was thankful that the end of slavery was in sight and that the abolitionists' "moral warfare" had made it possible. When an army camp for Negroes (with the ironic name, Camp William Penn) was established near Philadelphia in the neighborhood where she was living at the time, Lucretia Mott, to show her disapproval of the war, rarely visited the camp. But she found ways to give Negro soldiers gifts of cake. She also found a way to befriend their families by trying to help desegregate the horsecars that brought them from Philadelphia toward the camp. Though seventy years old, one day in a cold rain she rode with a black woman on an outside platform where blacks were supposed to ride until a conductor, begged by white passengers, invited both her and the black woman to come inside.[42] Such was Lucretia Mott's "war" work.

May, who was still a Unitarian pastor in Syracuse, was saddened by the war. He regretted that all peaceful "ecclesiastical, religious, moral" instruments had not been wielded as vigorously in abolishing slavery as the American Antislavery Society and the American Peace Society had advocated that they should be so as to prevent war. But since war had come, May hoped the Union would win. As for himself, while May admitted that the war shook his "confidence in the *extreme* principles of the nonresistants," he would not fight, and at least early in the war he refused to encourage anyone to enlist.

May helped collect boxes of clothing for federal soldiers and freed Negroes in the South, and himself was sent by a Syracuse relief committee to the front in Maryland and Virginia to distribute supplies; while there he dressed soldiers' wounds in hospitals. On a visit to a military camp he said, "Nothing but slavery seems to me so bad as war."[43] For May, as for Garrison, his antiwar position had been subordinated to his antislavery position, but he was still clinging uncomfortably to both.

The sophisticated author Lydia Maria Child, one of the leading women to organize fund-raising fairs for the Garrisonians, admitted, more frankly than most abolitionists, that advocating both peace and freedom led her into what appeared to be inconsistencies. At the beginning of the war, when she saw an American flag snapping in the breeze, she would turn from it with tears, not so much because she associated it with the war as because she associated it with the continued federal protection of slavery. Within a few months, when certain army commanders, despite Washington's policy, refused to send fugitive slaves who had fled to their lines back to their owners, Mrs. Child, pacifist or not, began to sew with her neighbors in Wayland, Massachusetts, for those commanders' troops. Yet she felt through much of the war that if slavery was to be abolished as a "war necessity," "everything *must* go wrong" because the nation, except for a few abolitionists, still had "no heart or conscience" on Negro rights.

During the war, in a plan agreed on with a neighbor, she hung on the gate of her house a white flag of peace—a memorable example of an independent woman's determination to do what she could to lift public opinion, like Lucretia Mott's carrying her little bag of free-grown sugar wherever she went. When some passers-by interpreted the flag to mean she was a Copperhead Democrat who wanted to bring the war to an end by compromising with slavery, she was indignant. She was for peace, but not at any price. She didn't want the war to end until slavery was abolished; and when she was bothered that this seemed inconsistent with her pacifism, she persuaded herself that ending the war in a compromise with slavery would only mean that "another bloody war must inevitably follow." Just after the war was over, she claimed that she had "never wavered" during the whole war in her conviction that society could not be truly civilized till it accepted "peace principles."[44]

Garrison's editorial assistant Charles K. Whipple, who had been adept in concocting nonviolent methods for abolitionists, insisted during the war that the Union should have found a better way than war to protect itself against the rebel South—a way that would include "unpalatable medicine" to the foe, but would stop short of injury and would be really designed to effect the foe's good. He recognized that such a nonviolent method, like war, might not succeed. But since the Union had not found such a nonviolent way, while Whipple said he could not participate in war himself and would advise no one else to participate, he believed, like Garrison, that for abolitionists to proselytize for peace now would be misunderstood as aiding the rebels. He therefore devoted much of his great space in the *Liberator,* as did Garrison and H. C. Wright, to urging support of the Union as the enemy of Southern slaveholders and in pushing the Union to become more antislavery. As the war neared its end, he reminded his readers that he hated war and every form of murder and therefore could not favor the execution of the rebel leaders.[45]

Also much like Garrison, Henry C. Wright, once the outspoken agent of the Nonresistance Society, during the war muted his nonresistance, emphasizing his abolitionism instead. While once he had said a Christian might as well be a robber as a soldier, now he said, in praise of a nephew who volunteered, "Some hearts must bleed, some homes must be made desolate, or slavery will rule the nation." Like Garrison, Wright by no means urged nonresistance on others at this time, but he made clear that he remained a nonresistant himself. Soon after the war began, he denied that abolitionists were swerving from their peace principles. Speaking in 1863 to a New England antislavery convention, he said he was pleased that Negroes were now becoming soldiers, but he himself was "not a military man"; "individually" he "believed in the making of war by ideas rather than bullets," he said, using a theme he repeated many times. Writing in the *Liberator* in 1864, he still said that every person should resist slavery and the rebellion "by such weapons as he deems right and most efficient." Near the end of the war, as he saw the abolition of slavery clearly in sight, Wright regretted that "our great work" could not have been "finished without the shedding of any blood but our own"; he blamed the failure on those who, twenty-five years earlier had the power to abolish slavery without bloodshed and would not use it.[46]

The second group of abolitionists, the hickory-tough New Hampshire radicals, Foster and Pillsbury, took a somewhat more antiwar stand than Garrison. While they were similar to Garrison in maintaining their personal nonresistance without urging it on others at this time, they actively agitated against enlistments, at least in the early years of the war, and they remained through the war more skeptical that the war could bring real freedom to Negroes.

Early in the war, the unconventional Foster—the speak-inner and the impartial protector of both fugitive slaves and slave hunters by nonviolent means—urged abolitionists to refuse to enlist in the army, not because war itself was wrong, but because the Union had still not abolished slavery. He wanted to use the withholding of support for the war as a lever to lift the Union up to complete abolition, and he still urged this policy even after the Emancipation Proclamation was issued; he remained through the war unwilling to concede that the Lincoln administration was doing all it could to secure equal rights for Negroes. At a meeting of the American Antislavery Society in the midst of the war, Foster insisted that he himself was still a nonresistant: "If you are battling with slavery upon the field of blood," he said, "you are not on my platform." He reminded the society, we pledged ourselves at the outset of the antislavery struggle never to use violence. "I cast . . . no reflections upon those who . . . resort to this mode of warfare; but for one, I will continue as I have ever done." Foster, in his fifties now, was still supremely confident, after having faced perhaps hundreds of mobs, that his rugged figure, piercing eye, and bold stance would protect himself and others nonviolently. He offered, much as he had before the war, that if the Union would completely abolish slavery, he would volunteer to lead the Union armies against the rebels in Carolina—"not with the sword of steel," however; only with the "sword of the spirit."[47]

While both the *Liberator* and the American Antislavery Society urged the federal government to abolish slavery as a matter of military necessity to help crush the rebellion, Parker Pillsbury—the church come-outer, the nonvoter, the staunch defender of Foster's speak-ins—objected to freeing the slaves in that way. Expressing a basic pacifist insight, he said, "We cannot cast out the devil of slavery by the devil" of war. Early in the war Pillsbury had doubts—more than most abolitionists—that the war would end slavery. In 1862 he said the war had been useless so far—100,000 men had been slaughtered for nothing—and he opposed enlistments so vociferously that the New York *Journal of Commerce* said he was as disloyal as the Southern rebels and should be sent South to join them. Even in 1864 and 1865, Pillsbury said God had no plan of saving the nation through slaughter, only by doing justice, and the nation did not even intend to do justice to the Negro.[48]

The third group of abolitionist leaders were more absolute in their opposition to the war than Garrison, not so much because, like Foster and Pillsbury, they doubted that war would really bring freedom to the Negroes, as more directly because of their antiwar principles. Though they agreed with Garrison in personally refusing to assist in the violence of the war, they would not emphasize as much as he did that the Union cause was just, and unlike Garrison they openly castigated the majority of abolitionists for acquiescing, if not participating, in the war. Among these openly antiwar abolitionists were many Quakers, such as Samuel Rhoads and Alfred Love. But particularly relevant here is to follow the non-Quakers, for whom adopting an absolutely antiwar position was more difficult because the American public could not tolerate them so easily: for example, the Tappanite Beriah Green, the independents Moncure Conway and Elihu Burritt, and the Garrisonians Adin Ballou and Ezra Heywood.

During the war Beriah Green remained pastor of the antislavery Congregational church in Whitesboro, New York, which as a come-outer he had helped to create. Green had presided at the 1833 convention that adopted the nonviolent Declaration of Sentiments and had been identified with Tappanites, but for many years he had not particularly emphasized nonviolence. From about the time that abolitionists allowed his Oneida Institute to close for lack of funds, Green had become more withdrawn, more dismal in his world outlook, more convinced of the corruption of government, and while many abolitionists were moving toward more violence, he was moving toward more nonviolence. When the rebellion came, he considered the North as wicked as the South, and though his congregation dwindled, he would not cooperate in suppressing the rebellion. He scolded Garrison for believing that meaningful emancipation would come through war. "Freedom, in any proper sense of the inspiring word, is not the child of violence," Green wrote the *Liberator* sharply. "Good must be built on good alone. . . . We shall derive *from* war what is characteristically involved *in* war, and nothing else."[49]

An antiwar abolitionist with quite a different background was the young aristocrat, Moncure Conway. Visiting his home town in Virginia in 1855, he was surrounded on the street by young men warning him to leave town because they knew that as a Harvard divinity student he had recently been converted to abolition. The next day he left, expecting never again to see his home and the Virginia countryside he loved. About a year later, as an advocate, like the

Garrisonians, that the North should separate itself peacefully from the South to free itself of the guilt of slavery, Conway was pushed out of his Unitarian pulpit in Washington, D.C., and he moved to a somewhat safer pulpit in Cincinnati. Early in the Civil War, Conway believed, as his mentor Emerson did, that this war was holy, willed by God to end slavery; conscious of the value of peace, he believed a war for liberty was the only kind that could possibly be justified. But as the war lengthened, Conway came to believe that it was brutalizing Northern soldiers and the North at large; in 1862 he wrote, if we continue the war long enough, we will become the vandals the South claims we are.

In the spring of 1863, when war between the United States and Britain threatened, Conway, with the encouragement of such friends as Garrison, Phillips, and Elizur Wright, sailed to England to persuade the English to be more tolerant of the American government. While there, learning that a Confederate envoy was in the country, Conway wrote him a peace offer. Conway promised that if the South would voluntarily abolish slavery, the abolitionists would oppose continuing the war, and added that since abolitionists held the balance of political power, he believed that this would stop the war. As Conway expected, the envoy refused the offer, saying that the Confederacy would not give up slavery. But when the envoy, to embarrass abolitionists, published Conway's peace offer, abolitionists —unwilling to approve of private negotiations with the enemy Confederacy—overwhelmingly repudiated his offer. Conway was shocked. He had expected that abolitionists would of course be delighted to see the war end if the South abolished slavery. As he explained, the American Antislavery Society, and "in particular its great chieftain Garrison, had for so many years been advocates of nonresistance principles, and had so unanimously opposed suppressing secession by bloodshed—until war had actually broken out— they had so constantly directed all their efforts simply to control and influence the horrible cyclone to the one end of extirpating its fatal source forever; that it had never occurred to me that now, if that source were at once removed, any of them would countenance bloodshed for the sake of political and economic interests."

Conway, humiliated and disillusioned, was driven toward an absolute antiwar stance. He wrote his wife that to slaughter men for any cause except for the holiest one of liberty was worse than treason and that he washed his hands of war forever. About this time he was drafted, and his wife, still in the United States, knowing, as Conway explained later, that "I would sooner be shot than shoot anybody," paid the $300 commutation fee for him. Meanwhile Conway decided that, having become an outright opponent of the war, he could do little in America; he would be "almost alone." Sending for his family to join him, he settled as a Unitarian pastor in London.[50]

More consistent than Conway in his opposition to the war was Elihu Burritt, the promoter of world peace congresses and the pledge of refusal to assist in any war. When the war came, Burritt opposed participation in it, even though he expected, like most abolitionists, that it would incidentally free the slaves. He was accused of treason in his own neighborhood in Connecticut; he feared being arrested. He tried to place antiwar articles in Northern publications—as he had done hundreds of times before—but found he no longer could. He grieved that churches both North and South were virtually unanimous in sustaining the war. He believed that this war would produce new evidence of "the utter unreality of any seeming good attained by the sword." Foreseeing, however, that if Northern soldiers freed slaves by force, Southern whites would later be cruel to Negroes in revenge, he hoped that the Confederacy would need the slaves in its armies so desperately that it would voluntarily free them. Meanwhile Burritt favored ending the war by a separation of the North and South,[51] much as Love, Conway, Ballou, and Ezra Heywood did.

Adin Ballou, who had been president of the Nonresistance Society, sorrowed that Garrison wished success to the Union armies, reminding him that once he had been sure that violence could not bring reform. Ballou considered Garrison and Foster inconsistent in calling themselves nonresistants at the same time that they urged the United States government to abolish slavery under its war powers. At an antislavery meeting Ballou reminded abolitionists who were peace men that if they were true to their beliefs, they could not glorify even an antislavery war, but, he said, they could strike their axes far deeper into the root of animal selfishness than abolitionists who were war men. In reply to a sermon in which Henry Ward Beecher pronounced nonreistants cowards, Ballou issued a pamphlet asking, how long will men stultify themselves with the "absurd twaddle" that Christians ought to kill their enemies provided they kill them "in pure love, with holy affection, for the sake of justice?" Ballou was proud that his Hopedale community continued to avoid cooperation with war-making government. The community abhorred both slavery and the rebellion, yet it explained in a formal statement: "We do not deem ourselves in any wise responsible for this terrible conflict, having done what we could in our humble way, by warning and example to prevent it . . . so that nothing now remains for us in relation to it but to abstain from all complicity with it, to bear patiently our portion of its ills, to relieve where we can the distresses of its victims, and to look forward with unwavering confidence in the all-wise providence of God to better days."[52]

The young Ezra Heywood, a graduate of Brown, had been converted to abolitionism by Garrison just three years before the war and had become almost at once a prominent abolitionist orator. In the first months of the war Heywood hoped, as did Garrison, that the Union would win, and while he said he did not believe in war himself, he urged those who did to fight. By the middle of the war, however, Heywood had come to oppose participation in the war not only for himself but for everyone. Addressing a Unitarian church in Boston, he quoted the antiwar sections of the Declarations of Sentiments of both the American Antislavery Society and the Nonresistance Society and predicted that these Garrison-written documents would some day stand higher than the Declaration of Independence. He called the war "immoral, impolitic, and unnecessary," and answering what many Garrisonians were saying—that slavery is a greater evil than war—Heywood said that to kill a man is surely a greater sin than to enslave him. At an antislavery meeting he demanded that slavery be ended not as a "military necessity, or as the gift of an irresponsible and despotic war power, but in the name of humanity and according to the law of the living God." In the *Liberator*, toward the close of the war, Heywood praised the conscientious objectors Pratt and Love for their "manly example," as few Garrisonians made a point of doing, and scolded Garrison for not recognizing that officials who enforced the draft law were as execrable as officials who enforced the fugitive slave law. Heywood became so outspokenly antiwar that a distinguished British peace leader called him the bravest man in the American Union.[53]

As the war advanced, the strongest non-Quaker abolitionist opponents of the war felt themselves increasingly isolated and ineffective. Green remained buried in his central New York small town. While Ballou continued to be elected as an officer of Garrisonian societies, he seldom emerged from Hopedale to take an active part in them. By 1863 both Conway and Burritt, despairing of a brutalized America, had settled in the more congenial England, at least for the duration of the war. By the last year of the war, orator Heywood had set himself so completely against the usual abolitionist acquiescence in the war that he found himself seldom invited to speak to Garrisonian meetings any more; he was reduced to speaking independently, under his own auspices. While many nonviolent abolitionists—particularly Quakers and Tappanites—found it possible to take part in relevant action, consistent with their beliefs, in military hospitals or in the privately organized but militarily coordinated relief and education of freed Negroes in the South, these few non-Quaker abolitionists who aggressively opposed the war found no organized movement in which they could freely take part.

It was only after the war was over that Heywood, Ballou, and Love were to help form a new peace movement—along with others who were wartime opponents of war in varying degrees, such as the venerable merchant J. P. Blanchard and the veteran Garrisonian H. C. Wright.[54] Their initiative was to lead to the formation of the radical Universal Peace Union, which opposed the post-war military occupation of the South and favored amending the Constitution to deprive the government of the power to make war. The abolitionist who was to emerge as the Peace Union's pre-eminent leader was draft refuser Alfred Love.

In December, 1863, the American Antislavery Society held a convention in Philadelphia to celebrate its founding in the same city thirty years earlier. By this time the Emancipation Proclamation was being put into effect, and many abolitionists were enthusiastically expecting that their long campaign for the abolition of slavery would soon end in a complete triumph.

Many aspects of the convention were familiar. Garrison's call for friends of the slave to attend the convention used the well-known words from the founding convention's Declaration of Sentiments, pledging the society to the "overthrow of prejudice by the power of love, and the abolition of slavery by the spirit of repentance," and added with comfortable assurance, if not accuracy, that the American Antislavery Society had always used those methods. At the convention itself, Garrison, still the head of the society, presided as usual. He asked that the declaration be read to the meeting, as he had asked at many previous meetings. Many of the faithful Quakers and Garrisonians were present, including eleven of the now elderly signers of the declaration.

But other aspects of this wartime convention were unfamiliar. Over the platform hung the American flag, which many Garrisonians had once viewed with distrust as a symbol of slavery but which now, since the Union had taken steps toward freeing some of the slaves, they chose to view as a symbol of liberty. Still more unfamiliar was the kind of guests the convention chose to honor. While a letter from Quaker Whittier was being read to the convention, saying that he set a higher value on his name signed to the Declaration of Sentiments than on his name signed to any of his books, the convention was interrupted by the arrival of a group of men in uniform—black soldiers from a nearby army camp. The convention greeted them with applause, and officials led them to honored seats on the platform, where they provided an ironic backdrop for a convention of a society dedicated to the methods of "love" and "repentance."

The emphasis of the convention was not so much sorrow that the society's nonviolent measures had failed—though that was mentioned several times—as joy that slavery was being overthrown regardless of the means. The Garrisonian Quakers Lucretia Mott, Oliver Johnson, and James N. Buffum said happily that abolition was near. Garrison, in introducing the soldiers seated on the platform, said that the government's arming of the blacks meant that "the utter overthrow of slavery" was coming. The once absolute pacifist C. C. Burleigh said that he was proud that black men had become soldiers and saw hope that slavery would be ended completely. Pastor May of Syracuse said, the work we undertook thirty years ago, "but found too hard for moral suasion . . . will now be done, thoroughly done" by war, as God, "in his righteous displeasure with us," has decided. Slavery will soon end, said Senator Charles Sumner in a letter to Garrison which was read to the convention: "It is sad to think that this infinite good is reached only through the fiery process of war—so contrary to all your desires and to all mine. But we have not been choosers. . . . To save the Republic—to save civilization . . . to save ourselves from participation in unutterable crime and baseness—it has been necessary to rally the country against a rebellion, whose single object is the exaltation of slavery. Never before in history was there a war so necessary and just."

Garrison asked the convention: "Do you wish to see this rebellion put down?"

Voices answered, "Yes, yes."

"What is it in this country that has rebelled?" Garrison asked; "Is it freedom?"

"No."

"Then it is slavery that is in rebellion, is it not?"

"Yes."

"Are you for the abolition of slavery?"

"Yes, yes."

"So am I," said Garrison; "it is a unanimous vote. Amen and Amen."

A hint that Garrison still retained some of his pacifism came out in his desire not to be vengeful. "In carrying this thing through," he said, "though first it must be through the desolation of war by the depravity and fiendish obstinacy of the South, carrying it through will not be a curse to the South, but to bless her with freedom and free institutions. . . . O, the . . . glorious hope of thus repaying the South for her oppression, not with vengeance but with love and good-will."

Garrison still would not aid the war directly himself, but he had led the American Antislavery Society to acquiesce in the war, if not quite to bless it, and at this convention none of the nonviolent abolitionists organized a revolt against him for doing so. Burritt and Conway had already gone abroad; Ballou and Heywood did not choose to come to the convention. Beriah Green, who had presided at the original convention thirty years earlier, was necessarily invited to come—though Garrison feared if he came he was more likely to condemn Lincoln than the Confederacy—but he also stayed away. At least two conscientious objectors were present—son Wendell Garrison, who served as a convention secretary, and Alfred Love, who served as a member of the business committee, but according to the convention record, neither of them disturbed the smooth course of the convention. Foster protested that Garrison had gone too far in trusting the Lincoln administration, and he argued against enlistments until all slaves were freed, but that was about all.[55] The black soldiers remained in honor on the platform, and most abolitionists' hearts remained with the Union soldiers, black and white, through the war.

By the election of 1864, while Foster, Pillsbury, and Phillips still hung back from support of the administration, preferring to put pressure on it until it freed all the slaves, and while the American Antislavery Society officially remained nonpartisan, Garrison had come to support Lincoln warmly. Early in 1865, with Lincoln and the abolitionists together urging it, Congress adopted a constitutional amendment extending emancipation to all slaves. Garrison regarded the amendment as a "glorious result" for the benefit of the North and South, black and white. When the requisite number of states had ratified the amendment, Garrison accepted it as a sign that the *Liberator*, after having advocated the abolition of slavery for thirty-five years, had accomplished its purpose and should stop publication.

With the end of the war in sight, Garrison—in an act difficult to reconcile even with his personal pacifism—accepted an invitation from Secretary of War Stanton to participate in a ceremony to raise the Stars and Stripes again over Fort Sumter. About the same time Lincoln said of emancipation: "I have been only an instrument. The logic and moral power of Garrison and the antislavery people of the country and the army have done all."[56]

20. Elusive Victory

◇◇◇◇◇◇◇◇◇◇◇◇

WHILE AT FIRST most abolitionists celebrated the war-induced abolition of slavery as a great victory, after the war was over, a considerable number of them, whether they had been violent or nonviolent during the war, gradually came to sense that the victory was hollow.

Within a month of the ending of the war, Foster said that the American Antislavery Society had long rejected the very kind of "forcible emancipation" which in fact had come about; because it was forcible, it would not last, he predicted. A few months later H. C. Wright was insisting that while slavery was dead, "its spirit and its results live," and, reasserting his pacifism, he said, never yet has military power protected human rights. By 1867, William Wells Brown, who had recruited blacks to fight for the Union, was admitting that by fighting against the Confederates, blacks had "gained the hatred of their old masters" and put themselves throughout the South in a very bad position." In 1868, Pillsbury was still saying—as he had many times during the war—that it was a grievous error for the nation to have freed the slaves as an act of military necessity rather than justice. That error, he said, and the further error, in the same niggardly spirit, of giving Southern Negroes the right to vote because of political necessity rather than justice were engendering hate in Southern whites which would "burn at the flames of hell for generations."

Garrison had foreseen just before the war began that war could not force Southern whites to give genuine freedom to Negroes, but during the war he had lost sight of it, and when slavery was finally abolished under the pressure of the war, Garrison regarded it as a complete and final victory. After the federal government had given up Reconstruction, however, Garrison was not quite so sure. He said that the North was abandoning Southern Negroes like "sheep" to Southern "wolves," and therefore, he admitted, "the battle of liberty and equal rights is to be fought over again."

Also after Reconstruction, the wartime convert to complete nonresistance, Moncure Conway, wondered what abolitionists who had died fighting for the Union would say if they could come back to the earth. Would they ask, "Was it well then to shed our blood in order that the Negro might be freely lynched?" By this time even the pro-violent Cassius Clay could see that force had not assured justice to the Negro. "Force has been tried," he said, "and like the storm in Aesop's fable of the sun and the winds, caused the traveler to bind his cloak the more closely around him—it was the chief cause of Southern [white] solidarity." At about the same time Frederick Douglass took at least a small step back toward his earlier nonviolent position. He recalled the advantage the British West Indies had in emancipating their slaves peacefully. By contrast, he saw that what Ballou and Burritt and Foster had predicted would be the result of the forcible freeing of the slaves in the United States had indeed occurred. "Liberty came to the freedmen of the United States," said Douglass, "not in mercy, but in wrath, not by moral choice, but by military necessity, not by the generous action of the people among whom they were to live, and whose goodwill was essential to the success of the measure, but by strangers, foreigners, invaders, trespassers, aliens, and enemies. . . . Nothing was to have been expected other than what has happened."[2]

As many abolitionists vaguely sensed, the war and the military occupation of the South that followed had merely given the slaves apparent legal freedom, but had not broken the determination of the nation—North or South—to deny Negroes genuine legal, economic, or political freedom. Violence had proved largely ineffective.

Before the war in neither the North nor the South had abolitionists been able to prepare most whites for giving genuine freedom to Negroes. In the North the abolitionists had persuaded most whites to concede that the slaves should be freed at some future time, but they had made only a little progress in persuading most whites to give equal opportunity to the Negroes who were already free. Just before and during the war most Negroes in the North were still confined to menial jobs, could not vote, could not serve on juries, sat in segregated theaters and restaurants, attended inferior separate schools, lived in inferior segregated housing, and were subject to insult in the streets; several Western states legally prohibited Negroes from coming to their states to live. Not even during the war had abolitionists been able to prepare whites for the fundamental economic and social revolution necessary to bring Negroes equality; although both the Garrisonians' American Antislavery Society and the Tappanites' American Missionary Association had advocated distributing large plantation lands to Negroes, they had not persuaded most Northerners to advocate it. It was possible for Lincoln to say in 1858, "I am not, nor ever have been, in favor of bringing about in any way the social and political equality of the white and black races"; at the time Lincoln opposed allowing free Negroes to vote or to serve on juries or to marry whites. The events of the war moved Lincoln and most Northerners only slightly toward more equality for the Negro. Lincoln came to favor giving the vote to the "intelligent" Negroes and to those who had fought in the Union forces, but he did not insist on it. As the war ended, Whittier was saying that four terrible years of war had not taught Americans as a people their lesson when Pennsylvania still did not assure equality to blacks on public conveyances, and Remond was saying, if Americans were asked if they were ready for the entire equality of Negroes, they would vote it down ten to one.[3]

From the short-range point of view, insofar as it is possible to separate abolitionist violence from abolitionist nonviolence, each had sometimes succeeded. Violence had succeeded in protecting some fugitive slaves, as at Christiana; it had achieved the limited victory of ending legal slavery through the Civil War. Similarly, nonviolence had succeeded in protecting some fugitive slaves, as under Thomas Garrett's aegis in Delaware, and it had improved educational opportunity for Negroes in many parts of the nation, North and South.

From the short-range point of view, both violence and nonviolence had also sometimes failed. Violence had failed to rescue Burns from being returned to slavery, and it had failed in John Brown's raid. Nonviolence had failed to keep Prudence Crandall's school open, and it had failed to protect Seth Concklin and the slaves he was rescuing.

But from the point of view of the twentieth century, the abolitionist efforts, mostly nonviolent before the Civil War and mostly violent during and just after the war, must be judged on the whole a failure. Whether abolitionists used direct or indirect action, separate or inter-racial action, legal or illegal action, violent or nonviolent action, they did not succeed in opening up a clear road for equal opportunity for Negroes. In the nineteenth century black-white relations threatened to destroy the nation, and they still do in the twentieth century.

If the nonviolent abolitionists did not achieve the total victory that many of them for a time claimed they did, at least they left a record of experiment and limited victories which provides a rich resource, still much unexplored, for later generations who are tortured, alas, with much the same problems.

Comparing the three schools of nonviolent abolitionists, the evidence examined for this study indicates that the Garrisonians were the most shrill, the most creative, and the most revolutionary. The Tappanites, the least absolute in their degree of nonviolence, were the most effective in appealing to the large numbers of Americans who were conservative in manners and religion. The Tappanites were also the most vigorous of the three groups in carrying their nonviolent abolitionism into the South, notably in the 1850's through the American Missionary Association. The Quakers were the most quiet and steady. Because of their long tradition of nonviolence, they were a source of inspiration and ideas to the other two groups. They provided notable exemplars of radical actionists without hate in Lucretia Mott, Thomas Garrett, and Isaac T. Hopper.

All three groups made significant contributions to nonviolent direct action. At times all associated as equals with those of another color—in sit-ins and ride-ins, by eating together and walking together. All three groups took part in pray-ins, coming out of churches, creating new schools, boycotting slave produce, and hiding fugitive slaves. Sometimes their action was legal and sometimes not; sometimes they took suffering on themselves and sometimes not. Often they coerced others, but usually they shared a distrust of reliance on coercion, even if it could be called nonviolent coercion. Often they wrestled with the terrible dilemma of either keeping their nonviolence pure or of accomplishing some immediate humanitarian goal by lapsing into violence.

In particular, the Quakers led in the Underground Railroad, which played a significant role not only in aiding individual slaves but also in showing Northerners the horror of slavery as it impinged on individuals. The Quakers also led in the boycott of slave produce, but its objectives were too diffuse and its costs too great to produce more than a slim result in relation to the energy expended on it. In education for Negroes the Quakers made a large, long-term contribution, both in the North and in the South, especially in the conservative form of creating and sustaining separate schools for Negroes.

The Tappanites proved to be the most vigorous of the three groups in attempting to abolish slavery by direct action relating to churches: they were active in refusing fellowship to slave owners as Christians, in withdrawing membership from slavery-acquiescing churches, in splitting such churches, and in creating new antislavery religious organizations. The Tappanites proved to be the most flexible of the three groups in their ability to increase educational opportunity for Negroes; they successfully created and sustained both Negro schools and interracial schools, and, unlike the other two groups, they even dared to create interracial schools in the South.

The Garrisonians helped develop particularly radical forms of non-violent direct action. Experimenting with alternative structures for society, they helped to create interracial socialist communities, like Northampton and Hopedale. In regard to churches, Garrisonians initiated a distinct form of nonviolent direct action in the speak-ins, but it was a form that most Garrisonians themselves rejected as interfering with the liberty of others. In regard to education, though the Garrisonians tried, they did not create any viable schools open to Negroes; however, they successfully developed the boycott as a means to desegregate public schools. They led in two notable desegregation campaigns in which they combined political action with direct action—the Boston school boycott and the Massachusetts railroad ride-ins. In the area of noncooperation with government, they developed the nonviolent direct action of refusing to vote or participate in political parties, as well as asking the North to secede from the South; they also led in experimenting with a wide range of ways to defy the 1850 fugitive slave law.

From early in the development of their movement, the nonviolent abolitionists were handicapped by the ambiguity of their pledges to nonviolence, as in their Declaration of Sentiments, and they allowed themselves to become even more ambiguous in their response to Lovejoy's use of guns. Moreover, they sometimes appeared ambivalent about their practice of nonviolence. Some nonviolent abolitionists denounced slaveholders in language that seemed violent in spirit. Some nonviolent abolitionists threatened slaveholders by saying that their slaves would inevitably revolt, though at the same time they advised slaves not to revolt. Some nonviolent abolitionists—especially Tappanites—used violence to defend themselves against antiabolitionist attack at the same time that they advised slaves not to use violence to defend themselves against white attack. Some of them, like Foster in his speak-ins and Lucretia Mott in her walk-alongs, insisted on continuing nonviolent actions that they knew invited retaliation by violence.

Despite such ambivalences, which doubtless could not be entirely avoided, the nonviolent abolitionists were often effective practitioners of positive nonviolence. They were not primarily passive. They were not essentially naïve. They were often tough and disciplined. They were often sophisticated in calculating the effect of their confrontations with those who sustained racial exploitation. More than historians have often admitted, they made direct confrontation a significant part of what they called "moral suasion." And at least grudgingly many of them—including at times Lundy, Tappan, Garrison, Foster, Thoreau, Douglass, Angelina Grimké, and John Fee—recognized the coercive character of some of their nonviolent direct action. They recognized its economic threat, its psychological force, its nuisance, or its disruption. But at least until the Civil War, for the most part they continued to insist that all their measures—whether incidentally coercive or not—were for the ultimate purpose of calling the nation to give justice to blacks willingly, not as a result of necessity; willing justice was the only kind, they usually believed, that would provide permanent racial peace.

The achievement of the nonviolent abolitionists is especially creditable in that they had relatively little tradition of nonviolent direct action to draw on. There was not yet available to them the successful example of women's long struggle for the right to vote by such methods as marching, mock elections, refusing to pay taxes, and inviting arrest, as there was by the early 1900's. There was not yet the example of Gandhi in leading a great people to freedom by nonviolent civil disobedience, as there was by the 1940's. There was not yet the deliberate development by small groups like CORE of the specific direct-action techniques effective in the desegregation struggle, such as sit-ins, swim-ins, and freedom rides, as there was by 1950. There was not yet the successful example of the 1955–56 Montgomery bus boycott, led by Martin Luther King, which mobilized masses of Negroes to walk, pray, and sing, without hate for their oppressors. Because they had little tradition of nonviolent direct action to guide them, the nonviolent abolitionists did not sufficiently see the direct action they took as central to their task of "moral suasion." They did not sufficiently accept direct action as controlled coercion; they didn't organize direct action enough, didn't incorporate it enough into their theory, didn't use it sufficiently on a mass scale to become well aware of its power.

Not always seeing quick, sure results from their use of nonviolence, many abolitionists drifted toward increasing acceptance of violence. The abolitionists were the most nonviolent in the early and mid-1830's, at the same time that they were personally the most subject to violence. Gradually as crises relating to slavery succeeded one another with mounting intensity—the Lovejoy crisis, the fugitive slave law crisis, the Kansas War, and the John Brown raid—they felt increasingly pushed toward using violence or at least toward tolerating violence in others.

The Mexican War provided a temporary break in the abolitionists' trend toward violence. Abolitionists were nearly united in opposing the Mexican War, which they believed was being fought to extend slavery; in this case their opposition to slavery and war reinforced each other. But during the Civil War, when most abolitionists came to believe the war would end slavery, their opposition to war and slavery clashed.

Under the pressure of the Civil War a majority of abolitionists came to acquiesce in the war as God's punishment of the nation for continuing slavery. Among the three groups of nonviolent abolitionists, the Tappanites, never having established a tradition of complete nonresistance, proved the least able to keep their nonviolence alive, and the Quakers, being more disciplined as a community and having a tradition of nonviolence that was better understood by the public, proved the most able. The Garrisonians, while generally supporting the government, preserved a moderate degree of their nonviolence: they gave conscientious objectors some support, and they continued in some degree to question the efficacy of war as a means of justice to Negroes.

Altogether, the major role of the completely nonviolent abolitionists, as a minority among abolitionists, was to provide moral leadership, much as the role of the completely nonviolent movement led by Martin Luther King did in the racial revolution of the mid-twentieth century. If one excepts its implication that the abolition of legal slavery was a final victory—a common error among abolitionists—the following graceful statement by the pro-violent abolitionist Higginson is helpful: "The Garrisonian . . . abolitionists represented the narrowest of the streams which made up the mighty river [of the abolition movement], but they undoubtedly represented the loftiest height and the greatest head of water. The Garrisonians were generally nonresistants, but those who believed in the physical rescue of fugitive slaves were nevertheless their pupils. The Garrisonians eschewed voting, yet many who voted drew strength from them. The Garrisonians took little part in raising troops for war, but the tradition of their influence did much to impel the army. . . . The forces at work during that great period of our country's life were too complex to be held in any single hand, but it was to Garrison more than to any other man, that the great ultimate result was remotely due."[4]

Perhaps the nonviolent movement was too absolutely idealistic, but a democratic society needs to be reminded repeatedly about its unrealized ideals. Perhaps nonviolent leaders like Garrison and Lewis Tappan would have been more useful if they had combined their aggressive noncooperation with slavery with a search for a series of gradual steps toward a solution that would have given hope of holding the community together; idealism needs to be tempered with concern for the realistic steps toward goals that have a reasonable chance to work in a world which is far from ideal. But when quieter abolitionists like Burritt and Whittier, and even Lincoln as well, proposed gradual compensated emancipation, few slaveholders would listen. Perhaps the Garrisonian leaders were mistaken in refusing to vote, futile as political action seemed to them in the 1840's and 1850's when they saw a relatively small number of Southern planters dominate the federal government; but most nonviolent abolitionists in fact did vote and still did not prevent war from coming. Perhaps the Garrisonians, Tappanites, and Quakers lacked the humility any reformers need when what they insist on may bring the whole community to chaos; but the question remains, if one must choose, is order always a greater value than justice? Perhaps Garrison and Foster and Douglass were too absolute, much as Luther was. Fierce rhetoric can help to produce violent reaction, and violence breeds more violence. But without Luther would the gentle irony of Erasmus have been felt? Similarly, without the thunder of Foster and Garrison and Douglass, would the gentle humanity of May and Lucretia Mott, or even the charity of Lincoln, have had as much meaning for their time? Without harsh judgments on slavery, would the majority of usually apathetic Americans ever have been stirred to abolish it?

Perhaps by 1859 it was already too late for nonviolence to abolish slavery within a united nation—given the weakness of the nonviolent abolitionists, the entrenched position of those who believed they profited from slavery, and the immaturities of men at large. Perhaps the South should have been allowed to secede peacefully, as most abolitionist leaders believed in early 1861, and this would eventually have led the South to abolishing slavery in its own interest, voluntarily. Is it clear that concern to preserve a united nation should have priority over concern for peace and voluntary emancipation?

History sometimes presents terrible dilemmas for which there are no solutions. There were terrible dilemmas in the racial turmoil before the Civil War just as there have been in the mid-twentieth century: dilemmas of law versus morality, of order versus justice, of liberty versus equality, of outsiders helping an oppressed people versus waiting for the oppressed to help themselves, of pushing quickly for justice by coercion versus accepting injustice till justice can come by consent. To meet such dilemmas we need not only clarity but also humility; we need not only determination but also wisdom; we need not only thunder but also awareness of the weaknesses of men. And having them in fair measure, we still may largely fail, as the abolitionists did before us.

Acknowledgments

IT IS A PLEASURE to acknowledge the help of many persons in gathering materials for this book and in putting it together. I can name only a few.

For their advice and encouragement, I thank Benjamin Quarles of Morgan State College and James McPherson of Princeton University.

For criticizing portions of the manuscript I thank Edwin Bronner, Haverford College; Leon Litwack, University of California, Berkeley; Larry Gara, Wilmington College, Ohio; Martin Oppenheimer and Philip Foner, Lincoln University, Pennsylvania; Howard Zinn, Boston University; Donald G. Mathews, University of North Carolina, Chapel Hill; and my colleagues at State University College, New Paltz, New York, Richard Hathaway, Donald Roper, and Gerald Sorin.

For many kinds of help I thank various members of my family, and particularly for her endless patience with details I thank my mother, Miriam Bentley Mabee.

For several grants that helped to make the necessary travel possible, I thank the Research Foundation of the State University of New York.

For permission to republish my article on the Boston school boycott in revised form as Chapter 11, I thank the *New England Quarterly*.

For permission to use their manuscripts, I thank the following:

LIBRARY	COLLECTIONS ESPECIALLY USED
American Antiquarian Society	Stephen S. Foster papers
Berea College	John G. Fee papers

Boston Public Library — William L. Garrison papers
Cornell University — Antislavery Collection
Fisk University — American Missionary Association papers

Harvard University — Henry C. Wright papers
Historical Society of Pennsylvania — Vigilant Committee of Philadelphia papers

Library of Congress — Lewis Tappan papers
Massachusetts Historical Society — Horace Mann papers
Edmund Quincy papers
Miscellaneous

New York Historical Society — Miscellaneous
New York Public Library — Gerrit Smith family papers
J. Miller McKim papers
Alvan Stewart papers

New York State Historical Association
Syracuse University — Gerrit Smith papers
Worcester Historical Society — Stephen S. Foster papers
Yale University — Amos Beman papers (in James Weldon Johnson collection)

Notes

•

These notes have been compressed to save space. In titles and quotations spelling and punctuation have occasionally been altered for clarity.

For convenience the following works are abbreviated:

Work	Cited as
A. H. Abel and F. J. Klingberg, eds. *A Side-light on Anglo-American Relations . . . Correspondence of Lewis Tappan and others with the British and Foreign Anti-slavery Soc.*, n. pl., 1927.	Abel and Klingberg
Vincent Y. Bowditch. *Life and Correspondence of Henry Ingersoll Bowditch*, Boston, 1902.	Bowditch I, II
New York *Colored American*	*Colored Am.*
Philip S. Foner. *The Life and Writings of Frederick Douglass*, N.Y., 1950.	Foner I, II, III, IV
W. Freeman Galpin. *God's Chore Boy, Samuel Joseph May* (unpublished MS at Syracuse Univ.), 1947.	Galpin, *God's Chore Boy*
Wendell P. and Francis J. Garrison. *William Lloyd Garrison*, N.Y., 1885.	Garr. I, II, III, IV
Boston *Liberator*	*Lib.*
New York *National Antislavery Standard*	*Nat. AS Stand.*
Lewis Tappan. *The Life of Arthur Tappan*, N.Y., 1870.	L. Tappan, *Life*
John Weiss. *Life and Correspondence of Theodore Parker*, N.Y., 1864.	Weiss I, II
Letters of Theodore Dwight Weld, Angelina Grimké Weld, and Sarah Grimké, N.Y., 1934.	*Weld-Grimké Letters*

For convenience the following organizations are abbreviated:

Organization	Cited as
American and Foreign Antislavery Society	Am. and For. AS Soc.
American Antiquarian Society	Am. Antiq. Soc.

American Antislavery Society	AAS
American Missionary Association	AMA
Boston Public Library	BPL
Cornell University	Cornell U.
Fisk University	Fisk U.
Harvard University	Harv. U.
Historical Society of Pennsylvania	H.S. of Pa.
Library of Congress	LC
Massachusetts Historical Society	MHS
New York Historical Society	NYHS
New York Public Library	NYPL
New York State Historical Association	NYS Hist. Assoc.
Syracuse University	Syr. U.
Worcester Historical Society	Worc. H.S.
Yale University	Yale U.

1. The author has chosen the term "complete nonresistant" and the comparable terms that follow, "limited nonresistant" and "occasional nonresistant," to permit using somewhat more precise terminology than was used among the abolitionists. The nonviolent abolitionists often called themselves "nonresistants," "peace men," or believers in "peace principles," but these terms were used differently by different abolitionists and do not convey clear differences in degrees of nonviolence.

1. V(ladimir) Tchertkoff and F(lorence) Holah, *A Short Biography of William Lloyd Garrison* (London, 1904), p. xii.

2. Garr. I, 76.

3. Bennington (Vt.) *Journal of the Times*, Dec. 12, Oct. 2, 1828.

4. Garrison to Jacob Horton, June 27, 1829, BPL. Referring to this incident in the *Genius of Universal Emancipation* (Sept. 16, 1829, p. 14), Garrison said he gave the militia clerk who ordered the fine both nearsightedness and nonresidence as reasons for his not appearing; he does not mention that he said anything about his beliefs on war.

5. *Ibid.*

6. *Lib.*, April 9, 1858, p. 57.

7. Samuel J. May, *Some Recollections* (Boston, 1869), pp. 35–37.

8. Nathan Glazer, in Stanley M. Elkins, *Slavery* (N.Y., 1963), p. ix.

9. *National Enquirer*, Nov. 9, 1837, p. 24; Garr. II, 163; May to Garrison, May 1, 1839, BPL.

10. Garrison, *The Infidelity of Abolitionism* (N.Y., 1860), p. 8.

11. John A. Collins, *Right and Wrong* (Glasgow, 1841), pp. 42–43.

12. Bronson Alcott, *Journals* (Boston, 1938), p. 191.

13. L. Tappan, *Life*, pp. 198–99, 44; L. Tappan, Notes on his Career, 1868, LC.

14. When he first came to Boston, L. Tappan fell into attending Channing's church because one of his brothers, John, already had a pew there (*Ibid.*, p. 53). Brother Charles joined the same church in 1818 (L. Tappan, Journal, March 1, 1818, LC).

15. (L. Tappan), *Memoir of Mrs. Sarah Tappan* (N.Y., 1834), p. 5.

16. L. Tappan, Journal, Feb. 15, 1817, July 3, 1819, March 3, 1820, Dec. 5, 1823, LC; Edson L. Whitney, *The American Peace Society* (Wash., 1928), p. 123. Unfortunately Bertram Wyatt-Brown, *Lewis Tappan,*

Cleveland, 1969, the first biography of Lewis Tappan, which I have seen only since my text was completed, not only does not explain how Tappan was influenced toward nonviolence but also almost ignores his nonviolence altogether.

17. (L. Tappan), *Letter from a Gentleman in Boston to a Unitarian Clergyman* (Boston, 1828).

18. L. Tappan, Journal, Nov. 23, 1827, LC; Weld to Tappan, May 21, 1836, NYHS.

19. *Harbinger of Peace*, May, 1829, pp. 17–18.

20. Whittier, "Justice and Expendiency" (1833), in Whittier, *Writings* (Boston, 1889), VII, 26.

21. L. Tappan, *Life*, pp. 129, 371.

22. *Lib.*, Jan. 5, 1838, p. 2.

23. L. Tappan to G. Smith, Jan. 13, 1844, Syr. U.

24. Merle Curti, *American Peace Crusade* (Durham, 1929), p. 116; *Advocate of Peace*, May, 1846, pp. 123–24.

25. L. Tappan to Lysander Spooner, Oct. 7, 1858, BPL.

26. L. Tappan to S. S. Jocelyn, May 17, 1858, Fisk U.

27. *Lib.*, Feb. 18, 1832, p. 25; NYC Antislavery Soc. *Address* (N.Y., 1833), pp. 46, 22.

28. S. J. May, pp. 89–90; T. W. Higginson, *John Greenleaf Whittier* (N.Y., 1902), p. 50; Garr. I, 396–97.

29. Garr. I, 399n; Whittier, "The Antislavery Conv. of 1833," *Atlantic*, Feb., 1874, p. 167.

30. *Proceedings of the A. S. Conv. Assembled at Phila.* (N.Y., 1833), p. 7.

31. *Lib.*, Jan. 5, 1838, p. 2, June 28, 1839, p. 102; S. J. May, pp. 95–96.

32. AAS *Procs. . . . at its Third Decade* (N.Y., 1864), p. 41.

33. L. Tappan, *Reply to Charges Brought Against the Am. and For. AS Soc.* (London, 1852), pp. 4–5, 21–22; L. Tappan in Am. and For. AS Soc. *An. Report*, (N.Y., 1851), pp. 51, 90; Edmund Quincy, *An Examination of the Charges of . . . Mr. Lewis Tappan* (Dublin, 1852), pp. 6–7; *Nat. AS Stand.*, May 15, 1851, p. 202; AAS *Procs. . . . at its Third Decade*, pp. 3, 7.

CHAPTER 3, *Absorbing Violence*

1. *Pa. Freeman*, Aug. 16, 1838.

2. Catherine H. Birney, *The Grimké Sisters* (Boston, 1885), p. 150; Wm. Goodell, *Slavery and Antislavery* (N.Y., 1853), pp. 437–38; *Trial of Reuben Crandall*, (Wash., 1836); *Lib.*, April 30,

1836, p. 71, May 7, 1836, p. 75, March 16, 1838, p. 43.

3. Russell B. Nye, *Fettered Freedom* (East Lansing, 1949), pp. 145–46.

4. *Lib.*, March 19, 1836, p. 46.

5. Jas. L. Smith, *Autobiog.* (Norwich, Conn., 1881), p. 64.

6. *Lib.*, Nov. 5, 1836, p. 180; L. Tappan, *Life*, pp. 196–97.

7. S. J. May, *Some Recollections* (Boston, 1869), pp. 152–53; T. W. Higginson, *John Greenleaf Whittier* (N.Y., 1902), pp. 56–57.

8. *Lib.*, March 4, 1864, p. 40; L.M. Child, *Letters* (Boston, 1882), pp. 249–50.

9. L.M. Child, *Isaac T. Hopper* (Boston, 1853), pp. 315–16.

10. Isaac Parrish, *Brief Memoirs of Thomas Shipley and Edwin P. Atlee* (Phila., 1838), pp. 8–11.

11. *Lib.*, Dec. 17, 1836, p. 203.

12. Anna Hallowell, *Jas. and Lucretia Mott* (Boston, 1884), pp. 128, 133–34.

13. *Lib.*, Sept. 26, 1835, p. 156; Nashville *Banner*, in *ibid.;* Augusta *Chronicle* in Samuel Brooke, *Slavery and the Slaveholder's Religion* (Cincinnati, 1846), p. 59.

14. Dresser's account of his experience was published in *Lib.* (Sept. 26, 1835, p. 156) and often republished.

15. *Weld-Grimké Letters*, pp. 522, 748, 706–707, 513, 206–207.

16. Benj. Thomas, *Theodore Weld* (New Brunswick, N.J., 1950), p. 104.

17. *Friend of Man*, July 26, 1837, p. 22.

18. *Lib.*, Aug. 29, 1835, p. 139.

19. *Lib.*, Oct. 31, 1835, p. 173, Oct. 24, 1835, p. 171, Nov. 7, 1835, pp. 178–79; Garr. II, 24.

20. Angelina Grimké, *Appeal to the Christian Women* (N.Y., 1836), p. 32; *Friend of Man*, Sept. 1, 1836, p. 41; *Lib.*, Feb. 13, 1836, p. 26.

21. Birney, *A Collection of Valuable Documents* (Boston, 1836), p. 12; *Colored Am.*, Sept. 30, 1837, p. 4.

22. *Pa. Freeman*, May 24, 1838, p. 3; Bowditch I, 100; *Lib.*, Oct. 22, 1836, p. 171, Nov. 5, 1836, p. 177, May 14, 1836, p. 77, Nov. 5, 1836, p. 178; S. J. May, pp. 167–69; *Nat. AS Stand.*, March 3, 1842, p. 154; *Liberty Bell*, 1842, pp. 151–52.

CHAPTER 4, *Lovejoy Tries Guns*

1. *Weld-Grimké Letters*, pp. 153–56; Clarence W. Bowen, *Arthur and Lewis Tappan* (N.Y., 1883), pp. 11–12.

2. N.Y. *Evening Post*, July 12, 1834; *Lib.*, July 19, 1834, p. 114.

3. Stewart to Jas. Dean, Oct. 20, 1835, NYS Hist. Assoc.; Luther Marsh in Alvan Stewart, *Writings* (N.Y., 1860), p. 16. Defensor (Wm. Thomas), *The Enemies of the Constitution Discovered* (N.Y., 1835), p. 94, confirms the armed defense of Stewart's house.

4. Beriah Green, *Sketches of the Life and Writings of Jas. Gillespie Birney* (Utica, N.Y., 1844), pp. 48, 66; Betty Fladeland, *Jas. Gillespie Birney* (Ithaca, 1955), pp. 127–28, 141.

5. Melvin Jameson, *Elijah Parish Lovejoy* (Rochester, 1910?), p. 39; *Lib.*, Nov. 10, 1837, p. 181.

6. Abby Kelley to Newbury Darling, Dec. 10, 1837, Worc. H.S.; *Friend*, Dec. 9, 1837, p. 80; *National Enquirer*, Nov. 23, 1837, p. 42; *Lib.*, Dec. 1, 1837, p. 194, Nov. 24, 1837, p. 191.

7. *Lib.*, Jan. 5, 1838, p. 3, Feb. 16, 1838, p. 26. Edmund Quincy, in *Liberty Bell* (1848, p. 249), said that Sprague, though a war veteran, became a "thorough-going peace man" before his death.

8. *National Enquirer*, Jan. 11, 1838, p. 70.

9. Dover *Morning Star* in *Emancipator*, Dec. 21, 1837, p. 131 (*sic*); *Lib.*, Feb. 16, 1838, p. 26.

10. *Lib.*, Feb. 16, 1838, p. 27, Jan. 5, 1838, p. 3.

11. Chas. Marriott to Garrison, Dec. 21, 1837, BPL. Marriott praised for their nonviolence the Mass. AS Soc., Benj. Lundy, Wm. Goodell, and H. C. Wright, but added, "From the spirit manifested by not a few abolitionists, slavery is not likely to be terminated by moral conflict only."

12. *Emancipator*, Dec. 28, 1837, p. 135.

13. *Lib.*, Jan. 5, 1838, pp. 2–3.

14. *Lib.*, Feb. 16, 1838, p. 26. The AAS *An. Report* (N.Y., 1835), p. 38, supports May's view by saying: "The American Antislavery Society, at its formation, published a full and explicit declaration of sentiments and measures, by which its members were pledged to seek the abolition of slavery only by moral, peaceful, and constitutional means."

15. *Nat. AS Stand.*, Feb. 3, 1842, p. 138. Similarly, the Quaker Jonathan P. Magill of Bucks County, Pa., wrote Garrison, Jan. 13, 1838 (BPL), that abolitionists in his region "Never supposed for a moment that abolitionists anywhere, starting as they did with the peaceful Declaration of Sentiments on their tongues, would prove recreant to the doctrines of that declaration, until the recent outrage at Alton." He said if the funds of the AAS were to be appropriated for "carnal defense," abolitionists in his region could no longer conscientiously act as part of the society.

16. *Lib.*, Jan. 5, 1838, p. 3.

17. Beriah Green, *The Martyr, A Discourse in Commemoration . . . of . . . Lovejoy* (N.Y., 1838), pp. 15–16; *Colored Am.*, Dec. 2, 1837, p. 3, Jan. 13, 1838, p. 2.

18. *Colored Am.*, Nov. 25, 1837, p. 2; *National Enquirer*, Nov. 30, 1837, p. 47.

19. *Lib.*, Jan. 26, 1838, p. 13; *Pa. Freeman*, March 22, 1838, p. 2.

20. *Friend of Man*, Jan. 31, 1838, p. 127; *Lib.*, Feb. 16, 1838, p. 26, Jan. 5, 1838, p. 2, Nov. 24, 1837, p. 191.

21. *National Enquirer*, Dec. 14, 1837, p. 55; *Lib.*, Dec. 8, 1837, p. 197.

22. *Lib.*, Nov. 24, 1837, p. 191.

23. Galpin, *God's Chore Boy*, pp. 117–19; *Pa. Freeman*, May 10, 1838, p. 2; S. J. May in *Nat. AS Stand.*, Feb. 3, 1842, p. 138; AAS *An. Report* (N.Y., 1838), pp. 7, 9.

24. S. J. May in *Nat. AS Stand.*, Feb. 3, 1842, p. 138; *Friend of Man*, May 16, 1838, p. 186.

25. Whittier in *Pa. Freeman*, May 10, 1838, p. 2.

26. *Nat. AS Stand.*, Feb. 3, 1842, p. 138.

27. *Nonresistant*, Aug. 12, 1840. Goodell said that if antislavery societies abandoned "the full length of the Quaker [peace] principle," he would abandon antislavery societies (*Friend of Man*, Sept. 22, 1836, p. 54). Later Goodell was afraid that in response to the Lovejoy affair, abolitionists generally might take up arms and violence would follow in which "abolitionists would be almost certain to be overpowered" (*Lib.*, Sept. 6, 1839, p. 141). In the War of 1812, Goodell had been a member of the R. I. Governor's bodyguard of cadets (*Principia*, July 30, 1863, pp. 1158–59; *In Memoriam, William Goodell*, Chicago, 1879, p. 13).

28. *Friend of Man*, May 16, 1838, p. 186.

29. *Ibid.*; AAS *An. Report* (N.Y., 1838), pp. 19, 45.

30. AAS printed forms, commissions to J. M. McKim as agent, Aug. 10, 1836, Sept. 9, 1837, Aug. 1, 1839, McKim papers, NYPL; *Emancipator*, June 21, 1838, p. 32. Birney said in 1839 that the declaration, while "possessing no obligatory force," was "the highest evidence that can be had, apart from the constitution, of what was intended by the body of the abolitionists in that instrument" (*Lib.*, June 28, 1839, p. 101).

CHAPTER 5, *Should Slaves Revolt?*

1. Jas. G. Birney, *A Collection of Valuable Documents* (Boston, 1836), pp. 41–53; *Lib.*, Sept. 12, 1835, p. 146; Wm. Oakes to Samuel

Sewall, Aug. 20, 1835, BPL; Wm. E. Channing, *Slavery* (Boston, 1835), pp. 131–32.

2. Whittier, "Justice and Expediency" (1833), in Whittier, *Writings* (Boston, 1889), VII, 33; Wm. W. Brown, *Narrative* (Boston, 1849), p. 135.

3. *Lib.*, Sept. 3, 1831, p. 143, Oct. 15, 1831, p. 163.

4. *Lib.*, Jan. 7, 1832, p. 2, June 30, 1832, p. 101.

5. Raymond and Alice Bauer, "Day to Day Resistance to Slavery," *J. of Negro Hist.*, 1942, pp. 390ff.; Kenneth M. Stampp, *The Peculiar Institution* (N.Y., 1956), pp. 101, 99; C. S. Sydnor, *Slavery in Miss.* (N.Y., 1933), pp. 45–48; Addison Coffin, *Life and Travels* (Cleveland, 1897), pp. 45–46; Douglass in *Lib.*, Aug. 2, 1850, p. 121.

6. Harriet Martineau, *The Martyr Age of the U.S.* (Boston, 1839), p. 11.

7. AAS *An. Report* (N.Y., 1835), p. 11. While Birney studied law in Philadelphia in 1810–14, he became a friend of the abolitionist Quaker merchant, Abraham Pennock. In 1844 when Birney was Liberty party candidate for the Presidency, in a letter to Pennock he condemned wars of conquest but not strictly defensive wars. However, in 1846 he proposed that the Liberty party work to abolish the army and navy (Betty Fladeland, *Jas. Gillespie Birney*, Ithaca, 1955, pp. 12, 232, 258–59).

8. Herbert Aptheker, "Militant Abolitionism," *J. of Negro Hist.*, 1941, p. 455; Jabez Hammond to G. Smith, May 18, 1839, Syr. U.; Ralph V. Harlow, *Gerrit Smith* (N.Y., 1939), p. 260.

9. *North Star*, May 11, 1849; Am. and For. AS Soc. *Address* (N.Y., 1843), p. 21; *Oberlin Evangelist*, March 16, 1842, p. 46, April 13, 1842, p. 62; Geo. Julian, *Life of Joshua R. Giddings* (Chicago, 1892), pp. 118–25 and *passim*.

10. *Nat. AS Stand.*, Feb. 24, 1842, p. 149. The New Eng. AS Convention issued a very similar *Address . . . to the Slaves* (Boston, 1843).

11. *Minutes of the . . . An. Conv. for the Improvement of the Free People of Color* (N.Y., 1834), p. 28; (Phila., 1835), pp. 18–19.

12. Information from a grandson, Leigh Whipper, an actor, of NYC, Dec. 27, 1966; M. R. Delany, *The Condition . . . of the Colored People* (Phila., 1852), pp. 95–96; *Friends Rev.*, Sept. 10, 1859, p. 14.

13. *Colored Am.*, March 3, 1838, p. 26.

14. Whipper, *Eulogy on William Wilberforce* (Phila., [1833]), pp. 23, 33; Whipper, "Address on Nonresistance," *Colored Am.*, Sept. 9, 16, 23, 30, 1837; Whipper in *Procs. of the Pa. Conv. Assembled to Org. a State*

AS Soc. (Phila., 1837), p. 53; Whipper in *National Reformer*, April, 1839, pp. 114–15.

15. In 1836 the American Moral Reform Society adopted a resolution, proposed by Whipper, that, if taken literally, clearly endorsed complete nonresistance (*Friend*, Sept. 10, 1836, p. 392, Nov. 19, 1836, p. 54). The *National Reformer*'s statement of purpose, in its first issue (Sept., 1838, p. 1), emphasized nonviolence. The 1838 annual meeting of the society unanimously adopted a resolution, introduced by Whipper, saying, "The principles of peace, in the British West Indies, have secured for the abolition of slavery a triumph more glorious than the . . . laurels of a Cesar, an Alexander, or a Napoleon," and hailing the success of "the Miss Grimkés in the cause of peace" (*National Reformer*, Sept., 1838, p. 9). Later Whipper said that while the American Moral Reform Society adopted peace resolutions at every annual meeting, the society "could not agree upon the principles on which it [peace] should be based" (*National Reformer*, March, 1839, pp. 104–105). This suggests that the American Moral Reform Society, like the American Antislavery Society after the Lovejoy murder, found itself unable to spell out precisely what it meant by "peace" or "nonresistance" in everyday practice.

16. *National Reformer*, Oct., 1839, pp. 155–56.

17. Henry Highland Garnet, *A Memorial Discourse* (Phila., 1865), pp. 19, 25–26, 30; John Cromwell, *The Negro in Am. Hist.* (Wash., 1914), p. 126.

18. *Walker's Appeal . . . and also Garnet's Address to the Slaves* (N.Y., 1848), pp. 93–96. In presenting this text of his address, Garnet said that the original text "has been slightly modified, retaining, however, all of its original doctrine" (*ibid.*, p. 89).

19. Beman to editor, March 6, 1863, clipping, *Anglo-African Weekly*, Beman Scrapbook II, 3, Yale U.; *Minutes of the National Conv. of Colored Citizens Held at Buffalo* (N.Y., 1843), p. 13.

20. *Lib.*, Sept. 8, 1843, p. 142.

21. W .W. Brown escaped from slavery with the help of a Quaker and in gratitude allowed him to give him the name Brown as his nonslave name. The first antislavery paper Brown read was Quaker Lundy's (Brown, *Narrative*, pp. 103–104, 107). As a Garrisonian, Brown became an eloquent lecturer and a resourceful direct actionist. No evidence is available that he ever became a complete nonresistant, but he generally advocated that abolitionists use nonviolent methods, and he believed that the antiwar and antislavery reforms blended harmoniously together (*Lib.*, July 27, 1849, p. 119).

22. Beman to Garnet, Dec. 15, 1844, in *Clarksonian*, clipping, Beman Scrapbook II, 81, Yale U.; *Minutes of the National Conv. of Colored Citizens Held at Buffalo*, pp. 23, 18–19, 24. The second vote, taken as the convention was beginning to break up, was 9 with Garnet and 14 with Douglass.

23. *Lib.*, Sept. 22, 1843, p. 151.

24. *Procs. of the National Conv. of Colored People* (Troy, N.Y., 1847), pp. 16–17, 31–32. Nevertheless, at this convention, Garnet apparently repeated his call for slave revolt; at any rate he gave an address to the slaves that, according to Nell, advocated "physical force" in opposition to "moral suasion" *(ibid.,* p. 10; *North Star*, Dec. 3, 1847, p. 1). According to Douglass, Garnet persisted, especially when talking to blacks, in favoring violence. Douglass and Garnet became hostile, partly over this issue *(North Star*, June 22, July 27, Aug. 10, 17, 1849).

25. Julian, p. 243; Anon., "The Insurrection and Its Hero," *Liberty Bell*, 1848, p. 1ff.

26. *North Star*, July 27, 1849. Garnet was adaptable enough to refer often to the value of peace; he even spoke at the World Peace Congress in Frankfort in 1850. Garnet continued to be regarded as a valued colleague by most nonviolent abolitionists.

27. State Conv. of the Colored Citizens of Ohio *Minutes* (Oberlin, 1849), p. 18; *Ram's Horn* in *Lib.*, Aug. 3, 1849, p. 122. *Ram's Horn* was edited in part by Thos. Van Rensselaer, who as a New York slave had run away from his master and settled in New York City where he became a businessman. In 1840 he was elected to the executive committee of the AAS. He was only an occasional nonresistant. When by mistake he received a notice to appear at militia training in New York City (by law blacks were excluded), he armed himself, appeared at the proper place, and offered to train, evidently enjoying making an issue over it, but the commander would not permit him to train.

28. Merle Curti, *Social Ideas of Am. Educators* (Paterson, N.J., 1959), pp. 128–30; *North Star*, Jan. 5, 1849.

29. *Minutes of the Eighth Anniversary of* [the] *Maine and New Hampshire Historical and Agricultural Soc.* (Portland, 1849), pp. 16, 3. This society was not Garrisonian; it endorsed the Free Soil party. Its founding convention in 1841 had already refused to label violent slave revolt unchristian.

30. *North Star*, Aug. 10, 1849; *Lib.*, May 11, 1849, p. 74.

31. *Lib.*, Sept. 21, 1849, p. 150; W. W. Brown, *Antislavery Harp* (Boston, 1849), p. 6.

32. *Lib.*, July 20, 1849, p. 114.

33. *North Star*, Aug. 4, 1848; *Lib.*, Aug. 17, 1849, p. 129; Amos Beman, *Address Delivered at . . . Hudson* (Troy, N.Y., 1847), pp. 13–14; *Lib.*, Aug. 17, 1849, p. 130; Broadside, "Hymns and Songs for the Anti-slavery Celebration of the Decl. of Indep., at Abington [Mass.], July 4, 1849," BPL.

Chapter 6, *The Nonresistance Society*

1. *Lib.*, Feb. 25, 1837, p. 35, Nov. 1, 1839, p. 176; Garrison to Wright, Oct. 1, 1844, BPL; Garr. III, 80n.

2. *Nonresistant*, April 8, 1840, Nov. 11, 1840, p. 82, March 11, 1840; Garrison to Eliz. Pease, July 2, 1842, BPL; Garrison to Wright, Oct. 1, 1844, BPL.

3. Before Wright met Garrison in Nov., 1835, Wright already favored secession of the North from the South (Wright, *Human Life Illustrated in My Individual Experience*, Boston, 1849, pp. 364, 377), and said that voting under the slavery-protecting Constitution was a vote to sustain slavery (*ibid.*, p. 365). Just after Garrison met Wright, Garrison wrote in the *Liberator* (Dec. 12, 1835, p. 197): "I ask no physical violence to be exerted for my protection, and I acknowledge no other government than that of the Most High." Garrison voted in 1834 but not again until 1871 (Garr. IV, 241).

4. The *Dict. of Am. Biog.* article on May is mistaken in saying the society was too extreme for May to support. Galpin, *God's Chore Boy*, p. 101, Garr. II, 327, and *Nonresistant*, Nov. 2, 1839, and Feb. 1, 1845, agree in indicating that May was active in the society.

5. Garrison to Geo. W. Benson, Sept. 29, 1838, BPL.

6. L. M. Child to F.G. Shaw, Dec. 7, 1841, Feb. 15, 1843, Cornell U.; L.M. Child to J. M. McKim, Jan. 26, 1842, Cornell U.

7. Garr. II, 327; L. Tappan to G. Smith, May 15, 1839, Syr. U.; *Emancipator*, May 2, 1839, p. 3, June 20, 1839, p. 30.

8. *National Reformer*, Jan., 1839, p. 66, Nov., 1839, p. 163; Chas. Spear, Journal, May 22, 1842, BPL.

9. Garrison to Richard D. Webb, Feb. 27, 1842, BPL.

10. *Nonresistant*, Nov. 11, 1840, p. 82. H. C. Wright, after visiting Smith, wrote him on Oct. 7, 1839 (Syr. U.), indicating that he had hope for Smith as a nonresistant. Wright wrote in his Journal on April 15, 1840, (Harv. U.): "Spent the evening with Bro. Smith's family conversing on nonresistance. I think Bro. Smith is influenced —it may be unconsciously by his [wealthy] pecuniary circumstances, in his conduct. His conscience and reason are with nonresist-

ance, but his circumstances battle against it." Smith never joined the Nonresistance Society.

11. Garr. II, 326–27; unsigned editorial, probably by Ballou, in *Nonresistant*, Feb. 1, 1845.

12. *Nonresistant*, Nov. 11, 1840; *Lib.*, Dec. 21, 1849, p. 204.

13. *Nonresistant*, May 13, May 27, Jan. 22, 1840.

14. H. C. Wright, "Fragments of Diaries," Jan. 29, 1835, Harv. U.

15. *Nonresistant*, Feb. 12, 1840. Wright and Ladd agreed on the inviolability of human life, but Ladd balked at Wright's views on government. On April 27, 1840, Wright noted in his Journal (Harv. U.) that he had just talked with Ladd. "He denies that any man or body of men are authorized to take the life of man for any cause. But he can hardly see how to apply it to government. He thinks there may be a system of . . . punishments without the life-taking power."

16. *Nonresistant*, Feb. 12, Oct. 28, Dec. 9, 1840.

17. *Lib.*, June 1, 1849, p. 86. Sumner, in an oration published by the American Peace Society *(The True Grandeur of Nations,* Boston, 1845, p. 8), said that "in our age there can be no peace that is not honorable; there can be no war that is not dishonorable." Logically this meant a rejection even of defensive wars and was so interpreted by contemporaries, but when pressed, Sumner acknowledged the right of defensive wars in extreme circumstances; thus he may be called an occasional nonresistant. Sumner was active in the peace movement until about 1849. After that, he continued his concern to avoid violence as much as possible, and he remained a vice-president of the American Peace Society throughout the Civil War.

18. *Lib.*, Dec. 7, 1849, p. 194.

19. *Nonresistant*, Dec. 7, 1839. The Shaker community at Watervliet, N Y., did not recognize distinctions of color (Kate E. R. Pickard, *The Kidnapped*, Syr., 1856, p. 388). H C. Wright visited Shaker communities near Cleveland, Ohio, and at New Lebanon, New York. He reported they opposed both slavery and war; he said Shakers thus far "have been the most successful communists in the world" *(Lib.,* April 21, 1854, p. 64, Aug. 27, 1858, p. 140).

20. *Nonresistant*, May 4, 1839. Whipple graduated from Amherst in 1831. In 1833 he studied medicine in Salem. By 1835 he had met the Garrisonians. In 1839 he "came out" of an orthodox church in Salem. In 1841 when he first heard Theodore Parker preach, he believed he heard the preaching of the gospel for the first time, and by 1845 he had joined Parker's church *(Lib.,* July 23, 1858, p. 120).

21. Garrison in *Nonresistant*, March 16, 1839, March 11, 1840.

22. *Nonresistant*, Oct. 12, 1841. I have ignored a resolution reported to have been proposed by Garrison, in *ibid.*, because it is either not clear or inconsistent with what Garrison was saying elsewhere at about the same time. During the Revolutionary War, when Pennsylvania law exempted conscientious objectors only on the payment of a fine, Quakers often opposed paying it, while Mennonites, also pacifists, were more willing to pay it (C. Henry Smith, *Mennonites of America*, Scottdale, Pa., 1919, pp. 108–109). Shakers wavered on whether to pay such fines (Edward D. Andrews, *The People Called Shakers*, N.Y., 1953, p. 212). The student peace society at abolitionist Oneida Institute would not permit any member to "support the system of war, neither by engaging in any military exercise himself, nor by proxy, nor by paying fines or taxes for that purpose" *(Friend of Man*, Aug. 18, 1836, p. 34). The society had 26 members when there were about 123 students at Oneida.

23. *Nonresistant*, Nov. 16, June 15, 1839.

24. At Oberlin, Cambell may have been a factor in founding the branch of the Nonresistance Society there, an event which profoundly disturbed the college community (Robert Fletcher, *History of Oberlin College*, Oberlin, 1943, pp. 272–75, 323–25). The establishment of the Oberlin branch, with John Orvis as secretary, was reported in *Nonresistant*, Sept. 9, 1840. The only other branch established was the New Hampshire branch, with Pillsbury, Rogers, Foster, and Amos Wood among the 26 original members *(Nonresistant*, Jan. 13, Feb. 24, 1841).

25. *Lib.*, April 20, 1849, p. 64; Chas. Spear, Journal, May 17, 1847, BPL; *Prisoners' Friend*, Sept., 1848, pp. 3, 32.

26. *Memoir of Samuel Joseph May* (Boston, 1873), 181–82.

27. *Nonresistant*, Nov. 16, 1839; (Eliz. P. Peabody), *Record of a School* (Boston, 1835), 143–46; F. B. Sanborn and Wm. T. Harris, *A. Bronson Alcott* (Boston, 1893), p. 228.

28. *Nat. AS Stand.*, Oct. 1, 1846, p. 75, Nov. 14, 1850, p. 98.

29. Edm. Quincy to Anne W. Weston, June 25, 1839, MHS; Chas. Spear, Journal, Oct. 13, 1843, BPL; *Nonresistant*, Aug. 12, 1840.

30. Garrison to Benson, July 8, 1842, BPL; Garrison to Wright, Oct. 1, 1844, BPL. Collins was influenced by Robert Owen, whom he met in Britain.

31. A call for a meeting in Skaneateles to plan the community was signed by four persons, Collins, N. H. Whiting, John Orvis, and J. O. Wattles *(Lib.*, Oct. 13, 1843, p. 163). All were abolitionists active in the Nonresistance Society. May and the Garrisonian Quaker Sarah

Pugh were among the legal trustees for the community, but May is not known to have been otherwise involved (Lester Wells, *The Skaneateles Communal Experiment*, Syr., 1953. p. 5).

32. John Humphrey Noyes, *Hist. of Am. Socialisms* (Phila., 1870), pp. 162ff.; *Nat. AS Stand.*, Aug. 20, 1846, p. 46; *Lib.*, Aug. 28, 1846, p. 139.

33. Garrison to wife, Jan. 12, 1844, BPL.

34. Alice McBee, *From Utopia to Florence* (Northampton, 1947), p. 51; *Lib.*, June 20, 1845, p. 100.

35. (Olive Gilbert), *Narrative of Sojourner Truth* (N.Y., 1853), pp. 114, 120; Frederick Douglass, *Life and Times* (N.Y., 1968), p. 275; Harriet Beecher Stowe, "Sojourner Truth," *Atlantic*, 1863, p. 480.

36. Chas. A. Sheffield, *History of Florence* (Florence, Mass., 1895), pp. 130–31; *Lib.*, Oct. 13, 1843, p. 164.

37. McBee, p. 51; *Nonresistant*, March 10, 1841, p. 19; Ballou, *History of the Hopedale Community* (Lowell, Mass., 1897), p. 394.

38. Noyes, p. 122–23; Wilbur H. Siebert, *Underground Railroad in Mass.* (Worcester, 1936), p. 55; Ballou, *History*, pp. 77, 142–43.

39. *Nonresistant*, Jan. 1, 1845, p. 5; *Lib.*, Nov. 23, 1849, p. 186; *Antislavery Bugle*, Feb. 22, 1851, p. 91; Phillips to Eliz. Pease, Aug. 29, 1847, BPL; Noyes, p. 119.

40. Oliver Johnson to G. Smith, Oct. 15, 1852, Syr. U. While Johnson seemed to attribute the distinction between injurious and noninjurious force to Ballou, it evidently did not originate with him. The Peace Society of Oneida Institute had already indirectly adopted the distinction between injurious and noninjurious force in 1836. According to its constitution, its members "forever discard all such resistance as shall cause personal injury to an assailant." The secretary of the society explained that this would allow a member, if assailed, to parry a blow or hold the assailant by superior strength *(Friend of Man*, Aug. 18, 1836, p. 34). H. C. Wright quoted this constitution, including the passage above, and said, "This is the Gospel principle" *(ibid.*, Sept. 8, 1836, p. 46). Similarly, in 1838, Wright, like Ballou, approved of the noninjurious restraint of children, as in preventing them from injuring one another or jumping into a boiling pot *(Lib.*, April 27, 1838, p. 66). Later Ballou approved of a nonresistant placing himself in front of an intended victim and covering his retreat until his own body is crushed, if necessary (Ballou, *A Discourse on Christian Nonresistance in Extreme Cases*, Hopedale, Milford, Mass., 1860, pp. 17–19). Whipple agreed that nonresistants did not object to all "physical force" but only to "injurious force" (Whipple, *Nonresistance Ap-*

plied to the Internal Defense of a Community, Boston, 1860, pp. 4, 20–21). For examples in which nonresistants seemed to justify their use of noninjurious force, see CHAPTER 16, the case of Williamson, and CHAPTER 17, the cases of Shadrach, Jerry, and Butman.

41. Lewis G. Wilson, "The Christian Doctrine of Nonresistance," *Arena*, Dec., 1890, pp. 4–5. About 1890, when Tolstoy was writing on nonresistance, he was influenced by Ballou (Alexandra Tolstoy, *Tolstoy, A Life of My Father*, N.Y., 1953, p. 307).

Chapter 7, *Regardless of Complexion*

1. *Colored Am.*, July 8, 1837, p. 1; *National Reformer*, Nov., 1839, p. 162.

2. *Lib.*, Nov. 19, 1836, p. 186; *Colored Am.*, Oct. 14, 1837, p. 1; Antislavery Conv. of Am. Women *Procs.* (Phila., 1838), p. 8.

3. Jas. and L. Mott to Anne W. Weston, June 7, 1838, BLP; *Weld-Grimké Letters*, p. 163; L. Tappan, *Life*, pp. 201–202; *Friend*, Aug. 1, 1840, p. 352.

4. *Weld-Grimké Letters*, pp. 273, 379–81. *Colored Am.*, Sept. 9, 1837, p. 2, June 2, 1838, p. 58.

5. L. Tappan and S. S. Jocelyn favored public association with Negroes as equals, but the majority of the AAS executive committee disagreed (L. Tappan, Journal, April 6, 1836, LC; L. Tappan to G. Smith, April 8, 1836, Syr. U.; *Weld-Grimké Letters*, pp. 270–77).

6. S. J. May, *Some Recollections* (Boston, 1869), p. 288; Antislavery Conv. of Am. Women *Procs.* (Phila., 1839), p. 6; H. C. Wright, in *Liberty Bell*, 1848, pp. 153–54.

7. Bowditch I, 138; *North Star*, May 25, 1849.

8. *North Star*, May 30, 1850; *Lib.*, June 8, 1849, p. 90.

9. *Colored Am.*, Sept. 2, 1837, p. 1, Sept. 22, 1838, p. 122.

10. *Lib.*, June 8, 1849, p. 90.

11. *Lib.*, Nov. 6, 1857, p. 170.

12. W. W. Brown, *The Negro in the American Rebellion* (Boston, 1867), pp. 364–65.

13. F. Douglass, *Life and Times* (Hartford, 1881), p. 467; *Lib.*, Feb. 11, 1848, p. 21.

14. *Lib.*, June 14, 1834, p. 91.

15. State Conv. of Colored Citizens of Ohio *Minutes* (Oberlin, 1849), p. 19; *Lib.*, Sept. 13, 1850, p. 147, June 11, 1847, pp. 94–95.

16. Lydia Maria Child, *Isaac T. Hopper* (Boston, 1853), pp. 448–49.

17. *African Repository*, March, 1853, pp. 82–84.

18. An account written by an official of the railroad company, in *Lib.*, June 8, 1855, p. 92.

19. S. A. M. Washington, *George Thomas Downing* (Newport, R.I., 1910), p. 6; *Lib.*, Oct. 12, 1855, p. 163.

20. *Lib.*, April 23, 1858, p. 67; Still, *Underground Railroad* (Phila., 1872), pp. 540–41; *North Star*, Oct. 6, 1848.

21. Mass. AS Soc. *An. Report*, 1846, p. 92; *Nat. AS Stand.*, Dec. 10, 1846, p. 111; *North Star*, Jan. 5, 1849; Bowditch I, 130–32.

22. *Colored Am.*, June 23, 1838, p. 70; Douglass to Francis Jackson, Jan. 29, 1846, BPL.

23. Watkins, in Still, pp. 758–60; Chas. Spear, Journal, Oct. 14, 1842, BPL.

24. *American Antislavery Almanac for 1843*, opp. page for June.

25. Nell, *Colored Patriots* (Boston, 1855), pp. 345–57.

26. *Colored Am.*, Oct. 14, 1837, p. 1; *National Reformer*, Feb., 1839, p. 83.

27. *Nat. AS Stand.*, Nov. 3, 1860, p. 2.

28. *Lib.*, Feb. 20, 1836, p. 29.

29. *Lib.*, Aug. 6, 1836, p. 126, July 19, 1834, p. 115, Nov. 26, 1852, p. 190; NYC AS Soc. *Address*, 1833, pp. 28–29.

30. *Lib.*, July 26, 1834, p. 119; *Emancipator*, Aug. 26, 1834; Wm. Jay, *An Inquiry* (N.Y., 1835), p. 147; David Ruggles, *The Extinguisher Extinguished* (N.Y., 1834), pp. 11–14.

31. *Lib.*, March 30, 1838, p. 52.

32. Garrison to Geo. Benson, June 25, 1844, BPL; *Lib.*, Oct. 15, 1841, p. 167, April 22, 1853, p. 62.

Chapter 8, *Railroad Ride-Ins*

1. Ruggles entered a white car of the Stonington-Providence railroad, but, he said, three men "forcibly ejected me from the car and forced me into what they called the pauper (or jim crow) car" (parentheses are Ruggles') *(Colored Am.*, Aug. 25, 1838, p. 107).

2. *Lib.*, July 9, 1841, p. 110, July 30, 1841, p. 122.

3. *Lib.*, July 23, 1841, p. 118, Aug. 6, 1841, p. 127.

4. *Lib.*, July 9, 1841, p. 110, Aug. 6, 1841, p. 127, Sept. 3, 1841, p. 143.

5. *Nat. AS Stand.*, Aug. 26, 1841, p. 46.

6. *Lib.*, Aug. 27, 1841, p. 139; *Nat. AS Stand.*, Sept. 2, 1841, p. 50.

7. Rogers in *Nat. AS Stand.*, Dec. 2, 1841, p. 102; Nell in *North Star*, Feb. 23, 1849; Nell to Garrison, Oct. 21, 1865 (printed letter), BPL. Rogers referred to Garrison's riding-in on the New Bedford Railroad and Nell to his riding-in on the Eastern Railroad.

8. *Nat. AS Stand.*, Dec. 2, 1841, p. 102. The New Bedford car in which Rogers and Garrison rode on this occasion was, according to Rogers, a Jim Crow car, and he considered that riding in it was daring; but in this case other whites also rode in it as if they did so customarily. It may have been both a Jim Crow car and a second class car for whites.

9. *Lib.*, Oct. 21, 1842, p. 166.

10. *Nat. AS Stand.*, Sept. 9, 1841, p. 55; Mass. AS Soc. *An. Report* (Boston, 1842), pp. 71, 73.

11. *Ibid.*, p. 72; *Lib.*, Oct. 15, 1841, pp. 165–66.

12. *Lib.*, Nov. 12, 1841, p. 184.

13. *Lib.*, Feb. 18, 1842, p. 28. At a meeting of the Bristol County Antislavery Society, the resolutions committee, of which Collins was a member, proposed a resolution that both whites and blacks should use their influence to do away with discrimination on railroads "not by physical or brute force, but by the means inculcated by our great Master, *viz.*, to return good for evil, and patiently submit until deliverance comes" *(Lib.*, Dec. 24, 1841, p. 205).

14. *Lib.*, Oct. 1, 1841, p. 157.

15. Dr. Mann later advocated resistance to the fugitive slave law in a violent form that Garrison opposed *(Pa. Freeman*, April 22, 1852, p. 65).

16. *Lib.* Aug. 27, 1841, p. 139.

17. *Lib.*, Oct. 15, 1841, p. 165.

18. Douglass, *Life and Times* (Hartford, 1881), p. 228; *Lib.*, July 22, 1842, p. 114.

19. *Nat. AS Stand.*, Oct. 14, 1841, p. 74.

20. New Eng. AS Conv. *Procs.* (Boston, 1834), pp. 17–18; *Minutes of the . . . An. Conv. for the Improvement of the Free People of Color* (N.Y., 1834), p. 15. Similarly, *ibid.*, (Phila., 1835), p. 14. Editor Cornish, after publishing a report that Negroes were mistreated on railroads and steamboats between New York City and neighboring cities like Newark, Philadelphia, and New Haven, recommended that blacks, if they did not have horses and vehicles of their own, stay home or go on foot *(Colored Am.*, June 30, 1838, p. 75). David Ruggles urged abolitionists to boycott the Stonington-Providence railroad because of its segregation *(Colored Am.*, Aug. 25, 1838, p. 107).

21. Mass. AS Soc. *An. Report,* 1842, p. 71. *Lib.*, Feb. 25, 1842, p. 30, April 28, 1843, p. 67.

22. *Lib.*, Dec. 24, 1841, p. 205. An exceptional antislavery society that did endorse the ride-in and sit-in method was that of Windham

County, Conn. It resolved: "We recommend to such abolitionists as believe it right for them to patronize a church, a railroad, or anything else, where a separate place is appropriated for the colored men, that they identify themselves with the injured party, and occupy with their abused brother, the station assigned for him" *(Nat. AS Stand.,* Oct. 14, 1841, p. 74).

23. *Lib.* July 22, 1842, p. 114, Oct. 22, 1841, p. 171, Nov. 26, 1841, p. 190.

24. *Nat. AS Stand.,* Sept. 23, 1841, p. 63; *Lib.,* Oct. 1, 1841, pp. 157–58; *Minutes of the First Colored Conv. Held in the City of Portland, Oct. 6, 1841* (Portland, 1842), p. 13.

25. *Lib.,* May 13, 1842, p. 73; S. J. May, *Some Recollections* (Boston, 1869), pp. 399–400. Barney had raised funds for the Nonresistance Society in Nantucket in 1839.

26. *Lib.,* Dec. 30, 1842, p. 206, Feb. 10, 1843, p. 22.

27. *Lib.,* April 28, 1843, p. 66. There was at least one relapse (Remond, in *Lib.,* April 28, 1843, p. 67).

28. *Lib.,* Dec. 1, 1843, p. 190; *Proceedings of a Crowded Meeting of the Colored Population of Boston . . . Bidding Farewell to . . . Garrison* (Dublin, 1846), p. 5.

29. *North Star,* June 22, 1849, March 10, 1848.

30. Nell to Garrison, Oct. 21, 1865 (printed letter), BPL. Additional railroad ride-ins, some of them probably inspired by the Massachusetts railroad ride-ins, are mentioned as follows: by Jabez P. Cambell in New Jersey and Pennsylvania *(Lib.,* April 28, 1843, p. 66); by W. W. Brown in Ohio ([Josephine Brown], *Biography of an Am. Bondman by His Daughter,* Boston, 1856, pp. 56–59; W. W. Brown, *The Negro in the Am. Rebellion,* Boston, 1867, pp. 370–73); by Douglass in Pennsylvania (Garr. III, 190; Foner I, 79); by Jeremiah Meyer in Rhode Island *(North Star,* April 14, 1848); by Garnet in New York *(North Star,* April 14, June 23, July 7, 14, 1848). For Garnet's advice in favor of violent ride-ins, see *North Star,* April 14, 1848.

Chapter 9, *Pray-ins and Pray-outs*

1. S. R. Ward, *Autobiog.* (London, 1855), p. 30. Catholic churches were exceptional in not segregating seating.

2. Antislavery Conv. of Am. Women, *An Appeal* (N.Y., 1837), pp. 59–60; *Colored Am.,* Aug. 19, 1837, p. 2; *North Star,* Feb. 25, March 10, 1848.

3. *Lib.,* June 4, 1831, p. 90; E. S. Abdy, *Journal of a Residence and Tour* (London, 1835), I, 135–36; Alice Henderson, *Hist. of the N.Y. State AS Soc.* (Ann Arbor, 1963), p. 292; *Colored Am.,* June 9, 1838, p. 63.

4. *Lib.*, April 2, 1858, p. 56; *Nonresistant*, May 27, 1840, p. 38; *In Memory, Angelina Grimké Weld* (Boston, 1880), p. 11.

5. Bowditch I, 123; L. Tappan, *Life*, pp. 194, 201; *Lib.*, Nov. 10, 1837, p. 181; *Colored Am.*, Oct. 28, 1837, p. 2; John Hooker, *Some Reminiscences* (Hartford, 1899), p. 23.

6. *Friend of Man*, Oct. 11, 1837, p. 65; *Colored Am.*, Sept. 19, 1840, p. 1.

7. L. Tappan, Journal, Feb. 25–26, March 19, 1836, LC.

8. Clipping, letter by L. Tappan, dated Aug. 24 and Sept. 11, 1837, in L. Tappan, Journal, pp. 123–28, LC.

9. *Lib.*, Aug. 6, 1841, p. 127; *Friend of Man*, May 30, 1838, p. 194; *North Star*, June 13, Sept. 5, 1850; *Lib*, May 28, 1831, p. 87; *Minutes of the National Conv. of Colored Citizens Held at Buffalo* (N.Y., 1843), pp. 10–12, 14–15.

10. *Lib.*, Dec. 8, 1854, p. 196; *Colored Am.*, Oct. 24, 1840.

11. *Weld-Grimké Letters*, p. 831; *Nonslaveholder*, Sept. 2, 1850, p. 206; Galpin, *God's Chore Boy*, p. 105.

12. *Lib.*, Jan. 22, 1858, p. 14.

13. Douglass, *My Bondage and My Freedom* (N.Y., 1855), pp. 350–53; *North Star*, Aug. 17, 1849.

14. *AS Record*, June, 1836, p. 4; *Colored Am.*, April 22, April 29, 1837, Oct. 24, 1840, Feb. 20, March 13, 1841.

15. *North Star*, Dec. 14, 1849; *National Reformer*, Sept., 1839, p. 133; *Colored Am.*, Feb. 6, 1841.

16. *North Star*, Jan. 8, March 10, 1848, March 9, June 15, 1849, May 30, 1850.

17. *Anglo-African Magazine*, 1859, p. 339; *North Star*, June 23, 1851; *Nat. AS Stand.*, Jan. 6, 1842, p. 123.

18. Ward, pp. 98–99. The skeptical Delany said that since there were no people in the United States more religious than Negroes and since Negroes were also the most poor and miserable, this proved that success in life did not depend on religious character (Delany, *The Condition . . . of the Colored People*, Phila., 1852, p. 39).

19. Ward, p. 29. Ward had been exposed to Quaker influences in his youth, and he was a protégé of the almost complete nonresistant Gerrit Smith. Ward believed in defending himself by violence from being forced back into slavery. But, regarding whites' responsibility for generations of oppression of blacks, he urged blacks to forgive whites, difficult as it was, and not to hate them. Said Ward, "How frequently have I heard a Negro exclaim, 'I cannot like a white man. He and his have done so much injury to me and my people for so

many generations.' " But, he said, I remind him that Christ forgave and so should we; "that just as surely as the whites were our enemies —a most palpable fact, of every day illustration—just so surely we must forgive them, or lie down for ever with them, amid the torments of the same perdition!" (Ward, pp. 84–85). Ward called himself a "peace man" (Am. and For. AS Soc. *An. Report*, 1850, p. 22).

20. State Convention of Colored People *Procs.* (Albany, 1851), pp. 14–15.

21. *Lib.*, Dec. 7, 1855, p. 196; *North Star*, July 14, 1848.

22. *Friend of Man*, May 9, 1838, p. 182; *Lib.*, April 7, 1848, p. 55; *North Star*, June 15, 1849; Geo. T. Downing *et al.*, *To the Friends of Equal Rights in R.I.* (Providence, 1859), p. 8.

Chapter 10, *Creating Schools*

1. *Minutes and Procs. of the First An. Conv. of the People of Color* (Phila., 1831), p. 18; Am. and For. AS Soc. *An. Report* (N.Y., 1848), p. 7; Antislavery Conv. of Am. Women *Procs.* (Phila., 1839), pp. 8, 13.

2. Jas. W. C. Pennington, *The Fugitive Blacksmith* (London, 1849), p. 56; Douglass, *Narrative* (Dublin, 1846), p. 37; Am. and For. AS Soc. *An. Report* (N.Y., 1850), p. 22.

3. Asa E. Martin, *The Antislavery Movement in Ky.* (Louisville, 1918), p. 83; W. W. Brown, *Narrative* (London, 1849), p. iv.

4. Angelina Grimké, *Appeal to the Christian Women* (N.Y., 1836), pp. 18–19; *Lib.*, Nov. 19, 1836, p. 186.

5. C. G. Woodson, *Education of the Negro* (N.Y., 1915), pp. 208–15.

6. *J. of Negro Hist.*, 1927, pp. 377, 381; John Malvin, *Autobiography* (Cleveland, 1966), p. 34.

7. *Lib.*, March 8, 1850, p. 39; Wm. Goodell, *American Slave Code* (N.Y., 1853), pp. 323–24; *Colored Am.*, April 29, 1837, p. 2.

8. *Am. Missionary*, Jan., 1857, p. 7, May, 1857, p. 105, Sept., 1857, p. 211.

9. Woodson, pp. 133–44, 266–67, 137; Henry Barnard, "Education in the D. of C.," *Am. J. of Ed.*, XIX (1870), 201, 206–209.

10. Margaret Douglass, *Personal Narrative* (Boston, 1854).

11. Garnet, *The Past and Present Condition . . . of the Colored Race* (Troy, N.Y., 1848), p. 19; *North Star*, Dec. 1, 1848.

12. New Eng. AS Conv. *Procs.* (Boston, 1834), pp. 13–14; *Nat. AS Stand.*, Dec. 23, 1841, p. 114.

13. *Lib.*, Oct. 15, 1836, p. 166; N.Y. State AS Soc. *Procs.* (Utica, 1835), p. 16; *Weld-Grimké Letters*, pp. 263–64.

14. *Lib.*, Jan. 30, 1836, p. 19; *Friend*, 1836–37, *passim;* Benj. Bacon,

Statistics of the Colored People of Phila. (Phila., 1859), pp. 5–6; *Friends Rev.*, May 21, 1859, p. 584.

15. Emma Thornbrough, *The Negro in Indiana* (Indianapolis?, 1957), pp. 167–73; *Friends Rev.*, 1858–60, *passim.* For examples of Friends teaching in Midwest Negro schools, see *Friends Rev.*, Oct. 27, 1860, p. 120, and Oct. 25, 1862, p. 121.

16. Thornbrough, pp. 167–68; *Friends Rev.*, Oct. 27, 1860, p. 120. "Some" blacks attended Indiana Yearly Meeting Friends schools *(Friends Rev.*, Dec. 13, 1862, p. 231). "Several colored children are reported to have attended our [Indiana Yrly. Mtg.] schools; and when they have been unable to pay their tuition fees, their school bills have been paid by the committees" *(Friends Rev.*, Nov. 14, 1863, p. 166). Marion Wright, *Education of Negroes in N.J.* (N.Y., 1941), p. 124, cites instances of Negroes studying in predominantly white Friends schools in New Jersey, but in that state as elsewhere, Friends gave more attention to separate schools for Negroes.

17. Senator Hiram H. Revels attended a Friends school in Indiana, probably Beech Grove Seminary, near Liberty, for one or two years beginning in 1844, and he was treated there without discrimination (Gerald E. Wheeler, *Hiram Rhoads Revels,* thesis, U. of Cal., no pl., 1949, p. 4; *J. of Negro Hist.*, 1938, p. 378).

18. Union's first principal (1846–55), a white, had been a student at Oneida and Oberlin; like those schools, Union was based on manual labor principles. During the Civil War the Negro principal left to enlist in the Union army—evidently he was not a Quaker (Thornbrough, pp. 173–77). Indiana Yearly Meeting—to which by this time the Antislavery Friends had largely returned—described Union as being "established for colored persons" and as "doing much good to that people" *(Friends Rev.*, Dec. 13, 1862, p. 231). Union closed in 1874.

19. Evidence that the few Friends colleges (Haverford, Earlham) or the numerous Eastern Friends academies admitted blacks is not available. Sarah Grimké reported in 1840 two unsuccessful efforts to enter black children in Philadelphia Friends schools for whites *(Weld-Grimké Letters,* p. 855). In 1865 the Friends school in Providence had never yet permitted blacks to enter but was considering it (Lillie and Arthur Wyman, *Elizabeth Buffum Chace*, Boston, 1914, I, 276–78).

20. Garr. I, 322–23; May, *Some Recollections* (Boston, 1869), pp. 39–72; May, *Letters . . . to Miss Crandall* (Brooklyn, Conn., 1833).

21. Wm. Oakes to Samuel Sewall, Sept. 27, 1834, BPL; *Lib.*, Sept. 5, 1835, p. 141, Oct. 3, 1835, p. 159.

22. Nell, *Colored Patriots* (Boston, 1855), p. 349.

23. *Lib.*, May 28, 1836, p. 87.

24. *Lib.*, Dec. 2, 1853, p. 190.

25. According to *Oberlin Evangelist*, May 10, 1843, p. 78, the Oberlin Peace Society's constitution, adopted after an animated debate of several days, said: "The necessity for even defensive war might be entirely obviated" among civilized nations if in their international disputes they appealed to arbitration or a congress of nations. It boldly urged clergymen not to sanction war by becoming military chaplains. It refused to approve the laws of the U.S. government respecting war, and said they felt bound "to yield obedience to civil authority so far as it does not seem to us to conflict with the authority of God and no farther." Officers included Oberlin professors John Morgan and Amasa Walker. On the motion of Pres. Mahan and Prof. Finney the society voted to arrange to debate the question, "Is all war sinful?" Prof. Geo. Whipple, later to be one of L. Tappan's closest associates, was a member of the society's nominating committee.

26. Delazon Smith, *Oberlin Unmasked* (Cleveland, 1837), pp. 57–58. By 1859, Smith was U.S. Senator from Oregon, naturally a Democrat.

27. L. Tappan to G. Smith, Dec. 2, 1862, Syr. U.

28. Ohio AS Soc., *Report* (Cincinnati, 1837), p. 61.

29. Ohio AS Conv. *Procs.* (Putnam, Ohio?, 1835), pp. 16, 34; *Lib.*, Nov. 3, 1854, p. 174. Wattles in 1836 became AAS agent to work with Northern blacks. In one project, in Mercer County, Ohio, Wattles bought farm land, induced blacks to settle there as farmers, and established a manual labor school especially for blacks but deliberately open also to whites (5 of the 30 pupils were white) *(Colored Am.,* March 2, 1839, p. 3; *Friend,* Dec. 26, 1840, p. 100). The school, which received some Quaker support, grew and still flourished in 1846 (Wm. and Jane Pease, *Black Utopia,* Madison, 1964, pp. 40–41).

30. Colored National Conv. *Procs... Held at Cleveland* (Rochester, 1848), pp. 14, 19; Am. and For. AS Soc. *An. Report* (N.Y., 1850), p. 123.

31. Colored National Conv. *Procs.* (Rochester, 1853), pp. 30–38, 40; *Lib.*, July 27, 1855, p. 120; Colored National Conv., *Procs . . . Held . . . 1855* (Salem, N.J., 1856), pp. 38, 10–11, 25–27.

Chapter II, *Boycotting Schools*

1. C. G. Woodson, *Education of the Negro* (N.Y., 1915), pp. 320–25, describes the desegregation of schools in Salem, Nantucket, and particularly Boston without mentioning the boycott as a method or

Nell as the Boston leader, giving credit to whites as leaders instead. Louis Ruchames stresses the Boston campaign in his "Race and Education in Mass." *(Negro Hist. Bull.*, Dec., 1949, pp. 53ff.); he gives due credit to Nell, but only mentions the boycott in one oblique reference. Leon Litwack, *North of Slavery* (Chicago, 1961), gives pages 143–50 to the Boston campaign but does not mention Nell or the boycott. As far as I know, the story of the Boston campaign was first comprehensively published in my article, "A Negro Boycott to Integrate Boston Schools" *(New England Quart.*, Sept., 1968), of which the text of this chapter is a fuller version.

2. *Colored Am.*, Sept. 28, 1839, p. 3, April 22, 1837, p. 2; *National Reformer*, Nov., 1839, pp. 163–68; *Weld-Grimké Letters*, 445–46; *Lib.*, May 26, 1854, p. 82; Robert Fletcher, *History of Oberlin College* (Oberlin, 1943), p. 184.

3. *Lib.*, Dec. 21, 1849, p. 201; *Report of the Minority of the Committee of the Primary School Board on the Caste Schools* (Boston, 1846), pp. 21–22; *Report of a Special Comm. of the Grammar School Board* (Boston, 1849), pp. 37, 57.

4. *Ibid.*, p. 39; *North Star*, May 25, 1849.

5. Charlotte Forten, *Journal* (N.Y., 1953), pp. 13–15; W. W. Brown, *The Black Man* (Boston, 1863), pp. 190–93; *Lib.*, Aug. 1, 1856, p. 122; *Nat. AS Stand.*, March 20, 1858, p. 3.

6. *North Star*, Sept. 22, 1848, Nov. 2, 9, Aug. 10, 17, Dec. 7, 21, 1849; Foner II, 40–41; Blake McKelvey, "Lights and Shadows in Local Negro History," *Rochester History*, Oct., 1959, p. 6.

7. S. A. M. Washington, *George Thomas Downing* (Newport, R.I., 1910), *passim.;* Irving Bartlett, *From Slave to Citizen, The Story of the Negro in R.I.* (Providence, 1954), p. 53; Amos Beman, in clipping dated Newport, March 24, 1863, Beman Scrapbook II, 5, Yale U.; Geo. T. Downing *et al., Will the General Assembly Put Down Caste Schools?* (Providence, 1857); Comm. on Education, Gen. Assembly of R.I. *Minority Report . . . on the Abolition of Caste Schools* (Providence, 1858); (Geo. T. Downing *et al.*), *To the Friends of Equal Rights in R.I.* (Providence, 1859).

8. Boston *Atlas*, June 28, 1844; *Report to the Primary School Committee . . . on the Petition of Sundry Colored Persons* (Boston, 1846), p. 20; *Report of a Special Comm.*, p. 3.

9. The result of the controversy over corporal punishment in the Boston schools was a reduction in its use by about 80 percent in about two years, of which Mann was proud (Mary P. Mann, *Life of Horace Mann*, Boston, 1865, p. 246). Mann's wife Mary was the sister of Eliz.

Peabody who had taught with Alcott and shared his interest in experimenting in nonviolent education.

10. Mary P. Mann, p. 239; Mann to S. G. Howe, May 11, 1845, MHS; *Lib.*, Aug. 28, 1846, p. 137, Dec. 24, 1847, p. 206, Feb. 11, 1848, p. 22; (Mass.) Bd. of Ed. *Twelfth An. Report* (Boston, 1849), p. 59.

11. Mann to Eliz. Peabody, Aug. 24, 1833, MHS; *Am. and For. AS Reporter*, Jan., 1845, p. 30; *Report of a Special Comm.*, p. 70; *Lib.*, Aug. 3, 1849, p. 122; May to Mann, Feb. 8, 1843, BPL; Mary P. Mann, p. 172; May, *Some Recollections* (Boston, 1869), p. 313.

12. Nell was sympathetic to Douglass' effort to uphold moral suasion as opposed to physical force (in *North Star*, Dec. 3, 1847, p. 1). Nell said that the idea of writing on Negro military service in the Revolutionary War was suggested to him by Quaker Whittier, who said that, while he did not wish to eulogize the shedding of blood, if white Revolutionary War heroes were to be honored, then black ones ought to be also. Nell's book first appeared as a pamphlet, *Services of Colored Americans in the Wars of 1776 and 1812* (Boston, 1851), then in an enlarged form under the same title (Boston, 1852), and then still more enlarged as a book, *Colored Patriots* (Boston, 1855). The Whittier statement appeared in all three of these editions in the preface.

13. *Lib.*, Oct. 5, 1849, p. 160.

14. *Lib.*, Dec. 28, 1855, p. 206; Boston *Pilot*, Oct. 6, 1855.

15. Boston *Bee*, Sept. 5, 1855; clipping, marked Boston *Mail*, Sept. 5, 1855, in Boston Public School for Colored Children, scrapbook, p. 26, BPL; *Lib.*, Sept. 14, 1855, p. 147.

16. Morris said slavery could not be abolished peaceably, only "by the strong arm" *(Lib.*, Aug. 13, 1858, p. 132). Morris "rather inclines to a military life, and has, on more than one occasion, attempted the organization of an independent [military] company" (W. W. Brown, *The Black Man*, p. 228). Morris was not commonly involved in Garrisonian abolitionist activities.

17. *Lib.*, Dec. 28, 1855, pp. 206–207.

18. Downing *et al.*, pp. 9–12; Colored National Conv. *Procs.* (Salem, N.J., 1856), pp. 28–29; *Anglo-African Magazine*, July, 1859, p. 223.

Chapter 12, *Boycott of Slave Produce*

1. Am. and For. AS Soc. *An. Report* (N.Y., 1853), p. 135.

2. *Nat. AS Stand.*, Nov. 11, 1841, p. 89; Chas. Marriott, *Address* (N.Y., 1835), pp. 4, 18.

3. *Genius of Universal Emancipation*, Oct. 30, 1829, p. 58; *Lib.*, May

28, 1831, p. 87, July 30, 1831, p. 121, June 11, 1836, p. 95.

4. Ohio AS Conv. *Procs.* (Putnam, Ohio?, 1835), pp. 9–11; *Emancipator*, July 28, 1836, p. 50; L. Tappan to G. Smith, July 5, 1836, Syr. U.; Requited Labor Convention *Minutes* (Phila., 1838), p. 17; L. Tappan to G. Smith, June 29, 1840, Syr. U.; L. Tappan to Henry Grew, April 15, 1844, LC.

5. Chas. H. Wesley, *Richard Allen* (Wash., 1935), pp. 239–40; Ruth Nuermberger, *The Free Produce Movement* (Durham, 1942), p. 119. Nuermberger is an indispensible source for the boycott, particularly on Quaker participation.

6. L. Mott to J. M. McKim, April 8, 1834, Cornell U.; W. W. Brown, *The Rising Son* (Boston, 1874), p. 407.

7. *Lib.*, July 2, 1836, p. 106.

8. *Lib.*, June 13, 1835, p. 95; *Quarterly AS Mag.*, July, 1836, pp. 398–9; Am. and For. AS Soc. *An. Report* (N.Y., 1853), p. 135.

9. Lewis C. Gunn, *Address to Abolitionists* (Phila., 1838), pp. 12–13; *Genius of Universal Emancipation*, Nov., 1835, pp. 120–22; *Quarterly AS Mag.*, Jan., 1837, pp. 168–69; *Colored Am.*, Sept. 15, 1838, p. 119.

10. *Weld-Grimké Letters*, p. 873; *Nonslaveholder*, May, 1846, p. 77.

11. *Friend*, May 14, 1836, p. 252, June 13, 1836, pp. 293, 296; Ohio Assoc. *Report* (Cincinnati, 1837), p. 14; Child to G. Smith, May 2, 1838, Syr. U.; Robert Fletcher, *History of Oberlin College* (Oberlin, 1943), pp. 249, 655–56. *Friends Rev.*, Oct. 2, 1852, p. 40, Dec. 24, 1859, p. 248, March 24, 1860, p. 461.

12. Wendell P. Garrison, "Free Produce Among the Quakers," *Atlantic*, 1868, p. 493; *Lib.*, Sept. 3, 1841, p. 143.

13. *Friend*, June 1, 1839, pp. 279–80; *Lib.*, Jan 5, 1855, p. 4. Jas. Mott is an example of a cotton merchant who as a result of his scruples against handling slave goods, stopped handling cotton, turning after 1824 to other forms of business (Mary Grew, *James Mott*, N.Y., 1868?), pp. 6–7.

14. Adin Ballou, *The Voice of Duty* (Hopedale, Milford, Mass., 1843), pp. 10–11; W. W. Brown, *Antislavery Harp* (Boston, 1849), p. 21.

15. John Woolman, *Journal* (N.Y., 1922), pp. 54–55; *Lib.*, April 29, 1853, p. 68.

16. Burritt to G. Smith, July 29, 1854, MHS; *Am. Missionary*, Jan., 1858, pp. 21–22.

17. Betty Fladeland, *Jas. Gillespie Birney* (Ithaca, 1955), pp. 270–71; *Weld-Grimké Letters*, pp. 885, 954.

18. Hinton R. Helper, *Impending Crisis* (N.Y., 1860 [c. 1857]), p. 155.

19. *Friends Rev.*, Jan. 21, 1860, pp. 311–13; *Lib.*, Jan. 1, 1858, p. 3, July 30, 1858, p. 122; Garrison to S. J. May, Jr., July 20, 1858, BPL; H. C.

Wright, *No Rights, No Duties* (Boston, 1860), pp. 26–27; *Lib.*, Jan. 18, 1861, p. 12, March 22, 1861, p. 47.

20. *Lib.*, Feb. 7, 1851, p. 22; *National Reformer*, Sept., 1839, p. 141; *Minutes of the First Colored Conv. Held in the City of Portland, Oct. 6, 1841* (Portland, 1842), p. 13; *Minutes of the State Conv. of Colored Citizens of the State of Mich.* (Detroit, 1843), p. 15.

21. *Nat. AS Stand.*, Nov. 18, 1841, p. 93.

22. New Eng. AS Conv. *Procs.* (Boston, 1834), p. 11; Nuermberger, pp. 71, 92, and *passim.;* Anna Hallowell, *Jas. and Lucretia Mott* (Boston, 1884), p. 88.

23. Free Produce Assoc. of Friends of Ohio Yrly. Mtg., *The Plea of Necessity* (Mt. Pleasant, Ohio, 1851), pp. 2, 11; *Friends Rev.*, Feb. 26, 1859, p. 393.

24. *Lib.*, Dec. 30, 1842, p. 205; *Genius of Universal Emancipation*, Oct. 30, 1829, p. 58.

25. Wendell P. Garrison, p. 492; *Lib.*, June 18, 1836, p. 98, July 16, 1836, p. 115.

26. Delazon Smith, *Oberlin Unmasked* (Cleveland, 1837), p. 59; *Lib.*, March 5, 1847, p. 38.

27. *Lib.*, Dec. 1, 1848, p. 190; *North Star*, Oct. 11, 1849, May 26, 1848.

28. *Friends Rev.*, Sept. 22, 1849, p. 9, Nov. 20, 1852, pp. 153–54.

29. Requited Labor Convention *Minutes* (Phila., 1838); Nuermberger, pp. 24–28; *Weld-Grimké Letters*, pp. 797, 944.

30. *Nat. AS Stand.*, Sept. 3, 1846, pp. 53–54; Nuermberger, pp. 103–104 and *passim.; Weld-Grimké Letters*, p. 944.

31. *Pa. Freeman*, May 20, 1852, p. 82; *National Reformer*, Jan., 1839, pp. 77, 79.

32. *Nat. AS Stand.*, Jan. 30, 1851, p. 141; *Lib.*, March 1, 1850, p. 36, June 28, 1850, p. 103, Jan. 5, 1855, p. 4; Wm. Still, *Underground Railroad* (Phila., 1872), p. 759. Foner (II, 566) says Douglass "strongly" endorsed the boycott, but gives no evidence except a reference to Nuermberger, who on page 75n. merely says - Douglass "strongly" endorsed the boycott without giving evidence.

33. Nuermberger, pp. 115–19; *Nonslaveholder*, April, 1847, p. 79.

34. O. B. Frothingham, *Gerrit Smith* (N.Y., 1878), p. 230; Otelia Cromwell, *Lucretia Mott* (Cambridge, 1958), p. 162; *Friends Rev.*, Sept. 14, 1861, p. 26.

Chapter 13, *Foster Speaks-In*

1. Parker Pillsbury, *Acts of the Antislavery Apostles* (Concord, N.H., 1883), pp. 133, 136–37, 281–82.

2. Pillsbury, p. 124; Stephen S. Foster, *The Brotherhood of Thieves*, (New London, 1843), p. 6.

3. Pillsbury, pp. 194, 271.

4. *Lib.*, July 15, 1842, p. 110.

5. Garrison to wife, Nov. 27, 1842, BPL; *Lib.*, July 15, 1842, p. 110.

6. Irving Bartlett, *Wendell Phillips* (Boston, 1961), pp. 109, 99-100; Lillie B. C. Wyman, "Reminiscences of Two Abolitionists," *New Engl. Mag.*, Jan., 1903, p. 541.

7. Frederick Douglass, *Life and Times* (N.Y., 1968), pp. 221-22; Oliver Johnson, *Garrison* (Boston, 1879), p. 332.

8. Pillsbury, pp. 146, 265-66.

9. Pillsbury, pp. 308-15.

10. *Lib.*, July 22, 1842, p. 114, July 29, 1842, p. 118; Mass. AS Soc. *An. Report* (Boston, 1843), p. 59.

11. *Lib.*, Oct. 28, 1842, p. 171, Oct. 21, 1842, p. 167, Nov. 4, 1842, p. 175; George Ramsdell, *Hist. Of Milford* (Concord, N.H., 1901), p. 107; Nathaniel P. Rogers, *Collection* (Concord, 1847), p. 241; Pillsbury, p. 320.

12. Edm. Quincy to Anne W. Weston, Oct. 19, 1842, MHS; *Lib.*, Jan. 6, 1843, p. 1; Mass. AS Soc. *An. Report* (Boston, 1843), pp. 60–61.

13. *Lib.*, April 20, 1838, p. 63; Rogers, p. 243.

14. *Lib.*, Dec. 30, 1842, p. 207; *Friend*, Dec. 16, 1843, p. 92.

15. *Nonresistant*, June 29, 1842, p. 48; Pillsbury, pp. 292-93.

16. *Nonresistant*, Feb. 9, 1842, p. 9; *Lib.*, Dec. 9, 1842, p. 194; Pillsbury, pp. 298-99.

17. *Lib.*, June 27, 1845, p. 102; Abby Kelley to Foster, April 1, 1844, Worc. H.S.; Thos. Drake, *Quakers and Slavery* (New Haven, 1950), p. 177.

18. *Pa. Freeman*, June 12, 1852, p. 95, June 26, 1852, p. 102.

19. *Pa. Freeman*, July 10, 1852, pp. 110-11, July 3, 1852, p. 105.

20. *Lib.*, Dec. 9, 1853, p. 192; *Nonresistant*, Nov. 10, 1841, p. 81; Thoreau, *Writings* (Boston, 1884-98), X, 147; *Lib.*, Feb. 11, 1853, p. 21; Pillsbury, p. 145.

Chapter 14, *Churchmen Come Out*

1. Gerrit Smith, *To the Friends of the Slave in the Town of Smithfield* (Peterboro, N.Y., 1844).

2. *Am. and For. AS Reporter*, Jan., 1845, p. 29.

3. Early Fox, *American Colonization Soc.* (Baltimore, 1919), p. 140.

4. Daniel A. Payne, *Recollections* (Nashville, 1888), pp. 50-51.

5. Foner I, 184.

6. New Eng. Yrly. Mtg. of Friends, *Testimony . . . Against Slavery* (Boston, 1847), p. 7.

7. *Lib.*, Aug. 13, 1841, p. 130; *Liberty Bell*, 1845, p. 98.

8. *Nonresistant*, Oct. 19, 1839; *North Star*, Dec. 3, 1847, p. 1, Dec. 29, 1848.

9. *Nonresistant*, Dec. 23, 1840, p. 96, Feb. 9, 1842, p. 9; *Lib.*, Feb. 19, 1841, p. 32.

10. Parker Pillsbury, *Acts of the Antislavery Apostles* (Concord, N.H., 1883), pp. 156ff.; *Nonresistant*, April 28, 1841;; *Lib.*, Oct. 1, 1841, p. 158, Oct. 21, 1842, p. 167.

11. Edm. Quincy to Anne W. Weston, July 16, 1840, MHS. The Tappanite come-outer Wm. Goodell, in his *Slavery and Antislavery* (N.Y., 1855), pp. 548–49, claimed that most AAS members probably remained in churches, especially liberal churches like the Universalist, Unitarian, Swedenborgian, and Friends.

12. *North Star*, May 26, 1848; *Lib.*, Oct. 8, 1841, p. 163.

13. *Lib.*, Feb. 2, 1849, p. 17, Dec. 21, 1849, p. 204.

14. (L. Tappan), *Proceedings of the Session of Broadway Tabernacle Against Lewis Tappan* (N.Y., 1839), p. 64; L. Tappan to G. Smith, Aug. 28, 1840, Syr. U.

15. L. Tappan to G. Smith, Sept. 9, 1843, Jan. 13, 1844, Syr. U.

16. Beriah Green, *Sermons and Other Discourses* (N.Y., 1860), pp. 229-37, 193.

17. Donald G. Mathews, *Slavery and Methodism* (Princeton, 1965), pp. 232–45; Roy Nicholson, *Wesleyan Methodism in the South* (Syr., 1933), pp. 27–29, 115, and *passim*.

18. Am. and For. AS Soc. *An. Report* (N.Y., 1850), p. 50.

19. Jas. T. Addison, *The Episcopal Ch. in the U.S.* (N.Y., 1951), pp. 192–93; John Jay, *Thoughts on the Duty of the Episcopal Ch. in Relation to Slavery* (N.Y., 1839); Madeleine Rice, *American Catholic Opinion in the Slavery Controversy* (N.Y., 1944), pp. 89, 152–54, 161. Neither of these two churches lent much assistance to the peace movement either.

20. *Colored Am.*, June 20, 1840.

21. Mass. AS Soc. *An. Report* (Boston, 1848), p. 70; Fee, *Non -Fellowship with Slaveholders* (N.Y., 1851), p. 52.

22. Pillsbury, *The Church as It Is*, pp. 50–51; Garr. III, 257, 275n., chap. 9; Rice, p. 152; *North Star*, Jan. 8, 1848; Weiss II, 118.

23. L. Tappan, *Reply to Charges Brought Against the Am. and For. AS Soc.* (London, 1852), p. 21; Am. and For. AS Soc., *Address* (N. Y., 1852), p. 10; Am. and For. AS Soc. *An. Report*, 1853, pp. 106, 114.

24. Clifford Griffin, "Abolitionists and the Benevolent Societies," *J. of Negro Hist.*, July, 1959, p. 210; *Lib.*, May 14, 1858, p. 78.

25. Am. and For. AS Soc. *Procs.* (N.Y., 1854), p. 6; Griffin, p. 216; *Am. Missionary*, June, 1857, pp. 131–33, June, 1858, pp. 130–32, July, 1859, p. 145.

26. L. Tappan to G. Smith, Jan. 19, 1842, Syr. U.

27. Clifton Johnson, *American Missionary Association* (thesis, U. of N. C., 1958), p. 186; *Am. Missionary*, Dec., 1859, p. 280; L. Tappan to S. S. Jocelyn, May 17, 1858, Fisk U.

28. *Am. Missionary*, Feb., 1857, p. 43.

29. *Am. Missionary*, May, 1859, p. 114, Oct., 1859, p. 234; Edwin Embree, "A Kentucky Crusader," *Am. Mercury*, Sept., 1931, p. 102.

30. *Am. Missionary*, Jan., 1860, p. 13; Fee, *Autobiog.* (Chicago, 1891), pp. 73, 28; Fee to G. Smith, Feb. 21, 1854, Syr. U.

31. L. Tappan to Fee, April 3, 1855, Berea College; Fee to G. Smith, May 18, 1855, Syr. U.

32. Fee, *Autobiog.*, p. 43; *Am. Missionary*, April, 1858, p. 89.

33. Fee wrote G. Smith, Jan. 4, 1856 (Syr. U.), "We have for months been talking about starting an academy and eventually look to a college—giving an education to all colors, classes, cheap and thorough." Fee reported in *Am. Missionary* (May, 1859, p. 114) that the trustees had already committed themselves to the creation of an interracial college.

34. *Am. Missionary*, Nov., 1858, pp. 269-70.

35. *Am. Missionary*, June, 1858, p. 139.

36. Nicholson, p. 70.

37. *Am. Missionary*, Dec., 1859, p. 277, Aug., 1858, p. 211.

38. Nicholson, pp. 95, 102–103.

39. *Am. Missionary*, March, 1860, p. 64.

40. Phillips, *Philosophy of the Abolition Movement* (N.Y., 1860), p. 25; *Procs. of the AS conv. Held at Rochester . . . 1857* (Auburn, N.Y., 1858), p. 57; L. Tappan, *Life*, p. 323.

41. *Lib.*, March 22, 1861, p. 47; *Procs. of the Conv. Held at Rochester*, p. 58; *North Star*, Feb. 8, 1850. In 1862 the Pennsylvania Antislavery Society at last conceded that the church was no longer the bulwark of slavery (Pa. AS Soc., "Minutes of the Exec. Comm.," entry for Oct. 25, 1862, H.S. of Pa.). In the same year, C. K. Whipple admitted that at last the great change of opinion in the country on slavery was making itself felt in the churches *(Lib.*, Oct. 31, 1862, p. 174).

42. Phillips, p. 22; L. C. Matlack, *The Antislavery Struggle and Triumph in the Methodist Episcopal Church* (N.Y., 1881), p. 144.

Chapter 15, *Noncooperation with Government*

1. Ballou, *Violations of the Federal Constitution* (Hopedale, Milford, Mass., 1861), pp. 28–29.

2. Ballou, *Christian Nonresistance* (Phila., 1846), pp. 216, 219, 227, 239. Garrison said few nonvoters were so as nonresistants; most nonvoters were so simply to oppose slavery *(Lib.,* June 6, 1856, p. 90). He said he himself refused to vote both because the Constitution sanctioned slavery and because it sanctioned war *(Lib.,* Sept. 29, 1854, p. 154).

3. *Lib.,* Nov. 3, 1848, p. 174.

4. L. Tappan, *Life,* p. 329.

5. L. Tappan wrote G. Smith, March 24, 1840 (Syr. U.), that, unlike Smith and Birney, he was not so much for politics as the chief work of abolitionists as he was for "moral suasion." Two years later Tappan was writing Smith (Feb. 7, 1842, Syr. U.) that he was voting the Liberty party ticket, but still did not "unite cordially and fully" with third party men. "Politics are so absorbing that little else is done by those who enter heartily in this scheme." Similarly Tappan wrote Samuel P. Chase, June 7, 1842 (H.S. of Pa.), that his sphere was not politics but "the religious and moral branches" of antislavery. By Dec. 9, 1843, however, Tappan proposed to G. Smith (LC) that all abolitionists rally under the Liberty party flag and all national antislavery societies be abandoned.

6. Garrison to H. C. Wright, Oct. 1, 1844, BPL.

7. Phillips, *The Constitution* (N.Y., 1844); Irving H. Bartlett, *Wendell Phillips* (Boston, 1961), pp. 122, 134.

8. *Lib.,* March 28, 1845, p. 51.

9. *National Reformer,* Nov., 1839, p. 163; Mass. AS Soc. *An. Report* (Boston, 1852), pp. 68–74.

10. Edm. Quincy, *An Examination of the Charges of Mr. John Scoble and Mr. Lewis Tappan* (Dublin, 1852), p. 9; Bartlett, p. 168; *Lib.,* Aug. 10, 1855, p. 127.

11. *Nonresistant,* Dec. 7, 1839; Garr. III, 100, 454–57, 485.

12. Maria Chapman, *Right and Wrong in Mass.* (Boston, 1840), p. 146; Wm. Goodell, *Slavery and Antislavery* (N.Y., 1855), pp. 519, 532–34; Garrison, *Principles and Mode of Action of the AAS* (London, 1853?), p. 12.

13. Goodell, pp. 532–33; *Platform of the AAS* (N.Y., 1853), p. 16; Mass. AS Soc. *An. Report* (Boston, 1846), p. 76.

14. *Lib.,* June 27, 1845, p. 103, July 7, 1848, p. 105, July 18, 1845, p. 115; Mass. AS Soc. *An. Report* (Boston, 1850), pp. 94–95.

15. *Ibid.*, pp. 14–15; Louis Filler, *The Crusade Against Slavery* (N.Y., 1960), p. 175; Abel and Klingberg, pp. 239–41.

16. *Nat. AS Stand.*, Jan. 14, 1847, p. 130, April 22, 1847, p. 186; Mass. AS Soc. *An. Report* (Boston, 1846), pp. 4, 8–9.

17. *Ibid.*, pp. 48–49; *Lib.*, July 4, 1845, p. 106; Garrison to May, July 17, 1845, BPL.

18. New Eng. Yrly. Mtg. of Friends *Testimony . . . Against Slavery* (Boston, 1847), p. 4; *Nat. AS Stand.*, May 13, 1847, p. 197, March 4, 1847, p. 158, Jan. 14, 1847, p. 130; *North Star*, Jan. 21, 1848.

19. *Nat. AS Stand.*, March 4, 1847, p. 158; Am. and For. AS Soc. *An. Report* (N.Y., 1848), p. 13; Garr. III, 211–15; Betty Fladeland, *Jas. Gillespie Birney* (Ithaca, 1955), pp. 262–65; L. Tappan to G. Smith, Nov. 18, 28, 1848, Syr. U.

20. Abel and Klingberg, pp. 220, 223, 241; *Oberlin Evangelist*, May 13, 1846, p. 79, June 9, 1847, pp. 91–92, Aug. 19, 1846, p. 135, July 21, 1847, p. 118.

21. *Advocate of Peace*, Jan.–Feb., 1847, p. 6, June, 1846, p. 130, July–Aug., 1847, p. 85; Wm. Jay, *Review of the Causes and Consequences of the Mexican War* (2d ed., Boston, 1849; no indication in the copies at Yale and NYPL when 1st ed. was published). Jay's book was written for an American Peace Society competition, and it was offered the prize provided Jay would expunge its censure of the Whig party, but he refused. Jay was president of the American Peace Society from 1848 till his death in 1858.

22. *Oberlin Evangelist*, Feb. 3, 1847, p. 21.

23. Parker, *A Sermon of War* (Boston, 1846), pp. 7, 39; Moorfield Storey, *Charles Sumner* (Boston, 1900), p. 48.

24. Mass. AS Soc. *An. Report* (Boston, 1847), pp. 58–59; Garrison to H. C. Wright, June 1, 1846, BPL.

25. *Nat. AS Stand.*, Jan. 14, 1847, p. 130, July 2, 1846, pp. 17–18; *North Star*, Aug. 31, 1849.

26. Mass. AS Soc. *An. Report*, 1847, p. 93; Am. and For. AS Soc. *An. Report* (N.Y., 1848), p. 7, (1847), p. 15; *Nat. AS Stand.*, Sept. 24, 1846, p. 66; *Friends Rev.*, Jan. 29, 1848, pp. 301–302.

27. *Advocate of Peace*, July–Aug., 1847, p. 83; Clayton Ellsworth, "Am. Churches and the Mexican War," *Am. Hist. Rev.*, Jan., 1940, pp. 314, 320–21, 326.

28. *Nat. AS Stand.*, Feb. 25, 1847, p. 155; Weiss II, 78.

29. *Nat. AS Stand.*, Feb. 4, 1847, p. 143; *Am. AS Almanac for 1847*, no paging, near end.

30. *Advocate of Peace*, Oct., 1846, p. 243; Merle Curti, *Am. Peace*

Crusade (Durham, 1929), pp. 152–53, 156; Foner I, 227, II, 13; *Lib.*, Dec. 7, 1849, p. 194; B. Green to G. Smith, Nov. 21, 1846, Syr. U.; Abel and Klingberg, p. 230.

31. National Conv. of Colored People *Procs.* (Troy, N.Y., 1847), pp. 16–17.

32. *Nat. AS Stand.*, Jan. 14, 1847, p. 130.

33. *Ibid.*, June 18, 1846, p. 11, June 25, 1846, p. 15, Jan. 14, 1847, p. 130; Cassius M. Clay, *Life* (Cincinnati, 1886), I, 110.

34. Am. and For. AS Soc. *An. Report* (N.Y., 1847), p. 5; Fee, *Autobiog.* (Chicago, 1891), p. 127; *Nat. AS Stand.*, Aug. 20, 1846, p. 45.

35. *Nonresistant*, June 15, 1839.

36. *Nat. AS Stand.*, Oct. 22, 1846, p. 82; Rogers, *Collection* (Concord, N.H., 1847), p. 308.

37. Garrison to Eliz. Pease, June 20, 1849, BPL; Oliver Johnson, *The Abolitionists Vindicated* (Worcester, 1887), p. 24; Bartlett, p. 243.

38. *North Star*, Jan. 5, 1849.

39. *Lib.*, July 21, 1854, p. 116.

40. Thoreau, *Writings* (Boston, 1884–1898), X, 143–44, 149.

41. *Nonresistant*, March 2, 1839; *Lib.*, May 21, 1841, p. 83; *Oberlin Evangelist*, June 23, 1841, p. 103; Colored National Conv. *Report of the Procs.* (Rochester, 1848), pp. 10, 16.

42. *Nat. AS Stand.*, Jan. 14, 1847, p. 130.

43. *Lib.*, Jan. 27, 1843, p. 16; Bronson Alcott, *Journals* (Boston, 1938), pp. 150–51; *North Star*, July 28, 1848.

44. *Lib.*, Dec. 16, 1853, p. 195; W. W. Brown, *The Black Man* (Boston, 1863), p. 256.

45. Oswald Garrison Villard, *John Brown* (Boston, 1910), pp. 134–35. Two black California businessmen refused to pay their taxes in protest against their not being allowed to vote, and a tax collector seized goods from them in payment. *Lib.*, July 3, 1857, p. 108.

46. For parallels between nonviolent direct-action methods on behalf of Negroes and on behalf of women, see Carleton Mabee, "Women and Negroes March," *Midwest Quart.*, Winter, 1965, pp. 163–74.

47. Thoreau, pp. 149–50.

Chapter 16, *Underground Railroad*

1. Jas. W. C. Pennington, *The Fugitive Blacksmith* (London, 1849), p. 30. In 1843, Pennington attended the World Peace Convention. In 1844 he wrote his master that while a slave under his control he had "deemed it my duty to get out of your hands by peaceable means"

(ibid., p. 79). In 1845, while still a fugitive himself, he said in a sermon that he did not wish to be defended by daggers (Pennington, *A Two Years' Absence,* Hartford, 1845, p. 4). By 1851 his freedom had been purchased.

2. *North Star,* Sept. 5, 1850; *Nat. AS Stand.,* Oct. 21, 1841, p. 78.

3. Henry Bibb, *Narrative* (N.Y., 1849), p. 177; Wm. Still, *Underground Railroad* (Phila., 1872), p. 517; clipping (1837?) in L. Tappan, Journal, p. 119, LC; *Nat. AS Stand.,* April 3, 1851, p. 179; *Lib.,* May 27, 1853, p. 93.

4. *Lib.,* June 22, 1855, p. 99; *J. of Negro Hist.,* 1926, p. 140; Lloyd Hennings, *American Missionary Assoc.* (thesis, Oberlin College, 1933), p. 92.

5. R. C. Smedley, *Hist. of the Underground Railroad* (Lancaster , Pa., 1883), pp. 276–77; AMA *An. Report,* 1861, p. 28.

6. *Lib.,* Aug. 17, 1849, p. 130; Garr. III, 324; Douglass, *Narrative* (Boston, 1845), pp. 101–102.

7. Theodore Parker, *The Boston Kidnapping* (Boston, 1852), p. 60; *Lib.,* May 28, 1858, p. 88; Still, p. 448.

8. Ballou, *Violations of the Federal Constitution* (Hopedale, Mass., 1861), pp. 17–18; Larry Gara, *Liberty Line, The Legend of the Underground Railroad* (Lexington, Ky., 1961), p. 193.

9. Colored National Conv. *Procs.* (Rochester, 1848), pp. 7, 14; *North Star,* May 19, 1848; Am. and For. AS Soc. *An. Report* (N.Y., 1848), p. 7; *Lib.,* Dec. 8, 1843, p. 193.

10. *Mirror of Liberty,* Jan., 1839, p. 20, July, 1838, p. 7.

11. Vigilance Comm. of Phila. "Minute Book," 1839–44, H.S. of Pa.; Smedley, pp. 355–58; Still, p. 711; Robert Purvis, *A Tribute to the Memory of Thos. Shipley* (Phila., 1836), pp. 9, 13. Note that when Purvis' father-in-law, James Forten, the sail manufacturer, died in 1842, Purvis praised him for fighting in the Revolutionary War, saying that by doing so Forten had given "the best evidence of his love for his country" (Purvis, *Remarks on the Life and Character of James Forten,* Phila., 1842, p. 11). Purvis' second wife was a Friend, and *Friends Intelligencer* (April 23, 1898, pp. 294, 299) reports his burial in a Friends burying ground. Henry J. Cadbury ("Negro Membership in the Soc. of Friends," *J. of Negro Hist.,* 1936, pp. 201–202) wrote that Purvis "was very likely a Friend, and certainly closely associated with Friends." I know of no solid evidence that he ever became a Friend and much to suggest that he did not. His funeral was preached by a Unitarian minister in a Unitarian church.

12. C. K. Whipple, *Nonresistance Applied to the Internal Defense of a Community* (Boston, 1860), pp. 17–18; L. Tappan, Journal, July 28, 1836, LC; *Emancipator,* June 1, 1837, p. 18.

13. *Colored Am.,* March 4, 1837, pp. 2–3, June 9, 1838, p. 61, March 3, 1838, p. 27, Aug. 19, 1837, p. 2.

14. *Colored Am.,* Aug. 26, 1837, p. 3, Sept. 9, 1837, p. 1; Jan. 12, 1839, p. 2; May 18, 1839, p. 2. Like some other Tappanites, Cornish and C. B. Ray had conventional rather than nonresistant views on war.

15. *National Reformer,* Oct., 1838, p. 23; *Lib.,* Aug. 6, 1836, p. 127; N.Y. [City] Comm. of Vigilance *First An. Report* (N.Y., 1837), pp. 73–77; *Colored Am.,* Dec. 9, 1837, p. 3, Feb. 3, 1838, p. 15. The debate was continued into a second session. Evidently supporting nonresistance were also the talented and tactful Philip A. Bell, who had recently been the proprietor of the *Colored Am.,* and Dr. John Brown, a lecturer on chemistry. Opposing nonresistance were Wm. P. Johnson, city agent of the *Colored Am.,* and the bright students Garnet and Thos. S. Sidney. Editor Cornish scolded Sidney, whom he called "one of the most talented youth of the age," for seeming at another meeting to favor violent "means of bodily emancipation" and giving a "bloody speech." Sidney denied it, saying that he favored, at least in working for Negro "civil rights," only the weapons of "truth and argument" *(Colored Am.,* March 3, 1838, p. 27, April 12, 1838, p. 46).

16. *Mirror of Liberty,* July, 1838, p. 5; *ibid.,* Aug., 1838, in Bella Gross, *Clarion Call* (N.Y., 1947), p. 38. For further hints of Ruggles' nonviolence, see Ruggles, *An Antidote* (N.Y., 1838), pp. 17–18, 20.

17. *Lib.,* June 6, 1851, p. 91.

18. Still; (Samuel May, Jr.), *The Fugitive Slave Law,* N.Y., 1861. Neither May's report nor Still's shows signs of being biased in favor of nonviolence. In fact, both clearly indicate respect for those who used violence. No doubt both also reflect the human tendency to notice violent incidents more than nonviolent ones simply because violent ones are likely to seem more exciting. Samuel May, Jr., although a cousin of Samuel J. May of Syracuse and an agent of the Mass. AS Soc., was nevertheless not a Garrisonian nonresistant.

19. Levi Coffin, *Reminiscences* (Cincinnati, 1880), pp. 112–20.

20. Eliz. Buffum Chace, *Antislavery Reminiscences* (Central Falls, R.I., 1891), pp. 34–36.

21. *Lib.,* Dec. 10, 1852, p. 198; Smedley, pp. 67–70.

22. Coffin, pp. 366–73; Harriet Martineau, *The Martyr Age* (Boston,

1839), pp. 40–41; *Lib.*, Aug. 6, 1836, p. 127.

23. Kate Pickard, *The Kidnapped* (Syr., 1856), pp. 389, 284, 297, 409; Still, pp. 31, 34.

24. Smedley, p. 173; *Lib.*, July 20, 1849, p. 115; Eliza Wigham, *The Antislavery Cause* (London, 1863), pp. 81–86.

25. Garr. IV, 252; Sarah Bradford, *Harriet Tubman* (N.Y., 1961), pp. 44–45; Still, p. 625.

26. *Lib.*, Oct. 14, 1853, p. 162; Still, p. 634.

27. Alexander M. Ross, *Recollections* (Toronto, 1875), pp. 9–11, 41, 8; Ross, *Memoirs* (Toronto, 1893), pp. 87–89; *Iowa J. of Hist. and Politics*, 1924, pp. 430–36.

28. *Lib.*, Feb. 2, 1849, p. 19, Feb. 16, 1849, p. 27.

29. Still, pp. 403–406, 536–38; *Lib.*, July 11, 1851, p. 112, Feb. 22, 1850, p. 31.

30. May, *Some Recollections* (Boston, 1869), pp. 301–302.

31. Still, pp. 86–92; AAS *An. Report* (N.Y., 1856), p. 29.

32. *Lib.*, July 25, 1845, p. 120; (Sam. May, Jr.), p. 65.

33. *North Star*, June 15, 1849; Anna Hallowell, *Jas. and Lucretia Mott* (Boston, 1884), pp. 310–11; Garrison to Eliz. Pease, June 20, 1849, BPL; Still, pp. 83–86.

Chapter 17, *Resisting the Fugitive Slave Law*

1. *North Star*, Oct. 24, 1850; Mass. AS Soc. *An. Report* (Boston, 1851), p. 103; *Am. Missionary*, Oct., 1850, p. 100; Nina Tiffany, *Samuel E. Sewall* (Boston, 1898), p. 79; Am. and For. AS Soc. *An. Report* (N.Y., 1851), pp. 17–18.

2. *Lib.*, Dec. 13, 1850, p. 199, Oct. 4, 1850 p. 158; Wm. Still, *Underground Railroad* (Phila., 1872), p. 370.

3. Powell said that his family's entire property at the sailors' home was destroyed during the 1863 draft riots and that he and his family had been prisoners of a mob for six hours. "As a man of peace," Powell wrote Garrison at that time, "I have religiously, and upon principles eternal as the heavens, never armed myself with deadly weapons of defense, and thus have been at the mercy of the blood-thirsty vandals" (*Lib.*, July 24, 1863, p. 118).

4. *Nat. AS Stand.*, Oct. 10, 1850, pp. 78–79. The following is an analysis of forty-seven declarations of meetings or organizations advocating disobedience to the 1850 fugitive slave law during the six months after the passage of the law, as reported in the Boston *Lib.*, Rochester *North Star*, New York *Nat. AS Stand.*, or the Salem (Ohio) *Antislavery Bugle.* Eleven statements on the whole favored violence

in disobeying the law, eight favored nonviolence, and twenty-eight did not make a clear decision. Comparing the states, Pennsylvania had the clearest record for nonviolence and New York for violence. Comparing declarations that were primarily black in origin with those that were not, the black ones were more violent.

5. Booker T. Washington, *Frederick Douglass* (Phila., 1906), p. 110; *North Star*, Aug. 4, 1848, Aug. 10, 1849; *Nat. AS Stand.*, Nov. 28, 1850, p. 107; *Frederick Douglass Paper*, Aug. 20, 1852.

6. *Lib.*, Oct. 25, 1850, p. 171, Sept. 27, 1850, p. 154.

7. *Lib.*, Oct. 11, 1850, p. 162.

8. May, *Some Recollections* (Boston, 1869), pp. 361–62.

9. *Lib.*, Dec. 13, 1850, p. 199.

10. *Lib.*, Jan. 10, 1851, p. 7; Am. and For. AS Soc. *An. Report* (N.Y., 1851), pp. 51, 90; *Nat. AS Stand.*, May 15, 1851, p. 202.

11. *Ibid.*, Oct. 10, 1850, p. 79, April 10, 1851, p. 182; *Pa. Freeman*, March 4, 1852, p. 38, Nov. 6, 1851, p. 2; *Lib.*, Oct. 11, 1850, p. 163, Feb. 6, 1852, p. 22.

12. *Lib.* Nov. 8, 1850, p. 178; Chas. Beecher, *Duty of Disobedience to Wicked Laws* (Newark, N.J., 1851), pp. 21–22; Still, pp. 736–37; *Nat. AS Stand.*, Oct. 31, 1850, p. 91.

13. *Lib.*, Nov. 8, 1850, p. 178, Nov. 22, 1850, p. 188, Feb. 7, 1851, p. 24, *Pa. Freeman*, Nov. 6, 1851, p. 1; Sumner, *The Antislavery Enterprise* (London, 1855), p. 27; *Nat. AS Stand.*, Oct. 10, 1850, p. 79; Am. and For. AS Soc., *The Fugitive Slave Bill: Its History* (N.Y., 1850), p. 21.

14. Wm. C. Whitcomb, *Discourse on the Recapture of Fugitive Slaves* (Boston, 1850), p. 34. *Lib.*, June 16, 1854, p. 95, June 23, 1854, p. 98; *Nat. AS Stand.*, Oct. 24, 1850, p. 87.

15. *Lib.*, Oct. 11, 1850, p. 164, April 11, 1851, p. 59; *Pa. Freeman*, May 20, 1852; *Nat. AS Stand.*, Nov. 28, 1850, p. 107, April 10, 1851, p. 182.

16. *Lib.*, Sept. 27, 1850, p. 155, May 23, 1851, p. 83, Jan. 31, 1851, p. 20; *North Star*, Oct. 24, 1850; *Nat. AS Stand.*, Nov. 28, 1850, p. 107.

17. Bowditch I, 206; *Lib.*, Nov. 1, 1850, p. 174; Jan. 31, 1851, p. 20, Oct. 31, 1851, p. 174, Weiss II, 95–103; *Nat. AS Stand.*, Nov. 28, 1850, p. 106, Dec. 5, 1850, p. 110.

18. Still, pp. 534–39; Francis Jackson to Edm. Quincy, Feb. 23, 1859, MHS.

19. R. C. Smedley, *Hist. of the Underground Railroad* (Lancaster, Pa., 1883), pp. 115–30; Still, pp. 348–68; Frederick Douglass, *Life and Times* (N.Y., 1968), p. 282.

20. *Lib.*, Sept. 19, 1851, p. 151, Sept. 26, 1851, p. 155; Pa. AS Soc. *An. Report* (Phila., 1851), p. 70.

21. *Pa. Freeman,* Dec. 25, 1851, pp. 2–3.

22. Still, pp. 736–39.

23. *North Star,* Jan. 16, 1851.

24. Mass. AS Soc. *An. Report* (Boston, 1852), pp. 10–11; Am. and For. AS Soc., *An Address* (N.Y., 1852), p. 8; *Lib.,* Feb. 21, 1851, p. 30.

25. *Memoir of Samuel J. May* (Boston, 1873), p. 221; *Lib.,* Oct. 12, 1855, p. 162; O. B. Frothingham, *Gerrit Smith* (N.Y., 1878), p. 236; May, pp. 377–78; Mass. AS Soc. *An. Report,* 1852, pp. 10–11, 30–35, 86–87.

26. Charlotte Forten, *Journal* (N.Y., 1953), p. 36; Bowditch I, 269–70.

27. Higginson, *Cheerful Yesterdays* (Boston, 1898), pp. 148, 145, 154; *Lib.,* June 2, 1854, p. 86; Weiss II, 131.

28. AAS *An. Report* (N.Y., 1855), p. 25; *Frederick Douglass Paper,* June 2, 1854; *Lib.,* June 2, 1854, p. 86.

29. *Lib.,* June 9, 1854, p. 90; Weiss II, 135.

30. *Lib.,* July 7, 1854, p. 106, June 9, 1854, p. 90, June 30, 1854, p. 102.

31. Foster to wife, Oct. 31, 1854, Am. Antiq. Soc.; Worcester *Mass. Spy,* Nov. 1, 1854; *Lib.,* Nov. 3, 1854, p. 174. For details of Foster's subsequent trial and imprisonment on the charge of inciting a riot in the Butman affair, see Worcester *Mass. Spy,* Nov. 22, 29, 1854. Foster refused to cooperate with his arrest, refused to give bail, and was literally carried to jail by officers *(Lib.,* Nov. 10, 1854, p. 179). He also refused to testify in his own defense *(Lib.,* Dec. 1, 1854, p. 190). After Foster's arrest in Worcester and Higginson's arrest about the same time for his part in the Burns affair in Boston, H. C. Wright declared that Foster and Higginson were the most popular men in Worcester *(Lib.,* Jan. 5, 1855, p. 2).

32. (Samuel May, Jr.), *The Fugitive Slave Law* (N.Y., 1861), pp. 103–107; J. Jeffrey Auer, ed., *Antislavery and Disunion* (N.Y., 1963), chap. 5; *Am. Missionary,* June, 1859, pp. 131–32; *Anglo-African Mag.,* July, 1859, pp. 209–16.

33. Anna Hallowell, *Jas. and Lucretia Mott* (Boston, 1884), pp. 387–91. The executive committee of the Pennsylvania Antislavery Society, of which Mrs. Mott was a member, decided to assume the expenses of the Dangerfield case (Pa. AS Soc., Minutes of the Exec. Comm., entry for April 13, 1859, H.S. of Pa.).

Chapter 18, *John Brown's Raid*

1. O. B. Frothingham, *Gerrit Smith* (N.Y., 1878), p. 233.

2. *Lib.,* July 27, 1855, p. 120, Sept. 14, 1855, p. 145, Jan. 4, 1856, p. 2.

3. Higginson, *John Greenleaf Whittier* (N.Y., 1902), p. 78; Lloyd

Hennings, *American Missionary Association* (thesis, Oberlin College, 1933), pp. 103–106, 196–97; Oswald Garrison Villard, *John Brown* (Boston, 1910), pp. 134–35; AMA *An. Report*, 1855, p. 82.

4. Garr. III, 439; Frothingham, p. 236; Garrison to May, March 21, 1856, BPL; L. Tappan to G. Smith, May 22, 1856, Syr. U.

5. L. M. Child to "Dear friends," July 9, 1856, Cornell U.; Weiss II, 190; G. Smith to Wm. Goodell, Aug. 15, 1856, NYPL; *Lib.*, Jan. 19, 1855, p. 11, Feb. 2, 1855, p. 18, Aug. 13, 1858, p. 132; *Procs. of a Conv. of the Colored Men of Ohio* (Cincinnati, 1858), p. 17.

6. Washington, *Frederick Douglass* (Phila., 1906), pp. 186–88; *Lib.*, Nov. 11, 1859, p. 177; Phila. *Press*, Oct. 29, 1860; Phillips, *Speeches* (2d ser., Boston, 1891), p. 308.

7. Thoreau, *Journal* (Boston, 1949), XII, 421, 437; Thoreau, *Writings* (Boston, 1884–1898), X, 227; Bronson Alcott, *Journals*, (Boston, 1938), pp. 315–16, 322–23; Moncure Conway, *Autobiog.*, (Boston, 1904), I, 299, 302; Philip and Elizabeth Wright, *Elizur Wright*, (Chicago, 1937), p. 337.

8. *Practical Christian*, Nov. 26, 1859, pp. 61–64, Dec. 10, 1859, pp. 65, 68. In 1855, Foster had already explained that he was no longer a nonresistant on principle but simply on expediency. He could protect himself better without resort to violence than with it, he said, but those who could not should use violence (*Lib.*, March 30, 1855, p. 50).

9. John Demos, "The Antislavery Movement and the Problem of Violent Means," *New Eng. Quart.*, 1964, p. 502; C. Vann Woodward, "John Brown's Private War," in Daniel Aaron, *America in Crisis* (N.Y., 1952), p. 122.

10. H. C. Wright, *Natick Resolution* (Boston, 1859), pp. 27–28; Samuel J. May, *Address Delivered before the Am. Peace Soc.* (Boston, 1860), p. 19; L. M. Child, *Letters* (Boston, 1883), pp. 104, 118; *Practical Christian*, Dec. 24, 1859, p. 70; Child to "Miss Osgood," Dec. 25, 1859, Cornell U.; Pa. AS Soc. "Minutes of the Exec. Comm.," entry for Feb. 1, 1860, H.S. of Pa.

11. Garr. III, 489; C. K. Whipple, *The Nonresistance Principle with Particular Application to the Help of Slaves* (Boston, 1860), pp. 21–24, 10.

12. *Nat. AS Stand.*, Nov. 3, 1860, p. 3; Jas. Redpath, *Echoes of Harper's Ferry* (Boston, 1860), p. 304; *Friends Rev.*, Oct. 29, 1859, p. 120; Thos. Drake, *Quakers and Slavery* (New Haven, 1950), p. 192; "John Brown among the Quakers," *Palimpset*, 1960, p. 43.

13. *Am. Missionary*, Dec., 1859, p. 280, Jan., 1860, pp. 13–14.

14. Ballou, *Violations of the Federal Constitution* (Hopedale, Milford, Mass., 1861), pp. 18–19, 43–44; Charles Northend, *Elihu Burritt* (N.Y., 1879), pp. 149–50; Burritt, *Ten Minute Talks* (Boston, 1873), pp. 46–49; Hugh Bailey, *Hinton Rowan Helper* (University, Ala., 1965), p. 54; W. H. Furness, *Put Up Thy Sword* (Boston, 1860), pp. 14–15, 21.

15. *Lib.*, Dec. 16, 1859, p. 198. Ballou *(Autobiog.*, Lowell, Mass., 1896, pp. 420–21) regarded this speech by Garrison as a desertion of his nonviolence. Merle Curti *(Peace or War*, N.Y., 1936, pp. 57–58) and recent biographers of Garrison have agreed with Ballou. It seems to me they exaggerate the extent of Garrison's change, as this chapter and the one following make clear.

16. *Lib.*, Jan. 4, 1861, p. 4, Feb. 15, 1861, p. 27; *Friends Rev.*, Feb. 2, 1861, p. 350.

17. *Lib.*, Feb. 15, 1861, pp. 26–27.

Chapter 19, *Peacemen Face War*

1. Merle Curti, *The Learned Blacksmith* (N.Y., 1937), p. 139; *Lib.*, Aug. 28, 1863, p. 140, Jan. 20, 1865, p. 12; *Friends Rev.*, Jan. 2, 1864, p. 280. Blanchard described conscription as "criminal compulsion of a person to enter an anti-Christian murderous service" *(Lib.*, April 8, 1864, p. 58). He made a survey to determine whether those who had signed the Burritt peace pledge were holding to it during the Civil War, and decided that only three out of eighty were doing so (Curti, *Peace or War*, N.Y., 1936, p. 60).

2. *Lib.*, June 7, 1861, p. 91, Jan. 22, 1864, p. 13, May 16, 1862, p. 79, Sept. 18, 1863, p. 152, June 6, 1862, pp. 90, 92, July 26, 1861, p. 120; Geo. Frederickson, *The Inner Civil War* (N.Y., 1965), pp. 123–24; Alfred Love, *Appeal In Vindication of Peace Principles* (Phila., 1862), p. 12.

3. *Lib.*, April 26, 1861, p. 67. However, by 1863, when Brown was promoting Negro enlistment, Negro Robert Morris was refusing to encourage enlistments while Negroes were not treated equally in the armed forces *(Lib.*, June 5, 1863, p. 91). For hints of similar Negro refusals, see Jas. McPherson, *The Negro's Civil War*, (N.Y., 1965), pp. 29, 177.

4. *Lib.*, March 20, 1863, p. 47; *Douglass Monthly*, April, 1863, p. 817.

5. Beman to ed., April 2, 1863, clipping, *Anglo-African Weekly*, Beman Scrapbook II, 4; Beman to ed., Feb. 4, 1864, clipping, *Anglo-African Weekly*, Beman Scrapbook II, 39, Yale U.; *Procs. of the Nat. Conv. of Colored Men* (Boston, 1864).

6. *Nat. AS Stand.*, July 4, 1863, p. 2; Wm. Still, *Underground*

Railroad (Phila., 1872), p. 740; *Lib.*, April 17, 1863, p. 62.

7. *Nat. AS Stand.*, June 20, 1863, p. 3.

8. *Am. Missionary*, July, 1862, p. 164.

9. *Advocate of Peace*, July–Aug., 1861, pp. 283–87, 274–76, May–June, 1863, p. 278; L. Tappan, *Life*, pp. 362–63, 375.

10. *Advocate of Peace*, July–Aug., 1861, p. 269. Similarly the American Peace Society said, we, like the Quakers, are required to "support the government in every way consistent with our principles" (*ibid.*, May–June, 1862, p. 88).

11. *Advocate of Peace*, Sept.–Oct., 1861, p. 303, March–April, 1863, pp. 254–56.

12. *Am. Missionary*, June, 1861, p. 130, Oct., 1861, p. 227.

13. *Principia*, Oct. 12, 1861, July 30, 1863, Feb. 11, 1864.

14. AAS *Procs. . . . at its Third Decade* (N.Y., 1864), p. 145; *Nat. AS Stand.*, July 4, 1863, p. 2; *Lib.*, March 25, 1864, p. 50; J. M. McKim, *An Address* (Phila., 1862), p. 16. An unsigned article in *Nat. AS Stand.* (June 20, 1863, p. 3), commenting on McKim's help in raising a black regiment, said McKim, "though an eminently peaceable man, is not a peace-man in any technical sense of the word."

15. *Library of the World's Best Lit.* (N.Y., 1902), XXIII, 9262.

16. Moncure Conway, *Autobiog.* (Boston, 1904), I, 335, 436; Frederickson, pp. 177–78.

17. Edward N. Wright, *Conscientious Objectors in the Civil War* (N.Y., 1961), pp. 209, 186; Curti, *The Learned Blacksmith*, p. 139; Garr. IV, 37; *Friends Rev.*, Jan. 4, 1862, p. 280.

18. *Lib.*, Feb. 15, 1861, p. 27, April 12, 1861, p. 58, May 24, 1861, p. 82.

19. *Lib.*, May 10, 1861, p. 76, Sept. 27, 1861, p. 156, March 1, 1864, p. 44, Sept. 16, 1864, p. 52, July 31, 1863, p. 124. By 1841, Brigham had become an antislavery come-outer from a Baptist church (Brigham, *Voice from Nazareth, A Letter . . . in Reply to a War Sermon*, Plymouth, Mass., 1865, p. 33). During the war Brigham refused to take any part in it, whether through his money, his influence, or his vote. In doing so, he said he stood "almost alone" (*ibid.*, pp. 7, 34). Extracts from *ibid.* were published in *Lib.*, Nov. 17, 1865, p. 184.

20. *Lib.*, Aug. 30, 1861, p. 140.

21. John L. Thomas, *The Liberator* (Boston, 1963), p. 422.

22. *Lib.*, June 14, 1861, p. 94, July 31, 1863, p. 122, July 12, 1861, p. 111, Feb. 7, 1862, p. 21; Garrison to O. Johnson, July 5, 1863, BPL; L. Tappan to G. Smith, Dec. 3, 1861, Syr. U.

23. Higginson, *Contemporaries* (Boston, 1899), p. 247; *Lib.*, Oct. 31, 1862, pp. 175–76, Aug. 26, 1864, p. 140, Oct. 30, 1863, p. 175, May 9, 1862,

p. 74, July 8, 1864, p. 112. When Samuel May, Jr., an agent of the Massachusetts Antislavery Society, publicly called for enlistments, a county antislavery society official, Joseph A. Howland of Worcester, condemned him for it, saying May stood "alone of the old guard" abolitionists in calling for enlistments (*Lib.*, Aug. 22, 1862, p. 136).

24. *Congressional Globe*, 1864, p. 575; *Lib.*, Sept. 6, 1861, p. 144, Aug. 23, 1861, p. 136, May 10, 1861, p. 74.

25. Garr. II, 231; *Lib.*, July 24, 1863, p. 118, May 6, 1864, p. 76.

26. *Lib.*, Sept. 19, 1862, p. 150, Sept. 26, 1862, p. 155, Oct. 31, 1862, p. 176.

27. *Lib.*, June 24, 1864, p. 102, July 8, 1864, p. 112. Among those present were the Quaker Garrisonians Thos. Whitson and Alfred Love, the Garrisonian Purvis, and Editor Theodore Tilton of the N.Y. *Independent*.

28. *Lib.*, Sept. 19, 1862, p. 150. J. Thomas (p. 422) and Curti (*Peace or War*, p. 58) consider Garrison's advice to nonresistants to pay the fee a compromise of his peace principles, as if approval of paying such fees had not long been a part of his principles.

29. Ballou, *Hist. of the Hopedale Community* (Lowell, Mass., 1897), pp. 317–20. Later, however, Ballou regretted his encouraging J. L. Heywood to pay the fee, having come to believe that his refusal to pay it even at the cost of his life would have been a clearer testimony against war (Ballou, *Autobiog.*, Lowell, Mass., 1896, pp. 449–50).

30. Benj. Thomas, *Theodore Weld* (New Brunswick, 1950), p. 245; AAS *Procs. . . . at its Third Decade*, p. 11; Chas. S. Weld to Theodore Weld, June 2, Sept. 25, 1862, U. of Mich. Charles was a selective conscientious objector only, not rejecting all war. He considered going to Mexico to fight for Maximillian.

31. Garr. IV, 84. Garr. IV, though written by Garrison's conscientious objector sons, Francis and Wendell, describes George's enlistment but not their own refusal to train or serve. Other biographies of Garrison, often heavily dependent on the sons' biography, do the same. Garrison's daughter, Fanny Garrison Villard, in her *William Lloyd Garrison on Nonresistance* (N.Y., 1924), p. 19, said: "My father's nonresistant principles were fervently embraced by all his children except his eldest son," that is, George, but she did not describe their response to the Civil War. As far as I know, the fact of Wendell's being a drafted conscientious objector has been buried in the files of the *Liberator* from Wendell's generation till now. I believe that the common failure to mention the two war-objecting Garrison sons and Garrison's support of their position, plus E. N. Wright's failure to

give non-Quaker abolitionist war objectors due consideration, plus the failure to recognize the space given in the *Liberator* to antiwar statements have contributed to a general failure to recognize the modest degree of nonviolence that persisted in the non-Quaker abolitionist movement through the war. Peter Brock, *Radical Pacifists in Antebellum America*, Princeton, 1968, which I have seen only since the text of this book was completed, helps to correct the record for the Garrisonians, but underplays the Tappanites.

32. Garrison to Francis Gardner, Jan. 13, 1864, BPL. J. Thomas (p. 422) gives half a sentence to this incident.

33. *Lib.*, Aug. 21, 1863, p. 134.

34. Love, p. 6; *Lib.*, Aug. 21, 1863, p. 136, Jan. 29, 1864, pp. 20, 18.

35. *Lib.*, Nov. 6, 1863, p. 179, April 1, 1864, pp. 56, 54.

36. *Lib.*,; April 8, 1864, p. 54; *Friends Rev.*, Feb. 27, 1864, p. 409; E. N. Wright, pp. 128–30.

37. *Lib.*, April 1, 1864, p. 54, July 8, 1864, p. 112.

38. *Congressional Globe,* 1864, pp. 255, 574–77; E. N. Wright, pp. 79–83. The law as adopted in Feb., 1864, provided that in the case of conscientious objectors paying the $300 fee, the money would be used for the benefit of sick and wounded soldiers. The law was revised again by July, 1864, with the provisions for objectors unchanged.

39. *Friends Rev.*, Feb. 27, 1864, p. 408, July 30, 1864, pp. 760–61; E. N. Wright, pp. 217, 165–66, 124–25; Cyrus Pringle, *Record of a Quaker Conscience* (N.Y., 1918), pp. 76–78; Jesse Macy, *Autobiog.* (Springfield, Ill., 1933), pp. 46–49.

40. Roy Nicholson, *Wesleyan Methodism in the South* (Syr., 1933), pp. 107–111; *Friends Rev.*, Nov. 21, 1863, pp. 178–82; N.C. Yrly. Mtg. of Friends, *Narrative of the Cruelties Inflicted Upon Friends of N.C. Yearly Meeting* (London, 1868), pp. 10–22; Fernando Cartland, *Southern Heroes, or The Friends in War Time* (Cambridge, 1895), pp. 305–306, 183–84, and *passim.;* E. N. Wright, pp. 171, 205.

41. *Friends Rev.*, June 27, 1863, p. 686. Higginson, in the *Independent* (Vol. 59 [1905], p. 1315), said that Whittier wavered in his nonresistance during the war as Garrison did not, and gave as an illustration that Whittier decorated his study with a bayonet from the field of Antietam, as Garrison would not.

42. Anna Hallowell, *Jas. and Lucretia Mott* (Boston, 1884), pp. 404, 407–408; AAS *Procs. . . . at its Third Decade*, pp. 64–67; *Lib.*, May 20, 1864, p. 82.

43. *Lib.*, May 24, 1861, p. 84; *Memoir of Samuel J. May* (Boston, 1873),

pp. 226–30; May to G. Smith, July 7, 1863, Syr. U.; Galpin, *God's Chore Boy*, pp. 276–77.

44. L. M. Child to G. Smith, Dec. 29, 1861, Jan. 7, 1862, Syr. U.; *Lib.*, Aug. 11, 1865, p. 125.

45. *Lib.*, Jan. 24, 1862, p. 16, Aug. 28, 1863, p. 140, May 13, 1864, p. 78.

46. *Lib.*, Jan. 2, 1863, p. 3, Aug. 23, 1861, p. 136, June 5, 1863, p. 90, Aug. 26, 1864, p. 140, Dec. 30, 1864, p. 211.

47. AAS *Procs. . . . at its Third Decade*, pp. 93, 59.

48. *Lib.*, April 11, 1862, p. 60, July 25, 1862, p. 119, Aug. 1, 1862, p. 121, June 10, 1864, p. 93, June 2, 1865, p. 87.

49. Green to G. Smith, *passim.*, Syr. U.; *Lib.*, May 17, 1861, p. 79.

50. Conway *Autobiog.*, I, 190–91, 241–48, 413–18, 436; Conway, *Golden Hour* (Boston, 1862), p. 31; *Nat. AS Stand.*, July 4, 11, 25, 1863; Mary Burtis, *Moncure Conway* (New Brunswick, N.J., 1952), pp. 81, 216, 105–106.

51. *Advocate of Peace*, July–Aug., 1861, pp. 276–83; Curti, *The Learned Blacksmith*, pp. 140, 146, 122; Burritt, *Lectures and Speeches* (London, 1869), p. 250; *Principia*, Jan. 18, 1862, p. 909.

52. Ballou, *Autobiog.*, p. 439; *Lib.*, Oct. 30, 1863, p. 175; Ballou, *Christian Nonresistance Defended Against Rev. Henry Ward Beecher* (Hopedale, Mass., 1862), pp. 9–10; Ballou, *Hist. of the Hopedale Community*, pp. 314–16.

53. *Lib.*, July 5, 1861, p. 106, July 17, 1863, p. 116, Oct. 30, 1863, p. 175, May 6, 1864, p. 76; Curti, *Peace or War*, p. 58.

54. This group, when it first met informally in Boston, decided to invite others of varying degrees of nonresistance to cooperate with them, including Quakers L. Mott and Eliz. Buffum Chace, H. H. Brigham, Geo. Beckwith, and Garrison *(Lib.*, Dec. 15, 1865, p. 199, Dec. 22, 1865, p. 202).

55. Garrison to McKim, Nov. 14, 1863, BPL; AAS *Procs. . . . at its Third Decade; Lib.*, Dec. 18, 1863, pp. 202ff.

56. N.Y. *Tribune*, Nov. 4, 1883, p. 13. For evidence of Garrison's continuing nonresistance beliefs after the war, see Garr. IV, 191, 247, 261, 271.

Chapter 20, *Elusive Victory*

1. *Lib.*, June 2, 1865, p. 85, Dec. 15, 1865, p. 199, Dec. 22, 1865, p. 202; W. W. Brown, *The Negro in the Am. Rebellion* (Boston, 1867), p. 355; *Revolution*, April 9, 1868, p. 211.

2. Boston *Traveller*, April 24, 1879; Moncure Conway, *Autobiog.*

(Boston, 1904), I, 222; C. M. Clay, *Life* (Cincinnati, 1886), I, 596; Douglass, *Life and Times* (N.Y., 1968), pp. 496, 503.

3. Lincoln, *Writings* (N.Y., 1905), IV, 1–2; *Lib.*, May 26, 1865, pp. 84, 81.

4. Higginson, *Contemporaries* (Boston, 1899), pp. 246–47.

Index